Why You Need This Book . . .

Why a tax-planning book for your bookshelf? Because if you use it, you'll pay less tax.

Why now? Because the way to pay less tax is to know enough to make tax-smart decisions year round. That's true whether you do your own tax return or pay someone else to do it for you.

But why, if you turn to a professional, do you need to worry about the ins and outs of the law? You don't need to know the intricacies, of course, but a pro's work can be only as good as the information you provide. Yes, a key part of his or her job is to ask you the questions to get that information. But the more you know, the more likely you'll seek advice *before* you make a costly, irreversible mistake. (Every accountant has a catalog of sorry stories about clients who came in *after* committing such an error.)

And, face it, tax pros aren't perfect. A recent study showed that while about 6% of taxpayer-prepared returns included errors that led them to pay too much tax, nearly *12%* of the returns prepared by certified public accountants and attorneys contained errors that cost their clients money. Consider these episodes:

- When I was promoting an earlier version of this book on a television show in New York, we broke for a commercial just after I mentioned a special break for owners of inherited property. (It's discussed in Chapter 10.) I was pointing out the often-overlooked fact that this tax saver could apply to widows and widowers who had owned property jointly with their husbands or wives. During the break, the interviewer told me she had sold a home two years earlier following the death of her husband. The accountant who did her tax return didn't mention the break, nor did she know to ask about it. Would it have saved her money? A quick review of the circumstances made it clear she had overpaid her taxes, but her distress disappeared when I told her she could reclaim her money by filing an amended return (as discussed in Chapter 2). The host opened the next session of the show with the

NOTE: *As this book was going to press, Congress seemed likely to approve a new tax bill. To get a free summary of the new rules, if any, as they apply to your 1996 tax planning, write to Tax Book, 1729 H St., N.W., Washington, DC 20006, or e-mail your request to taxbill96@aol.com.*

best promotion I could hope for: "Kevin just saved me thousands of dollars. Read this book."

- The second case also involves a home sale, but a very different tax rule. As discussed in Chapter 9, two great tax breaks protect homeowners from the Internal Revenue Service when they sell. One—the rollover rule—lets you put off the tax on profits from one sale if you buy another, more expensive home; the other tax break—the exclusion—wipes out the tax on up to $125,000 of profit. There are all sorts of p's and q's to be watched, of course, but a critical one is that the $125,000 break can be used only once in a lifetime. In a sad case that recently wound up in court, an accountant used it to eliminate the tax on a $7,000 profit from a home sale, even though the rollover was available because the taxpayer bought a new home. Later, when that new house was sold, the exclusion was gone and, because a replacement house was not purchased, so was the rollover option. The taxpayer was stuck with the tax bill on more than $100,000 of profit. The accountant's error cost her tens of thousands of dollars.

The point is not that you can't trust accountants or other tax practitioners. Many—probably the vast majority—are highly competent. One of the strongest arguments favoring the massive simplification of the tax law discussed next, in fact, is that it would free thousands of brilliant and creative men and women to turn to more productive pursuits than helping clients navigate the tax maze.

The point is that the more you know about the tax law, the more you can help your tax preparer help you limit your bill to the legal minimum. The more you know, the more your tax pro will have to be on his or her toes. That's good for you.

So, whether or not you do your own return, you'll profit from this book. Whether the issue is a home sale, a retirement plan, an investment sale, a nanny or a hobby, there's a good chance the IRS is interested, and how you handle things could make a big difference in how much tax you owe. *Kiplinger's Cut Your Taxes* will help you do just that.

KIPLINGER CUT YOUR TAXES

BY KEVIN McCORMALLY

EXECUTIVE EDITOR
KIPLINGER'S PERSONAL FINANCE MAGAZINE

KIPLINGER
TIMES BUSINESS

RANDOM HOUSE

KIPLINGER
BOOKS

Published by
The Kiplinger Washington Editors, Inc.
1729 H Street, N.W.
Washington, D.C. 20006

This publication is intended to provide guidance in regard to the subject matter covered. It is sold with the understanding that the author and publisher are not herein engaged in rendering legal, accounting, tax or other professional services. If such services are required, professional assistance should be sought.

Printed in the United States of America.
Sixth edition. First printing.

Book designed by S. Laird Jenkins Corp.

I am a reporter, not a tax attorney or an accountant.

That's not a disclaimer, but rather an indication of the debt I owe others for the completion of this book. During the nearly 20 years that I have covered taxes for *Kiplinger's Personal Finance Magazine,* I've enjoyed and benefited from the generous counsel and advice of scores of accountants, attorneys, financial planners, tax preparers, members of Congress and their aides, and Internal Revenue Service employees, from commissioners to auditors to public affairs officers. I had the questions, they supplied the answers that fill this book. I thank them.

Just as important is the source of those questions: the thousands of our readers who have showered the magazine with questions about their taxes. Their demand for practical advice on real life issues gets credit for this book's focus on down-to-earth realities rather than highfalutin technicalities.

My thanks to Steve Ivins and Peter Blank of *The Kiplinger Tax Letter.* Their keen knowledge of the tax law has been an enormous benefit. Thanks, too, to David Harrison, director of Kiplinger Books, for his insightful editing, to Dianne Olsufka for her careful proofreading and to Karmela Lejarde for her editorial assistance. Oh, yes: Three cheers for the cartoonists whose works brighten the pages.

Finally, my thanks to my children—Niamh Anna and Patrick Henry—for their patience during all the nights and weekends Dad worked on "The Book." And, most of all, to my wife Anne, for her unwavering faith and encouragement, and more than a few good ideas.

Kevin McCormally

Contents

WHY YOU NEED THIS BOOK i

PART ONE   SETTLING WITH UNCLE SAM

CHAPTER 1   Preparing Your Tax Return 2

A SPECIAL OVERVIEW: 31
50 Ways to Save on Your 1995 Return

CHAPTER 2   Amended Returns 43

CHAPTER 3   The Self-Employment Tax 47

CHAPTER 4   The Alternative Minimum Tax 51

PART TWO   YEAR-ROUND TAX-SAVING STRATEGIES

CHAPTER 5   Tax Planning & You 60
            Your real tax bracket 64

CHAPTER 6   What's Taxable, What's Not 71
            Fringe benefits 79

CHAPTER 7   Pay as You Go 88
            Boost your take-home pay. 92

CHAPTER 8   Your Family & Your Tax Bill 106
            Filing status 106
            Exemptions 111
            The kiddie tax 119
            Income splitting. 123
            Marriage tax penalty. 130
            Divorce. 132
            Death in the family 137
            Tax rules for household help 141

CHAPTER 9   Home Sweet Tax Shelter 148
            Home equity loans 158
            Refinancing. 161
            Over 55 & selling? 171

Vacation homes 177
Equity sharing. 183

CHAPTER 10 Investment Income & Expenses . . **186**
Capital gains. 187
Basis 191
Mutual funds 196
Stocks. 207
Bonds 211
Rental property 232
Life insurance. 246
Savings accounts. 250
Interest & expenses 252

CHAPTER 11 Retirement Plans: Do It Yourself . . **256**
Individual Retirement Accounts 256
Keoghs. 281
Simplified Employee Pensions 289

CHAPTER 12 Retirement Plans:
With Help from the Boss **291**
401(k)s 291
Company pensions & profit sharing. . . . 296
Social security 311

CHAPTER 13 Business & Employee Expenses . . . **315**
Automobiles. 316
Computers & other business equipment 326
Home offices 330
Travel & entertainment 338
Job hunting 346
Education 347
Hobbies 350
Child care 353
Health insurance. 353

CHAPTER 14 Write-Offs: Adjustments to Income 356
IRAs 357
Moving expenses 357
Self-employment tax. 359
Self-employment health insurance 359
Keoghs & SEPs 361
Alimony. 361

CHAPTER 15 **Write-Offs: Itemized Deductions** . . **363**
    Medical 368
    Damages 378
    Taxes 378
    Interest 383
    Charitable contributions 388
    Casualty & theft loss 402
    Miscellaneous deductions 410

CHAPTER 16 **Tax Credits** **414**
    Child & dependent care 414
    Overpaying social security 419
    Taxes paid by a mutual fund 420
    Foreign tax 420
    Credit for the elderly or disabled 421
    Earned income credit 422

CHAPTER 17 **Year-End Tax Tips** **425**
    Defer income 426
    Accelerate deductions 427
    Bunching 430
    Investment moves 431
    Interest 436
    Your business 436
    Retirement plans 441
    Give money away 443
    Get married? 444
    Watch your withholding 445

CHAPTER 18 **Estate & Gift Taxes** **446**

CHAPTER 19 **Surviving a Tax Audit** **463**

    APPENDIX **475**
    Tax rates for 1995 475
    Tax forms & IRS publications 476
    Glossary 481

    INDEX **489**

PART

ONE

Settling with
Uncle Sam

Preparing Your
Tax Return

This chapter should really be the last one in this book, since your tax return is the culmination of your year-round tax-planning efforts, the place to show off how successful you've been in trimming the amount you owe the government. But if you're like most people, you're buying this book in the shadow of April 15, when your top priority is tackling your return for 1995. Even at this late date, though, there's plenty you can do to save time, anxiety…and money. (See pages 31 to 42 for a quick rundown of last-minute money-saving tips.)

Once you've settled your accounts with the Internal Revenue Service, you can turn your attention to the rewarding task of finding and implementing ways to save on next year's return.

Of course, if you're cracking this book in November or December, there's still time. Turn first to Chapter 17, where you'll find year-end moves that can pay off handsomely. If it's after April 15, plan to revisit this chapter early next year.

But, first things first.

You have to give the folks at the IRS credit. Each year in early December they send out millions of sets of tax forms; then they ask the Postal Service to sit on the packages until the last week of the year. After all, Uncle Sam doesn't want to get blamed for flooding the mails at Christmastime and delaying your cards and gifts. But the government does want you to receive its package right after the holidays—perhaps as much to beat the Christmas bills' claim on your income as to give you a head start on completing your return.

Do You Have to File?

That's the first question, and the answer doesn't have anything to do with your age. You're never too young or too old to fall into the grasp of the IRS. The key is how much money you make, and the table at right shows the trigger points for 1995 returns. The figures will rise in future years to reflect inflation. The various filing statuses are discussed in Chapter 8.

Special Rules for Dependents

If you can be claimed as a dependent on someone else's return—a situation most likely to occur when children are claimed by their parents or elderly parents are claimed by their adult children—special rules apply. You must file a tax return even if you have less income than shown in the table. A dependent child, for example, must file if *earned* income—from a job or self-employment—exceeds $3,900 in 1995. The threshold drops lower still if the child has any so-called *un-*

earned income, which is basically income from investments (including interest on a savings account) rather than from a job. In that case, a return must be filed if the child's total income exceeds $650 in 1995. Someone who is 65 or older and is claimed as a dependent must file if unearned income exceeds $1,600, if single, or

Who Must File 1995 Returns?

Filing Status and Age	Gross Income
Single	
Under 65	$6,400
65 and older	7,350
Married filing jointly	
Both under 65	11,550
One 65 or older	12,300
Both 65 or older	13,050
Married filing separately	
Under 65	2,500
65 or older	2,500
Surviving spouse	
Under 65	9,050
65 or older	9,800
Head of household	
Under 65	8,250
65 or older	9,200

Note: Gross income does not include tax-exempt income from social security, for example, or interest from tax-free municipal bonds. If you can be claimed as a dependent on someone else's return, see the accompanying discussion for special rules that demand returns at lower income levels than shown here.

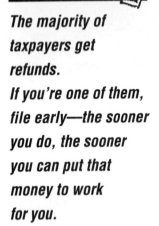

$1,400, if married. (Social security benefits that aren't taxed don't count for this test.)

There's another twist, too. In some cases, income of a child under age 14 can be reported on his or her parents' return, a move that eliminates the need for the child to file. See pages 12 and 22 for details.

And, if you're self-employed, you may have to file a return even if you owe no income tax. If income from self-employment is $400 or more, you must file in order to pay the self-employment tax that pays for social security and medicare. That's discussed in Chapter 3.

In some cases, you may want to file even if you don't have to; it's the only way to get a refund if taxes were withheld from your pay.

Getting Started

The tax forms are usually the first of the flood of tax-related mail to arrive. January's mail is sprinkled with papers that remind you of income to report to the IRS: the W–2 form from your employer, showing how much you were paid; the 1099–DIV forms, listing stock dividends; the 1099–INT forms, showing interest earned; the 1099–B form from your broker, showing the proceeds of your sales; the 1099–Gs, showing a state tax refund, perhaps, or unemployment compensation; the 1099–MISC, for various other types of income; and on and on.

Unfortunately, the IRS isn't nearly as concerned that you remember your deductible expenses. You should get a 1098 form from your mortgage lender, showing how much mortgage interest you paid. Beyond that, you're pretty much on your own. The success of all your tax-planning efforts during the year rests on how well you've kept your records.

Pulling together all the necessary paperwork isn't an appealing prospect. But it makes sense to answer the call of the tax return as early in the year as possible. There's no point in dallying, and procrastination can cost you money. If you deserve a refund, as the vast majority of taxpayers do, you're making what amounts to an interest-free loan to

Uncle Sam. The earlier you file, the sooner you can put that money back to work for you. Get your return in the mail by the end of February and you'll probably be banking—or spending—your refund while your neighbors are burning the midnight oil to meet the April 15 deadline.

If you're among the unhappy minority that owes more tax, getting started early still makes sense. Why risk missing a trick that could trim your tax bill because you ran out of time? Tackling your return early in the filing season is insurance against a bleary-eyed, last-minute rush into a costly shortcut.

Remember that preparing your return doesn't mean you have to mail it right away. If you owe extra tax, you can hold on to your return—and your check—until April 15. On the other hand, if your bottom line shows that you owe so much that you face a penalty, as discussed later in this chapter, the earlier you file the less you'll owe.

A good way to gear up for your return is to review all the forms and schedules you used to settle with Uncle Sam last year. That's a quick reminder of what's ahead. Sort through the papers you plan to use to back up your deductions, exemptions, adjustments and credits. The idea is to reacclimate yourself to the subject of taxes, to get your mind on the right track. There's a more tangible advantage, too: Reviewing last year's return can call your attention to holes in this year's records. For example, if you deducted $8,000 in real estate taxes on last year's return, but your records show you paid only $4,000 this year, perhaps you've misplaced a check.

Of course, you can't follow your old tax return exactly. Your circumstances may have changed significantly. Or, perhaps more likely, the tax law may have changed significantly. This is another reason why an early start is important. You may simply need more time to grapple with this year's forms than you needed last year.

The right form for you

Your first decision is which of three basic forms to use: the baby-blue 1040 long form, the pastel-pink 1040A short form or the even shorter light-green 1040EZ. You

Money Saver

Review last year's return for clues to possible holes in this year's records.

don't necessarily have to file the one you get in the mail. In some cases you're not permitted to; in others, choosing a different form will save you money. The forms package you get from the IRS is the agency's best guess of what you need, based on your previous year's return.

©1993 Stayskal—Tampa Tribune

The EZ route

The 1040EZ (as in *easy*, get it?) will probably be used by more than 20 million taxpayers this year—about one in six. If you can join them, filing is a breeze. The EZ has just a dozen numbered lines and there are no supplementary forms to file. All the instructions fit on the back of the single-page form.

Before you become too enamored of all that simplicity, consider the restrictions that put the EZ out of reach of most taxpayers. It's available only if you don't itemize deductions, have no dependents and if your taxable income is under $50,000. You *can't* use the form if you have any income from dividends or capital gains, self-employment income or more than $400 in interest income to report. Nor can you use the 1040EZ if you want to claim a deduction for a contribution to an individual retirement account or if you have a taxable pension, social security benefits or alimony to report.

A touch-tone option

Beginning in 1996, millions of taxpayers across the nation will be offered an even easier alternative: filing by telephone. Phone filing is available only to single taxpayers who qualify to file the 1040EZ. If you qualify for this simplest-ever option, you'll get a special packet from the IRS.

Basically, a taxpayer using TeleFile calls a toll-free number and uses the telephone keypad to "punch in" his or her social security number, wage and interest income and amount of tax withheld. The IRS computer will go to work, subtracting the standard deduction amounts and coming up with a verdict: Does the taxpayer owe more tax or deserve a refund? If a refund is due, the check should arrive within three weeks. If more tax is owed, the taxpayer can send it in anytime before April 15 with the voucher that came with the IRS packet. The toll-free call takes about five minutes. You send in your W–2 through the mail.

The 1040A

Between the EZ and the standard 1040 long form stands the 1040A—the form of choice for about 25 million taxpayers. This return can be used if you file as married, single, head of household or as a qualified widow or widower. Taxable income is limited to $50,000, but, unlike the 1040EZ, in addition to wages it can include any amount of interest, dividends, unemployment compensation, pension and annuity income, IRA distributions and social security benefits. You can also use this form to claim dependents, write off an IRA contribution and claim the child-care tax credit and credit for the elderly. But you can't use it if you have any alimony or capital gains to report.

The 1040 long form

If you have income that doesn't fit on the 1040EZ or the 1040A—income from self-employment, capital gains, or rent, for example—you must use the 1040 long form. It's also required if you itemize deductions or claim adjustments to income, such as the write-off for alimony paid or the penalty paid for early withdrawal of savings from a certificate of deposit. About 75 million of us use this form each spring. Sure, it's more complicated than the other forms, but on the bright side, it includes more opportunities for savings.

Never pass up a tax break simply to avoid using the long form. You can skip any lines that don't apply to you. Using the 1040 usually involves completing extra forms and schedules, too. The IRS paperwork collection—and what each form is for—is detailed in the appendix.

Money Saver

If you're single and file the 1040EZ, you can now file by telephone.

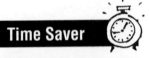

The rest of the paperwork blizzard

Another reason to get an early start on your return is that there's a good chance you'll need forms that don't come in the mail. The 1040 package mailed out routinely by the IRS contains the most commonly used forms, but you may well require others.

You may be able to find the forms you need at a bank, post office or public library. If you have time, you can call the IRS and have the agency mail the forms to you. The IRS has a nationwide, toll-free number for ordering forms and instructions: 800–TAX–FORM. If you can't get through, find the number for a local IRS office in the phone book under U.S. Government. You can also order what you need by mail, using the order form that comes with the tax package. In either case, allow a couple of weeks for the forms to arrive. If you plan to drop by a local IRS office, call first to make sure it has the forms you need. If you use computer software to prepare your tax return, as discussed later in this chapter, you don't have to worry about missing forms. The programs automatically print out IRS-acceptable versions.

If you have a computer and a modem, you have another option: downloading the forms you need from IRS computers. Forms and instructions are available online on "IRIS" on the FedWorld bulletin board (703–321–8020) and on the Internet's World Wide Web at *http://www.ustreas.gov.*

Don't Be Afraid of the IRS

Before you even begin gathering your tax records, check your attitude. Are you afraid of the IRS?

Sure, we're all supposed to have a healthy respect for the tax agency. The ever-present threat that the IRS can use part of its multi-billion-dollar budget to scrutinize anybody's financial affairs is supposed to keep us all in line. There has to be a method to force the unscrupulous to comply with the law. Otherwise, as a former IRS commissioner concedes, the tax system would allow the taxpayer "with the least conscience to get the best result."

Nobody wants that. But neither should taxpayers be scared into making costly mistakes on their tax return. Excessive worry makes some taxpayers reluctant to claim legitimate deductions. They pass up tax savings rather than risk arousing the suspicions of what they see as a sinister Big Brother. In effect, they try to buy peace of mind by overpaying their taxes. Don't fall into that trap. Don't be intimidated into paying more tax than you owe.

You have every right to attack this annual chore aggressively. Know your tax bracket (which you will after you read Chapter 5) so you can put a price tag on each deduction you find. Throughout the record-gathering phase, collect any documents that might help reduce your tax bill. It's better to hold on to a paper, even if it doesn't translate into tax savings, than to discard one that could shave your bill. At this stage, at least, make all close calls in your favor. When questions arise, check the index in this book to find out where to turn for answers. Be sure to make a note about any missing receipt, canceled check or other item. That way a temporarily misplaced paper won't become a permanently lost deduction.

As you get ready to prepare your return, put your records together as though the IRS were coming to visit. This is the best time to collect the documentation you need to substantiate deductions you'll claim, since the necessary records are readily accessible. Holes in your records now could come back to haunt you later. It could be two years or longer before this year's returns are audited, and trying to reconstruct records then can be a real pain.

Waiting for a Refund

Q: *I have a big refund coming. When can I expect to get it?*

A: The earlier in the filing season you mail your return, the sooner you should get your check. File by mid-February and you should have your refund within three or four weeks. Even last-minute filers should have their refunds within eight weeks. If you file by April 15 and the IRS hasn't mailed the refund by June 1, the government has to pay you interest on what it owes you.

Getting the Help You Need

Considering that federal income taxes take one of the largest bites out of the family budget, it's no wonder that we have an insatiable appetite for help with this annual chore. Such assistance comes in all forms and at all prices.

Written Help

For do-it-yourselfers there's a library of written material. Most visible is the garden of hardy perennial paperback tax-return guides that blooms in the bookstores from around Christmas until mid-April. Frankly, though, you probably don't need one of those guides at all— because you already own this book. Although the overall emphasis of *Kiplinger's Cut Your Taxes* is tax planning, within these covers you'll find what you need to complete your return.

Straight from the IRS

If you're interested in more detailed line-by-line instructions than you find in the IRS packet, get a copy of the IRS's own entry in this field: *Your Federal Income Tax,* also known as "Publication 17." You might be somewhat skeptical about the publisher's motives, but you can't complain about the price: it's free. You can get a copy by contacting your local IRS office or calling 800–TAX–FORM.

Publication 17 is thorough and well-organized, has a good index and should answer most of your questions about filling out the forms. Especially helpful is a filled-in, hypothetical tax return. Nearly every line of each form and schedule is keyed to the page in the guide that offers information on the issue at hand. In fact, most commercial guides draw heavily from Publication 17. One of the best selling is a word-for-word reprint, annotated with the publisher's comments and tips.

One drawback of Publication 17 is its tone. The commercial tax guides generally come with the exciting promise to steer you to tax breaks and save you money. *Your Federal Income Tax* makes no such pretense. The information is there, but don't expect flashing neon lights to call your attention to money-saving tips.

You also have to keep in mind that what you're getting is the official IRS view of the tax law. In most cases, that's all that counts, but on some matters courts have taken a position that is more favorable to taxpayers. If the IRS is sticking with a position despite having been whipped in court by a taxpayer, you won't find any reference to the case in Publication 17, whereas a commercial guide might alert you to the conflict. You don't have to worry about missing a chance to save, however, if you use Publication 17 in conjunction with this book.

In addition to Publication 17, the IRS offers a library of booklets focusing on specific tax issues. They are listed in the appendix and are also free.

If you still want to consider buying one of the fat annual guides, choose among the field by testing books on a specific tax question. This isn't bedtime reading. The key to a book's value is how easily you can find what you're looking for, how much information is provided and how clearly the book presents it. Check the index for its thoroughness and ease of use.

Letting Software Do the Hard Part

As your tax return becomes more complex—whether because of changes in the law or new complications in your financial life—you may be drawn more and more to the idea of forsaking do-it-yourself status and turning your return over to a professional preparer. First, though, you may want to consider a middle ground that a growing number of taxpayers find appealing: putting their home computers to work on the IRS forms.

Several tax-preparation programs have been around long enough to have had the bugs worked out. They've kept up with the changing tax law, and most have become both better and cheaper, too. Some fans of this genre of software actually claim it makes doing a tax return fun. That's probably going too far, but a good program can speed the process along. And one with good built-in help can save you money as well as time.

Time Saver

Cut the drudgery with computer software.

Before you rush out to buy software, recognize what it *can't* do. There's no magic involved. You still have to gather all the information about your income, deductions, credits and so forth. That's the scut work, and it is inescapable whether you do your return with a pencil, use a computer or turn the whole mess over to a professional preparer. GIGO—garbage in, garbage out—applies as much to tax-return programs as anything else.

Nor is computer technology a substitute for thinking. This software is a labor-saving tool, not a brain substitute. Still, the computer can be an amazing accessory for this tedious job. The more you know about the tax law, the better you can imagine how a program can help. The less you know, perhaps the more you stand to benefit from a computer's help.

- **Did your son or daughter earn more than $650 in 1995,** with any part of it being investment income such as interest on a savings account? If so, the child must file a return. If the investment income exceeds $1,300, the kiddie tax rears its head, as discussed in Chapter 8. That means filling out an extra form. Good tax software not only reminds you of what's required but also handles the calculations with aplomb.

- **Do you own rental property?** If so, you not only have to report the income or loss on your Form 1040 but you also need a Schedule E, plus a Form 4562, to figure your depreciation, and a Form 8582 if you show a loss. A good program will handle all the necessary calculations based on your input.

Tax programs don't stop at doing your arithmetic and transferring data among related forms—although their facility in these realms removes much of the drudgery from return preparation. If you report self-employment income on Schedule C, for example, the software not only carries it over to the proper line on the Form 1040 but also generates a Schedule SE that shows whether you owe any self-employment tax. If so, the program will figure the amount and transfer it to the proper line on the 1040.

One of the great virtues of these programs is the ease with which they let you correct mistakes. Almost everyone has had this experience: Just as you're ready to mail your completed return, you discover a receipt that earns you an extra deduction. If you do your return by hand, you may decide to punt—forgo the tax savings rather than redo the arithmetic and start from scratch on all the affected forms. But with a tax program you enter the new deduction and almost instantly your computer does all the recalculations.

The most popular programs generally cost $50 or less. As with all software, choosing the right program is a subjective matter. The program one person swears by may be the one another taxpayer only swears at. (Not surprisingly, our favorite program is *Kiplinger TaxCut.* But we're not alone. Independent reviewers have consistently cited it as tops in the field for both its power and ease of use.)

The cost of tax software can be deductible. It's considered a miscellaneous expense, deductible to the extent that your total write-offs in this category exceed 2% of your adjusted gross income, as discussed in Chapter 15.

One thing a tax preparation program can't do is allow you to file your return electronically and directly to the IRS. Only government-authorized services can file returns over the telephone lines. But you needn't have a professional prepare your return to take advantage of electronic filing. If you use a leading computer program, you can send your return information—via a modem or on a disk—to an authorized service which, for a fee, serves as a middleman between you and the IRS. The instructions

Shorted on a Refund

Q: *When I got my refund check, it was for $188 less than I had requested on my return. I don't know why the IRS shorted me. If I cash the check, does that mean I agree with them?*

A: No. Cashing the check wouldn't prevent you from disputing the IRS on whatever issue is involved. There's a good chance that the difference between what you expected and what you got is due to a mathematical error or other simple mistake—such as using the incorrect tax rates for your filing status—that was caught by the IRS. You should receive a notice from the agency explaining why the change was made. It sometimes arrives after the check because they are sent by different offices.

with the software will explain how to do it. For more on electronic filing, see page 21.

Human Help

Sometimes books and computers just don't cut it. If you have a question, you want to talk to someone about it.

"I THINK THAT'S GOOD...IT MEANS TWO-THIRDS OF OUR GUESSES ABOUT THE NEW TAX FORMS ARE RIGHT!"

© 1988 Stayskal—Tampa Tibune

Perhaps you suffer from that common tax-time malady: *form phobia.* Or maybe you just don't trust yourself to capture all the tax breaks you deserve. After all, it was Albert Einstein who, after jousting with his tax return, commented: "This is too difficult for a mathematician. It takes a philosopher." Many taxpayers today unabashedly declare that one of their best investments is paying someone else to do their tax returns. About half of all returns are prepared by someone the taxpayer hires to do the deed.

There's no doubt that as a nation of taxpayers we're willing to spend a bundle for help figuring out how little we can send to the IRS. A few years ago, a study estimated the annual bill for tax help at between $3 billion and $3.4 billion. That's cash out of pocket and doesn't include a dime for the two billion or so hours we spend doing returns or gathering the records so someone else can finish the job. If you're looking for help, you have plenty of choices—so many, in fact, that picking the right kind can be a real challenge.

Before you begin your search, face this inescapable fact: No matter how much you're willing to pay, a lot of the work just can't be done by an outsider. It's up to you to pull together the information that translates into tax savings. Even if you hire someone to ask all the right questions, you must supply the records that provide the answers. There's no guaranteed correlation between price and perfection, nor does paying for tax help guarantee a lower bill. Also, no matter who prepares your return, the IRS holds you responsible for its accuracy.

How about the IRS?

To some folks, going to the IRS for tax help makes as much sense as donning a cement overcoat for a swim. Although such cynicism is unwarranted, it is true that on close calls the government's employees are likely to rule in the government's favor. (Don't kid yourself, though: The same goes for some paid preparers.) Still, a telephone call to the IRS might produce the answer you need to do your own return. The IRS has offices around the country and operates a toll-free telephone service to respond to taxpayer inquiries.

Such assistance is free and, in recent years, its quality has improved. A few years ago, government investigators posing as taxpayers put IRS phone service to the test, and it failed miserably: Almost half the answers given were incorrect. The accuracy rate is much better now, up to almost 90%. But considering the millions of calls that are fielded each year, the IRS is still dishing out plenty of bum advice. If an answer you receive seems off the mark, ask to speak to the employee's supervisor for clarification.

If you call the IRS for help, take this precaution: Write down the name of the employee who answers your question, the date of the call, your question and the advice you receive. That way, if the advice turns out to be wrong and, by relying on it you underpay your taxes, you probably won't be penalized for the error. You'll have to pay any extra tax, but the agency will probably waive the normal penalties. Although that may seem only fair, the IRS doesn't have to forgive the penalty. That has been the policy in recent years, however.

There is a downside to the increased IRS accuracy: Getting its advice takes longer. In 1994, only one in four callers got through to the agency on their first try. The rest got busy signals. When using the IRS phone service, the

Money Saver

Protect yourself from IRS errors. If you call the agency for help, note the name of the person you talk to.

earlier in the January-through-April crunch you call the better your chances of getting through. The best time to call is between 8 AM and 11 AM on Tuesdays, Wednesdays and Thursdays. Fridays are bad as taxpayers try to prepare for a weekend with their forms; Mondays are busy as the taxpayers try to resolve all the problems they encountered over the weekend. Lunchtimes are always bad.

Commercial preparers

Anyone can hang out a shingle declaring him- or herself a tax preparer. If that sounds like a warning, it is. There are no federal standards for commercial preparers. In fact, the IRS staunchly opposes any kind of testing or licensing program. However, all paid preparers are covered by rules aimed at rooting out the unscrupulous or incompetent. A preparer can be fined for deliberately or negligently understating a taxpayer's liability. Notice, though, that there's no penalty if the preparer's goof causes you to *overpay* your taxes.

Commercial preparers generally fall into two categories: the independents, and those associated with a national firm, such as H&R Block. Block is the nation's single largest tax preparer, with about 8,000 offices open around the country during the January-through-April filing season. The company handles about ten million individual returns each year. The cost is relatively modest, averaging around $60 for a Form 1040 with itemized deductions and an accompanying state return. Simpler returns cost less, more complicated ones cost more. Price can range all over the lot with independent preparers.

An advantage of a national firm is that employees—who often work only temporarily during the filing season—are given substantial training in the tax law to

---

Jury Fees

· ·

Q: *When I was called to jury duty for two weeks last year, my employer continued my salary but required that I turn over the $250 in jury fees I received. The IRS instructions say I have to report jury fees as taxable income, but that doesn't seem fair because I really didn't get the money. What can I do?*

A: You report the income on line 21 of the Form 1040, and then offset it by claiming the amount you turned over to your employer as an adjustment to income on line 30 of the form. You get this write-off even if you don't itemize other deductions.

keep them up-to-date with changes. With an independent preparer, training and experience can range from nonexistent to extensive.

Be wary of tax-preparation operations that pop up in the spring and disappear just as quickly in mid-April. Some local services offer first-rate help, but others fall in the category dubbed "drugstore cowboys." It's up to you to evaluate the preparer's qualifications.

Can you trust a commercial preparer? You've probably read stories about tests in which someone posing as a taxpayer visits several preparers, provides the same data to all of them and is presented with tax returns that have widely disparate bottom lines. The results probably say as much about the complexity of the tax law as the competence of the preparers. Also, preparers have argued that in such tests the "taxpayers" are deliberately reticent—unwilling to volunteer any information that might reduce their tax bill. In the real world, they say, it's the taxpayer's job to help.

Certainly, some commercial preparers are better than others. If you go this route, these tips should help you get the most for your money.

- **Go early**. One criticism of commercial firms is that they rush taxpayers in and out to build a high-volume operation. If you're part of the last-minute rush, you might be shortchanged.

- **Find out how much you'll be charged** at the outset for federal and state forms. You don't want any surprises.

- **Ask the preparer about qualifications and experience.** If you get the feeling you know as much about taxes as the preparer, go elsewhere.

- **Be suspicious of a preparer who doesn't ask you a lot of questions.** His or her job is to probe into your financial affairs to get you all the breaks you have coming.

- **Check your completed return carefully** when you get it. Be certain all the forms and schedules the preparer discussed with you are included.

Time Saver

Order a social security number for a newborn before you leave the hospital.

Beyond return preparation

If all you want is someone to figure out what you owe and fill out your forms correctly, a commercial preparer may be just the ticket. Paying higher fees to an accountant or other tax professional might buy you nothing extra except, perhaps, status. Face it: Once you sit down to do your return, it's too late for nearly all of the tax-saving maneuvers a certified public accountant or other tax pro might steer you toward.

The real question is whether you need more than tax-return preparation. Depending on your income and the complexity of your financial life, you might benefit handsomely from year-round tax help, with the mechanics of filling out the forms merely frosting on the cake. That kind of broader assistance is what accountants, enrolled agents and certified public accountants (CPAs) can offer. (Although some attorneys specialize in federal taxes, few handle actual preparation of tax returns—except as a courtesy to valued clients.)

Even if your tax life has been simple, a tax adviser might come up with some valuable tax-saving maneuvers that complicate tax preparation. As income increases, so does the importance of the tax angles of financial planning. Many taxpayers prize their tax advisers for knowing how to exploit the gray areas of the tax law and guide them

---

Lost Return

● ●

Q: *I filed my return in mid-February, and now, in mid-July, I still haven't received my refund. I'm afraid the return is lost. Do I have to file some special form now?*

A: No. To check the status of your refund, telephone the number in your Form 1040 instruction packet. (If you can't find it, call 800–829–1040 and ask for the number for Automated Refund Information for your area.) You will need to punch in your social security number, filing status and the exact amount of your expected refund. Don't call every day. The IRS updates the data only on the weekends. If the IRS hasn't received your return by now, you can assume it's lost. In that case, send a copy of the return, marked "duplicate," to the service center where you originally filed, along with a letter explaining what has happened. Since you have a refund coming, you won't be penalized for filing late.

If you had owed money, however, you would include with your duplicate return evidence that you had filed earlier—a copy of the checkbook register showing the date on which you wrote the check for the taxes due, for example. Indicating that the return was filed on time but lost in the mail should deflect any late-payment penalty.

through what's been called the "fairyland of confusion" of the tax law.

Although tax-return season is a lousy time to initiate a tax-saving strategy for the previous year, it can be the perfect time to begin a relationship with a tax pro. Preparing your return will give him or her a detailed look at where you stand, and once the April 15 rush has passed, you and your accountant can map out a strategy for the year ahead.

If you decide you want more than simple tax preparation, you'll pay more—perhaps a lot more—than the fees at H&R Block. CPA charges vary widely, with hourly fees ranging from $25 to $250 or more. National firms are likely to charge more than smaller, local firms, but it is not unusual for a tax return and related services to cost several hundred dollars.

Clearly, you'll be cheating yourself if you pay that kind of freight for fill-in-the-blanks return preparation. There are choices between commercial preparers and high-powered CPAs: public accountants. Those who specialize in this area—many do not—are likely to be year-round tax advisers who haven't passed the exams or met the experience requirements demanded of CPAs. In most states public accountants must be licensed, but in some anyone can claim the title.

Enrolled agents. Also bidding for your tax business are enrolled agents, the only tax practitioners who must meet IRS standards. The 15,000 or so enrolled agents earned their status by passing a tough IRS exam or having worked for the tax agency. Public accountants and enrolled agents usually charge less than CPAs, but count on a minimum of $100 to $150 and perhaps far more depending on the complexity of your return.

Regardless of what level of help you choose, you have to bare your financial soul to your tax preparer. What's to prevent him or her from blabbing it all over town? Preparers are required by law to keep the information confidential. It's against the law to divulge it, except under court order. Note this, though: there is no accountant-client privilege similar to attorney-client privilege. Your accountant can be forced to disclose in court information that you give him or her in connection with your tax return or other matters.

Shopping for Professional Help

If you decide to seek a tax pro's help, start your search early. By early in the filing season, many firms have all the work they can handle. Some will take on new clients at this point only if you agree to get an extension of time to file—discussed later in this chapter—so your return can be done during the summer. Since you're after more than return preparation, you should count on investing some time in making the right choice.

Hiring a CPA is a lot like choosing a doctor. You want someone who is smart and with whom you feel comfortable. Start by asking your friends and business associates for recommendations. The most useful references are likely to come from people whose financial and business situations are similar to your own.

Before you sign on with an accountant, take the time to interview him or her. Ask about professional education, and find out how the accountant keeps up with tax-law changes. Is the firm computerized? Will your financial data go into a computer for quick retrieval if you need an answer to a question about the tax ramifications of a potential investment? Ask for a few examples of ideas the accountant has come up with to save other clients money.

Some CPAs wonder whether colleagues who work alone or in small firms can possibly keep up with the growing complexity of the tax law and financial universe. Others dismiss such concerns, saying that because taxpayers so seldom need a true specialist, what's important is to have a CPA who's astute enough to know when other kinds of help are needed and who has access to assistance. Ask the accountant you're considering where he or she turns when stumped.

Because tax planning is probably a key element of what you'll be buying, ask what your accountant offers. Is the firm among those branching out more and more into financial planning? You may also want to ask for copies of transmittal letters that accompanied other clients' completed tax returns last year so you can review the suggestions that were made. What you need to find out, of course, is how aggressive the accountant is in offering advice and encouraging you to ask for it.

Be sure to talk fees. Ask for an estimate of what a full year's service is likely to cost, from return preparation through year-end planning.

Shopping for either a public accountant or an enrolled agent is similar to the search for a CPA. Rely on recommendations and interviews. If you consider a public accountant, ask why he or she has not become an enrolled agent with the privilege of representing clients before the IRS. The National Society of Public Accountants encourages all of its members to take the IRS test. You can get a list of enrolled agents in your area by contacting the National Association of Enrolled Agents at 800–424–4339.

If you haven't been referred to the tax pro by a client, ask for the name of one you can call and chat with about the accountant's services. Ask that person about the availability of the accountant, whether work is delivered on time and for a general impression of the adviser's creativity and financial-planning skills.

If that sounds like a lot of work, remember that the stakes are high. Picking the right kind of help for your taxes is a major financial decision.

The Dubious Value of Electronic Filing

The IRS continues to beat the drum for electronic filing, the system that zaps your tax information almost instantly to IRS computers over telephone wires rather than on paper forms that slog their way through the mail. And a lot of taxpayers are listening. About 12 million returns—nearly one in ten—were filed electronically in 1995.

What's the appeal?
For the taxpayer who has a refund coming, filing elec-

tronically promises to get you your check within three weeks. If you have the IRS deposit your money directly in your bank account, you can speed up the refund by a couple more days. That compares to the four to eight weeks you have to wait for a refund if you use an old-fashioned paper return.

What's the drawback?

You have to pay extra to have your return filed electronically—and that's true even if you prepare your return on a computer. Only IRS-authorized firms can send data directly to IRS computers. Last year, H&R Block handled more than half of the electronic returns filed and charged about $30 to send each one. Assuming that same fee applied to all returns filed electronically, taxpayers shelled out about $300 million for this service.

Although $30 may seem like a modest charge, it's probably more than it's worth. If you figure what your money could earn in a bank account during the extra three to four weeks you'd have it to invest, you need a refund of $7,500 or more to justify the cost of electronic filing.

The IRS also allows people who owe money with their returns to file electronically, although it's even more difficult to imagine why anyone would want to go this route. As with refund-due returns, you have to pay someone to file your return electronically. You're still stuck with the April 15 deadline to pay what you owe. You have to *mail* a check for the balance due to the IRS, along with a voucher (Form 9282) showing that the return data was sent electronically. Whether you have a refund coming or owe more money with your return, you'll have to sign a statement (Form 8453) that says your return is accurate. That form and your W-2 wage statement are also *mailed* to the IRS.

Despite the dubious advantage to taxpayers, the IRS will continue to push for electronic filing. The agency likes it because of savings on processing and storing returns. And forms sent in over the phone lines have proven to be far less error-prone than conventional paper returns, mainly because no one at the IRS has a chance to goof when typing your figures into the agency's computers.

To overcome some of the objections to electronic filing, the agency is working to make the system truly paperless, so that taxpayers could "sign" their returns electronically, too, and not have to send in their W–2s.

Rapid-Refund Loans

The advent of electronic filing has led to a booming business in what are called rapid-refund loans. These deals, usually offered through tax preparers, promise to put a tax refund in your hands within a couple of days if you file electronically. Unless you desperately need the money though, don't bite.

The quick refunds are really very short-term, *very* expensive loans. Here's how they generally work: Once the IRS acknowledges that it will process a return it has received electronically, the firm offering the rapid refund will give you a check for the amount you've got coming. You agree that the refund will be used to repay that loan.

Sounds nifty, but it's an extremely expensive way to borrow money. Officials in one state closed down an operation accused of charging the equivalent of 1,000% interest on rapid-refund loans. That was an extreme case, but even when relatively modest fees are charged, the interest-rate equivalent is sky-high because the loan is outstanding for such a short time. If you pay $30 to get a $300 refund loan, for example, you're paying more than 100% annual interest on what amounts to a three-week loan. Even if you need the money immediately, you should be able to find a cheaper source of credit.

The Consequences of Being Late

Everyone knows the deadline for filing tax returns is midnight, April 15—unless that date happens to fall on a Saturday, Sunday or legal holiday, which pushes the deadline to the next business day. If you can't get your tax forms completed, signed and in the mail by the deadline, you can buy extra time. Each year, millions of taxpayers do so.

Money Saver

Rapid-refund loans are short-term, very expensive loans. Even if you need the money, find a cheaper source of credit.

Delaying the Inevitable

You can put off the filing deadline by four months—to August 15—by filing Form 4868, *Application for Automatic Extension of Time to File U.S. Individual Income Tax Return.* Note that glorious word "automatic" in that mouthful of IRSese. This is a no-questions-asked deal. You don't have to offer any explanation of why your return will be overdue. Each year, more than five million procrastinating taxpayers file this one-page form by April 15 rather than a completed tax return.

There is, alas, a catch. Although the extension gives you more time to file your return, it doesn't put off the deadline for paying the tax you owe. In the past, in fact, the *automatic* extension was denied automatically if the form wasn't accompanied by a check for the amount you figured you owed. Now, however, you can buy extra time without sending a check.

You still have to estimate how much you owe, though, and that's what complicates the otherwise simple Form 4868. There's a line for your estimated tax liability—a figure that's tough to come up with unless you've already done most of the work necessary to complete your return. If you don't pay the amount due with your Form 4868, you'll owe interest on the unpaid balance from April 15 on. The IRS interest rate is set each quarter in line with what it costs the government to borrow money. It was 9% for the last half of 1995, but has reached as high as 20% in the past.

If you're short by 10% or more, you'll probably also be hit with a late payment penalty, which builds up at ½ of 1% of the amount due each month. If you owe an extra $1,000 with your return, for example, the penalty would be $5 for each month (or part of a month) you fail to pay up after April 15. If you procrastinate too long and ignore IRS notices to pay, the penalty can double to 1% of the balance due each month. In no event can this penalty exceed 25% of the tax due, however.

Failure to file

Although that penalty may seem modest, getting

an extension lets you avoid a much stiffer one, too: the failure-to-file penalty. If you file neither your return nor a Form 4868 by April 15, this penalty is 5% of the tax due for each month your return is late. A $1,000 balance due on a return four months late, for example, would trigger a $200 penalty.

If your return is more than 60 days late, the failure-to-file penalty is a minimum of $100 or 100% of the tax due, whichever is less. By accurately estimating and paying your tax with your Form 4868, you avoid interest and both penalties during the extra four months you get to complete your return.

File the request for an extension by April 15 with the IRS service center to which you send your return. When you file your completed return, attach a copy of the Form 4868 and *be sure to give yourself credit*—in the payments section of the Form 1040—for any amount you paid with the Form 4868.

> ## Computerized Filing
> ●
>
> **Q:** *I bought a tax-preparation program for my computer and want to send my return to the IRS electronically. How do I do that?*
>
> **A:** You can't do it yourself. Only authorized parties can file returns over the phone lines, so you'll have to pay one for this service even if you complete your own return. That will probably cost at least $20 or so. The IRS says going this route will get you your refund within three weeks. You can gain an extra couple of days by having the IRS deposit your money directly into your bank account. Unless you have a pressing need for the money, you're better off filing your return the old fashioned way—with a 32 cent stamp.

What If You Owe, But Can't Pay?

If you find yourself in that unenviable position, you should still file a return. That protects you from the late-filing penalty that otherwise would keep digging you deeper into a hole. As noted above, that penalty mounts up at a rate of 5% of what you owe *per month*. You avoid that penalty by sending in your return, even if you don't enclose a check for the balance due.

Attach to your tax return a Form 9465—*Installment Agreement Request*—asking the IRS to set up a monthly payment plan to pay off what you owe. That's not as unusual as you might imagine: About 2.5 million taxpayers are current-

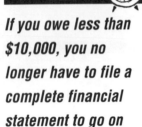

Time Saver

If you owe less than $10,000, you no longer have to file a complete financial statement to go on the installment plan.

ly paying off their bills under such an arrangement, and recently the IRS made it easier to qualify. In the past, before the IRS would okay an installment plan, the agency demanded a look at your finances—your assets, liabilities, cash flow and so on—so *it* could decide how much you could afford to pay. That's no longer required in cases where the amount owed is under $10,000 and the proposed payment plan doesn't stretch over more than three years.

Don't think the IRS is a patsy, though. You may be better off if you can borrow the money to pay your bill, rather than go on an installment plan that means, effectively, borrowing from the IRS. The IRS interest rate on late payments was 9% at the end of 1995 and can change quarterly. That might not sound bad, but that's not all you have to pay, either. There's also the 0.5% a month late-payment penalty, which hikes the effective cost to 15% a year. If you can borrow the money to pay your tax bill elsewhere for less, you're better off doing so.

Note this, too: In the past, the IRS set up installment agreements for free. Now the agency charges $43 for this "service."

Filing beyond August 15

Pushing the filing deadline beyond August 15 is possible, but you need a good reason. You can apply for an extra two months by filing Form 2688, *Application for Additional Extension of Time to File U.S. Individual Income Tax Return.*

If it appears you'll need to push the deadline back to October 15, try to file Form 2688 well before August 15. That way, if the IRS turns down your request, you'll still have a chance to file on time. If the IRS okays the extra time, you'll get a notice approving the extension. Attach that notice to your return when you finally file.

Automatic exemptions

U.S. citizens who live outside the country, those whose main place of business is beyond our borders, and military personnel who are stationed abroad on April 15 automatically get an extra two months to file their returns and pay their tax. If you qualify, you don't have to file any forms to request the additional time, but you should include with your return a statement explaining that you qualify for the June 15 deadline.

If You're Due a Refund

For most taxpayers, the deadline doesn't really matter, anyway.

That may come as a surprise—and the IRS would just as soon this not become common knowledge. But the vast majority of taxpayers do not really have to file by April 15. Notice in the discussion above that the penalties for failing to meet that deadline are based on the amount of tax you owe with your return. But the vast majority of taxpayers don't owe a dime with their returns. Instead, they get refunds. Hmmmmm. If there's no tax due on which to levy a penalty for late filing, then . . .

That's right: Even without an extension, there is no penalty for missing the deadline *if* you're due a refund. That piece of knowledge might come in mighty handy if you find yourself scrambling to finish things up in mid-April. If you're certain you have a refund coming, you may be able to skip that late-night rush to the post office. But don't procrastinate too long. You do have to file a return, and failing to do so until after the IRS figures you're late—and asks you about it—could mean a penalty.

Of course, if you have a refund coming you should be making every possible effort to file early—so you can get your money back—rather than putting things off. Generally, the IRS has to pay interest on refunds that aren't paid to taxpayers by June 1. (The rate is 1% less than the rate charged on underpayments, making it 8% during the last

Could I have a receipt for the IRS?

From the Wall Street Journal,
Permission, Cartoon Features Syndicate.

Time Saver

Keep only the records you need; toss the rest.

half of 1995.) That rule doesn't apply if you file your return late, though. In that case, if the IRS pays the refund within 45 days of the time you file, you get no interest.

(Most states also have provisions for extending their income-tax-filing deadlines. If you're going to be late, be sure to check with state income tax officials for specific requirements.)

Record Keeping

Over and over again in this book you'll read about the importance of keeping records. Of course, nothing can drive home the point better, or more unequivocally, than an invitation to an IRS audit. Unfortunately, at that point the revelation is of little help. When you're called before an auditor, a missing receipt—something you may have tossed away as a meaningless scrap of paper—can cost you dearly. What you can expect in a tax audit and how to survive the experience are discussed in Chapter 19.

Tax-return time is when you have all your records together. What do you need to keep, and for how long? It's simple: Keep whatever you need to persuade the IRS that everything on your return is accurate. And hang on to the evidence for as long as the IRS has the right to question your return.

Your record-keeping system doesn't have to be elaborate. What is important is to have a system and the discipline to keep your files up-to-date. The better organized you are, the easier it will be to put your hands on the information you need to complete your return. Your tax forms themselves can serve as an outline for what you need.

Set up files for your itemized deductions: medical, taxes, interest, etc. Save any bills, receipts and canceled checks that correspond to those deductions. If you write off the cost of a business car, you'll need a logbook recording your trips as well as evidence of the costs you incur. If you have rental property, you need another folder for all income and expenses. Do you claim someone as a dependent who's not your child? If so, keep a separate file for the evidence that you provide more than half of the person's support. Homeowners need a file for the house to keep track of additions to the basis that will affect the taxable profit when they ultimately sell the place.

Investors face special demands. You need to hang on to the documents that show when you bought every investment and what you paid for it.

How Long Is Long Enough?

But how long do you have to save all this stuff? That depends on what's involved.

The general rule is to keep your tax records until the statute of limitations on your tax return has expired. In most cases, that's three years after the due date of a return. Your return for 1995 is due April 15, 1996, so the auditing period ends April 15, 1999. If you haven't been alerted to an audit by then, it's probably safe to toss most of the records.

In some cases, though, the IRS gets six years to come after you. The extended jeopardy applies if you fail to report income that is 25% or more of the amount of gross income you do report. And if you fail to file a return or the IRS can prove that you committed fraud, there's no limit. Using the six-year rule, April of 1996 is the time to toss returns for 1989 and earlier years.

You can't pitch things willy-nilly, though. Although most of the paperwork can be thrown away, some of the financial papers connected with your tax return have a life beyond the statute of limitations. For example:

- **You need to hang on to brokerage statements and other papers that help you establish the tax basis of assets you still own.** Since the basis is the value from which any gain or loss will be determined when you sell the asset, these papers will figure in a return sometime in the future.

The basic six-year rule is also somewhat misleading because items on one return often carry over to future years. For example:

- **If you file a return reporting the sale of one home and the purchase of another**—in which the profit from the first home is rolled over into the second, as discussed in Chapter 9—the return should be kept indefinitely, along with the pertinent documents.

• **If you make nondeductible contributions to an individual retirement account** and file Form 8606, as discussed in Chapter 11, you need to keep that form and related information from your IRA sponsor until all funds are withdrawn from your IRAs.

• **If one year's return includes losses you can't deduct because of the passive-loss rules** (discussed in Chapter 10) hang on to the return and associated records until after you dispose of the passive activity and get to use the loss. Then you should keep the records for another three or six years until the statute of limitations on the return reporting the loss has expired.

• **Unused losses from home-office expenses** (see Chapter 13) can also be carried forward, so you need to keep the records substantiating them until after the loss has been used.

When you're cleaning out your tax files, err on the side of caution—particularly when it comes to your investments.

What about your tax forms themselves? Six years is probably long enough to hold on to them—except those that have a bearing on future returns. That's as long as the IRS keeps its copies of your returns.

50 Ways to Save
on Your Return

The real goal of this book is to help you drive down the tax bills you'll owe in the future. But in early 1996 there are still ways to save on your 1995 return, the one that's due April 15, 1996. Take this quick, guided tour of the tax forms in search of last-minute savings. At most stops along the way, you'll be directed to where you can find more information about the subject at hand so you can devise money-saving strategies for future returns.

Form 1040

✎ **1. Filing status (lines 1—5)** You may have more choice in determining your filing status than you think. If you're single or legally separated from your spouse, you may qualify as a head of household. That puts more of your income in lower tax brackets than if you file an individual return. And you get a bigger standard deduction: $5,750 versus $3,900. That alone saves over $500 if you're in the 28% bracket. Head of household filing status requires that you provide a home for someone in addition to yourself—usually a parent or child. It's often used by divorced taxpayers. *See Chapter 8.*

✎ **2. If your spouse died during 1995 you can still file a joint return for the year to take advantage of the lowest tax rates.** If your spouse died in 1993 or 1994 and you have a dependent child, you can probably file as a qualifying widow or widower, which also allows you to use joint-return rates. *See Chapter 8.*

✎ **3. Exemptions (line 6)** Each one you claim knocks $2,500 off your taxable income, saving $700 in the 28% bracket. A person doesn't have to be related to you to be your dependent. You may be able to claim someone who lives with you if you provide more than half of his or her support. In an attempt to short-

Form 1040 (cont'd.)

circuit attempts to claim pets or non-existent people as dependents, the law now demands that you provide the social security number for almost any dependent you claim. The only exception is for newborns. Babies born November 1 or later in 1995 don't have to have a social security number to be claimed on your 1995 return. Bad news for some: If you can be claimed as a dependent on someone else's return—such as your parents'—you can't claim a personal exemption. That costs $375 in the 15% bracket. Also, if your adjusted gross income exceeds certain levels—$172,050 on 1995 joint returns and $114,700 on single returns, for example—the tax-saving value of exemptions is gradually phased out as income rises. *See Chapter 8.*

4. Interest (line 8). If you report a lot of taxable income here, it may be a sign that you should consider tax-free bonds or mutual funds. A 5% tax-free yield is worth almost as much as a 7% taxable return if you're in the 28% bracket and more than 8% if you're in the 39.6% bracket. And, that doesn't count any possible state tax savings. *See Chapter 10.*

5. Don't include tax-exempt interest reported on line 8b in your taxable income. So, why report it at all, if the IRS doesn't get a shot at it? The government wants this information because there might be tax ramifications. Tax-free interest finds its way into the formula for taxing social security benefits, for example, and some of it may be hit by the alternative minimum tax. *See Chapters 12 and 4.*

6. State tax refunds (line 10). Think twice before you report a state tax refund as taxable income. Yes, your state sends both you and the IRS a notice of how much you got back in 1995. But refunds are tax-free for most taxpayers. That includes you if you didn't itemize deductions on your 1994 federal return. Even if you did itemize, part of the state refund may dodge the IRS. *See Chapter 15.*

7. Capital gains and losses (line 13). Be sure to revive any capital losses you couldn't use in 1994. The law won't let you deduct more than $3,000 of net capital losses in any year. If that rule means you had leftover losses in 1994, they may cut your taxes now. Use carryover losses first to offset 1995 capital gains on Schedule D, then use any excess to deduct up to $3,000 more against other income. *See Chapter 10.* (If Congress changed the rules for capital gains for 1995 after we went to press, write or e-mail us for an update. *See page i.*)

8. Capital gains distributions (line 13). Although there's no longer a special line for reporting capital gains distributions from your mutual funds, you show them here—*if* your only capital gains for the year are from such distributions and you

Form 1040 (cont'd.)

have no losses to report. If you have to file a Schedule D anyway, report the distributions there. Don't confuse a capital gains distribution—which, like a dividend, is a payout by a mutual fund—with the results of the redemption of mutual fund shares. Profit or loss on such a sale must be reported on Schedule D. *See Chapter 10.*

9. IRA payouts (line 15). This one might seem confusing if you rolled over part or all of your IRA last year. You must report on line 15(a) every dime you took out of individual retirement accounts during 1995. The amount to show on 15(b) as taxable income is what you *didn't* roll over (minus any amount that represents a return of nondeductible contributions). Although it may seem like useless paperwork to report a tax-free rollover, failing to do so will make the IRS question why you didn't pay tax on the distribution. Who needs the hassle? *See Chapter 11.*

10. Rental real estate, royalties, partnerships (line 17). You may be able to reduce the amount of income reported here by deducting a passive loss carried over from an earlier year. Basically, losses from passive activities, such as rentals and partnerships, are deductible only against income from passive activities. Any excess losses are suspended for use in future years when you have net passive income to offset. Also, if during

1995 you sold a passive investment that had generated suspended passive losses, those losses can now be used to offset any kind of income. *See Chapter 10.*

11. Social security benefits (line 20). Don't report more of your benefits as taxable income than you have to. This complicated calculation adds insult to injury, considering that only a few years ago all benefits were tax-free. Now, depending on your income, up to 85% of your benefits can be nicked by the IRS. Basically, if your adjusted gross income plus half your benefits total less than $25,000 on a single return or $32,000 on a joint return, all your benefits are safe. If your income is over $34,000 on a single or $44,000 on a joint return, up to 85% of the benefits are vulnerable. When income falls between those ranges, no more than half of your benefits can be taxed. *See Chapter 12.* (As this book went to press, Congress was considering changing the rules on this issue again to reduce the tax on benefits received by higher-income retirees. If changes are made that affect 1995 returns, write or e-mail us for an update. *See page i.*)

12. Other income (line 21). Don't be intimidated by the all-encompassing sound of "other income." Although the IRS might like a shot at every dollar that passes through your hands, there are limits. Things *not* to report here: inheri-

33

50 Ways to Save

Form 1040 (cont'd.)

tances, life insurance benefits or new-car rebates. All are tax-free. This catchall category covers income from a lottery or other gambling, the value of prizes, and jury fees. *See Chapter 6.*

13. IRA deduction (line 23). The IRA holds out the hope for a retroactive tax break. If you qualify to deduct contributions, deposits made right up to April 15 can be deducted on your 1995 return. You can deduct all or part of a contribution unless you or your spouse is covered by a retirement plan at work *and* your adjusted gross income is over $35,000 on a single return or $50,000 on a joint return. An entry on this line guarantees tax savings: In the $28% bracket, a $2,000 IRA deduction saves $560. If both you and your spouse can contribute and deduct the maximum, your savings double to $1,120. *See Chapter 11.*

14. Moving expenses (line 24). Until recently, only itemizers got to deduct their job-related moving expenses. Now, everyone who moved in 1995 to take a new job qualifies. To earn the deduction, the move must be in connection with taking a job at a new location and the new job has to be at least 50 miles farther from your old home than your old job was. Making this write-off available to those who use the standard deduction could be especially important to new graduates who moved to take the first job. *See Chapter 14.*

15. Self-employment tax deduction (line 25). To ease the pain of the self-employed tax, the self-employed get to deduct half of what they pay. The tax—the equivalent of the social security and medicare taxes paid by employees and employers—was 15.3% of the first $61,200 of 1995 self-employment income and 2.9% of income over $61,200. For every $1,000 paid, the 50% deduction saves $140 if you're in the 28% bracket. *See Chapter 3.*

16. Self-employed health insurance (line 26). This is an on-again/off-again tax break that Congress allowed to expire and then restated several times in recent years. In 1995, the lawmakers finally found the gumption to make the break permanent. It allows self-employed taxpayers to deduct 30% of the cost of health insurance for themselves and their families as an adjustment to income. That's valuable because, otherwise, the cost is added to other medical expenses and written off as an itemized deduction only to the extent that total medical costs exceed 7.5% of adjusted gross income. *See Chapter 14.*

17. Keogh and SEP (line 27). Here's another chance for a last-minute tax break. If you had self-employment income during 1995, you can shelter part of it inside a Keogh plan or Simplified Employee Pension (SEP). Contributions to either type of account—basically 13% to 20% of income up to a top pay-in of $30,000 a year—can be made as late as the filing

Form 1040 (cont'd.)

deadline and still earn a 1995 write-off. Although a Keogh plan had to have been opened during 1995 to qualify for a 1995 deduction, you can open a SEP right up to April 15, 1996, and still get credit for a 1995 contribution. *See Chapter 11.*

18. Jury fees (line 30). You'd never know it from looking at line 30—since it's labeled as a place to simply add figures that come above it—but this is where you may be able to deduct jury fees you were paid during 1995. If you served on a jury, your employer may have continued your full salary but required you to turn over the jury fees. The law demands that you report the jury fees as income, though, so you need to claim a deduction here to protect yourself from being taxed on money that really only passed through your hands. Include such jury fees in the total you enter on this line for total adjustments to income. *See Chapter 14.*

19. Foreign tax credit (line 43). You don't have to work at Rick's Place in Casablanca to earn the foreign tax credit. You may deserve it, for example, if you own shares in a mutual fund that invests in foreign securities. If information from the fund shows that foreign taxes were paid on your behalf, you can treat that amount as an itemized deduction or file Form 1116 to claim this credit. The credit is almost always worth more, since a credit offsets your tax liability dollar for dollar. *See Chapter 16.*

20. Alternative Minimum Tax credit (line 44). Folks who were hit by the alternative minimum tax (AMT) in the past but who are out from under the yoke this year may deserve a credit here. If you qualify, you can reclaim part of the AMT paid in earlier years. The credit is figured on Form 8801. *See Chapter 4.*

21. Self-employment tax (line 47). The self-employment tax is more painful than ever. The 15.3% rate to pay for social security and medicare applies to the first $61,200 of self-employment income in 1995. From that point on, the 2.9% medicare part of the tax applies. The time-saver here is the streamlined Schedule SE. Most taxpayers who owe social security tax on their earnings from self-employment can use this abbreviated version of this form. Remember, too, that half of what you pay in self-employment tax is deductible on line 25. *See Chapter 3.*

22. Retirement plans (line 51). There are penalties for taxpayers who break the retirement plan rules. But don't jump to the conclusion that you're guilty of an early withdrawal, say, if you took money before age 59½. It's okay to take money from a company retirement plan as early as age 55, if you get the money after you leave the job. And you can get company plan or IRA money at any time, without penalty, if the payout is part of a string of annual payments based on your life expectancy. One of the toughest penalties is reserved for

50 Ways to Save

Form 1040 (cont'd.)

taxpayers who fail to take the minimum required amount from an IRA after reaching age 70 ½. The penalty claims 50% of the amount you should have withdrawn, but didn't. But note this: If you have a good excuse, the IRS can waive the penalty. *See Chapter 11.*

23. Taxes for household help (line 53). This is a big time-saver if you have household help, such as a housekeeper or a caretaker for your children. If that person is considered your employee and you pay more than $1,000 a year, you're responsible for paying social security and medicare taxes for your employee. You may also have to pay federal (and state) unemployment taxes. In the past, you were subject to these taxes if you paid a household employee more than $50 in a calendar quarter and payments of the social security tax had to be made quarterly. Now the trigger is $1,000 a year and you pay the taxes with your own Form 1040 (or 1040A). You figure the taxes on the new Schedule H, which replaces the four quarterly social security tax payments and the annual employment tax payment. *See Chapter 8.*

24. Estimated tax payment (line 56). Memory jogger: Rather than claim a refund due on your 1994 return, did you have the IRS apply the amount to your 1995 tax bill? Remember to take credit for that payment here, along with any quarterly estimated tax payments you made.

25. Social security tax credit (line 59). Did you have more than one job in 1995? Did the combined pay exceed $61,200? If you answered *yes* to both questions, too much social security tax was withheld from your paychecks. To even things out, you get a credit. How much? The difference between what you paid in social security taxes (6.2% of your wages) and $3,794.40, the maximum amount anyone was supposed to pay in 1995. Check your W–2 forms.

26. Fuel-tax credit (line 60). Did you buy a new diesel-powered car or light truck during 1995? If so, you have a rebate coming from the government. The one-time credit, worth $102 (for cars) or $198 (light trucks), is to compensate you for a hike in the diesel fuel tax that was aimed at commercial users. *See Chapter 16.*

27. Underpayment penalty (line 66). If you owe $500 or more beyond what you've paid via withholding and estimated tax payments—and the amount due is more than 10% of your tax bill for the year—the IRS will assume you also owe a penalty for failing to pay enough during 1995. But there are exceptions to the penalty. Most taxpayers are spared, for example, if they paid in as much during 1995 as they actually owed for 1994. Check the exceptions before you pay a penalty. *See Chapter 7.*

Schedule A–Itemized Deductions

✎ **28. Medical and dental expenses (line 1).** Although medical expenses are deductible, most taxpayers don't get to deduct them. This oxymoron is due to the little catch that allows the write-off only for expenses that exceed 7.5% of adjusted gross income. When figuring whether your medical costs exceed the threshold, don't overlook the cost of getting to the doctor. The cost of trips to see out-of-town specialists and at least part of the cost of lodging when you're out of town to get medical care count toward the 7.5%. *See Chapter 15.*

✎ **29. Real estate taxes (line 6).** If you bought a home during 1995, you may deserve a bigger deduction than you think. If the seller paid real estate taxes in advance for a period during which you actually owned the home, include that amount in your deduction—whether or not you reimbursed the seller for the taxes. *See Chapter 15.*

✎ **30. Personal property tax (line 7).** Depending on where you live, you may be able to write off part of what you pay for auto license tags as a personal property tax. Any part of the fee based on the value of your car is deductible. This helps residents in about one-third of the states. If you're not sure, call your local department of motor vehicles. *See Chapter 15.*

✎ **31. Mortgage interest (line 10).** It's likely that all the interest paid on a mortgage secured by your home is deductible. If

you bought a home during 1995, points you paid to get the mortgage should be included on the 1098 form you received from the lender. If so, those points—including points paid by the seller on your behalf—are deducted along with the interest you paid on the mortgage during the year. *See Chapter 9.*

✎ **32. Mortgage interest, additional payments (line 11).** If you bought a house during 1995, you may have paid more mortgage interest than shows up on the year-end statement from the lender. Your settlement sheet should indicate whether you reimbursed the seller for interest paid during the time you actually owned the house. If so, you get to deduct that amount. Also, if the seller took back a mortgage that is secured by the house, the interest you're paying on that loan is deductible, too, even though it was not reported to you on a Form 1098. You do, however, have to report the name and social security number of the person you're paying so the IRS can be sure he or she is reporting and paying taxes on the interest income. *See Chapter 9.*

✎ **33. Mortgage payments in December (line 11).** You can claim the interest portion of a December mortgage payment mailed during the final days of the year, even if it doesn't show up on the lender's year-end statement. *See Chapter 9.*

✎ **34. Mortgage points (line 12).** Points you paid to get a mortgage should be

50 Ways to Save

Schedule A–Itemized Deductions (cont'd.)

reported on the 1098 form you got from your lender, in which case, you'd deduct them on line 10. In some cases, though, points don't show up on the 1098. That doesn't mean they're not deductible. You just have to report them separately. This includes any points you're writing off over the life of your mortgage (as may be the case if you refinanced your home mortgage) and, perhaps, points that a seller paid on your behalf at closing. Such points are now deductible by the buyer. *See Chapter 9.*

35. Investment interest (line 13). Despite a widespread belief that only mortgage interest is deductible, the law still allows investors to deduct interest on loans used to make investments. Such interest is deductible to the extent of your investment income. *See Chapter 10.*

36. Charitable gifts (lines 15 and 16). Congress is a suspicious group. That's why the lawmakers told the IRS that it can no longer consider a canceled check proof of a contribution of $250 or more. You must have a receipt from the charity to back up such a write-off. That applies to a single gift—of cash or property—of more than $250. If you gave your church fifty $25 contributions during the year, for a total of $1,250, you wouldn't need a receipt; your canceled checks are good enough. If you don't have a receipt for a donation, ask for it now. You're sup-

posed to have it before you file your return. *See Chapter 15.*

37. Charitable gifts, adding up the little things (line 15). Make sure your generosity during 1995 pays off as much as possible by rounding up all of your write-offs. The big contributions—which translate to the big deductions—are hard to overlook: what you give your church or synagogue or alma mater. But little expenses from your good-deed-doing can also mount up. Whether it's out-of-pocket contributions to a bell-ringer or what you pay for supplies while you're doing charitable work, if the money is going to help a qualifying charitable organization, you get a deduction. If you drive your own car while doing volunteer work, you can deduct 12 cents a mile. If your charitable work takes you out of town overnight—as the official delegate to a church meeting, for example—you can deduct the cost of transportation and the cost of your meals and lodging. *See Chapter 15.*

38. Charitable gifts, giving stock or mutual funds (line 16). There's a special break if you donate property—such as stock or mutual fund shares—to charity. If you owned the asset for more than a year, you get to write off it's value on the day that you made the gift, not what you originally paid for it. You don't have to pay tax on the appreciation while you owned the stock, either. In

Schedule A–Itemized Deductions (cont'd.)

the past, that untaxed appreciation could fall victim to the alternative minimum tax, but no more. Take advantage of this break now if you donated appreciated property last year, and keep it in mind in the future. Whenever you make substantial contributions, consider using appreciated property instead of cash. What if you really want to keep the stock, for example, in your portfolio? Donate the shares you own and use the cash you would have given to buy shares on the open market. The advantage is that you'll owe tax only on profit that accrues after you repurchase the shares. *See Chapter 15.*

39. Miscellaneous expenses (lines 20, 21 and 22). Don't assume the worst. Although you get no tax benefit unless these expenses add up to more than 2% of your adjusted gross income, there are so many possibilities that you may be able to vault over the threshold. Include job-related car and education expenses, union and professional dues, the cost of small tools and special workclothes, and job-hunting costs (including the cost of travel). Investment-related costs such as safe-deposit box rental and IRA custodial fees count, too, as does what you paid in 1995 for tax preparation help, including the cost of this book. *See Chapter 15.*

Schedule B—Interest and Dividends

40. Bonds: Don't pay tax on someone else's interest (line 1). The price you paid for bonds purchased in 1994 may have included an amount for interest accrued while the previous owner held the bonds. You don't have to pay tax on that amount, even if it was paid to you as part of the first interest payment in 1995. You do have to report the full amount of interest, though. How do you avoid being taxed on too much? You get to subtract out the "accrued interest." *See Chapter 10.*

41. Dividends (line 5). This can be confusing because although you have to report capital gains and nontaxable distributions as part of your total dividends on line 5, you break out the same amounts on lines 7 and 8 so you can subtract them to arrive at your taxable total. Don't skip the subtraction part, though. Otherwise you'll overpay your taxes because the capital gains distributions have to be reported elsewhere and the nontaxable distributions are really supposed to be tax-free. *See Chapter 10.*

Schedule C–EZ

42. Save time if you qualify to use this streamlined form. The C-EZ devotes almost as much space to explaining who can use the form as it does gathering information. After reporting your business name and address, you might get by with entering just three numbers: business income, business expenses (you don't have to itemize them) and net profit. Only the simplest of businesses can use the short form, but completing this form is a breeze for the lucky ones. *See Chapter 13.*

Schedule D—Capital Gains and Losses

43. Mutual funds: Don't overpay tax on your profits (lines 1 and 9). This is a major threat if you redeemed shares during 1995. The fund will tell you how much you received, but it's up to your records to show your cost or other "tax basis." You subtract that from the amount received to figure whether you have a gain or a loss. If you reinvested dividends over the years, your basis includes the amount reinvested. Many taxpayers apparently overlook this fact and overpay the tax. If your records are incomplete, call the fund—most have toll-free numbers—and ask for help. Investing a little extra time on this point can really pay off. *See Chapter 10.*

44. Inherited assets: Take advantage of stepped-up basis (line 9.) If you sold assets that you inherited, you deserve a very special tax break. Inherited property enjoys a "stepped-up" basis, that is, your basis is generally the value of the property when the previous owner died. The tax on any appreciation during his or her lifetime is forgiven. You're taxed only on appreciation after you inherit the asset. And if the asset has declined in value since you inherited it, you may claim a tax-saving loss deduction even though you're clearly financially ahead. The gain or loss from the sale of inherited property is automatically considered long-term, even if you didn't hold on to the asset for more than one year. *See Chapter 10.*

45. Capital loss carry-overs (lines 6 and 15). Don't forget to take advantage of capital losses you were unable to use on your 1994 return. Check last year's Schedule D for any losses you carried over. Those losses can be used here to offset 1995 capital gains, and up to $3,000 of excess loss is deductible against other 1995 income such as salary, interest or dividends. *See Chapter 10.*

Form 8814—Reporting a Child's Interest and Dividends

46. Child's income: An offer you can probably refuse. This form is designed to let you avoid slogging through Form 8615—the one designed to enforce the kiddie tax that applies the parents' tax rate to the investment income of their children under age 14. If your child's only income is from interest and dividends—and the total is $5,000 or less—you can report the income on your own return. You don't just add all your child's income to your own. The first $500 is tax-free and the next $500 is taxed at 15%. Beware that this procedure to save paperwork could result in a slightly higher federal tax on the child's income and raise your family's state tax bill. *See Chapter 8.*

Form 2441—Child-Care Credit

47. Child-care bills paid by Uncle Sam. If, to enable you to work, you pay for the care of a child age 12 or younger, this credit can cut your tax bill by several hundred dollars. Note that if a child turned 13 during 1995, what you paid for care up until his or her birthday counts toward the credit. If you have the option to use a reimbursement account at work to pay for child care, consider whether paying your child-care bills that way might be a better deal. Money that goes through a reimbursement account avoids federal income and social security taxes and, in almost all states, state income taxes as well. The combined benefit generally exceeds the savings offered by this credit. *See Chapter 16.*

Form 4972—Lump Sum Distribution

48. Retirement plan pay outs. If you received a lump-sum distribution from a retirement plan during 1995—and received it after you were 59½—you might qualify for forward averaging, a special tax break that can significantly cut the tax due on the pay out. If the distribution was less than $70,000, in fact, averaging makes part of the distribution tax-free. If you rolled over the distribution into an individual retirement account, no tax is due until you withdraw your money from the IRA. *See Chapter 12.*

Form 4562—Depreciation

✎ **49. Business-expense write-offs.** The law allows business owners to deduct immediately the cost of up to $17,500 worth of qualifying property that otherwise would have to be depreciated over several years. Known as "expensing," this could permit you to deduct the full cost of a computer used in your business at once, for example, rather than gradually over six years. *See Chapter 13.*

Getting Your Return to the IRS

✎ **50. First class mail is usually the way to go.** After all the effort invested in preparing your return, the last thing you want is for it to be lost in the mail and have the IRS accuse you of failing to file on time. So, should you take the precaution of sending the completed forms by certified mail, with return receipt requested? For most taxpayers, that's a needless hassle and expense. It's extremely rare for a return to be lost in the mail and even if yours is misplaced or destroyed, the chances are good that the IRS will believe that you filed on time if you have a copy of the signed and dated return. If you have a refund coming, there's no penalty for filing late anyway.

However, if you owe a substantial amount of extra tax or are making an election that the law says has to be made by the due date, using certified mail—which provides you with a receipt showing when the letter was mailed—may make sense. The penalties for late filing rise with the amount of tax owed with your return, so the more money potentially at stake, the more the peace of mind purchased by using certified mail is worth. Filing your return electronically to speed up the receipt of your refund is usually not worth the cost. If you move after filing, you should advise the IRS of your change of address by filing Form 8822, to insure you get your refund and any other mail the IRS sends you.

Starting this year, if you owe money with your return, you may have to send a 1040-V payment voucher in with your check. And if you file a Schedule C business return, you'll mail your payment separately from your tax return. This is supposed to make it easier for the IRS to cash your check quickly. And speaking of checks, don't make yours payable to the IRS. It's too easy for someone to change the IRS to MRS and cash it as a check to MRS. John Jones. Write out Internal Revenue Service.

Amended
Returns

Confession, so they say, is good for the soul. It can also pay off for the pocketbook if you're admitting to the IRS that you made a mistake on your tax return. Although blowing the whistle on yourself might sound like unsound tax strategy, hundreds of thousands of taxpayers who do it each year are rewarded with refunds. Why? Because they correct errors that caused them to overpay their tax with the original return.

The amended tax return, filed on Form 1040X, can be a handy weapon in your tax arsenal. With it you can apply newly discovered tax-saving knowledge to returns filed in previous years. That means a once neglected tax advantage isn't irretrievably lost.

Something—or things—you learn in this book could easily prompt a money-saving amended return. You might need to file a 1040X, for example, if you discover you reported too much capital gain on the sale of a mutual fund or overlooked an itemized deduction or credit on your 1994 return. Sometimes, you have to file an amended return because Congress or the IRS changes the rules retroactively to permit a tax break that can save you money, as discussed later.

A missed deduction last year can't simply be claimed on this year's forms. That would be too simple. (Also, it might lead to folks forgetting write-offs in years they are in low tax brackets and remembering them when they are in higher ones.) No, if you want to retroactively take advantage of a tax break, you must file a 1040X for the year involved.

Of course, the 1040X isn't designed as a one-way street. You're supposed to use it to correct any errors or

oversights that resulted in paying less than you really owed in an earlier tax year. Each year, taxpayers file about 1.5 million amended returns.

You generally have three years from the due date of a return to file an amended version, although the period can stretch to seven years if the revision involves a bad debt or worthless security. The three-year limit means that 1995 returns, due April 15, 1996, are usually open for amendment until April 15, 1999.

How to Do It

You don't have to redo your entire return to make a change. The 1040X asks for totals of income, adjustments, deductions and so on. When you make a change, you adjust the total—by adding $1,000 to your itemized deductions, for example—then send in a revised version of Schedule A showing the correct amount of itemized deductions.

When figuring your tax on the revised income amount, be sure to use the tax rates for the year of the return you're amending. Since tax brackets change every year, even if rates don't, using the wrong year's rates will guarantee another mistake.

If your 1040X shows the government owes you money, the form serves as a request for refund, and you ought to get your money within two months. The IRS pays interest going back to the original due date of the return (assuming you filed it on time). The rate can change each quarter, and was 8% for the last half of 1995. If your amended return shows that you owe more tax for the year involved, send a check along with the form. The IRS will bill you for the interest due.

Note this about 1995 returns: If your original return called for a refund and—before you get the check—you discover an error that requires an amendment that will bring you even more money, hold off on the 1040X until you get the first refund. Having two returns in the system at the same time can really foul things up. But if the change means you owe the IRS money, file the 1040X as soon as possible to limit the amount of interest you'll owe on the late payment.

When It's the Government's Fault

Sometimes a 1040X is required through no fault of your own. Here are two examples:

Self-employed medical insurance deduction. As discussed in Chapter 14, self-employed taxpayers can qualify to deduct part of what they pay for medical insurance as an adjustment to income, which is much more valuable than deducting that cost as an itemized deduction. That break is now permanent and allows a write-off of 30% of qualifying cost. In the past—when the deduction was for 25% of the premiums—the break was allowed to expire, then reinstated retroactively. If the deduction "didn't exist" when returns were filed but was later reinstated, those taxpayers must file a 1040X to get the tax-saving deduction.

This could put money in your pocket if you paid qualifying expenses during the last half of 1992 or during 1994 and didn't claim the deduction because it had expired at the time you filed your return for the year involved. In both cases, Congress retroactively reinstated the deduction. If you missed the 1992 deduction, you have only until April 15, 1996, to file your 1040X to claim it. That's the deadline for changes to 1992 returns. If you missed the 1994 deduction, you have until 1998 to file your 1040X, but the sooner you file, the sooner you'll get your money.

Seller-paid points on home mortgages. This is an IRS flip-flop that might save you money. As noted in Chapter 9, in 1994 the agency had a change of heart on the subject of points paid in connection with the purchase of a home. Before that time, the rule was basically that points paid by a buyer could be deducted by the buyer but points paid by the seller could not be deducted by anybody. In 1994, though, the IRS decided that even if the seller paid the points, the expense could be deducted by the buyer. The rule change was made retroactive to 1991, setting off a flood of amended returns.

Because of the three-year limit for amended returns, 1991 returns can no longer be changed. But if you bought a house in 1992—and the seller paid points for you—you have until April 15, 1996, to file a 1040X and claim a retroactive refund. A $2,000 seller-paid points deduction is worth $560 to you if you're in the 28% bracket—plus interest back to April 15, 1993. If you bought a home in 1992 or 1993, check the settlement papers carefully to see if you qualify for this break.

Begging for an Audit?

Is it risky to file a 1040X? If you use one to ask for an extra refund, are you begging for an audit, too? The IRS says the answer is no, and although that's what you might expect to hear from the tax agency, there's no reason to believe a 1040X marks your original return for audit. That's the word from accountants who have filed amended returns for clients.

You can get a copy of the 1040X and the instructions for filing it from your local IRS office or by calling 800–TAX–FORM. Send the completed form to the IRS Service Center for the area where you now live, even if the return you're correcting was filed to a different center.

The Self-Employment Tax

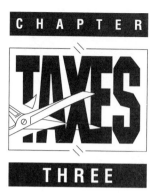

How would you like to send an extra 15.3% of your income to Uncle Sam—on top of what you pay in income taxes?

That's what you could owe in social security and medicare taxes if you earn self-employment income. It doesn't matter whether the earnings come from a full-time business, say, or occasional moonlighting. If that net income is $400 or more, say hello to the self-employment tax. It's officially known as the SECA tax, the *Self-employment Contribution Act* tax, and it pays for social security and medicare.

Employees don't have to worry about this levy. Instead, they pay for social security and medicare via the FICA (*Federal Insurance Contribution Act*) tax. Employers with-hold half of that tax from employees' pay and pay the other half. When you're both the employer and the employee, you have to figure the tax and pay the full amount yourself.

Considering the big bite that the self-employment tax takes, it's important to know exactly what income it applies to and what income escapes.

Self-employment income is basically the net income you report on Schedule C, *Profit (or Loss) From Business or Profession.* If you are a member of a partnership that carries on a trade or business, your share of partnership income counts as self-employment income, too, and any losses reduce the income subject to this tax. But if you're

Money Saver

Don't pay the self-employment tax on rental or investment income.

an investor in a limited partnership, your share of income and losses don't come into play for purposes of the self-employment tax.

This tax does *not* apply to investment income, such as interest, dividends or capital gains, or to rental income (unless you're a real estate dealer or you provide hotel-like services in connection with the rental).

Unlike the income tax, there is a limit on how much income is vulnerable to the self-employment tax. The amount rises each year, however, and to complicate things further, different parts of the self-employment tax apply to different amounts of income.

Anatomy of the Tax

This tax really has two parts: 12.4% pays for the social security retirement benefits; the other 2.9% goes to pay for medicare. Until 1991, the difference was rather academic to the taxpayer: Since both parts applied to the same amount of income, it was fine to think of it as a single tax, with a 15.3% rate.

Now, however, if your income is more than $61,200 you have to know there are two parts. Here's why:

For 1995, the full 15.3% tax applies to the first $61,200 of self-employment income. At that point, the 12.4% social security part of the tax stops, but the 2.9% medicare tax continues regardless of how high your income rises. (The extension of the medicare tax affects employees, too. The FICA tax withheld from their checks includes 1.45% for medicare—their employers pay the other half—and that levy applies to all of their wage income. The 6.2% withheld for social security applies only to the first $61,200 of wages.)

The $61,200 cap is 1995's limit. It's $62,700 for 1996.

For purposes of the income cap, "income" includes net self-employment income *and* any wages earned on a job on which social security taxes are withheld. If you have a job as an employee and earn $45,000 on which FICA is withheld, for example, the full 15.3% self-employment tax would apply only to the first $16,200 of self-employment income. (That amount, plus the $45,000 of wages, would bring you up to 1995's $61,200 cap.) Additional self-employment income would be hit by only the 2.9% medicare tax.

Figuring the Tax

The social security/medicare split isn't the only thing that complicates the self-employment tax, as you'll discover when you go through the rigmarole required to figure how much you owe. You can't just multiply the appropriate tax rate times your self-employment income. There's more to it than that, but at least the extra effort is likely to save you money.

First of all, you get to reduce net self-employment income by 7.65% before applying the tax rate. Say, for example, that your net self-employment income is $50,000. That's the amount you report as taxable for income tax purposes on Form 1040. But when figuring your self-employment tax on Schedule SE, *Computation of Social Security Self-Employment Tax,* the taxable amount is $46,175. (On the form, you handle this by multiplying income by 0.9235, which is the equivalent of subtracting 7.65%.) Not paying the 15.3% tax on $3,825 difference in this example saves you $585. (The savings are phased out at higher income levels. When self-employment income hits $66,270, for example, even after the 7.65% reduction, the 15.3% rate applies to the maximum $61,200. Above that level, then, the reduction saves not the full 15.3% but only the 2.9% medicare portion of the tax.)

Extra Cash

•••••••••••••••••••••••••

Q: *In addition to my job, I do a little carpentry work on the side. Last year, I made about $1,000 doing odd jobs for neighbors. I know it's taxable but I'm not sure where to report it. Do I count it as "other income" on the Form 1040?*

A: No. It's self-employment income, and you should report it on a Schedule C or C-EZ. On the plus side, that will also permit you to deduct the cost of any materials you used, plus the cost of transportation to and from the jobs. Since your self-employment income was more than $400, you may also have to file a Schedule SE and pay the 15.3% social security tax on the income.

Money Saver

Deduct from your income 50% of the self-employment tax you pay.

Income tax deduction

Another money saver is the right to an *income tax* deduction for 50% of the self-employment tax you pay. Again, consider an example that assumes you have $50,000 of self-employment income. The self-employment tax would be $7,065 and that generates a $3,533 income tax deduction. In the 28% bracket, that saves you almost $1,000.

You claim the income tax deduction on line 25 of the Form 1040 as an adjustment to income, so you get the benefit even if you don't itemize your deductions.

When you work on the Schedule SE, you'll notice a discussion of optional methods for figuring the tax due. It's doubtful that you'll want to spend any time trying to see if an alternative technique can save you money. The options are available only to those with small amounts of self-employment income and are designed to permit individuals to pay *extra* self-employment tax. The point is that by doing so a taxpayer may be able to increase the income base used to set his or her social security benefits.

If you're hit by the self-employment tax, you should include what you'll owe when figuring your quarterly estimated tax payments, as discussed in Chapter 7.

The Alternative Minimum Tax

It's sometimes said that AMT stands for *A Magic Tax*. That's because taxpayers who think they've done a great job whittling down their income tax bill are sometimes astonished to see their savings disappear when the IRS pulls a new set of rules out of a hat. Actually, AMT is the acronym for the alternative minimum tax, a levy that grew out of congressional embarrassment over reports that numerous millionaires were playing the tax game so shrewdly that they could pull their tax bills down to $0, or shockingly close to it.

The point of the AMT is to ensure that taxpayers with substantial income pay at least a reasonable amount of income tax. To accomplish that, Congress created what amounts to a separate tax system, lurking in the shadows and ready to spring into action if you benefit too much from tax breaks offered by the regular tax rules.

Unfortunately, there's no easy answer to the question of who needs to be concerned about the AMT. While it's not reserved solely for millionaires, it generally hits only the most affluent, those with incomes well into the six figures. Only in rare circumstances will it reach down and bite a taxpayer with income under $100,000.

A couple of things are certain:

- First, if you are subject to the AMT, you're almost sure to need professional help with your tax return. The rules here are so complex that they make other parts of the tax law seem crystal clear.

- Second, the AMT throws a major-league curve at traditional year-end tax planning.

To know whether you have anything to worry about, you have to do your tax return twice: first applying the regular rules, then recalculating everything for the AMT. Things are rigged against you, too: You're stuck with whichever method produces the *bigger* bill.

The AMT is close to a flat tax, with only two rates: 26% for taxable income up to $175,000 and 28% for income above that level. (For married-filing-separately taxpayers, the 28% bracket kicks in at $87,501.)

So what's the big problem? Even at 28%, the AMT rate is more than ten percentage points lower than the top income tax rate. How can a lower rate produce a higher tax bill? That's the tricky part of the AMT: It applies to more income than the regular tax. Many of the deductions and other tax breaks that are perfectly proper for holding down regular taxable income aren't permitted under the AMT rules.

"What makes you think I'm filing a frivolous tax return?"

From the Wall Street Journal;
Permission, Cartoon Features Syndicate.

Figuring AMT Income

The first step toward determining whether you have to worry about the AMT is to pinpoint your AMTI— alternative minimum taxable income. The starting point is your regular taxable income. Not surprisingly, almost all the adjustments demanded by the AMT increase that amount. Here are the ones most likely to affect you:

Personal exemptions

They aren't permitted to reduce AMT income. Since they pulled down your regular taxable income, you must add them back.

Itemized deductions

Many of the write-offs that reduce regular taxable income don't count for AMT purposes. Add back deductions claimed for the following:

- **State and local taxes.**

- **Miscellaneous itemized deductions above the 2% threshold.**

- **Medical expenses not in excess of 10% of adjusted gross income.** (The threshold for regular tax purposes is 7.5%.)

- **Certain mortgage interest.** Under the regular tax, you can use a home-equity loan to skirt the law's crackdown on the deduction of personal interest, as discussed in Chapter 9. For the AMT, however, you can generally deduct interest only on loans used to buy, build or substantially improve your first or second home. Also, if your regular mortgage deduction included an amount on a loan used to buy a boat, that amount doesn't count for AMT purposes. A boat can't qualify as a first or second home under the AMT.

Depreciation

The AMT has its own set of depreciation rules, which generally result in smaller write-offs than the deductions you get under the regular tax. To the extent that regular depreciation exceeds what you are allowed under the AMT, you have another add-on to your AMTI. It's possible, however, that the special depreciation rules will reduce AMTI. That happens if you deserve a bigger write-off using the AMT approach than you do by following the regular tax rules.

For example, residential real estate put in service after 1986 is depreciated over 27.5 years for the regular tax but over 40 years for the AMT. If you're depreciating a $500,000 building, annual write-offs for the regular tax would be $18,182 ($500,000 ÷ 27.5) but just $12,500 ($500,000 ÷ 40) under the AMT. You'd have to add the $5,682 difference to your regular taxable income when toting up your AMTI. If you still own the building after 28 years, it would be fully depreciated for regular tax purpos-

> *"And it came to pass in those days, that there went out a decree from Caesar Augustus, that all the world should be taxed."*
>
> —ST. LUKE

es, but you'd still have a dozen years' worth of $12,500 annual depreciation write-offs under the AMT. In those years, you'd get to subtract that $12,500 from regular taxable income when calculating your AMTI.

These rules promise to greatly complicate your record keeping. The different depreciation schedules mean your adjusted basis in the property (basically, that's cost minus depreciation) will be different for AMT versus for regular tax purposes. That, in turn, will affect your gain or loss when you sell. If you're subject to the AMT, you'll have to keep separate sets of books tracing the tax basis of the property under each system.

Taxable tax-free interest?
• •

Q: *My broker suggested I invest in "private activity bonds," which he said are municipal bonds that pay a premium yield because the interest is taxable under the Alternative Minimum Tax. Why would anyone want a muni bond that pays taxable interest?*

A: It can make sense if you are among the vast majority of taxpayers who don't have to worry about AMT. Interest on private activity bonds—which basically are bonds issued by states or municipalities for nongovernmental purposes—is tax-free under the regular income tax. If you're hit by the AMT, however, interest on such bonds issued after August 7, 1986, is taxable at either 26% or 28%.

Incentive stock options

Here's an AMT preference item that doesn't show up on the regular tax return at all. When you exercise an incentive stock option, you get to buy shares for less than current market value. The bargain element is ignored by the regular tax, but it is considered part of your AMT income. Including in AMTI the difference between what is paid for shares and their market value when the option is exercised is often the event that pushes a taxpayer into the grasp of the AMT.

In the year you sell the stock, however, you'll get to reduce AMTI by the same amount. That's because your shares have a different basis for regular and AMT purposes. Since you don't report the bargain element as income under the regular tax, your basis in the shares is what you pay for them. Under the AMT, however, your basis is what you paid *plus* the amount you had to report as an AMT preference item. The higher basis means you have a smaller taxable profit—for AMT purposes—when you sell. The larger profit is included in regular taxable income, so you subtract the difference when calculating AMT income.

Tax-exempt interest

Thanks to the AMT, there's such a thing as *taxable* tax-free interest. Tax-exempt interest on certain "private activity bonds" issued after August 7, 1986, is a preference item to be added to AMTI. Interest on such bonds— basically those issued by states or municipalities for nongovernmental purposes—is still tax-free under the regular tax. The issuer, or the broker trying to sell you the bonds, should be able to tell you whether the AMT threatens the interest.

Charitable contributions

One significant add-on to AMTI has been eliminated in recent years. As discussed in Chapter 15, under the regular tax rules, gifts of appreciated property can earn you a deduction for the full market value of the property while letting you avoid the tax on the gain that would be due if you sold the property. But before 1993, such untaxed appreciation was a "preference" item and had to be included in AMTI. For gifts made in 1993 and later years, however, such appreciation is tax-free under the AMT, just as it is under the regular tax.

The AMT Exemption

Once you arrive at your bloated AMTI figure, you get to subtract an exemption amount based on your filing status: $45,000 if you're married filing jointly or a surviving spouse; $33,750 if you're single or a head of household; $22,500 if you're married filing a separate return.

The exemption is phased out, however, for taxpayers whose AMTI exceeds certain levels. It begins to disappear when AMTI hits $150,000 for taxpayers filing joint returns, $112,500 for those who file as an individual or head of household, and $75,000 for marrieds filing separately. For every $100 of excess income, the exemption

Money Saver

The AMT no longer applies to the untaxed appreciation of charitable gifts.

shrinks by $25 until it's completely phased out at the income levels shown in this table:

Filing Status	Exemption Amount	Phaseout Begins	Exemption Wiped Out
Married filing jointly	$45,000	$150,000	$330,000
Single or head of household	33,750	112,500	247,500
Married filing separately	22,500	75,000	165,000

After you subtract the exemption, you know how much is subject to the alternative minimum tax rates of 26% on the first $175,000 and 28% on amounts over $175,000 ($87,500 if married filing separately).

The only tax credit available for AMT purposes is the foreign tax credit. If you claimed that credit on your regular tax return, you can use it here, too (although it can't offset more than 90% of your AMT bill). The result is known in tax parlance as your *tentative* minimum tax.

Compare it to your regular tax bill. If the minimum tax is higher, the difference between the two is actually your alternative minimum tax. You pay it in addition to your regular tax.

The AMT Credit

Ready for more confusion? Part, if not all, of the extra tax you're forced to pay by the AMT may be refunded to you in the future via an AMT credit to offset your regular tax liability. This surprising generosity stems from the fact that the AMT attacks two different kinds of tax benefits: those that defer your tax liability, such as accelerated depreciation and the bargain element of incentive stock options; and those that wipe out part of your tax bill completely, such as itemized deductions. The AMT credit is Congress's way of refunding to you in a later year the amount attributable to the "timing preferences," that is, the tax the AMT forces you to pay sooner rather than later.

Figuring the credit requires yet another set of calculations. After you know how much alternative minimum tax you owe, find what the bill would be if the only add-ons to regular taxable income were from these preferences: disallowed itemized deductions, depletion allowances and tax-exempt income from private-purpose bonds. These are the breaks that permit the permanent avoidance of the regular tax and therefore don't count toward the credit.

The difference between the AMT figured this way and the amount you actually have to pay is your minimum tax credit.

Say, for example, that your regular tax is $10,000 and the AMT calculation delivers a $14,000 bill. Assume the entire difference is attributable to your inclusion in AMT income of the bargain element of incentive stock options—a timing preference. In this case, the full $4,000 alternative minimum tax becomes an AMT credit for the future.

There is a catch, though. You can use the AMT credit only in a year when you're not subject to the AMT. If you find yourself facing the AMT year after year, the credit will be of no use. Also, you can use the credit to pull your regular tax liability below the AMT liability in a future year. Remember that reducing the regular tax bill below the AMT obligation would toss you back into the AMT quagmire. You can carry forward any unused part of the AMT credit to future years, however, when you might have regular tax to offset.

Money Saver

Part of the extra tax you're forced to pay by the AMT might be refunded via a credit in future years.

PART

TAXES

TWO

Year-Round
Tax-Saving Strategies

Tax Planning & You

A wry observer once said that the ten most feared words in the English language are: "I'm from the federal government, and I'm here to help." So it's no surprise that taxpayers are skeptical each time Congress sits down to rewrite the tax law—as our lawmakers seem destined to do every year. Despite promises to make the law fairer and simpler and, of course, to make our tax bills smaller, we often wind up with more complexities and inequities . . . the near-constant change in the law keeps the Internal Revenue Service desperately behind in its effort to write regulations explaining what the rules mean. Is it any wonder that half of all Americans pay someone else to do their tax returns? Or that former President Jimmy Carter described the system "a disgrace to the human race?"

It's enough to make you throw up your hands in frustration and, assuming there's no way to win, abandon all efforts to hold down your tax bill.

That would be a costly mistake. IRS research shows that nearly one in ten taxpayers overpays his or her taxes because of errors on tax returns. Millions more undoubtedly pay more than they should because they fail to take advantage of tax-saving opportunities during the year. That's what tax planning is all about: identifying opportunities and capturing tax savings. Remember that the tax bill you owe each spring is based on the saving, investing, spending, business and other personal decisions you made during the previous year.

The stakes are enormous, a point that is driven home each year when the Tax Foundation, a private research group in Washington, D.C., announces Tax

Freedom Day. That's the date by which the average American will have earned enough to pay all of his or her federal, state and local taxes. For 1995, the group's economists pinpointed May 6 as Tax Freedom Day, the latest in the year it has ever fallen. The idea is that every dime earned during the first 126 days of the year—from January 1 to May 6—went to pay taxes. About two-thirds of the tax tab was owed to Uncle Sam; the rest to state and local governments.

The accompanying table shows how Tax Freedom Day has shifted over the last four decades, so that it now arrives more than a month later than it did in 1950.

The aim of this book is to help you take advantage of the tax rules rather than be victimized by a higher-than-necessary tax bill. The goal is to make your personal tax freedom day come earlier each year.

How We Got Here

Although it is difficult to imagine, the income tax didn't start out to be oppressively complex. It's taken a long, tortuous road since 1913 when the 16th Amendment to the Constitution authorized the government to impose such a tax. At first, it was really a simple law. The first $3,000 of a single person's income was tax-free; the first $4,000 for married couples. For perspective, if we adjust these amounts for all the inflation since then, the tax-free figures would be around $30,000 and $40,000 today. The basic tax rate was a whopping 1%, but there was a "super tax" on the rich that claimed as much as 7% of incomes above half a million dollars. The first Form 1040 was four pages—including the instructions. Very few Americans had to fool with the form at all. Less than 1% of the population had to pay the tax.

From a few pages tucked inside a tariff bill in 1913, the Internal Revenue Code has grown to over 2,000 pages of the proverbial small print. There are thousands of pages of IRS regulations and volumes of public and private IRS rulings to explain what the law means and how it applies in various circumstances. Thousands of court decisions further mystify the riddle of the tax law as they

Tax freedom day:

1950	April 3
1955	April 9
1960*	April 17
1965	April 15
1970	April 28
1975	April 28
1980*	May 1
1985	April 30
1990	May 3
1991	May 2
1992*	May 2*
1993	May 3
1994	May 6
1995	May 6

* Leap year

Source: Tax Foundation

support, contradict, expand or narrow the IRS view of the taxpayer's world.

From the straightforward 1040 form that made its debut for 1913 returns, the IRS now serves up an impressive arsenal of forms. The "principal" ones are gathered each year and presented in Package X. It's now printed in three volumes, crammed with well over 100 forms and schedules and their instructions.

From the graduated rates of 1913—ranging from 1% to 7% on the theory that the higher one's income, the greater proportion of it he or she could afford to pay in tax—Congress has pushed the rate over the 90% mark. The top bracket was 70% as recently as 1981. It's officially 39.6% today although, as noted later in this chapter, it can bite even deeper.

Over the years, the income tax has undergone a metamorphosis, from a simple means of raising revenue to the government's largest source of funds and, simultaneously, one of the central tools for manipulating and fine-tuning the economy. One Congress after another has peppered the law with scores of exclusions, deductions, exceptions and credits—granting preferential treatment to encourage certain activities considered socially desirable or in the pursuit of the illusive goal of fairness.

Piece by piece, amendment by amendment, the Internal Revenue Code has become the monstrosity it is today. In the process, it has spawned a massive industry of tax planners. Ingenious men and women spend their careers dreaming up ways to tie together seemingly unrelated nooks and crannies of the tax code. Excavating the tax law for nuggets that can save money has become a national pastime.

Why Tax Planning Is for You

The fact that federal income taxes are one of the biggest annual expenditures of most families underscores the importance of tax planning. It's a serious mistake to think of tax planning as the province of the wealthy. Instead, draw your inspiration from this comment from a high-priced tax attorney: "The best and finest tax planning is done by people who have more money than they'll ever spend or be able to give away to any meaningful purpose. The worst tax planning is done by nice middle-class people who have middle-class virtues, those who have to work hard and save and sacrifice."

If you're in the latter group, this book can help you. As you move through the chapters ahead, keep in mind the clarion call of tax planning issued by Federal Judge Learned Hand in 1947. In a ruling in which he rejected the IRS's position that a taxpayer's maneuvers were part of a "reprehensible scheme to lessen" his tax bill, Judge Hand wrote these comments that you'll find framed in the offices of many accountants and tax attorneys:

Over and over again courts have said that there is nothing sinister in so arranging one's affairs as to keep taxes as low as possible. Everybody does so, rich or poor; and all do right, for nobody owes any public duty to pay more than the law demands: Taxes are enforced exactions, not voluntary contributions. To demand more in the name of morals is mere cant.

Don't Get Mad, Get Even

If you need extra incentive to invest time and effort to hold down your tax bill, consider this: Even if you take advantage of every possible break, you have to pay more tax than you should. Why?

Because millions of your fellow citizens cheat.

A recently released study shows that almost 40% of returns filed in 1988 (the latest year for which data is available) understated the amount of tax due. The average underpayment? Almost $800. All told, those "mistakes" cost the government more than $30 billion—money that has to be made up by other taxpayers. And $30 billion is only the tip of the "tax gap"—the difference between what's owed in taxes and what's paid. Some estimates put the gap at $150 billion or more. Considering that the income tax brings in about $800 billion, that would mean that for every $1,000 collected, almost $200 falls through the cracks.

"The income tax has made more liars out of the American people than golf has."

—WILL ROGERS

Know your marginal tax rate. All extra deductions you come up with produce tax savings at that high rate.

That isn't to suggest you should join the cheaters, only that you should redouble your efforts to take advantage of every legitimate tax break.

Tax Rates and Your Tax Bracket

A key to tax planning is knowing your marginal tax rate. That's the rate that applies at the margin, to your top dollar of income. Under our graduated tax system, as income rises, both the size of your tax bill and the percentage of income claimed by the government increase. The theory is that the more money you have, the greater portion of it you can do without.

Knowing your marginal rate is essential because it tells you how much of any extra earnings—from investments, a raise or moonlighting—you get to keep. It also measures the saving power of deductible expenses. Only if you know your tax bracket can you pinpoint what a charitable contribution or business expense really costs you after you take your tax savings into account.

Unfortunately, this is an area of great confusion. The accompanying table presents the official tax rates for 1996. (See the Appendix for tax rates for 1995.) We say official because, as noted later, there's more here than meets the eye. In the table for joint returns, you'll see that taxable income between $40,100 and $96,900 falls in the 28% bracket. Does that mean if you make $60,000, 28% of it—$16,800—goes to Uncle Sam? Absolutely not.

Part of your earnings isn't taxed at all. If you claim four exemptions on your 1996 tax return—one each for yourself, your spouse and two dependent children—that knocks $10,200 off taxable income because exemptions are worth $2,550 each in 1996. Deductions will reduce taxable income by at least $6,700 more. That's the standard deduction for 1996 joint returns; if you itemize deductions, even more of your income will escape tax. (Note: The 1996 values for exemptions and the standard deduction are higher than those that applied in 1995 because they are increased each year to account for inflation.) So your $60,000 of earnings is pared down to no more than

$43,100. Does the government get 28% of that amount—$12,068? Nope.

On a joint 1996 return, the tax bill on $43,100 of taxable income will be $6,855. That's about 16% of $43,100, and just 11.4% of $60,000.

While you're said to be in the 28% bracket, the portion of your income that falls in the 15% bracket—the first $40,100 on a 1996 joint return—is still taxed at 15%. Only the dollars that fall in the 28% bracket—the $3,000

1996 Tax Rates

Taxable Income	Tax
Single	
Up to $24,000	15% of every dollar
$24,001 to $58,150	$3,600 plus 28% of amount over $24,000
$58,151 to $121,300	$13,162 plus 31% of amount over $58,150
$121,301 to $263,750	$32,738.50 plus 36% of amount over $121,300
Over $263,750	$84,020.50 plus 39.6% of amount over $263,750
Married Filing Jointly and Surviving Spouses	
Up to $40,100	15% of every dollar
$40,101 to $96,900	$6,015 plus 28% of amount over $40,100
$96,901 to $147,700	$21,919 plus 31% of amount over $96,900
$147,701 to $263,750	$37,667 plus 36% of amount over $147,700
Over $263,750	$79,445 plus 39.6% of amount over $263,750
Heads of Household	
Up to $32,150	15% of every dollar
$32,151 to $83,050	$4,822.50 plus 28% of amount over $32,150
$83,051 to $134,500	$19,074.50 plus 31% of amount over $83,050
$134,501 to $263,750	$35,024 plus 36% of amount over $134,500
Over $263,750	$81,554 plus 39.6% of amount over $263,750
Married Filing Separately	
Up to $20,050	15% of every dollar
$20,051 to $48,450	$3,007.50 plus 28% of amount over $20,050
$48,451 to $73,850	$10,959.50 plus 31% of amount over $48,450
$73,851 to $131,875	$18,833.50 plus 36% of amount over $73,850
Over $131,875	$39,722.50 plus 39.6% of amount over $131,875

between $40,100 and $43,100 in this example—are clipped by the 28% rate.

Unless you're affected by one of the bubble brackets discussed starting on the next page, you should still keep the 28% rate in mind for tax-planning purposes. Because that's the marginal rate, 28% of any extra taxable earnings will go to the IRS. And extra deductions—such as a deposit to an individual retirement account or a charitable gift—will produce tax savings at a rate of 28%. For example, a $2,000 deductible IRA contribution would knock $560 (28% of $2,000) off your tax bill.

Inflation's Good Deed

The tax brackets are adjusted each year for inflation, so that as dollars you earn decline in purchasing power so will the government's take. Basically, for example, if the inflation rate in 1996 is 3%, the 15% bracket for 1997 will be extended by 3%. On a joint return, that would push the top of the bracket from $40,100 to $41,300. (The adjustments are rounded down to the nearest $50.) This means an extra $1,300 would be taxed at 15% rather than 28%. That would save you $169. The top of the 28% bracket would also advance, delaying the start of the 31% bracket. And so on.

As noted earlier, personal exemptions and the standard deduction are also indexed for inflation. To see the impact, consider the example above in which $60,000 of 1996 taxable earnings will produce a $6,855 tax bill. In 1995, that same amount of earnings would have triggered a tax of $7,103—because the exemptions and standard deduction were worth less and, since the 15% bracket was smaller, more of the income fell in the 28% bracket. The $248 difference is a tax cut delivered by inflation.

As you might imagine, such automatic tax cuts bug some members of Congress. Abolishing indexing, or at least squeezing the size of annual changes, is often mentioned as a possible step toward balancing the budget. For an idea of what's at stake, consider this: If indexing is skipped for just 1996, the IRS would take in more than $50 billion in extra taxes over the next five years! Inflation would quietly impose a tax increase by pushing more and more income into higher brackets.

Bubble Brackets

The nice, neat, five-rate schedule is the official line. Unfortunately, reality can be more painful. Due to the interaction of various parts of the tax law, you could face a much higher "unofficial" marginal rate.

Say hello to the bubble brackets. These are hidden rate increases used to take away certain benefits from taxpayers whose incomes fall within various income ranges. At certain income levels, each extra dollar you earn adds more than $1 to the amount the IRS gets to tax. That hikes your effective marginal rate—the share of that extra dollar that winds up going to the IRS.

Drawing by Richter; © 1990
The New Yorker Magazine, Inc.

The 31.93%, 37.08% and 40.79% bubbles

As discussed in Chapter 15, if your 1996 adjusted gross income (AGI, which is basically income before subtracting exemptions and deductions) is over $117,950, the law takes away part of your itemized deductions. The trigger point is $58,975 if you're married filing a separate return. For every $1,000 that you're over the threshold, you lose $30 worth of deductions—so the IRS really gets to tax an extra $1,030. The result is the same as raising the tax rate—to 31.93% if you're officially in the 31% bracket, 37.08% if you're ostensibly in the 36% bracket and 40.79% if you're in 39.6% bracket. This bubble applies until 80% of your deductions for taxes, interest, charitable gifts and miscellaneous expenses are wiped out. Only then does your rate fall back to its advertised level.

The 32.56% and up and up bubbles

When AGI passes another threshold—$117,950 on a single return, $176,950 on a joint return, $147,450 on a head of household return or $88,475 on a married filing separately return—the law begins gnawing away at the value of your exemptions, as explained in Chapter 8. Ostensibly, each exemption you claim for yourself and each dependent knocks $2,550 off your 1996 taxable income. But for every $2,500 your AGI exceeds the trigger point for your filing status, you lose 2% of each exemption's value. Two per cent of $2,550 is $51. And, letting the IRS tax $2,551 for every $2,500 of extra income is the same as hiking the 31% rate by 0.63%. If you're in the 36% bracket, it adds 0.73% to the rate and in the 39.6% bracket, the exemption squeeze is the same as boosting the rate by 0.81%—for every exemption you claim.

When this phaseout hits a single person in the 31% bracket, the real effective rate is 32.56%—31% + 0.93% for the deduction phaseout discussed above + 0.63% for the exemption phaseout. For a married couple with five children—and therefore seven exemptions—who think they're in the 36% bracket, the effective 1996 tax rate is actually 42.19%—36% + 1.08% + 5.11% (which is seven times the 0.73% surcharge). This bubble lasts for $125,000 over the threshold amount, by which point the full value of exemptions has been devoured.

The 39.2% bubble

This rate bulge takes away the deduction for contributions to an individual retirement account. As discussed

---

Fingering a Tax Cheat

• •

Q: *I'm getting sick and tired of listening to a neighbor brag about all the ways he finagles to beat the IRS. Is it true the IRS offers rewards to people who turn in tax cheats?*

A: Yes. The law authorizes the IRS to pay rewards to informants whose tips lead to the detection and punishment of someone guilty of violating the tax law. Although the IRS says only a small percentage of the tips it receives actually pan out, it has paid informants millions of dollars over the years. The reward can be as much as 10% of the tax recovered. The IRS sets the exact amount depending on how important the information you provided was to catching the tax cheat.

in Chapter 12, if you or your spouse is covered by a retirement plan at work and your adjusted gross income on a joint return is between $40,000 and $50,000, every $100 of extra income squeezes your allowable IRA deduction by $40. (This assumes you and your spouse each make the maximum $2,000 contribution.) An additional $100 of income lets the IRS tax an extra $140 in the 28% bracket. That costs you $39.20, for an effective tax rate of 39.2%. If you file a single return and your income is in the IRA phaseout range—$25,000 to $35,000—the effective rate is 33.6%. It's lower because, since you have only one IRA deduction to lose, each $100 of added income reduces the write-off by just $20. This bubble ends when income is $10,000 above the threshold and the full value of the IRA deduction has been eliminated.

The 42% and 51.8% bubbles

If you receive social security benefits, you could face a marginal rate of 42% or 51.8%. As discussed in Chapter 12, above certain levels, extra income causes social security benefits to lose their tax-free status. When income—defined to include 50% of social security benefits—is between $25,000 and $34,000 on a single return or between $32,000 and $44,000 on a joint return, earning an extra dollar causes 50 cents' worth of benefits to be taxed. Adding $100 to your income, then, could allow the IRS to tax $150. In the 28% bracket, that costs you $42—the same as applying a 42% rate to the extra $100 of income.

If your income is higher than the ranges cited above, an extra $100 of income can make $85 of benefits taxable. Taxing $185 at 28% costs you $51.80, the same as taxing your extra $100 of earnings at 51.8%.

If your income is below the $32,000 or $44,000 threshold, no more than half of your social security benefits can be taxed. Even above those levels, no more than 85% of your benefits can be taxed. Once your income hits the point at which the maximum percentage has been taxed, the 42% and 51.8% bubbles end.

The capital gains bubble

As discussed in Chapter 10, the law sets 28% as the maximum tax rate on long-term capital gains. But don't believe it. Because a capital gain will raise your income—and therefore possibly push you into a bubble bracket—the IRS can claim more than 28% of your investment profits. If a gain pushes more of your social security benefits into the taxable category, for example, the effective tax rate could be 42% or 51.8%.

The bottom line is this: knowing how high your tax bracket really is can greatly energize your tax-planning efforts by enhancing the potential rewards.

What's Taxable, What's Not

Although a central premise of this book is to avoid legalese at all costs, it seems appropriate here to quote what must be the IRS's favorite part of the tax law, Internal Revenue Code Section 61(a). It's exceptionally straightforward in presenting the government's definition of gross income:

Except as otherwise provided in this subtitle, gross income means all income from whatever source derived . . .

Whew! Were it not for that glorious introductory phrase—except as otherwise provided—you might ruefully conclude that tax planning is a cruel, no-win game. Fortunately, though, our lawmakers have crammed "otherwises" into the law, provisions that spare certain kinds of income altogether and, just as important, opportunities to use deductions and adjustments to income to whittle away at the amount of income that is really taxed.

Taxable Income

Let's start with the bad news, the kinds of income that fall squarely within the sights of the IRS. (See Chapter 10 for detailed discussion of investment and rental income.)

Wages and salaries

This is the most common kind of income and the

easiest to keep track of, for both you and the government. Just after the close of each year, you get a W–2 form from your employer showing how much you were paid. In addition to your salary, this includes commissions, bonuses, vacation pay, sick pay or severance pay. It also shows amounts that never find their way into your take-home pay, such as the 7.65% of earnings whisked away to pay your share of social security and medicare taxes. (On the bright side, the W–2 doesn't include in taxable income any part of your salary you contribute to a 401(k) retirement plan—see Chapter 12—or to a medical or child care reimbursement account, as discussed later in this chapter.) The IRS gets the same information.

Self-employment income

If you work for yourself, either full time or as a sideline to a job as an employee, the net profit from your activity is taxable.

Rental income

You pay tax on income that exceeds your deductible expenses.

Alimony

Payments you receive are taxed, if your ex-spouse deducts the amount on his or her return.

Awards

An award you receive for your work on the job is generally taxable. If you get goods or services—such as an all-expense-paid trip to Fargo, N.D.—you include the fair market value in your income. An exception permits tax-free gifts of property worth up to $1,600—such as a gold watch—in recognition of length of service or safety achievement. Cash or gift certificates don't qualify for this exception.

Barter

You don't have to get cash to pique the IRS's interest. If you receive property or services in exchange for your work, you're taxed on the fair market value of what you get. If you are a member of a barter exchange, your barter income will be reported to you and the IRS each year on a Form 1099B.

Damages

Damages won in lawsuits that compensate you for lost income or profit are generally taxable, as are punitive damages in a case not involving personal injury or sickness. In 1995, the Supreme Court ruled that damages received in age discrimination suits are also taxable. On the other hand, payments for damages for physical injury or sickness, damage to your character or alienation of affection are generally tax-free.

Taxing Good Fortune

Q: *Our church raffled off a $14,000 car as part of a fund-raising drive. I was the lucky winner. Am I right in assuming that prizes awarded by churches are tax-free?*

A: Dream on. The fair market value of the car counts as taxable income to you. (You get to deduct what you paid for the raffle tickets, though, if you itemize deductions.) The taxable amount is the value of the car, which may be less than the sticker price—such as what the dealer who provided the car to the church would have been willing to pay you for it immediately after you won the raffle.

Disability payments

Benefits under a plan paid for by your employer are generally fully taxable. If you paid the premiums for disability insurance, benefits under the policy are tax-free. Veterans disability benefits are also tax-free.

Gambling winnings

This includes everything from multimillion dollar lottery winnings to the value of the basket of booze raffled off in the church hall. You can deduct gambling losses—

including your wagers and the cost of those raffle tickets—if you itemize deductions.

IRA withdrawals

Generally, withdrawals are fully taxable. If you made nondeductible contributions to your IRA, though, part of the payout is tax-free, as discussed in Chapter 11.

Jury fees

Payment you receive for doing your public duty is taxable, but you get a deduction for any part of the fees you pay over to your employer in exchange for continuing your salary while you're on the jury.

Pension and annuity payments

These are generally taxed, although a portion may be tax-free as explained in Chapter 12.

Prizes

From the Nobel prize to the value of your winnings on Wheel of Fortune, the IRS expects a share of your good fortune.

Severance pay

If you receive a cash payment based on your years of service, for example, the payment is taxable.

State Tax Refund

Q: *I got a $600 state tax refund last year and see that I'm supposed to report it as income on my federal return. That doesn't seem fair, since the refund just made up for my overpayment of state taxes. Do I have to pay tax on it?*

A: Maybe, maybe not. If you did not itemize on your federal return last year, none of the refund is taxable. If you itemized, however, the deduction you claimed for state taxes paid whittled down your federal taxable income and, therefore, the amount you paid Uncle Sam. In a sense, the refund from the state is evidence that you claimed too big of a deduction for state taxes. Rather than make you file an amended return for the previous year, the IRS gets even by having you report part or all of the refund as income.

Tips

All tips are taxable; you must report tip income of more than $20 a month to your employer, who will withhold taxes and report the tips to the IRS along with your wages.

Unemployment compensation

Although it may seem like giving with one hand and taking with the other, jobless benefits are fully taxable.

Tax-Free Income

Now to the good part: Some income gets a wink and a nod from the taxman.

Auto rebates

The IRS considers them a reduction in the car's price rather than income to you.

Car-pool receipts

Payments you receive from fellow workers you drive to and from work are considered tax-free reimbursement of your expenses.

Casualty insurance proceeds

Reimbursements for a loss—after an auto accident or a home fire, for example—are almost always tax-free. See Chapter 15 for the exceptions.

Child-support payments

Unlike alimony, this is tax-free.

Combat pay

All pay for enlisted personnel and noncommissioned officers while serving in a combat zone is tax-free, as is a portion of pay received by commissioned officers.

Damages

Damages won in lawsuits for damages for physical injury or sickness, damage to your character or alienation of affection are generally tax-free. Damages that compensate you for lost income or profit are generally taxable, as are punitive damages in a case not involving personal injury or sickness.

Garage Sale "Income"
. . . .

Q: *I had a fabulously successful garage sale and pocketed over $1,500. A neighbor tells me I have to report that amount as income on my tax return. I tell her she's crazy. Who's right?*

A: Receipts from such sales are not taxable, except in very unusual circumstances where an item sells for more than you paid for it. Otherwise, pocket the money in good conscience.

Disability payments

If you paid the premiums for disability insurance, benefits are tax-free. So are veterans' disability benefits. But benefits under a plan paid for by your employer are generally fully taxable.

Dividends on a life insurance policy

Dividends are usually a tax-free refund of an overpayment of your premium. If the total of such dividends surpasses the total of premiums paid, however, the excess is taxable.

Employee death benefits

Up to $5,000 paid by the employer can be tax-free, although Congress is considering ending this break.

Gifts

Whether it's a few dollars or tens of thousands, a gift is not taxed. To qualify, the gift must be given out of true generosity. A television given to you by a bank as an incentive to deposit funds in a certificate of deposit, for example, doesn't count. Its value is taxable income. Don't be confused by the federal gift tax, which is one of Uncle Sam's most misunderstood levies. When that tax is owed—which is rare—payment is the responsibility of the giver of the gift, not the recipient. See Chapter 18.

Health and accident insurance benefits

Reimbursement for medical expenses or compensation for the permanent loss of the use of part of the body or permanent disfigurement is tax-free.

Inheritances

Money or property that you inherit is tax-free. (Note, however, that if you inherit an individual retirement account or company retirement benefits, the money is generally taxable to you just as it would have been to the deceased.) If you sell inherited property, the sale may result in a taxable profit or a deductible loss, as discussed in Chapter 10.

Life insurance

Proceeds are tax-free, but if you choose to have the insurance company pay the proceeds in installments over a number of years, the part of each year's payment that represents interest earned on your account is generally taxed. However, a surviving husband or wife whose insured spouse died before October 23, 1986, may exclude from taxable income up to $1,000 of such interest each year.

Money Saver

Don't worry if someone gives you money. No matter how much it is, it's tax-free to you.

Money Saver

Payments for damages for physical injury or sickness, damage to your character or alienation of affection are generally tax-free.

Municipal bond interest

Interest on bonds issued by state and local governments is usually excluded from taxable income. Interest on certain bonds is taxed if you're subject to the alternative minimum tax. See Chapter 4.

Profits on the sale of a home

For qualifying individuals age 55 and older, up to $125,000 of profit on the sale of a principal residence is tax-free. See Chapter 9.

Scholarships and fellowship grants

The value of tuition and such related expenses as books, supplies and required equipment is tax-free, but the value of room and board and any other perquisites is generally taxed. The details are in Chapter 8.

Social security

For about 75% of recipients, benefits are totally tax-free. However, for those whose income—including 50% of their benefits—exceeds $25,000 on a single return or $32,000 on a joint return, up to 85% of the benefits can be taxed. See Chapter 12.

State tax refunds

If the refund is for a year you did not itemize deductions on your federal return, it's tax-free. If the refund is for a year you did itemize, part of it may be tax-free. See Chapter 15.

Veterans' benefits

Veterans Affairs disability payments are tax-free.

Workers' compensation

Compensation for a job-related injury is tax-free. If you turn the payments over to your employer who continues to pay your salary, you're taxed only on the amount by which your salary exceeds the compensation.

Fribge Benefits

Fringe benefits often deliver double benefits. Not only does your employer foot all or part of the cost, but the value of most of these benefits comes to you tax-free. Even when that value is included in your taxable income, you come out ahead.

Assume, for example, that your firm has a vacation resort that you can use free of charge. If you take advantage of such generosity, the law demands that you include in taxable income the fair market value of the accommodations. If the value is set at $1,000 for your two-week stay, for example, an extra $1,000 will show up on the W–2 form for the year and you must pay tax on the extra income. For someone in the 31% tax bracket, the tax cost of the vacation would be $310 (31% of $1,000).

That's a good deal, compared to the $1,000 it would have cost you otherwise. But it's even better than it appears. If you had to pay the

---

This Number for help

• •

Q: *I'm having a terrible problem with the IRS. I received a notice accusing me of failing to pay the amount due with my last return. In fact, though, I have the canceled check that proves I paid. After sending a copy of the check, I received one letter telling me everything was straightened out. Then, a couple weeks later, I got another letter saying I'd better pay up right away. Is there any way to get this resolved?*

A: Begin by calling your local IRS office and asking to talk with the problem resolutions officer. The Problem Resolutions Program (PRP) exists to rescue taxpayers who are getting the run-around or are being steamrolled by the bureaucracy. The PRP can pry loose late refunds, straighten out problems such as yours, overrule computer-generated penalty notices and delay IRS seizure of property while a case is being reviewed. If you don't get satisfaction within four weeks of talking with a problem resolutions officer, take your complaint to the head of the program: the taxpayer ombudsman. As this book went to press, that job is held by Lee Monks. You can write the ombudsman directly at Room 3003, Internal Revenue Service, 1111 Constitution Ave., N.W., Washington, DC 20224. The phone number is 202–662–6100.

$1,000 out of pocket, it would really cost you more because you'd be spending after-tax dollars. In the 31% bracket you must earn $1,450 to have $1,000 left after the IRS gets its share.

The tax appeal of fringe benefits can even make it a smart move to ask your employer to cut your salary, with the pay cut being diverted to pay for fringe benefits. Suppose your company has a plan that permits you to shift $300 a month into an account that it will use to reimburse you for $3,600 you have to pay for child-care expenses. You more than break even by funneling money through the company plan. It would take $5,000 of taxable earnings, in the 28% bracket, to have the $3,600 after taxes you need to pay for child care.

Deduct This Book?

● ●

Q: *Is the cost of this book deductible?*

A: Perhaps. Not so long ago, itemizers could fully deduct the cost of tax-planning books, as well as fees paid to professional tax advisers and return preparers. Now you can write off such costs only to the extent that they and all your other miscellaneous itemized deductions exceed 2% of your adjusted gross income. If your qualifying expenses exceed the threshold, then you can deduct what you paid for *Kiplinger's Cut Your Taxes.*

Remember, too, that the tax-saving value of fringes is often boosted when you take state income taxes into account.

Cafeteria plans

More and more companies let employees select from a menu of fringe benefits—which often includes the choice of cash as an entree—to tailor personalized benefits packages. The plans have become increasingly popular with the rise of two-earner married couples. Husbands and wives with duplicate benefits can trade in unnecessary items, such as double medical coverage, for more desired benefits, such as additional life insurance or dental coverage.

If you choose cash under such a plan, it's taxable income. If you choose tax-free benefits, their value is not included in your salary, and you therefore avoid the extra tax.

A popular selection on some menus—and sometimes a stand-alone benefit—is a **reimbursement account**. Also known as a **flexible-spending account**, these plans are funded through employee salary reduction, with the money going to pay certain expenses, such as medical and child-care costs. Say, for example, that your employer has a plan that permits you to divert $4,000 a year into a reimbursement account through which you will pay for child care. The advantage to giving up part of your salary is that you can pay necessary bills with pre-tax income. Put another way, this arrangement works like a tax deduction for the full $4,000 paid for child care. Actually, it's better than a deduction, since the money channeled through the program escapes the social security tax as well as the income tax.

These plans require an employee to elect in advance how much salary to deflect for designated benefits. Another condition is that the employee must forfeit any amount left in the account at year-end. The use-it-or-lose-it stipulation makes it somewhat risky to use such an account for uncertain expenses—such as medical and dental bills. But there's little danger for such predictable costs as child-care expenses. Also, the tax benefits are so great that, depending on your tax bracket, you could forfeit 20% or more of the salary diverted to the plan and still come out ahead.

Child care

Expenses paid by your employer for the care of children under age 13—whether for a care provider you hire or for the value of care at facilities provided by your employer—are tax-free, up to $5,000 a year.

Company-provided car

This is a true sign that you have arrived, and it usually carries a tax liability. You're taxed on the value of your personal use of the vehicle, but the value assigned to your business use of the car is tax-free. If you can't use the car for personal trips, but drive it to and from work, your personal use is assigned a flat $3-a-day value because

Money Saver

Salary funneled through a reimbursement account avoids both income and social security taxes.

commuting is considered personal use. Your employer is responsible for determining the value to be assigned to your personal use of the car and has to include it on your Form W–2 as income.

De minimis fringes

These are little things, the cost of which is so small that it's unreasonable to keep track. Included in this tax-free category: use of the office copying machine, supper money or taxi fare paid in connection with overtime work, the value of office parties and employer-provided sports or theater tickets.

Educational assistance programs

Company-provided educational expenses are tax-free if the course is designed to maintain or improve skills for a job you already have (rather than to qualify for a new job) or if your employer requires it. An on-again-off-again break allows employers to pay up to $5,250 worth of non-job-related educational expenses as a tax-free fringe. Unfortunately, that break expired at the end of 1994 and, at the time this book went to press in late 1995, Congress had not gotten around to reinstating it. For an update on this issue, write or e-mail the author at the address listed on page i. We'll respond with a factsheet explaining any changes enacted into law.

Employee discounts

Discounts of as much as your employer's profit on products and as much as 20% on services are tax-free to you.

Employee stock-purchase plans

Options granted under these plans, which are similar to incentive stock options (discussed on page 84), let employees buy company stock at a discount, often 15% below market value. You don't have to report any income when you get the option or when you exercise it to buy shares. When you sell the stock, you're taxed on the difference between what you paid and what you get.

Employer-provided travel

The fact that your employer pays your way on business trips is no great shakes, but you may be able to squeeze a valuable benefit out of on-the-job travel. Of course, what your firm pays for airline tickets and hotel and restaurant bills while you're on assignment is not taxable income. That remains true even if you tack a vacation on to the end of your trip. If you go to the coast for a three-day meeting, your airfare is the same whether you rush back to the office or hang around for a holiday. If you take the family along, you have to pay for your spouse's fare and the kids', but working things so you get a tax-free trip from the firm could significantly cut the cost of the trip. Since many hotels let spouses and children stay for reduced or no cost, the time you're on business with your company footing the hotel bill can produce tax-free accommodations for the rest of the family.

Free parking

Congress has slapped a limit on your employer's generosity when it provides free parking. For 1996, if the value of parking is more than $165 a month, the excess counts as taxable income. The amount will increase in the future to keep up with inflation. (The trigger point was $160 in 1995.)

Group term life insurance

The cost of up to $50,000 of coverage provided by your employer is tax-free. Coverage above that level results in taxable income, but it's still a real bargain. The follow-

Money Saver

For 1996, the first $165 a month your employer pays for parking is a tax-free fringe benefit.

ing table shows how much taxable income you will be assigned when coverage exceeds $50,000.

Your Age	Annual Rate per $1,000 Coverage
Under 30	$ .96
30 to 34	1.08
35 to 39	1.32
40 to 44	2.04
45 to 49	3.48
50 to 54	5.76
55 to 59	9.00
60 to 64	14.04
65 to 69	25.20
70 and older	45.12

A 50-year-old who gets $200,000 of company-provided insurance, for instance, would have to report as extra income the IRS-assumed cost of $150,000 of coverage. At $5.76 per thousand, that's $864, which in the 28% bracket would cost the employee $242 in taxes.

Incentive stock options (ISOs)

Often a part of executive compensation packages, ISOs offer the opportunity to buy company stock at a set price over a period of time as long as a decade. You can wait for the price to rise before exercising the option, thus locking in a sure profit. There's no taxable income when an employer grants you the option or when you exercise it to buy stock, even if the shares are worth more than the option requires you to pay. You incur tax only when you ultimately sell the shares. (Different rules apply if you're subject to the alternative minimum tax. See Chapter 4.)

Interest-free or bargain-rate loans

The option to borrow from your employer is a rare but sweet perquisite. To the extent that you get a break on the interest rate, though, the IRS says you have taxable income.

Meals and lodging

Your employer can provide food and housing tax-free if specific conditions are met. Basically, to qualify as a tax-free fringe benefit rather than a noncash addition to your taxable compensation, the meals must be offered at your employer's place of business—a company cafeteria, say, or at the restaurant where you're a chef or waitress. The meals must also be for your employer's "convenience," a test it can meet if, for example, a short lunch hour or lack of local eateries makes it unreasonable for you to eat elsewhere. Housing involves an extra requirement: The lodging must be a condition of your employment—as it might be if you're a motel manager, for example, or a ranch foreman.

Special rules apply to members of the clergy whose congregations give them a house or a housing allowance as part of their pay. That value is not taxable. There are also special rules for the tax treatment of on- or near-campus housing provided for professors and other employees of educational institutions.

Fouled up W–2?

Q: *When I got my W-2 form, it showed that I earned $48,000 last year. I know that's wrong because I remember how proud I was when I got my raise to $50,000. I checked and the new salary was in effect for the full year, so I really made $50,000. What do I have to do to get it corrected?*

A: Don't jump to a conclusion that could force you to overpay your taxes. Remember, any amounts you contributed to a 401(k) retirement plan should not show up on your W-2 as taxable earnings. Ditto for amounts you paid in to a child-care or medical-reimbursement plan. A great thing about those fringe benefits is that salary that you divert into such plans is not reported as taxable income to the IRS. If you didn't make such contributions, though, your W-2 might be wrong. In that case, ask your company's payroll office for a corrected copy.

Medical and dental

Insurance premiums paid by your employer for you and your family are tax-free, although there is often talk in Congress about limiting how much an employer can pay, with excess amounts being considered taxable income to the employee.

No-additional-cost services

You're not taxed on services that have value to you but don't cost your employer anything. Included are such benefits as free space-available air or train travel for airline or railroad employees. If your employer operates a subsidized eating facility, the difference between what you have to pay for meals and what they would cost at an independent cafeteria or restaurant is a tax-free fringe as long as the employer charges at least enough to break even. And the law includes the use of an on-site athletic facility on the list of tax-free perks.

© *Reprinted by Permission Tribune Media Services*

Outplacement services

The value of services paid for by an employer who is letting you go is a tax-free fringe. This might include motivational seminars, resumé writing and counseling aimed at helping you find a new job.

Retirement plans

Often the most valuable and most important fringe benefit, money set aside for your retirement is not taxed until you actually get your hands on it. See Chapter 12.

Stock bonuses and bargain purchases

If your company gives you stock or lets you buy it for less than market value, you receive taxable income to the extent that the stock is worth more than you pay for it. However, if there is a risk that you might have to forfeit the stock—such as a requirement that you return it to the company at the price paid if you quit your job within a certain number of years—you don't have to report any taxable income until those restrictions expire. At that time, you'd report as income the difference between what you paid for the stock and its value when the restrictions expire.

Transit passes

In 1996, employees can get up to $65 a month tax-free to cover the cost of getting to and from work via public transit. This benefit can take the form of bus, subway or train passes or tokens or reimbursement. The limit was $60 in 1995.

Working-condition fringe benefits

You're not taxed on such benefits as the value of a company car provided for business use or the cost of subscriptions to professional journals paid for by your employer.

Pay as You Go

Despite all the worrying and grousing we do about high taxes—and all the planning and conniving we do to minimize what we owe—the vast majority of us let the government dip deeper into our pockets during the year than we have to. The evidence is incontrovertible: The tens of millions of tax-refund checks the Treasury mails out each spring are proof positive that employees routinely have too much withheld from their paychecks.

This chapter will show you how to keep your withholding down to the legal minimum. Ditto if investment or self-employment income requires you to pay estimated taxes during the year. The point is for you to get the use and enjoyment of more of your money when you earn it rather than making an unintentional—albeit generous—interest-free loan to the government.

The extent of overwithholding is as massive as it is ironic. In the spring of 1995, the government churned out about 75 million tax-refund checks. The total amount sprinkled on appreciative taxpayers was more than $85 billion. The average size of the checks was almost $1,150. (The interest you could earn each year on the average overpayment in regular savings account would pay for this book many times over.)

On the flip side of the coin, having too little withheld or failing to pay enough estimated tax trips up a growing number of taxpayers each year. This is a particular problem for two-earner married couples. If underwithholding is your problem, you'll find here the formula for dodging the expensive penalty the IRS slaps on those who fail to meet its pay-as-you-go expectations.

Undoubtedly underpayment penalties hit some tax-payers who really don't have to pay them. The law includes exceptions, but because the IRS computers don't know who might have a valid excuse, penalty notices go to those who appear to be guilty. Filing the right form can deflect the fine and turn the IRS away empty-handed, as discussed later.

How the System Works

Giving Uncle Sam a crack at your paycheck before you get it is the linchpin of the federal income-tax system. Although ours is widely hailed as a "voluntary" tax system, it works best when there is the least opportunity not to volunteer. Congress put us on the pay-as-you-go system in 1943. Before then, the tax bill for one year was due in installments during the following year. During World War II, however, the government introduced withholding to speed collection of needed revenues and in recognition of the fact that millions of citizens—to whom the tax applied for the first time—were probably spending most if not all of their income as they earned it. Expecting them to come up with cash for the IRS the following year could cause problems.

So, although we think of April 15 as tax day, taxes are actually due as income is earned, and employers have become the country's primary tax collectors by withholding taxes from our paychecks. Of the $620 billion collected in individual income taxes in 1994, for example, more than $430 billion was withheld from employees' paychecks. The government also expects its share of income not covered by withholding—including income from self-employment, investments and alimony—in installments during the year. Social security taxes as well as income taxes are due on a pay-as-you-go basis.

Money Saver

Overwithholding is nothing more than an interest-free loan to the government. Withhold only what you must; invest the rest for yourself.

*Review your
withholding
allowances at least
every couple of years,
especially if you get a
big refund or you owe
a healthy amount
when you file.*

The Form W-4

The amount withheld from your pay is determined by two things: how much you make and the information you provide your employer on the Form W-4, Employee's Withholding Allowance Certificate. Your employer knows how much you're being paid; the form shows whether you're married or single and how many withholding allowances you want to claim. The more allowances, the less tax withheld.

You get a W-4 when you start a new job and often never see one again. It's wise, however, to review your withholding allowances at least every couple of years. The tip-off that something is amiss happens when you get a big tax refund (over $500) or owe a healthy amount (more than 10% of your total tax bill) when you file.

To understand the financial power of the W-4, consider the case of a married employee with a nonworking wife and two children and a $50,000 salary in 1995. If his W-4 claimed four allowances, the same number of exemptions he claims on his tax return, his employer would withhold $422 each month for the IRS. A new W-4 claiming ten allowances would knock withholding down to $235—and put an extra $187 a month in his pocket. That's an extra $2,244 a year.

It's not found money, though. The number of withholding allowances you claim has no impact on your tax bill for the year, only how much you shell out in installments each payday. Assuming the $2,244 in our example would otherwise have found its way into a springtime tax refund, adjusting withholding effectively lets the taxpayer claim the refund ahead of time in installments—by not overpaying in the first place.

Each allowance you claim exempts from withholding the same amount of income that an exemption knocks off your taxable income—$2,550 in 1996. The following table is a rough guide to approximately how much each extra allowance you claim in 1996 will trim withholding and add to your take-home pay each month.

Marital Status	Salary	Monthly Value of Each Withholding Allowance
Single	Up to $24,000	$32
Married	Up to $40,100	
Single	$24,000 to $58,150	$60
Married	$40,100 to $96,900	
Single	$58,150 to $121,300	$66
Married	$96,900 to $147,700	
Single	$121,300 to $263,750	$77
Married	$147,700 to $263,750	
Single	More than $263,750	$84
Married	More than $263,750	

Alas, you can't just make up a number for your W-4. IRS regulations control how many you can claim, and the agency can slap you with a $500 fine if you deliberately claim more than you deserve. It's clear from all the refunds, however, that most taxpayers claim too few allowances rather than too many. If you're in that group, take the time to closely match withholding to your actual tax bill.

Sure, more accurate withholding would mean giving up that luscious tax refund check in the spring. Undoubtedly, there are plenty of willing victims of overwithholding, including taxpayers who see it as a convenient means of forced savings. In fact, the national tax-preparation firm of H&R Block offers—for an extra fee—to help taxpayers file a W-4 designed to produce fat refund.

There are plenty of better ways to save, though. And, perhaps more costly than the fact that Uncle Sam doesn't pay interest, overwithholding can play games with your psyche. You've surely heard this joyous springtime comment: "Oh, I didn't owe any tax this year. I'm getting money back."

Of course, the gratified taxpayer had paid hundreds—perhaps thousands—of dollars in tax and simply

Money Saver

Claiming two extra withholding allowances could boost your take home pay by $120 a month.

recouped funds that had been overpaid. This delusion can inflict financial pain if it leads you to lower your guard when you're preparing your return. There's a good chance you'll work harder to shave the amount of extra tax due than to pump up a refund.

How to Change Your Withholding

Ask your employer for a blank Form W-4 and, while you're at it, check on how many allowances you claim now. Now figure out whether you can legitimately claim more. (If your employer doesn't have the form, contact the IRS at 800–TAX–FORM for a copy.)

Count your allowances.

Start by shaking off the notion that all you need to do is count the number of bodies around the house. You probably get an allowance for each exemption you claim on your tax return, but that's just the beginning. The only taxpayers who aren't guaranteed an allowance for each exemption claimed are those whose adjusted gross income exceeds certain levels—$117,950 on single returns in 1996, for example, and $176,950 on joint returns. Above those levels, the tax-saving value of the exemptions is phased out, as explained in Chapter 8. A worksheet in IRS Publication 919, *Is My Withholding Correct?*, shows how to take this into account when adding up W-4 allowances. If you don't have to worry about that—most taxpayers don't—claim an allowance for each exemption you claim and add extra ones if:

- You're single and have only one job;

- You're married, have one job and your spouse isn't employed; or,

- Your wages from a second job or your spouse's wages are $1,000 or less.

You also get an extra allowance if you have at least $1,500 of child- or dependent-care expenses and will claim a tax credit for these costs. And, you may take an additional allowance if you file as a head of household.

Estimate your tax-saving write-offs.

Next, determine if you can claim extra allowances for the itemized deductions and adjustments to income that will cut your taxable income. The W-4 comes with a worksheet for that figuring, but it might shortchange you. Basically, the worksheet asks for an estimate of your itemized deductions and adjustments to income, then has you reduce that amount by non-wage income—such as dividends and interest not covered by withholding—before determining how many allowances you should claim to reflect your tax-saving write-offs.

What the worksheet does not indicate is that you can also take anticipated losses into account. If you expect a deductible loss from a business or rental activity or investment, for example, you can adjust your withholding to account for the resulting reduction in your tax bill. Every $2,500 of net loss buys an extra withholding allowance. Such losses are first used to reduce any estimated tax payments you must make, but if a loss will more than wipe out your estimated tax liability, you can use the excess to curtail withholding.

Taxpayers whose adjusted gross income exceeds a certain level—$117,950 in 1996 ($58,975 for those who are married filing separately)—must take into account the fact that the law restricts their itemized deductions, as discussed in Chapter 15. A worksheet in Publication 919 shows how this affects withholding allowances.

Making all those estimates might sound like more trouble than it could possibly be worth, but IRS restrictions can simplify the job. Begin with your tax return for the previous year. If you can reasonably expect your write-offs to be at least as high for the current year, you can use last year's figures for the W-4. You can use higher figures only if you can point to something that justifies the increase, such as in the following examples:

- **You buy a new home for which mortgage interest and property-tax payments will be higher** than your previous write-offs in those categories.

- **You are divorced this year and have to pay alimony,** a tax-deductible expense you didn't pay in earlier years.

Money Saver

If you suffer a deductible loss from a business or investment, adjust your withholding to account for the resulting reduction in your tax bill.

• **You suffer a substantial loss in the stock market**—so bad that you'll be in the red even after accounting for profits you expect to take before the end of the year. You may use your estimated net loss to raise the number of allowances claimed.

The rules don't permit adjusting withholding in anticipation of a tax-saving event. If you're simply worrying about a stock loss or considering making a big charitable contribution, for example, you can't use your fears or intentions to reduce withholding. If the IRS challenges the number of allowances you claim, you'll have to show that you used a reasonable method to arrive at the number.

Working couples

If both you and your spouse have jobs, figure how many allowances you're entitled to together, then split the number however you choose. They're usually worth more—in terms of reduced withholding—when claimed by the higher-paid spouse.

Unfortunately, though, *under*withholding rather than *over*withholding is the bane many of married couples. The W-4 takes this notorious reality into account with a second worksheet for working couples. Based on the income of each spouse, this worksheet walks you through the process of eliminating allowances the other rules say you deserve.

Although negative allowances may seem like a penalty, this is the IRS's way of trying to accurately match withholding to a couple's tax bill. It's possible that claiming zero allowances might still leave you underwithheld. Don't worry, the IRS has a solution. The W-4 worksheet will show how much extra tax to ask your boss to withhold each payday.

Filing a revised W-4

Whether you decide you need more or less money withheld from your pay, filing a new W-4 with your employer—not the IRS—will trigger the change, usually within a month. That guarantees a quick payoff if your efforts cut withholding.

Although the IRS usually never sees W-4 forms,

employers must send the government a copy if you claim more than ten allowances. If a review of previous tax returns doesn't convince the tax collectors you deserve the allowances claimed, they may ask for an explanation. If you can't provide convincing support for your claim, the IRS can order your employer to ignore the W-4 and withhold at a much higher rate. Don't be intimidated by the possibility of IRS scrutiny. If your calculations show you should claim more than ten allowances, do so.

Part-Year Withholding

There is a special brand of withholding that's tailor-made for new college graduates who get their first full-time job around mid-year. The *part-year method* sets withholding according to what you'll actually earn during the part of the year you work, rather than on 12 times your monthly salary. That can make a significant difference in how much your employer holds back from your checks.

The part-year method can be used by anyone who expects to work no more than 245 days—approximately eight months—in continuous employment during the year. It could also pay off handsomely, for example, if you land a high-paying summer job.

You must give your employer a written request that the part-year method be used. Employers don't have to comply, but if yours does, you'll get more of your pay as you earn it.

Exemption from Withholding

In the past, students could often avoid withholding altogether on earnings from summer jobs. Now, however, the rules make it tough to dodge withholding if your income for 1996 will exceed $650. If your parents can claim you as a dependent on their return and if you have any "unearned" income—even $1 of interest on a savings account counts—you can be exempted from withholding only if your total income for the year will be $650 or less. The low level applies because, as discussed in Chapter 8, taxpayers claimed as dependents can't claim their own

Money Saver
If you don't work full time all year, explore part-year withholding; it can significantly reduce how much your employer holds back from your checks.

personal exemption. And their standard deduction is reduced. The double squeeze means they owe tax on less income than nondependent taxpayers.

If no one can claim you as a dependent, you can make much more and still be exempted from withholding, if you owed no federal tax for the previous year and expect to owe none in the current year. For 1996, for example, a single person who is not a dependent can have up to $6,550 in taxable income before any tax is due.

If you make $200 a week or more and claim the exemption from withholding on your W-4, your employer has to send the form to the IRS. As with taxpayers who claim more than ten allowances, the IRS may ask you to justify your claim.

Withholding Hits More than Wages

Withholding on tips

If you receive more than $20 a month from tips, that income is subject to withholding, too. You report the tips to your employer, who takes them into account when figuring how much to withhold from your wages.

Because Congress believes that a lot of tip income goes unreported, there are special rules to encourage *voluntary* compliance. Basically, the law assumes customers tip at an average rate of 8%. If restaurant and bar employees don't report to their employer tips totaling at least 8% of the establishment's gross receipts, the employer has to do it for them.

The shortfall between what's reported to the employer and the 8% level is allocated among the employees—but only for the purpose of a report to the IRS. No money will change hands, and waiters and waitresses are still expected to report their actual tip income, whether it's more or less than their share of the 8% kitty. Those who report less, however, should prepare more than ever for questions from the IRS. (The tip-allocation rule applies only to establishments with ten or more employees where tipping is customary.)

Retirement income

If you receive regular payments from a company pension or annuity, the payer may or may not withhold the tax. The same goes for withdrawals you take from an IRA. Believe it or not, it's almost always up to you whether part of the money will be skimmed off for the IRS. (As in the past, for 1996, there is no withholding on social security benefits, even though those benefits are sometimes taxable, as discussed in Chapter 12. Starting in 1997, however, voluntary withholding will become available for taxpayers who ask for it.)

If you want to forbid Uncle Sam from dipping into your retirement checks, all you have to do is file a form with the payer. The company that pays your pension or annuity should periodically remind you of your option to block withholding and tell you how to do it.

Note, though, that withholding on these payments isn't necessarily a bad thing, since it stretches the tax bill over the entire year rather than leaving the bill to be paid all at once at tax-return time. Withholding might make life easier if the alternative is to make quarterly estimated tax payments, discussed later. If you allow withholding, the amount held back from pension and annuity checks is based on information you provide on a form W-4P, just as withholding on wages is controlled by a W-4.

You don't have to retire for these rules to affect you. If you roll over funds from one IRA account to another, as discussed in Chapter 11, the company that makes the payment will withhold 10% unless you tell it not to.

Pension payout trap

There's an exception to the no-withholding rule that can trip up employees who get lump-sum payments from company retirement plans—the kind you might receive not only when you retire, but also if you quit or are laid off.

Before 1993, withholding on such payments was voluntary. The best course for most taxpayers, in fact, was to say "no" to withholding, take the money and roll it over into an individual retirement account (IRA). Doing so

Money Saver

If you're getting a lump-sum payout from a retirement plan, avoid withholding by directing your employer to send your money to an IRA.

within 60 days meant no tax was due on the payout, so there was no need for withholding. (See Chapter 12 for details on IRA rollovers.)

Now, however, if you take the money, 20% of it is automatically withheld for the IRS. That's true even though a rollover will still allow you to avoid the tax. In that case, the IRS would have the money you don't owe until you file a tax return for the year and demand a refund.

Congress set the 20% withholding trap to raise money—an estimated $2 billion over five years. But only unsuspecting taxpayers will pay it because there's an easy way around withholding: Simply ask your employer to send the money directly to a rollover IRA. As long as you don't get your hands on the money, there's no withholding. (It's considered a direct rollover even if you handle getting the check from your employer to the IRA sponsor…as long as the check is made out to the IRA, not to you personally.)

"…let us think of this instead as Harry's ultimate 'tax freedom' day."

© 1991 Beattie Blvd. reprinted by permission of
Newspaper Enterprise Association, Inc.

Even if you intend to spend some of the money right away, your best bet is still to ask your employer to make the direct IRA transfer. Then, when you withdraw funds from the IRA, it's up to you whether there will be withholding. See Chapter 12 for more on this issue.

Lotteries, bingo and bonuses

If you score big at the track or hit the winning number in the state lottery, you're not the only one who's lucky: so is the IRS. The winnings are taxable and, if high enough, subject to withholding at a flat 28% rate.

Withholding is required if you win more than $5,000 from a state lottery, a sweepstakes or other lotteries, including church raffles. Withholding also kicks in if you win more than $5,000 from other wagering, such as dog and horse racing or jai alai. Bingo or slot machines winnings are exempt from withholding.

If you're in the 15% tax bracket, the 28% withholding will be more than you actually owe in taxes. You'll get back the excess when you file your return for the year of your good fortune. You should get a copy of form W-2G showing the amount you won and how much the payer withheld. The IRS gets a copy, too.

If you get a bonus on the job, your employer will withhold a flat 28% for the IRS. Again, if you're in the 15% bracket, this means the government claims almost twice as much as the tax that will actually be due.

Backup withholding

The IRS would love to get a crack at your dividends and interest income before you do. In the early 1980s, in fact, Congress actually approved a plan to withhold 10% of such earnings as a prepayment of the tax due. But the lawmakers backed down in the face of a fierce taxpayer protest. Still, it is possible for a bank or business to claim a chunk of your interest or dividend payments as "backup withholding." The rate is a flat 31%.

Backup withholding applies when the bank or other payer doesn't have, or doesn't think it has, your social security number—the taxpayer identification number used to report the income to the IRS. If you forget or refuse to give the bank or business your social security number, or the IRS tells the payer that you provided an incorrect number, 31% of your dividends or interest will be diverted to the IRS. The IRS can also order backup withholding if it concludes you failed to report on your tax return interest or dividends you received during the previous year. Backup withholding shouldn't cause you any trouble if you've been reporting all your interest and dividend income properly—although foul-ups inevitably trip up some taxpayers. The rules also mean more forms to fill out and sign when you open an account, to certify that you've provided the right social security number and that you're not subject to IRS-ordered backup withholding.

> *"To tax and to please, no more than to love and to be wise, is not given to men."*
> —EDMUND BURKE

Estimated Tax Payments

There are plenty of sources of income not nipped by withholding: income from self-employment, investments, rents, alimony, prizes, etc. But avoiding withholding doesn't mean escaping the pay-as-you-go taxing system.

If you expect to owe $500 or more in tax when you file your return—beyond the amount of tax withheld from wages—the IRS expects you to make quarterly estimated tax payments. The $500 triggering point is a general rule and taxpayers can often ignore it, as discussed later.

You use Form 1040ES, *Estimated Tax for Individuals,* to calculate whether and how much estimated tax you owe at various times during the year. This involves time-consuming estimates of your projected taxable income for the year, the amount of income and social security tax you'll owe and how much, if any, of it will be paid via withholding. The easiest way to make your estimate is to use your previous year's return as a guide. Take a stab at how income and deductions are likely to differ in the current year and apply the latest tax rates to the best guess of your taxable income. If self-employment income is involved, be sure to take into account what you'll owe for social security taxes, too, as discussed in Chapter 3.

If the gap between what you expect to owe and the amount you expect to be withheld is $500 or more, you *might* have to make estimated payments.

Mid-year withholding adjustment

· ·

Q: *We just bought our first home, and paying interest on the $120,000 mortgage means we'll be itemizing deductions for the first time. Will this have an impact on the amounts withheld from my paychecks?*

A: It can make a big difference. Deducting about $10,000 of mortgage interest will cut your tax bill significantly, and you can get the benefit right away by telling your employer to withhold less from your checks. You do that by filing a new Form W-4 that claims extra withholding allowances. An extra $10,000 in deductions translates to four extra allowances. That will cut withholding by nearly $250 a month if you're in the 28% tax bracket. If you get an extra allowance or two to reflect your deduction for local property taxes, withholding will fall—and your take-home pay will rise—even more.

Those payments are due only if failing to make them would subject you to the penalty for paying too little during the year. That means shaving estimated payments to a minimum—a worthy goal that lets you keep more of your money working for you during the year—demands that you understand the underpayment penalty and the exceptions to it.

The penalty is the IRS's not-so-subtle reminder that taxes are due as income is earned, not just on April 15 of the following year. Basically, it works like interest on a loan, with the penalty rate applied to the amount of estimated tax due but unpaid by each of four payment dates during the year. The penalty rate is set by the IRS and can change each quarter. It was 9% for the last six months of 1995.

The IRS generally expects you to pay your estimated tax bill in four installments during the year. If any payment is short or late, the IRS applies the penalty rate on a daily basis until you pay up. If you ignore the first payment and double up on the second, for example, you would still owe a penalty based on the number of days the skipped payment was overdue.

Your estimates don't have to be precise to avoid the penalty; as long as your payments cover 90% of your actual tax liability, the penalty doesn't apply. Assume you figure that you'll owe $4,000 more in tax than will be withheld from your paychecks. The minimum quarterly payments would be $900 ($4,000 ÷ 4 x 90%).

Exceptions that Save You Money

In several situations, even the 90% rule is thrown out.

You owed no tax last year.

If you owed no tax in the previous year—and were a U.S. citizen or resident for the whole year—you don't have to make estimated payments regardless of how much tax you'll owe. This applies only if you had no tax liability in the previous year, not if you just didn't have to pay extra tax with your return.

Your payments this year equal last year's tax bill

If your payments for the year equal your tax bill for the previous year, the IRS generally waives the penalty—no matter how much you owe with your return. Even if your income jumps, thanks to a big profit on an investment, say, this exception lets you ignore estimated taxes if the amount withheld on your salary will be at least equal to your tax bill for the previous year.

There is an exception to the neat 100%-of-last-year's-tax exception. If your AGI for the year is more than $150,000 ($75,000 if married filing separately), you have to pay in at least 110% of last year's tax liability to avoid the underpayment penalty.

The annualized income exception

Although the general rule calls for taxpayers to make estimated tax payments in equal, quarterly installments, the law does recognize that in some cases that would make no sense. Say, for example, that the only reason you need to make an estimated payment is a $50,000 profit on a stock sale in mid November. Why should you make an estimated tax payment on that income the previous spring? You shouldn't and you don't have to.

Under the "annualized income" exception to the underpayment penalty, you base the amount due on each payment date on the actual amount of taxable income you have received at that point during the year. Although it does involve some extra number crunching, the annualized income approach can save you from a penalty due to a bulge in income during the latter part of the year.

Last-minute withholding

Employees have an extra, and particularly potent, way to avoid the penalty. Say you discover in October that you should have been making estimated payments all along on your investment income. Even if you make up for the oversight with a big estimated payment for the final quarter, the IRS will stick you with the penalty for missing earlier installments.

However, if your employer will increase withholding from your salary so that the total withheld will cover 90% of your tax bill (or 100%/110% of the previous year's liability, as discussed previously), you can retroactively eliminate the underpayment penalty. Unlike estimated payments, which are considered paid when they are paid, the IRS treats withholding as though it is taken out evenly throughout the year. To initiate penalty-saving overwithholding, you need to file a new W-4 form with your employer. (If you use this technique, remember to file another W-4 in January to bring withholding down to the proper level.)

Farmers and fishermen

Taxpayers who earn at least two-thirds of their gross income from farming or fishing—professions for which projecting income is notoriously difficult—are covered by special rules. Rather than being required to make estimated payments during the year, farmers and fisherman can pay their estimated taxes in a single payment, due January 15 of the following year. To avoid the underpayment penalty, that payment must be just two-thirds of the actual tax liability for the year, or 100% of the tax owed on the previous year's return. Farmers and fishermen can even skip the January 15 payment without penalty if they file their returns and pay the full tax due by March 1.

When and How to Pay

Never accused of oversimplifying things, the IRS doesn't break the tax year into four three-month quarters. The first quarter is three months (January 1 to March 31), but the second "quarter" is just two months (April 1 to May 31), the third is three months (June 1 to August 31) and the fourth covers the final four months of the year. The installment payments are due on April 15, June 15, September 15 and January 15 of the following year. You can skip the final payment if you will file your return and pay all the tax due by February 1. If a due date falls on a weekend or legal holiday, it's pushed to the next business day.

Time Saver

Save yourself the hassle of writing checks for estimated payments by using a tax refund due to pay the first installment and perhaps even the second.

As mentioned earlier, you don't have to make any payment until you have income on which estimated taxes are due. If you know early in the year that you must make estimated payments, each of the four payments should be 25% of the amount due.

But what if you receive income during the third quarter that, for the first time, makes you liable for estimated tax payments? Your first payment would be due on the third installment date—September 15—and the IRS expects you to pay 75% of the tax that is due.

To hold your payments to a minimum, base each installment on what you have to pay to avoid the penalty, using any exceptions that benefit you.

If you have a tax refund coming from the IRS, you can elect on your return to have part or all of the money applied to your estimated tax bill. Although the IRS doesn't pay any interest on such advance payments, it may make sense to use the refund to pay the first installment (due April 15) and perhaps even the second (due June 15) just to save yourself the hassle of writing and sending in the checks.

The first time you pay estimated tax you have to get a copy of the Form 1040-S (call 800–TAX–FORM for a copy) and complete and send in a payment voucher. After that, the tax agency will send you a package of preprinted vouchers showing your name, address and social security number. You make the payments to the IRS service center for your area.

Penalties: Real and Mistaken

When you file a tax return showing that you owe $500 or more in additional tax, and the amount due is more than 10% of your tax bill for the year, the IRS assumes you're guilty of underpayment.

If you are, you can figure the penalty on Form 2210, *Underpayment of Estimated Tax by Individuals,* and pay it when you send in your return. Completing the form is a challenging and time consuming task, though, and the IRS will do it for you. If you don't send a Form 2210 in with your return, the IRS will compute the penalty and send you a bill. Since the clock stops running on the penalty when you pay your tax—with your return—letting the IRS figure the penalty not only saves you time and aggravation, it also puts off for a bit the time you will have to part with money to pay the penalty.

The Form 2210 also has a more benevolent purpose: It can exonerate you by showing which of the exceptions shelters you from the penalty.

If you're safe but don't file the Form 2210, you'll probably get a bill from the IRS. The official notice demanding prompt payment can be intimidating. It can also be mistaken. The IRS computers don't know whether you can squeeze into one of the safety zones and—no surprise here—assume you can't.

Before responding to a penalty notice with a check, take the time to work through Form 2210, searching for an exception that might reduce or eliminate the penalty. IRS Publication 505, *Tax Withholding and Estimated Tax,* includes worksheets and hypothetical cases that can help. If you qualify for one of the exceptions, send the IRS the completed Form 2210.

Your Family & Your Tax Bill

When it comes to family tax planning, Uncle Sam is an enigmatic relative—in some ways, kind and generous, in others, crotchety and demanding. And, because the rules are always changing, you have to stay on your toes. As 1995 drew to a close, in fact, Congress was wrangling over several new tax breaks for families. One would give parents a $500 tax credit for each child under 18. Another would provide a modest tax credit to mitigate the so-called marriage tax penalty, which is discussed later in this chapter. Unfortunately, at our deadline, Congress and the President were still wrangling over the final shape of a tax bill. If, in the end, there are changes, we'll promptly prepare a free update for you. To get it, write or e-mail the author at the address in the front of this book.

Filing Status

Like most relatives, Uncle Sam has his favorites, so the tax law treats different taxpayers differently. Begin with your filing status. There are four separate sets of tax rates, and what you owe the government varies significantly depending on which one applies to you. Consider the tax bite on $50,000 of taxable income in each tax bracket.

TAX ON $50,000

Filing Status	1995	1996
Single	$10,972	$10,880
Married filing jointly	8,937	8,787
Head of household	9,945	9,821
Married filing separately	11,559	11,440

Glancing at the bottom lines, you might conclude that the government will reward you for tying the knot. And seeing that a single taxpayer pays nearly 25% more tax on $50,000 income than a married couple does, you may wonder about all the griping you hear about the *marriage tax penalty*. But as with so much in the tax arena, things aren't necessarily what they seem. There really *is* a marriage tax penalty, as discussed on page 130. First, though, consider the categories into which Congress places various taxpayers. Here, too, things aren't as straightforward as you might think.

Money Saver

If you were married during any part of the year and widowed at year end, you can file a tax-saving joint return.

Married Filing a Joint Return

If you are married on the last day of the year, you can file a joint return. This applies even if you are separated from your spouse and pursuing a divorce. Unless the divorce is final by the end of the year, the IRS considers you married, and you can't file a return as a single taxpayer. If you were married for any part of the year but were widowed at year-end, you file a joint return for yourself and your deceased spouse.

Unmarried Individuals

You fall in the "singles" category if you aren't married at year-end and don't qualify to use the lower surviving-spouse or head-of-household rates.

Surviving Spouse

For up to two years after the year in which your spouse dies you may be able to continue using the joint-return rates rather than moving immediately into higher brackets. Not every widow and widower qualifies, though. Most, in fact, do not.

To be a qualifying surviving spouse—sometimes called a *qualified widow or widower*—you basically must have a child living with you. There are four tests:

- You must have been eligible to file a joint return for the year your spouse died.

- You must not have remarried. (If you did, of course, you can use the joint-return rates by filing with your new spouse.)

- You must have a child, stepchild or foster child who qualifies as your dependent (which is explained on page 112).

- You must have paid more than half the cost of keeping up your home, which is the principal residence of the child for the entire year (except for temporary absences).

In other words, if your children are grown and have already moved out of the nest when your spouse dies, you're out of luck.

Head of Household

This category causes a lot confusion, particularly among young people starting out on their own. If you're the only member of your household, you must be the *head*, right? Not as the IRS sees it.

To earn the head-of-household title and the right to use the lower-than-single tax rates, you basically have to be providing a home for a child or other relative. To qualify:

- **You must be unmarried at the end of the year.** (Even if you're legally married at year-end, you can pass this test under a special "abandoned spouse" rule if your spouse didn't live with you during the last six months of the year.)

- **You must pay more than half the cost of keeping up the principal home for yourself and a child or other relative you can claim as a dependent.** If the child (including a grandchild, stepchild or adopted child) is unmarried, he or she doesn't have to qualify as your dependent to earn you head-of-household status. Any other relative living with you, however, must pass the dependency tests, outlined beginning on page 112.

Generally, head of household status is used by divorced women with small children at home. But it can also pay off for divorced or widowed parents whose grown children return to the nest after college or following a divorce. Since the dependency test doesn't apply when single children are involved, you can claim this tax-saving status regardless of how much money the boomerang child makes—as long as you meet the other tests.

In most cases, you and the child or other relative must share the same house for more than six months of the year. There is an exception, however, if you are paying more than half the cost of maintaining a home for your *dependent* mother or father for the entire year. In that case, he or she does not have to live with you for you to qualify for head-of-household tax status. If you are paying more than half the cost of a nursing home for your dependent parent, for example, you can qualify.

When figuring whether you pay more than half the cost of maintaining a home, count such expenses as rent or mortgage interest, taxes, insurance on the home, repairs, utilities, domestic help and food eaten at home. Don't count what you pay for clothing, education, medical treatment, vacations, life insurance or transportation.

Note: If you qualify as a surviving spouse, you may be able to meet the head-of-household test once your two-year use of the joint rates runs out. Head-of-household rates are lower than those that apply to singles.

Married Filing Separately

This filing status almost never makes sense. The rare circumstances in which it can pay off usually involve a husband and wife with similar incomes who by splitting the income on separate returns can claim deductions that would elude them on a joint return. One often-cited reason for filing separate returns, for example, is if one spouse has significant medical bills. Such expenses are deductible only to the extent that they exceed 7.5% of adjusted gross income. Splitting income on separate returns might squeeze out a bigger medical deduction for one spouse, but only in very

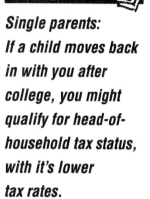

Money Saver

Single parents: If a child moves back in with you after college, you might qualify for head-of-household tax status, with it's lower tax rates.

special circumstances would the tax savings offset the cost of skipping the advantages that come by filing a joint return. There are plenty of disadvantages to filing separately:

- **One spouse can't claim the standard deduction if the other itemizes.** If one itemizes, both must. The squeeze on itemized deductions, discussed in Chapter 15, begins when 1996 AGI passes $117,950 for all filing statuses *except* married filing separately. On these returns, deductions are squeezed when AGI passes $58,975. (For 1995, the thresholds were $114,700 and $57,350.)

- **On separate returns, you can't claim the child-care credit.**

- **The $25,000 passive-loss allowance** for active rental real estate investors, discussed in Chapter 10, is not allowed on separate returns.

- **If you receive social security benefits,** filing separately guarantees that 85% of your benefits will be included in taxable income. On a joint return, benefits are partially taxable only when income exceeds $32,000, as explained in Chapter 12.

- **Filing separately doesn't get around the phaseout of IRA deductions discussed in Chapter 11, either.** On a joint return, taxpayers who have a retirement plan at work lose the deduction as income rises between $40,000 and $50,000; on a separate return, the deduction is phased out between $0 and $10,000. (At our deadline, Congress was considering changing the phase-out ranges. For a free update on this and other matters, write or e-mail the author at the address in the front of this book.)

Some of these separate-return disadvantages don't apply if you and your spouse don't live together at all during the year for which you file separate returns.

Although filing separate returns seldom makes sense at the federal level, don't assume the same applies to your *state* tax return. In some states, choosing married-filing-separately status can cut your tax bill significantly. Check the instructions with your state return carefully.

Exemptions

Although there may be fleeting fame attached to the first baby born in a new year, tax-savvy expectant parents are likely to prefer a New Year's Eve birth to a New Year's Day baby. After all, a child considerate enough to arrive before the year ends delivers to his or her parents a nice tax break, valuable enough to go a long way toward outfitting the nursery. A baby born before midnight December 31 earns the folks a full year's dependency exemption.

Each exemption you claim on your return shelters income from the IRS—$2,550 in 1996 and $2,500 in 1995—and the amount will increase in the future to keep up with inflation. In the 28% bracket, each $2,550 exemption for 1996 reduces your tax bill by $714.

Paper-Route Income

• •

Q: *Our 16-year-old son has a paper route and earns about $200 a month. Does he have to file a tax return and pay tax on that money?*

A: If that's his only income, he doesn't have to file a return. But if he has any "unearned" income—interest on a savings account, say—he must file. His standard deduction would be large enough to cover the paper-route earnings, but the unearned income would trigger a tax bill.

As the value of exemptions has risen in recent years—they were worth just $1,080 each in 1986—Congress has introduced new restrictions. In the past, for example, extra exemptions were granted to senior citizens and blind taxpayers. No more. The law also now denies children who are claimed on their parents' return—and older parents who are claimed as dependents on their children's return—the chance to claim their own personal exemptions. And there's a *recapture* system to obliterate the value of personal exemptions for upper-income taxpayers. In the face of these crackdowns, it's up to you to make sure you claim all the exemptions you have coming.

Regardless of what kind of return you file, you can claim a personal exemption for yourself—unless someone else can claim you as a dependent on their return, as explained on page 117. On a joint return, both husband and wife claim a personal exemption.

Beyond that, you must earn these valuable tax-savers by passing a series of tests to claim someone as your dependent. That's not difficult when it comes to a minor child who lives with you. The IRS almost takes that for granted, in fact. It's not so simple as children grow older or when you try to claim adult relatives—your parents, say—or unrelated people as your dependents.

Who Qualifies as Your Dependent?

There are five hoops you must jump through to win the right to claim someone as a dependent on your tax return:

- Member-of-household or relationship test
- Citizenship test
- Joint-return test
- Gross-income test
- Support test

The last two are the ones most likely to trip you up, but review all five.

Member of household or relationship

Perhaps the most important thing to note about this test is that someone needn't be related to you to qualify as your tax dependent. If you pass the other four tests, then, a friend you are supporting can be your tax dependent.

When an unrelated person is involved, the IRS demands that he or she be a member of your household, which means living with you for the entire year. When it comes to relatives, the IRS doesn't demand that they live under your roof for you to qualify for the tax break, and it's relatively broad-minded when defining relatives. Included are:

- Children, grandchildren or other lineal descendants;
- Stepchildren;
- Brothers, sisters, half brothers, half sisters, stepbrothers, stepsisters;

- Parents, grandparents or other direct ancestors (but not foster parents);

- Stepfathers, stepmothers;

- Brothers or sisters of your mother or father (your dad's brother—your uncle—counts, for example, but not his wife—your aunt);

- Sons or daughters of your siblings; and

- Fathers-in-law, mothers-in-law, sons-in-law, daughters-in-law, brothers-in-law, sisters-in-law.

The list probably contains about everyone you think of as a relative—except perhaps your cousins. To claim a cousin as your dependent, he or she must live with you for the entire year.

Citizenship
A person really *doesn't* have to be a citizen to pass this test. Someone can qualify if he or she is a U.S. citizen, resident or national, or a resident of Canada or Mexico.

Joint return
This test usually raises its ugly head only in the year a son or daughter you've been supporting gets married. The law prohibits claiming a dependency exemption for someone who files a joint return. Thus, if the new bride or groom files a joint return, you can lose a dependency exemption—even if you meet all the other tests. There's an exception to this rule. If the couple owes no tax but files jointly simply to reclaim money withheld from paychecks during the year, the joint return doesn't scotch your right to claim the exemption.

Gross income
Someone who earns more than the exemption amount—$2,550 in 1996 and $2,500 in 1995—generally can't be claimed as someone else's dependent. Say your elderly mother lives with you and the value of the food and lodging you provide and medical bills you pay amount to far more than 50% of her support. If she earns more than

the exemption amount—say from interest on her life's savings—you can't claim her as your dependent.

Here's an important exception: The income test does *not* apply to a son or daughter under 19 years old or to a child under age 24 who is a full-time student for at least five calendar months of the year. That means you usually don't have to worry about the gross-income test until your kids are out of college. Regardless of how much a child under 19 at the end of the year or a full-time student under 24 earns, you can claim him or her as a dependent if you pass the other tests.

"You have reached the IRS tax question answering service. To blow off steam, press one; to beg and plead, press two…"

From the Wall Street Journal; Permission, Cartoon Features Syndicate

Because too much income can obliterate your right to a dependency exemption, it's important to know what's included in gross income—and what is not. Essentially, gross income is all income that's not exempt from tax. Earnings from a job or taxable investments count; social security benefits don't, unless they are taxed under the rules discussed in Chapter 12. Gifts and insurance proceeds are not included, either, nor is tax-free interest.

If someone's interest income is tripping you up here, consider whether it would make sense to suggest a switch to tax-free bonds. Although there may be little or no tax benefit to a low-bracket investor, the exemption could be worth more to you than the amount of income lost to a lower yield.

Support test

To claim someone as a dependent, you must provide more than half of his or her support. With children living at home, there's generally no question that the parents pass this test. However, as the kids get older and get jobs to generate their own spending money, the 50% test can topple your right to the exemption.

When figuring the support you provide for someone living with you, include the fair rental value of the housing you provide. That means what you could expect a stranger to pay for it. Count what you spend for food, clothing, transportation, education, medical bills and wedding costs. That's right, you can include what you pay for your child's wedding. If you buy your son a state-of-the-art stereo system for his birthday, the cost is included in what you paid for his support.

You get the idea. A person's total support is what it costs for him or her to live during the year; your share is the amount of the total that came out of your pocket. If your son or daughter receives a college scholarship, you don't have to count its value as support provided by someone else, so it can't tip the support-test scales against you.

When you tote up what the person paid for his or her own support, don't assume it includes everything earned during the year. Money that goes into savings—whether it's summer job earnings put in a college account or social security benefits set aside for a rainy-day—does not count as support.

Special rules apply to the children of divorced parents. Generally, the parent with custody gets the exemption. For more details, see the discussion of divorce starting on page 132.

Multiple-support agreement. There's an exception to the hard-and-fast rule that you provide more than half of someone's support to claim that person as a dependent. When two or more persons *together* provide more than half of someone's support, one of the providers can claim the exemption if the others agree not to.

Disappearing Exemptions

●●●●●●●●●●●●●●●●●●●●●●●●

Q: *I understand that the law now takes away the right to claim dependents on my tax return. What's going on?*

A: Some taxpayers do lose the tax saving power of exemptions. The squeeze begins when adjusted gross income (AGI) passes certain thresholds. AGI is basically income before subtracting deductions and exemptions. For 1996, the value of exemptions is phased out as AGI passes $117,950 on individual returns and $176,950 on joint returns.

The multiple-support agreement generally comes into play when two or more adult children support a parent. Assume a brother and sister each provide 40% of their mother's support and that either one could claim her as a dependent if it weren't for the 50% test. Form 2120, *Multiple Support Declaration,* will permit one of them to claim the tax-saving exemption. The form is filed with the tax return of the person claiming the exemption and must be signed by the other provider, certifying that he or she provided more than 10% of the dependent's support and could have claimed her on his own return except for the 50%-support stipulation.

If more than two persons are involved, the one claiming the exemption must have a Form 2120 form signed by each person who provided more than 10% of the dependent's support. You can decide who will claim the exemption and it doesn't have to be the one who provided the greatest share of support. You can assign it to the provider in the highest tax bracket—to whom the exemption is worth the most—or rotate the tax break from year to year. You have to file 2120 forms each year you claim a dependent under the multiple-support agreement.

Social security number

There's one more requirement for claiming a dependent on your tax return. The person you're claiming—even an infant—must have a social security number. For 1995, this applies to any child who was at least two months old at the end of the year. For 1996 and future years, you need a social security number if the child was at least one-month old at the end of the year for which the return is being filed. Failure to provide the number triggers a $5 fine.

If you need a number for a child, ask your local social security office for a Form SS-5. (The form might also be available at a local post office.) In addition to completing the SS-5, you'll have to provide evidence of the child's age, identity and U.S. citizenship. The easiest proof of age and citizenship is the child's birth certificate. The Social Security Administration demands the original, though; not even a notarized copy will do. It will accept a religious certificate showing date and place of birth, such as a baptismal certificate.

In addition, you'll need one other proof of identity such as a nursery school or vaccination record or a Cub Scout or Brownie identification card. Check with the local office for specific demands. Once you apply for a card you should receive the child's number within two weeks.

To simplify this task for new parents, the Social Security Administration has introduced a program that lets parents order a number for a newborn before they leave the hospital. All they have to do is check a box on birth-record forms. State bureaus of vital statistics will pass the information on to social security. The agency will set up an account for the child, assign a number and mail the card to the parents.

If registering newborns strikes you as silly, keep in mind that the aim is to prevent taxpayers from claiming dependents they don't deserve. Apparently it's working. Between 1986 (the last year the numbers weren't required) and 1987 (the first year they were), 7 million dependents disappeared from tax returns. The mystery of the vanishing dependents sparked audits, of course, and the first 50 that were completed brought in an average of more than $2,000 of extra taxes and penalties.

Death of a Dependent

If a person who qualifies as your dependent dies during the year, you may claim the exemption on your return for that year. As long as the various requirements were fulfilled during the part of the year the person was alive—even if it was just part of one day—you qualify to claim the full exemption.

No More Double-Dipping

A person who can be claimed as a dependent on someone else's return can't claim a personal exemption on his or her own. This primarily affects children claimed on

Money Saver

If a dependent dies during the year, you can still claim the full exemption on your return for that year.

their parents' returns, but it also applies to anyone who can be claimed as a dependent, such as elderly parents who are being supported by their children. The loss of the exemption means more children must file returns because, without the exemption to shelter income, it's more likely their taxable total will be high enough to require a return.

Taking It Back

Congress has also decided that once your income reaches a certain level, you don't need the tax-saving assistance delivered by exemptions. If your adjusted gross income exceeds the levels shown in the table below your exemptions are in jeopardy. (These trigger points apply in 1996. The thresholds were slightly lower in 1995.)

LOSS OF EXEMPTIONS

Filing Status	Begins When AGI Passes
Married filing jointly	$176,950
Single	117,950
Head of household	147,450
Married filing separately	88,475

For every $2,500 your AGI exceeds the threshold for your filing status, you lose 2% of your exemptions. If you claim just one exemption, each additional $2,500 of AGI reduces the value of your exemption by $51 (2% of the 1996 exemption value of $2,550). If you claim ten exemptions, each additional $2,500 of AGI cuts the value of your exemptions by $510 (2% of $25,500).

The discussion of bubble brackets in Chapter 5 explains how this phaseout affects your marginal tax rate. By the time AGI reaches $125,000 above the trigger point, the full value of exemptions has been wiped out.

The phaseout can be extremely painful because the law demands that you lose 2% of your exemptions' value for every $2,500 *or fraction thereof* by which your income exceeds the trigger point. Say, for example, that you claim six exemptions on a joint return and your AGI is $176,951. That $1 over the threshold means you lose 2%

of $15,300 (6 x $2,550), the value of your exemptions. That adds $306 to your taxable income. . .and $110 to your tax bill in the 36% bracket. That's a heavy penalty for that extra dollar of income.

Kiddie Tax

Not so long ago, families had a golden opportunity to save on income taxes by spreading the wealth among family members. Such "income splitting" was at the heart of many college savings plans and is most easily explained with an example.

Assume you have $25,000 to invest and can buy bonds yielding 10% to produce $2,500 of income a year. As recently as 1986, if you were in the 50% tax bracket the IRS would claim $1,250. However, if you transferred ownership of the bonds to your son or daughter—either with an outright gift or in a trust—that $2,500 of annual income would have been taxed to him or her. The tax bill could have been as low as $162. The family saved $1,088. Multiplied over a number of years, the tax savings delivered by income splitting could make a significant dent in tuition bills.

Congress isn't against higher education, but it is opposed to tax maneuvering to get Uncle Sam to help pay for it. For one thing, denying children the right to claim their own personal exemptions trimmed the tax-saving potential of income splitting. The inability to shelter income with the exemption translates to a higher tax bill. And Congress took direct aim at income splitting by creating a set of rules immediately dubbed the "kiddie tax." Basically, investment income earned by a child under 14 is taxed in his or her parents' top tax bracket.

The kiddie tax disappears on the child's 14th birthday. If your child celebrates his or her 14th birthday anytime during the year—even on New Year's Eve—the tough taxing rules don't apply for any part of the year.

The distinction between *earned* and *unearned* income turns on whether the income is compensation for work performed. Salary, tips and self-employment income, for example, are considered earned income. Almost all other

Money Saver

No matter how much your son or daughter earns while on the job, the income is always taxed in the child's bracket— not yours.

kinds of income—including interest, dividends, capital gains, rents, and trust income—fall in the unearned income category and are vulnerable to the kiddie tax.

Not all of a child's unearned income is covered. On 1996 returns, only investment income over $1,300 can be taxed in the parents' bracket. The first $650 is tax-free, because up to $650 of a child's standard deduction can be used to shelter unearned income. The next $650 is taxed at the child's 15% rate. Excess unearned income is nicked by the parents' rate. (The $650 and $1,300 trigger points are the same for 1996 as they were for 1995. They may increase in the future with inflation.)

If your son or daughter has earnings from a job, that earned income is always taxed in the child's bracket. Here are some examples of how the kiddie tax applies to children under age 14:

- **Melody's only income is $400 of interest.** The federal tax bill is $0. No tax—kiddie or otherwise—is due because $650 of the standard deduction is available to shelter the income.

- **James has $900 of dividend and interest income and no earned income.** The first $650 is tax-free thanks to the standard deduction. The remaining $250 is taxed at James's 15% rate.

- **Jennifer receives $1,500 of interest and dividends and has no earned income.** The first $650 is tax-free and the next $650 is taxed at 15%. Then the kiddie tax kicks in, taxing the remaining $200 in her parents' bracket.

- **Tony has $700 earned income from a paper route and $300 from interest on a savings account.** His standard deduction is $700—the higher of earned income or $650—and is applied first to the $300 of unearned income. The

---

Copy of Missing Return

Q: *Going through my tax files, I discovered that I have misplaced a return I filed two years ago. Is there any way I can get a copy?*

A: Yes. The IRS generally holds onto returns for six years before destroying them. You can request a copy of your forms by filing Form 4506 with the IRS service center where you filed the missing return. The charge is $14.

remaining $400 of Tony's standard deduction shelters $400 of earned income. The remaining $300 of earned income is taxed in Tony's tax bracket. The kiddie tax doesn't come into play.

- **Anne has $700 of earned income and $1,500 of unearned income.** She gets a $700 standard deduction (based on earned income), with $650 of it offsetting unearned income. That leaves $850 of unearned income to be taxed: $650 at Anne's 15% rate and the remaining $200 at her parents' rate. The leftover $50 of the standard deduction offsets earned income, leaving $650 to be taxed in Anne's bracket. Bottom line: Of $2,200 of income, $700 is spared from tax by the standard deduction, $1,250 ($650 unearned and $600 earned) is taxed at Anne's 15% rate and $250 is taxed at her parents' top rate.

How to File

There's a special form—Form 8615—for figuring the kiddie tax. It must be filed with the return of each of the half a million or so "kiddies" to whom the rules apply. Although children's returns once were among the easiest to complete, those that involve the kiddie tax are now among the most difficult. When developing the Form 8615, the IRS estimated that completing the single-page form would add nearly a full hour to the return-preparation chore.

A costly shortcut

You may be able to skip the form. In some cases, parents may report a child's unearned income on the their return, avoiding the need for Form 8615, and letting the child escape filing altogether.

This alternative is available only if your child's entire income is from interest and dividends, and the total is less than $5,000. Also, of course, the child must be under age 14 at the end of the year. To use this streamlined method, you must fill out and file Form 8814 with your own return. The form makes it clear that you do not simply add all the

Money Saver

Skip the shortcut that lets you report a child's interest and dividend on your return. It will probably cost you money.

Saving money for college in your child's name reduces the tax on the earnings. A child could have more than $20,000 in an account yielding 6% without having to worry about the kiddie tax.

child's unearned income to your own taxable income. The first $500 of the child's income is tax-free and the next $500 is taxed at the child's 15% rate. The rest is added to your income and taxed in your tax bracket.

Beware, however, that a fluke in the law means opting for this time-saving shortcut may cost you money. Remember, when a child files a Form 8615, the first $650 of unearned income is tax-free and the next $650 is taxed at the child's rate. If you report the income on your tax form, those amounts drop to $500 and $500—meaning more income is taxed and more is taxed at your rate. The discrepancy is due to the fact that although Congress indexed the basic kiddie-tax levels to rise with inflation, the lawmakers forgot to do the same when it okayed the streamlined method. The $500 amounts are stuck at that level until the lawmakers get around to fixing their goof. (A fix was under consideration at the time we went to press. For a free update, write or e-mail the author at the address in the front of this book.)

There are other reasons to be leery of the shortcut. For one thing, reporting a child's income on your return will increase your AGI, and that could cost you tax-saving deductions. As discussed in Chapter 15, medical and miscellaneous expenses are deductible only to the extent they exceed a certain percentage of AGI. The higher your AGI, the fewer of those expenses you can deduct. The right to deduct IRA contributions is also tied to AGI, as is the phaseout of exemptions discussed earlier in this Chapter and the phase out of itemized deductions detailed in Chapter 15.

Even if the AGI traps don't snare you, reporting a child's income on your return could hike your family's *state* income tax bill. Many states are more generous than the federal government when it comes to how much income a child can earn tax-free. If you report the income on your federal return, though, you might have to report otherwise tax-free income on your state return, too. Check state tax instructions carefully.

Income Splitting Still Lives

Despite all the efforts to block the tax advantage of income splitting, there are still ways it can save your family money. If you're planning to help pay for your children's college education, starting to give them the money for tuition long before the first bill comes due can still get Uncle Sam to help pay the bill.

Remember that the first $1,300 of unearned income escapes the kiddie tax in 1996. A child could have more than $20,000 in an account yielding 6% without having to worry about the kiddie tax. If $1,300 is the child's only income in 1996, the tax bill will be just $97.50. If the same $1,300 were taxed in the parents' 36% bracket, for example, the tax would be $468. The $370.50 savings is the IRS contribution to the college fund.

Deferring investment income

Since the kiddie tax disappears when a child reaches age 14, consider giving your kids investments that defer income until that time. U.S. savings bonds are a natural choice because income can be deferred until the bond is cashed. If that's after the child reaches 14, even the interest that accrued during his or her younger days is taxed at the child's own rate. Note, though, that a special tax-saving twist for savings bonds could make it a better deal to buy the bonds in the parent's name rather than making the child the owner. When parents own the bonds and cash them in to pay a child's college tuition and fees, the interest on the bonds can be totally tax-free. See Chapter 10 for details.

Growth stocks, which generally throw off little, if any, current income in the form of dividends, are another way around the kiddie tax. As the stock appreciates, there is no tax on the paper profit. If the stock is sold after the child is 14, the profit is taxed in the child's bracket. Note that if a child invests in growth-stock mutual funds, rather than individual stocks, the fund will pay out capital-gains distributions each year based on trading within the fund. Such income would be subject to the kiddie tax if the child's unearned income exceeds $1,300 in 1996.

Money Saver

Growth stocks, which generally throw off little, if any, dividend income, are a way around the kiddie tax.

Making your child the owner

For income splitting to work, the child must actually own the assets that generate the income. If you want your son to pay taxes in his bracket on $1,000 of interest income generated by a $15,000 savings account, you can't simply give him the $1,000. You must give him the $15,000 in the account. Only then will the income it produces be his for tax purposes.

The easiest way to make such a gift to a minor child is to set up a custodial account under your state's Uniform Gift to Minors Act (UGMA) or Uniform Transfer to Minors Act (UTMA). Banks, savings & loans, credit unions, mutual funds and brokerage firms offer such accounts. All you need is a social security number for the child and a custodian to manage the account until the minor comes of age. You can name yourself custodian, but if you are also the donor and you die before the child reaches majority, the gift will count as part of your estate for federal estate-tax purposes.

An important point about custodial accounts is that your gift is irrevocable—you can't get it back. Once the child reaches the age set by your state's UGMA or UTMA law—typically 18 or 21—adult supervision of the account ends and the child can do anything he or she wants with the money. If sandy beaches are more enticing than ivy-covered walls, well…

You don't need a custodial account if you invest the child's money in U.S. savings bonds. Just buy the bonds in the child's name. Don't name yourself co-owner, though, or the income will still be taxed to you when the bonds are cashed.

Giving away a tax bill

Another move with income-splitting potential is

© 1988 Gorrell—Richmond News Leader

to give your child appreciated securities. The tax bill on the increase in value of the stocks or bonds passes along to the recipient along with the gift. Assume that stock you bought for $2,500 is now worth $5,000 and that you have a tuition bill coming due. If you sold the stock, you'd owe tax on the $2,500 gain. That would cost $700 in the 28% bracket.

Alternatively, you could give the shares to your college student. When sold, the same $2,500 would be taxed, but at the child's rate (assuming he or she isn't a prodigy who's in college before age 14). In the 15% bracket, the tax on the profit would be $375. Bottom line: a $325 tax savings. And if you didn't really want to part with the stock, you could reinvest in the shares with the cash that otherwise would have gone for tuition. You'd be taxed only on appreciation from that time on.

The gift tax

All this attention to generosity demands a brief mention here about the federal gift tax. The law permits you to give up to $10,000 each year to any number of people without having to worry about the gift tax. If you're married, you and your spouse can give up to $20,000 each year to each person on your gift list. Gifts above those levels are subject to the gift tax, which is imposed on the giver of gifts, not the recipient. However, there's a substantial tax credit that makes it doubtful you'll ever have to pay a dime in gift taxes. See Chapter 18 for more on the gift tax.

Hiring the family

If you have your own business—either full- or part-time—you have another income-splitting opportunity. Put your children on the payroll, working in the evenings and on weekends during the school year and during the summer. What you pay them is a business deduction for you and earned income for them. That shifts income out of your tax bracket and into the child's. Because it's earned income, the kiddie tax doesn't come into play. Although a child can use only $650 of the standard deduction to shelter unearned income in 1996, the full deduction— $4,000 on 1996 individual returns and more in future

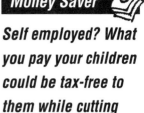

Money Saver

Self employed? What you pay your children could be tax-free to them while cutting both your income and self-employment tax bills.

years—can offset earned income. If your child's only income during the year is $2,000 earned working in the family business, for example, the child's tax bill would be zip. The $2,000 business deduction would save you $620 in income taxes if it otherwise would have been taxed in the 31% bracket.

To be deductible, the wages have to be reasonable and for real work your child performs for your business. Claiming a deduction for paying your 8-year-old $100 an hour to clean your office on Saturday mornings would be asking for trouble. But paying a reasonable wage for cleaning, serving as your answering service, filing documents, making deliveries, acting as your resident computer whiz, or performing other necessary services is a legitimate way to save on taxes and help build a college fund.

To protect your deduction, you need to handle the employment of your child in a businesslike manner. Keep careful records of the work done, the number of hours worked and the hourly wage. Pay with a check drawn on the business account. If you pay a child $600 or more during the year, you must file a form W-2 reporting the earnings to the IRS.

In addition to trimming your income tax bill, putting your kids on the payroll can save you a substantial amount of self-employment tax. As discussed in Chapter 3, that tax claims 15.3% of the first $62,700 of net self-employment income in 1996. Because you get to deduct wages you pay as a business expense, you avoid the social security tax on that amount. Every $1,000 of income you shift to a child via wages saves you $153 in social security taxes. Assuming you operate your business as a sole proprietorship rather than a corporation, your children under age 18 are not subject to the social security tax.

If you own rental property, consider hiring your children to mow the grass or help with other maintenance or repairs. What you pay them reduces the amount of rental income taxed in your bracket and the wages could be tax-free to the child. As noted above, earned income up to the standard deduction amount—$4,000 for single taxpayers in 1996—is sheltered by the child's standard deduction.

Become your child's landlord

Here's another income splitting and real estate combination that some parents have found valuable in paying for college. They pull together the down payment for a house or condo in the college town. The child gets a roommate or two and they all pay rent to the parents, who report it as income but also get to deduct mortgage interest, property taxes and depreciation. The parents also hire their child to manage the apartment—finding tenants, collecting rents, taking care of maintenance and repairs. What they pay him or her is deductible from the rental income. If the rental property shows a loss, and if the parents qualify for the $25,000 exception to the passive-loss rules discussed in Chapter 10, that loss can shelter other income. Any profit when the parents sell the home after graduation is an added sweetener.

Money Saver

Kid going away to school? Buy a place for him or her to live with roommates; collect rent, deduct interest, taxes and depreciation. After graduation, sell and deduct any loss or enjoy any gain.

Scholarships and Fellowships

First, the good news: For degree students, the value of grants for tuition and course-related expenses for books, supplies and equipment is tax-free.

Now, the bad news: Any part of a grant that goes for room, board or incidental expenses is taxable income for the student. And, nondegree students are taxed on the full value of any scholarship, including the amount that covers tuition. Also taxable are amounts received for teaching, research or other services, whether the student is paid in cash or through a tuition-reduction program. If tuition is discounted in exchange for a graduate student serving as a teaching assistant, for example, the amount that's shaved off tuition counts as taxable income.

There's a bit of a silver lining: The taxable part of a scholarship or fellowship qualifies as earned income, so at least even dependent students can use their standard deductions to offset part of it.

Family Loans

With today's house prices, this is an increasingly probable scene: Your son and his wife come over for dinner, fill the air with friendly chitchat and finally mumble sheepishly what's really on their mind: They've found their dream house and need help with the down payment.

No, they're not so brash as to ask for a $20,000 gift. Just a loan. A loan with *very* lenient terms—like no interest and an extremely flexible repayment schedule.

As you discuss the request, be aware that Uncle Sam may want to horn in on this congenial family scene. The government's interest in intrafamily loans stems from having been burned by no-interest loans designed to dodge taxes. Wealthy parents could *lend* money to a child in a low tax bracket and, in the best of income-splitting traditions, the child would invest the money so the income would be taxed at the child's lower rates. The government has closed that loophole.

The law now treats such loans as though the lender is charging interest on the deal and simultaneously making a gift to the borrower of the amount needed to pay that interest. This fiction has a very real tax consequence: The lender has to report as taxable income the phantom interest the loan did not produce. (If the amount of foregone interest exceeds $10,000, the lender may be liable for federal gift taxes, too.)

Don't turn down your kids' request straightaway, though, because—as usual—there are exceptions that can protect your intrafamily loan from the IRS.

- **If the amount of the loan outstanding at any time is $10,000 or less, the IRS will ignore it.** Under that test, husband and wife are considered to be one lender and the $10,000 limit applies.

- **A second exception protects even bigger low-interest or no-interest loans.** For loans up to $100,000, the IRS won't get involved as long as the borrower's investment income is less than $1,000. If it goes over $1,000, the "imputed" interest that the lender should report is limited to the amount of the borrower's investment income. In other words, you can go ahead and lend your children $20,000 interest-free for their down payment, but they'd better use most of their own savings, too. If their investment income for the year surpasses the $1,000 threshold, the imputed-interest rules could sting your friendly arrangement.

Both the $10,000 and the $100,000 exceptions are voided if the purpose of the loan is to save taxes. If the recipients use the borrowed funds to acquire income-producing assets, for example, the loan automatically falls victim to the imputed-interest rules. That doesn't block loans for such purposes as a house down payment, college tuition or to help a child start a business.

If you make a loan that fails to meet one of the exceptions, the amount of imputed interest on the deal is based on IRS-set rates that reflect what it costs the government to borrow money. These "applicable federal rates" are adjusted periodically. In late 1995, the long-term AFR was about 7%. Call your local IRS office to learn the current AFR. If you charge a low interest rate, rather than no interest, the imputed interest is the difference between what you actually charge and the amount due using the prevailing applicable federal rate.

Bad Debts

What if the family loan goes sour? Sure, you can count on your daughter the scholar to repay your loans after she gets her Ph.D., but what about your brother-in-law the taxidermist? If he stiffs you, can you write off the bad debt and thereby get Uncle Sam to subsidize your loss?

Perhaps, but the IRS is particularly suspicious of bad-debt deductions when the transaction involves relatives. Whether the borrower is your child or someone else, however, you can earn a bad-debt deduction if you can prove a true debtor-creditor relationship existed and that you fully expected to be repaid. That means you should go through the formalities of drawing up a note specifying repayment terms. If the borrower stops payments, you have to make an effort to collect, enough of an effort that you

Money Saver

If your family loan is under $10,000, don't worry about the imputed interest rules.

can convince an IRS auditor that there is no hope of collecting. You also have to be able to show that the debt became worthless in the year that you're claiming the deduction. Did the borrower file for bankruptcy, for example, or skip the country?

Clearly, it's difficult to qualify for a bad-debt deduction growing out of an unpaid family loan. If you can pass the tests, you can treat the bad debt as a capital loss and deduct it on Schedule D. As with other capital losses, bad debts are deducted first against capital gains and then against up to $3,000 of ordinary income.

Changing My Name

• •

Q: *I was married during the year and took my husband's last name. Do I have to report my name change to the IRS?*

A: No, but you should advise the Social Security Administration. You use Form SSA–5 to change your name on your social security records. Because the IRS uses the social security number as your taxpayer identification number, confusion could result; it could delay any refund you have coming if name and number don't match.

Marriage Tax Penalty

You might as well add Uncle Sam to the guest list for your wedding because the government has a financial stake in your nuptials. You and your bride or groom will wind up owing *either* more or less tax after the ceremony. Whether matrimony is for better or for worse on the bottom line of your tax return depends on how much each of you earns.

If your spouse has little or no income, marriage is sure to cut the family tax bill. But if you have similar incomes, you're likely to pay more tax as a couple.

Enter the marriage penalty. It's simple to understand, if not to accept. On a joint return, a husband's and wife's income are combined. Since our graduated tax system applies higher tax rates to higher incomes—under the theory that the more you earn, the more you can afford to pay—your combined income can be nudged up into a higher tax bracket. This is so even though the tax brackets are wider for joint returns than for single returns. The extra tax you pay on a joint return, compared to the combined bill if you and your spouse were filing individual returns, is the marriage tax penalty.

How It Works

In 1996, for example, the 15% bracket covers income up to $24,000 on single returns. If you and your betrothed each reported exactly that much, you'd each owe $3,600 in tax, for a total of $7,200.

On a joint return, the 15% bracket covers income up to $40,100. Although that's much higher than on a single return, it's not twice as high. Combining the two $24,000 incomes gives you a total of $48,000, shoving $7,900 out of the 15% bracket and subjecting it to the 28% rate. The tax on $48,000 on a joint 1996 return will be $8,227—$1,027 more than the combined levy on two single returns reporting the identical taxable income.

That's the marriage penalty.

It can really get brutal when two high income individuals marry, thanks to the new rate structure. When Congress decided to impose the 10% "millionaire's surtax" to create the 39.6% bracket, the lawmakers decided to apply it starting at the same taxable income level for both single and joint returns. For 1996, the trigger point is $263,750. (Yes, the surtax starts well below $1 million, but no one said you had to know math to be elected to Congress.)

Consider what this means for a betrothed couple, each of whom has a cool, quarter million of taxable income. On separate returns, they'd pay $79,070.50 each, for a total tax of $158,141. On a joint return reporting $500,000, however, the tax bill would be $173,000—$14,859 more.

The marriage penalty also comes into play when pairing two incomes hikes your AGI to a level that causes you to lose the benefit of personal exemptions (as discussed earlier in this chapter) or itemized deductions (see Chapter 15).

As noted at the beginning of this chapter, at our deadline, Congress was considering mitigating the marriage tax penalty by creating a special tax credit for two-

The marriage tax penalty gets all the attention, but for some couples, tying the knot can cut the tax bill.

earner couples. The proposed credit wouldn't do much, frankly, but for folks burned by the marriage tax penalty, any relief would be appreciated. For a free update on this matter, write or e-mail the author at the address in the front of this book.

The marriage bonus

Moving from single filing status to a joint return doesn't always work to your disadvantage. Assume, for example, that one of the betrothed has a taxable income of $50,000 and the other has no income at all. On a single return, the breadwinner would owe a tax of $10,880 for 1996. Marriage to a nonearning spouse would slash that bill. On a joint return, the tax would be $8,787, for a marriage bonus of $2,093.

Although far from romantic, cranking the income tax consequences of marriage into your wedding plans could pay off handsomely. If it's a toss-up whether you'll go to the altar just before Christmas or right after New Year's, take a look at how Uncle Sam views your union.

Divorce

As if divorce were not difficult enough, the tax laws complicate matters and demand your attention, too. At the simplest level, getting a divorce changes your filing status. If the divorce is final before the end of the year, the IRS considers you single for the whole year. You can't file a joint return with your ex-spouse even if you were married for the first 364 days of the year. It's your marital status on December 31 that matters to the IRS.

More importantly, the way the IRS treats various parts of the financial arrangements that accompany the split can play a major role in the structure of those arrangements. Careful tax planning can produce a settlement with the most favorable tax consequences for both parties—leaving more for each of you by limiting the government's share. If your differences keep you from addressing the tax issues, the only winner on this front will be the IRS.

Alimony/Child Support

The tax distinction here is enormous. Payments that qualify as alimony are deductible by the ex-spouse who pays them and taxed as income to the one who receives the money. Child support, on the other hand, is neither deductible nor taxed.

Generally, to qualify for the deduction, alimony must be paid in cash and be required by a written divorce agreement. If you and your ex just amicably decide that one will pay the other "alimony," forget the deduction. The payer must be obligated to make the payments to earn the tax deductions.

There are rules to prevent transfers that should be classified as child support or property settlements—neither of which is deductible—from sneaking through as deductible alimony.

Until a few years ago, support payments from one spouse to the other could be treated as alimony unless the payments were specifically called child support. Now, regardless of how the divorce agreement classifies the payments, they are treated as nondeductible child support if the payment is contingent on a future occurrence involving the child. If the agreement will reduce or eliminate the payment when a child reaches a certain age or completes school, for example, that part of the payment can never be claimed as alimony.

In the past, alimony was usually a long-term obligation to pay an ex-spouse, often until he or she remarried or died. The trend now, however, is toward so-called rehabilitative maintenance for only a few years. Such payments are often designed to help the recipient get training and then a job.

Although the government has nothing against such arrangements, there's concern that big payments in the first few years after a divorce may really be an attempt to disguise a nondeductible property settlement as deductible alimony. To prevent that, the law provides for "recapture" of alimony deductions under certain circumstances, depending on how much the payments to the ex-spouse vary during the first three years.

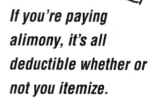

Money Saver

If you're paying alimony, it's all deductible whether or not you itemize.

You don't have to worry about recapture at all if alimony payments are $15,000 or less a year. As long as you meet the other requirements for alimony, the payments are fully deductible. A single $15,000 cash payment can qualify as deductible alimony. When larger payments are involved, however, they may trigger the recapture rules. If the payment in the first year exceeds the average payment in years two and three by more than $15,000, the excess is recaptured. Also, if the payment in the second year exceeds the payment in the third by more than $15,000, the excess is recaptured.

The impact is easiest to see in an illustration. Assume a divorce settlement calls for a $50,000 payment in the first year and no payments in years two or three. If the entire $50,000 was deducted as alimony in the first year, $35,000 of it would be recaptured in the third year—the amount by which $50,000 exceeds by more than $15,000 the average payment in the second and third years ($0 in this example). Under the rules, the payer would have to report the $35,000 as taxable income. And the recipient—who had to report the entire $50,000 in year one—gets to claim a $35,000 deduction to even things out.

Because the new rules cover just three years, it is possible to cram a substantial cash settlement into just 13 months and treat the full amount as deductible alimony. You could make the first payment in December of 1996, for example, the next sometime during 1997, and the third and final payment in January of 1998. If all three payments were equal, there would be no recapture.

Also, there is no recapture if payments drop off in the second or third year because the recipient dies or remarries.

You can call it alimony—or not

Although conventional wisdom suggests that a divorce agreement should classify payments whenever possible as alimony—because traditionally the payer was in a higher tax bracket than the recipient—that's not necessarily so these days. With more working couples, it's more and more likely both spouses will be in the same tax bracket—no more writing off alimony in the 50% bracket and reporting it in the 20% bracket.

The law gives divorcing taxpayers the leeway to declare that qualifying payments will *not* count as alimony. That means the payer can't deduct the payments and the recipient doesn't have to report them as income. The recipient, of course, may be willing to accept smaller payments if they're tax-free. Since the deduction is worth less to the payer in a lower tax bracket, a profitable compromise may be attainable. You need to work out the best overall deal with your attorneys.

Reporting requirements

If you do pay alimony during the year, you can deduct it whether or not you itemize your other deductions. It's considered an adjustment to income, as discussed in Chapter 14. You must include your ex-spouse's name and social security number on your tax return. That demand is designed to insure that if you're claiming a deduction, somebody is reporting the same amount as income. There's a $50 fine if you fail to include your ex's social security number.

Property Settlements

Thanks to the tax law, in a divorce settlement one piece of property can be worth far more than another with exactly the same market value. The reason is that when property changes hands as a result of a divorce—whether it is the family home, a portfolio of stocks or other assets—the tax basis of the property also changes hands. The basis is the amount from which gain or loss will be figured when the property is sold. Because the new owner gets the old owner's basis, he or she is responsible for the tax on all the appreciation *before* as well as *after* the transfer.

This rule means you have to look carefully at the tax basis of property that may be part of a settlement. For example, $100,000 worth of stock with a basis of $90,000 is worth significantly more than $100,000 worth of stock with a $50,000 basis. The maximum tax on the sale of the first stock would be $2,800 (28% of the $10,000 gain). The tax on the sale of the second block of stock could be as high as $14,000 (28% of the $50,000 gain).

Money Saver

In a divorce settlement, watch the basis of the assets. If two properties of equal value are involved, try to get the one with the higher basis.

Letting the noncustodial parent claim a child as a dependent can pay off if he or she is in a higher tax bracket.

Exemptions for Children

For years, the question of which spouse should claim the exemption for dependent children of divorced parents caused nothing but trouble. Often, the custodial parent would claim the exemption, and so would the other parent who was providing child support.

To simplify things, the law now generally gives the exemption to the custodial parent named in the divorce decree. If the decree doesn't name either parent, the custodial parent is the one with whom the child lives for the greater part of the year. It's possible, however, for the noncustodial parent to claim the exemption, which could be beneficial if he or she is in a higher tax bracket than the custodial parent.

The noncustodial parent gets the exemption if the custodial parent signs a waiver pledging that he or she won't claim it. Form 8332, *Release of Claim to Exemption for Child of Divorced or Separated Parents,* is provided for waiving the right to the exemption. The custodial parent must sign that form each year the exemption is shifted, and the noncustodial parent who is claiming the exemption must attach the form to his or her return.

For taxpayers divorced before 1985, if the divorce decree awarded the right to claim the dependency exemption to the noncustodial parent, he or she need not file a Form 8332 each year. Instead, there is a box on the tax return to check to indicate that a pre-1985 agreement controls the exemption.

Whether or not a divorced parent can claim a child as a dependent, the amount he or she pays for the child's medical care counts when the parent totes up medical costs to see if they are deductible. (Such costs can be written off only to the extent that they exceed 7.5% of adjusted gross income, as discussed in Chapter 15.)

Legal Fees

Although legal fees and court costs involved in a divorce are generally nondeductible personal expenses, you can deduct the part of your attorney's bill attributable to tax advice. If you are receiving alimony, you can deduct the portion of the fee the lawyer ascribed to setting the amount. It's tougher than ever to get any tax savings here, though, since these costs fall into the category of miscellaneous expenses that are deductible only to the extent that the total exceeds 2% of your adjusted gross income. Still, be sure your attorney provides a detailed statement that breaks down his fee so you can tell how much of it may qualify for a deduction.

Death in the Family

Death and taxes may be equally inevitable, but the taxman demands the last word. Death does not excuse a final accounting with the IRS. In fact, taxes can further complicate the lives of survivors. Federal estate taxes are discussed in Chapter 18. At issue here is the final income-tax return.

When a taxpayer dies, a new taxpaying entity—the taxpayer's estate—is born to make sure no taxable income falls through the cracks. Income is taxed either on the taxpayer's final return, on the return of the beneficiary who acquires the right to receive the income, or, if the estate receives $600 or more of income, on the estate's *income* tax return.

The chore of filing the taxpayer's final return usually falls to the executor or administrator of the estate, but if neither is named, a survivor must do it. The return is filed on the same form that would have been used if the taxpayer were still alive, but *deceased* is written after the taxpayer's name and the date of death entered on the name-and-address space. The filing deadline is April 15 of the year following the taxpayer's death.

Reporting Income

Only income earned between the beginning of the year and the date of death should be reported on the final return. For taxpayers who use the cash method of accounting, as most do, income is considered earned as it is actually received or at least made available to them. Taxpayers who use the accrual method of accounting, on the other hand, count income as earned when they actually earn it, regardless of when they receive it.

The distinction is important because some income that might logically seem to belong on the decedent's final return is considered *income in respect of a decedent* and is taxable either to the estate or to the person who receives it. Consider these examples.

Joe Jones owned and operated an orchard. He used the cash method of accounting. He sold $2,000 worth of fruit to a customer but did not receive payment before his death. That amount is not reported on Joe's final return. When the estate was settled, payment had still not been made and the right to receive it went to Joe's niece. When she collects the money, she will report it as taxable income.

If Joe had used the accrual method of accounting, the $2,000 would have been considered earned on the date of the sale and therefore included on his final return. His niece would not have to include the money on her return when the payment was actually received.

"And do you promise to love, honor, and cherish each other, and to pay the United States government more in taxes as a married couple than you would have paid if you had just continued living together?"

Drawing by Levin; © 1993 The New Yorker Magazine, Inc.

Mary Smith was entitled to a large salary payment at the date of her death, to be paid in five annual installments. Her estate collected two payments and then gave the right to the remaining three payments to her grandson. None of the income would be included on Mary's final return. The estate would include in its taxable income the two payments it received. Her grandson would include the other three payments in his taxable income—as income in respect of a decedent—on the returns for the years he received the money.

What about investment income?

Income in respect of a decedent encompasses only income that the decedent had a right to receive at the time of death but that is not reported on the final return. It does not include earnings on savings or investments that accrue after death.

Say a taxpayer who has a substantial amount in money-market mutual funds dies June 30. Only interest earned up to that date would be reported on the final tax return. Earnings after that date are taxable to the beneficiary of the account, or to the estate. That can create some hassles since the payer—a mutual fund, bank or broker, for example—will report income to the IRS on a 1099 form. Although you should try to get ownership of the account changed as quickly as possible after the death of the owner, the 1099 income report may well show more income assigned to the decedent than it should. In such cases, you must report the entire amount on Schedule B of the decedent's return and then deduct the amount that is being reported by the estate or other beneficiary who actually received the income.

Remember that money you inherit is not subject to the federal income tax. If you inherit a $100,000 certificate of deposit, for example, the $100,000 is not taxable. Only interest on it from the time you become the owner is taxed. If you receive interest that accrued but was not paid prior to the owner's death, however, it is considered income in respect of a decedent and *is* taxable on your return.

There's a special rule for U.S. savings bonds, income on which generally accrues tax-free until the bonds are cashed. When the bond owner dies, the accrued interest may be treated as income in respect of a decedent. In that case, the new owner of the bonds becomes responsible for the tax on the interest accrued during the life of the decedent. (The tax isn't due, however, until the new owner cashes the bonds.) Alternatively, the interest accrued up to the date of death can be reported on the decedent's final tax return. That could be a tax-saving choice if he or she is in a lower tax bracket than the beneficiary. If that method is chosen, the person who gets the bonds includes in his or her income only interest earned after the date of death.

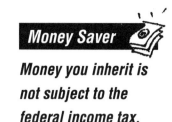

Money Saver

Money you inherit is not subject to the federal income tax.

Reporting Deductions

On the deduction side of the ledger, all deductible expenses paid before death can be written off on the final return. In addition, medical bills paid within one year after death may be treated as having been paid by the decedent at the time the expenses were incurred. That means the cost of a final illness can be deducted on the final return even if the bills were not paid until after death.

If deductions are not itemized on the final return, the full standard deduction may be claimed, regardless of when during the year the taxpayer died. Even if the death occurred on January 1, the full standard deduction is available. The same goes for the taxpayer's personal exemption.

Filing the Final Return

If the taxpayer was married, the widow or widower may file a joint return for the year of death, claiming both personal exemptions and the full standard deduction and using joint-return rates. The executor usually files a joint return, but the surviving spouse can file it if no executor or administrator has been appointed.

If an executor or administrator is involved, he or she must sign the return for the decedent. When a joint return is filed, the spouse must also sign. When there is no executor or administrator, whoever is responsible for filing the return should sign the return and note that he or she is signing on behalf of the decedent. If a joint return is filed by the surviving spouse alone, he or she should sign the return and write *filing as surviving spouse* in the space for the other spouse's signature.

If a refund is due, there's one more step. You should also complete and file with the final return a copy of Form 1310, *Statement of Person Claiming Refund Due a Deceased Taxpayer.* Although the IRS says you don't have to file Form 1310 if you are a surviving spouse filing a joint return, you probably should file the form anyway to head off possible delays.

If the person filing the final return is the decedent's court-appointed representative, he or she must attach a copy of the form certifying the appointment. When a return calling for a refund is filed by anyone other than a court-appointed representative or a surviving spouse filing a joint return, Form 1310 must also be accompanied by a copy of the taxpayer's death certificate or other proof of death.

Basis of Inherited Property

It's important to note that the basis of any property owned by a taxpayer at the time of death is "stepped-up" to its date-of-death value. Since the basis is the amount from which any gain or loss will be figured when the new owner ultimately sells the property, this means that the tax on any appreciation that occurred during the taxpayer's life is forgiven. The person who inherits the property—a house, say, or stocks and bonds—would owe tax only on appreciation after the time of death. See Chapter 10 for details.

Tax Rules for Household Help

Does someone work in your home—as a housekeeper, for example, or to take care of your kids? If so, you probably have a special set of tax paperwork to deal with, as well as extra taxes to pay.

Say hello to the *Nanny Tax*, the complicated web of rules for domestic employees that gained prominence in 1993 when several people President Clinton wanted to name to important jobs (including two potential Attorneys General) lost their chance when it was discovered they had failed to pay the proper social security, medicare and unemployment taxes for their household employees.

Yes, the rules have been simplified—a bit—since all that controversy, but the fact is, far more people will pay the tax starting in 1996 than ever before. Not that more people are legally obligated to pay, but the taxes are now much harder to ignore. In the past, the IRS figured 75% or so of the people who should have paid did not, and few of them were caught. Now, however, if you owe the tax, you pay it along with your Form 1040—not with four separate payments during the year. It's going to be hard for folks

Money Saver

If you inherit property—a house, say, or stocks and bonds—you owe tax only when you sell— and only on any appreciation after you became owner.

who owe the tax to ignore the new line on *their* tax returns—which must be signed, under penalties of perjury, to declare that the form is complete and accurate.

Hiring Household Help

Q: *Is it true I can be fined if the person I hire to look after my children is not a citizen?*

A: No. The caregiver does not have to be a citizen, but you are required to make sure anyone you hire has a legal right to work in the U.S. You're supposed to complete a **Form I–9**, Employment Eligibility Verification, and list on it the documents the employee provided to prove citizenship or other eligibility to work in the U.S. You can be fined for hiring an illegal worker. You can get copies of the I–9 from the Immigration and Naturalization Service by calling 800–755–0777.

Are You an Employer?

The first step to see if you're caught up in these rules is to determine whether the person working in your home is your *employee* or an *independent contractor*. If he or she is an employee, you're stuck with the paperwork and the expense of the Nanny Tax. If not, you can breathe easy.

Unfortunately, the distinction is often unclear. Here, though, are three quick tests to clear things up:

- **Control.** The more you have to say over when, where and how the person works, the more likely he or she is an employee.

- **Chance for profit or loss.** When the person you hire can lose money on the deal, he or she is considered self-employed. But when there's no risk for loss, the person usually looks like an employee to the IRS.

- **Continuity.** The more often someone works for you and the longer the arrangement exists, the more likely the person is your employee.

Someone you hire to care for your children in your home while you work is almost sure to be your employee. A part-time housekeeper may or may not be. If the housekeeper supplies the equipment and materials and works in numerous homes, he or she might qualify as a self-employed, independent contractor who's responsible for the various tax liabilities that go along with the job.

When you hire someone through an agency that treats that person as *its* employee, you're clearly off the hook. (These distinctions don't matter when the person working in your home is your parent. An exception almost always lets you ignore the employment-tax rules in that case.)

How Much Did You Pay?

Assuming the person is your employee, how much you pay him or her controls whether you owe employment taxes and, if so, which taxes you owe.

If you paid $1,000 or more during the *year*, you're responsible to pay both social security and medicare taxes for your employee. (Until 1994, the wage threshold was $50 per calendar quarter.) An exception to the $1,000 trigger point applies if the employee is under age 18, assuming his or her principal occupation is *not* household work. In that case, you don't have to worry about the Nanny Tax rules regardless of how much you pay. This exempts, for example, the high school student who regularly looks after your children or your lawn. If that person were to drop out of school and make child care or gardening his or her full time job, however, you'd owe the Nanny Tax if you paid $1,000 or more during the year.

If you paid the employee $1,000 or more during any *calendar quarter* during the current or previous year, you're also responsible to pay federal unemployment taxes for the employee.

You Need a Number

If you owe employment taxes, the first thing you need is an employer identification number (EIN). And you need it well before the filing deadline for the tax return on which you'll pay the tax. The EIN must be shown on the Form W-2 you must give your employee by January 31, as explained later.

Apply for an EIN by filing Form SS-4 with the IRS. (Call 800–TAX–FORM to order a copy of the form or download one from the IRS at the addresses listed in the

Money Saver

If you hire a student under age 18 to watch your kids or help around the house, don't worry about the Nanny Tax.

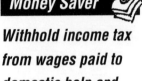

Money Saver

Withhold income tax from wages paid to domestic help and you'll put off paying part of the wages until next April.

appendix.) It takes about a month to get your EIN by mail but, if time is short, once you fill out the form you can call the IRS (the number's listed in the SS-4 instructions) and have an EIN assigned over the phone.

Social Security Taxes

If you owe social security and medicare taxes, the rate is 15.3% of the first $62,700 paid in 1996. (The limit was $61,200 in 1995.)

You and your employee share this burden. You're supposed to split the 15.3% rate evenly, each paying 7.65%. But it's up to you, as the employer, to see that the government gets its money. You can withhold 7.65% from your employee's pay or, as many household employers do, simply pay the full freight. Note that if you pay the employee's share, that amount is considered extra taxable income to the employee.

For example, assume that you pay a child-care provider $5,000 during the year and, rather than withhold social security taxes, you pay the full tax yourself. The 7.65% employee share would be $382.50, so as far as the IRS is concerned your employee earned $5,382.50 for income tax purposes. (The social security tax doesn't clip the value of food, lodging or other noncash benefits, which may count as income to the employee for income tax purposes.)

Income Tax Withholding

You don't have to withhold income tax from your employee's wages, but you can if the employee asks you to. Although that might sound like a hassle, it's not much trouble if you're already withholding social security taxes, and it actually lets you put off paying part of the wages until you file your return.

If you agree to withhold, have your employee complete a Form W-4, *Employee's Withholding Allowance Certificate.* You'll also need a copy of IRS Publication 15, *Circular E, Employer's Tax Guide,* which explains how to figure how much to withhold.

Note that the amount on which you withhold income tax may be different from the amount subject to the social security tax. For income tax purposes, you generally must count the value of food, lodging, clothing or other non-cash items provided to an employee, as well as cash wages paid. However, the value of food and lodging provided in your home and for your convenience is not considered income. This exception generally exempts from the income tax the value of food and lodging that you provide to a household employee who lives in your home.

Say, for example, that on $200 a week of wages, you withhold $17 for social security and income taxes. Basically, that means you'd pay just $183 each week and make up the difference by paying $850 (50 weeks worth of withholding) with your tax return the following April.

Earned Income Credit

If your employee earns less than about $27,000 a year, he or she may be eligible for a special tax break: the earned-income credit (see Chapter 16). In that case, you should give the worker a copy of IRS Notice 797, *Notice of a Possible Federal Tax Refund Due to the Earned Income Credit,* which is available from the IRS. The employee can give you a W-5 form, the *Earned Income Credit Advance Payment Certificate,* which requires *you* to pay the credit in installments each payday. The money comes out of the social security and income taxes you would otherwise pay with your return.

Federal Unemployment Tax

FUTA (for Federal Unemployment Tax Act) pays for your employee's unemployment insurance. As the employer, you're subject to the tax if you paid wages of $1,000 or more in any calendar quarter during the current or preceding year. Note that paying less than $1,000 during a quarter does not necessarily exempt you from FUTA on those wages. It still applies if you paid wages of $1,000 or more during any quarter of the current or previous year.

(FUTA does not apply to wages paid to your spouse, parents or children under age 21.)

The FUTA tax is 6.2% of the first $7,000 of cash wages paid during the calendar year, but you'll probably pay just 0.8% after a credit for paying your state's unemployment tax. When you hire a household employee, contact your state's employment-tax office for information on paying the state's tax and getting the reporting number you'll need to get federal credit for the state tax paid. Unlike the social security tax, the employer must pay this levy entirely. You can't withhold part of it from your employee.

Keeping My Name
● ●

Q: *Rather than take my husband's surname, I decided to keep my own. Will that cause us problems with the IRS when we file a joint return?*

A: It shouldn't, particularly now that the tax form provides separate lines for each spouse's name and social security number.

Deadlines and Paperwork

As an employer, you have to give your employee a Form W–2 showing how much you paid during the year and how much tax was withheld—just like the one you get from your boss. If you've paid taxes for domestic help in the past, you should automatically receive the necessary form from the IRS in January. But if this is your first time, pick up a W–2 at a local IRS office or order one by calling 800–TAX–FORM. You're supposed to give your employee a completed W–2 by January 31 and file a copy with the Social Security Administration by the end of February. If you have more than one household employee, the copies of the W–2s sent to Social Security must be accompanied by a Form W–3, *Transmittal of Wage and Tax Statements.*

If your employee leaves during the year, you can give him or her a W–2, and file the copy with Social Security, as soon as you make the final wage payment. You don't have to wait until the following January.

You'll report the social security, medicare and unemployment taxes you owe on a new Schedule H, which you should get in your regular package of tax forms. If you paid an earned-income credit, it reduces the amount of employment taxes you owe.

The total due figured on Schedule H is carried over to your Form 1040 or 1040A and added to the income tax you owe for the year.

As noted in Chapter 7, generally if you owe more than $500 when you file your return, you can be hit with a late-payment penalty. For 1995, 1996 and 1997 returns, however, employment taxes you owe for household help don't count for purposes of that penalty.

Starting in 1998, however, employment taxes are to be paid during the year, via quarterly estimated tax payments or increased withholding on *your* paychecks. Even before then, you may want to ask your employer to increase withholding on your checks enough to cover the Nanny Tax you'll owe with your return, so you don't get hit with an unexpected tax bill. See Chapter 7 for a discussion of how you can alter withholding on your checks.

State Tax Headaches

Although the feds have done away with quarterly payments for taxes on household help, your state may still require quarterly payments of unemployment taxes. Check with your state unemployment tax agency to make sure you don't run afoul of state rules. IRS publication 926, *Household Employer's Tax Guide*, includes a listing of the appropriate agencies in every state. Call 800–TAX–FORM for a copy.

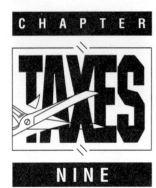

Home Sweet Tax Shelter

Your home—probably the biggest investment of your life—is likely to be the best tax shelter, too. Uncle Sam is standing by to serve as a generous partner in your investment, ready to subsidize your mortgage payments and willing to turn a blind eye to the profit you make when you sell the place—so long as you buy another home.

Given the favored status of homeownership in America, it's no surprise that the deductions for mortgage interest and local property taxes have survived as other deductions have gone the way of the dodo bird. Yes, there is a limit on mortgage-interest write-offs, but it kicks in only when mortgage debt exceeds $1 million. And the interest deduction can be nicked by the restriction that applies to taxpayers whose adjusted gross income exceeds $117,950 in 1996 ($114,700 in 1995). That's discussed in Chapter 15. It's impossible to say exactly how this will affect any specific taxpayer, since it depends on AGI and the makeup of your deductions. For that reason, the discussion that follows generally assumes that all of your mortgage interest will remain deductible.

Home Buyer's Subsidy

If you're considering buying your first house, you can be confident that doing so will cut your tax bill. As veteran homeowners know, it will just as surely complicate your tax life.

If you don't itemize deductions already, you're almost sure to begin once you purchase a home. After all, the mortgage-interest portion of the first 12 monthly payments on a $100,000, 8%, 30-year mortgage comes to almost $8,000. That's $1,300 more than the $6,700 standard deduction in 1996 for married couples. You'll also get to deduct state and local property taxes.

Once you begin itemizing your deductions, other expenses that are of no value to non-itemizers—such as state income taxes, charitable contributions and, possibly, medical bills—are automatically transformed into tax-saving write-offs.

The opportunity to trade nondeductible rent payments for mostly deductible mortgage payments is a powerful lure pulling tenants out of their apartments and into the housing market. Whether you're looking for your first home or planning to move up, the number crunching necessary to determine how much house you can afford demands two sets of books: one for your actual monthly outlays, the other for the true, *after-tax* cost.

Breakdown of Home Mortgage Payment

• •

The figures here, showing what part of each year's payment goes to reduce the principal on the loan and what part is tax-deductible interest, are based on a $100,000, 30-year fixed loan at 8%.

Year	Annual Payments	Principal	Interest
1	$8,805	$ 835	$7,970
2	8,805	905	7,900
3	8,805	980	7,825
4	8,805	1,061	7,744
5	8,805	1,149	7,656
10	8,805	1,712	7,093
15	8,805	2,551	6,254
20	8,805	3,800	5,005
25	8,805	5,661	3,144
30	8,811	8,441	370

In the early years of a home mortgage nearly all of every monthly payment you make is interest. That's disappointing from the standpoint that it means you are paying off just tiny bits of loan principal. But it's terrific in terms of tax savings.

Look again at a $100,000, 30-year, 8% mortgage. The monthly payment would be $733.76, and the accompanying table shows the breakdown in various years between principal repayment and deductible interest.

In the first year, $7,970 of your monthly payments—fully 90%—would be deductible as mortgage interest. Even in the 15th year, 71% of your payments would be deductible. In fact, only in the unlikely event that you live in the house for 22 years would the scales tip so that less than half of the total paid during the year would be tax-deductible.

Just what the deductions are worth to you depends, of course, on your tax bracket. If you are in the 28% bracket, every $1,000 of deductible interest and taxes translates to a $280 subsidy from Uncle Sam. In our $100,000 mortgage example, assume that in addition to the $733.76 monthly mortgage payment you also pay $150 a month for local property taxes. During the first 12 months, you pay a total of $10,605—about $884 a month.

But $9,770 is deductible—the $1,800 of property taxes plus the $7,970 of interest. In the 28% bracket that generates tax savings of $2,736 and pulls down the first-year after-tax cost to $7,869, or about $656 a month. In the 36% bracket, the tax savings total $3,517, bringing the real cost to about $590 a month. The tax savings built into the home-buying equation is why you can afford to make higher mortgage payments than your current rent payments without squeezing your budget. As disgruntled renters often complain, tenants enjoy no similar tax subsidy. In this example, the after-tax cost of a home payment of $884 a month is equivalent to rent at $656 or $590 a month, depending on your tax bracket. Of course, owning the house could present you with repair bills a renter doesn't have to worry about, but on the other hand, as an owner you reap all the appreciation on the value of your home.

Adjust withholding

What good is the tax subsidy if you're worrying about coming up with the cash needed each month to make the mortgage payment? Fortunately, you don't have to wait until the following year when you file a tax return to cash in on the savings. As soon as you purchase your first home or buy a new house that carries higher deductible expenses, you can direct your employer to begin withholding less from your paychecks. If you are self-employed, you can scale back your quarterly estimated tax payments. In either case, your cash flow can increase almost immediately to help cover the mortgage payments. Chapter 7 explains how to adjust estimated payments or trim withholding. (If you have problems coming up with the down payment, see the section on equity-sharing arrangements that begins on page 183.)

Record Keeping

Buying a home may be your introduction to the endearing term *tax basis*. That's the home's value for tax purposes. Keeping track of it is as demanding as it is important. The basis of your home is the figure you'll compare to the amount you get when you sell the place to determine whether you have a taxable profit that piques the interest of the IRS.

Although the basis of a home begins simply enough—as what it costs you to buy the house—it can change often before you sell. As discussed later, the basis of each home you own affects the basis of the next one you buy. You must keep track of all adjustments to the basis—for your entire home-owning career—to ensure that you don't overpay your tax.

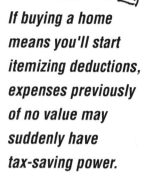

Money Saver

If buying a home means you'll start itemizing deductions, expenses previously of no value may suddenly have tax-saving power.

Closing Costs

The record-keeping chore begins with sorting out the tax consequences of the closing costs you pay at settlement. Although a few of these expenses may be deducted right away, most are considered part of the cost of acquiring the house and are therefore included in the basis.

First, consider the deductible closing expenses because they have the most immediate financial impact.

Points

A "point" is a fee—1% of the loan amount—that the mortgage lender charges up front. Assuming the charge is for the use of the borrowed money—as it clearly is when the number of points charged affects the interest rate on the mortgage—rather than a fee to cover loan-processing costs, it qualifies as prepaid interest. And, when the mortgage is to buy or build your principal residence, points enjoy a special tax status: You can deduct the amount in full in the year you pay it. Paying three points on a $100,000 loan to buy your home costs $3,000, and it creates a $3,000 deduction that saves you $840 in the 28% tax bracket.

Until recently, this was a controversial and confusing area. In addition to the requirement that you pay points in connection with a loan for your principal residence, you had to follow a bunch of other rules: Charging points had to be routine in your area; what you paid had to be in line with what other homebuyers paid; you couldn't use borrowed money or have the seller pay them for you; and on and on. A standard piece of advice, in fact, was that homebuyers write a separate check to pay the points, as proof that they didn't roll the expense into the mortgage.

Fortunately, though, the IRS has simplified things. Officially, there's still a lengthy list of rules, but in practice only a couple of things matter.

- **The charge must be based on a percentage of the loan amount and it must be clearly labeled on the settlement statement,** as *points, discount points* or *loan origination fee,* for example.

- **At or before closing, you have to provide at least enough cash to cover the points.** This can include your down payment, escrow deposits or earnest money. If you make a $20,000 down-payment, for example, you can actually roll the points into the mortgage amount and still deduct the points in the year you buy the house. The IRS will assume that you paid the points with part of the down-payment, rather than with the money you borrowed.

Seller-paid points. In an even more unexpectedly generous move the IRS has declared that points paid by the seller on behalf of a buyer can be deducted by the *buyer.* The basic conditions must still be met—primarily

---

Retroactive Tax Break

• •

When the IRS made the seller-paid points switch in 1994, the new rule was made retroactive to 1991. It's already too late to amend 1991 returns, but if you bought a house in 1992 or 1993 and the seller paid points on the deal, you probably deserve a retroactive refund. You can file an amended return for 1992 up until April 15 of 1996; the deadline for 1993 returns is April 15, 1997. If you file an amended return to claim an extra deduction, the IRS will refund the amount by which you overpaid your tax and, believe it or not, the tax agency will pay you interest back to the due date of the return. See Chapter 2 for details on amended returns.

that the buyer puts enough money into the deal to cover the points—but the IRS has decided to recognize the reality of the situation. When a seller pays points, that expense is probably built into the price of the house. So now, the tax agency will treat seller-paid points as though the seller gave the money to the buyer and the buyer paid the points . . . and therefore, the buyer gets the deduction.

There is an impact on basis, too. The IRS will assume the purchase price of the house is reduced by the amount of seller-paid points deducted by the buyer and that means the buyer must reduce the basis by that amount.

When the house isn't your home. Different rules apply to points charged for a mortgage used to buy a vacation home or a rental property. That expense is still deductible, but only in bits and pieces over the life of the loan.

On a 30-year mortgage, for example, one-thirtieth of the points generally would be deducted each year. In the first year, though, an even smaller amount would be deductible, depending on when during the year you bought the house. An alternative method for figuring the annual deduction would give you somewhat higher write-offs in the early years of a mortgage, but that's probably more trouble than it's worth. It involves finding what percentage of the total interest due on the loan is paid each year and deducting that same portion of the points in that year.

Whichever method you use, it's up to you to remember to claim this deduction each year. And, if you sell the house and pay off the mortgage early, you can fully deduct any undeducted points in the year of the sale.

Prepaid interest and property taxes

If your settlement costs include reimbursing the seller for interest or taxes he or she paid in advance for a period you will actually own the house, you may deduct those amounts as though you paid the bills directly. Such adjustments ought to be spelled out on your settlement sheet.

Even if you don't reimburse the seller for such payments, you can still deduct those costs as itemized deductions on your return. The costs are considered to be built

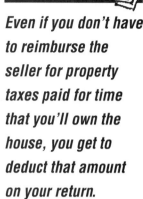

Money Saver

Even if you don't have to reimburse the seller for property taxes paid for time that you'll own the house, you get to deduct that amount on your return.

into the price of the house, and you should reduce your basis by the amount you deduct.

Other Closing Costs

Other closing costs and acquisition expenses are generally not deductible, but many can be added to the purchase price to hike your tax basis. Because additions to basis don't produce any immediate tax savings, you might be tempted to dismiss them. But that would be a costly mistake. Sooner or later you're going to have to know the adjusted basis of your home. The higher the basis when you sell, the smaller any potentially taxable profit.

Maintaining detailed records from the beginning is the best way to assure accuracy. It's also a lot easier than trying to reconstruct the basis later on. As you begin the running tab on your adjusted basis, add the following costs to the purchase price:

- **Attorney and notary fees**

- **Recording and title-examination fees**

- **State and county transfer taxes**

- **Property inspection fees**

- **Title insurance premiums**

- **Utility connection charges**

- **Amounts owed by the seller that you agree to pay,** such as part of the real estate agent's selling commission or back taxes and interest.

- **The cost of an option to purchase under a rent-with-option-to-buy arrangement.** It is also possible that part of the rent payments that were made prior to closing may be

---

Splitting the Commission

● ●

Q: *After arduous negotiations, we agreed to pay half the real estate commission owed by the couple who sold us our home. That cost us $5,000. Can we deduct it?*

A: No, but since it's basically an addition to the purchase price, it does increase the basis of your new home by $5,000. That means it will effectively offset $5,000 of taxable profit when you sell the house.

---

added to the basis if the payments were applied to the purchase price.

Cashing in on Your Annual Deductions

It's easy to take advantage of the basic tax benefits—the write-offs for mortgage interest and property taxes. If a financial institution holds your mortgage, you'll receive a Form 1098 early each year showing how much deductible interest you shelled out in the previous year. (The IRS gets a copy, too.) The statement will also show how much you can deduct for property taxes if you make those payments through an escrow account that your lender handles. Otherwise, copies of tax bills and your canceled checks provide the information you need to claim that deduction.

Your tax situation is more complicated if an individual holds your mortgage or you are buying with the help of some sort of "creative financing." The specifics of your arrangement control what part of your payments qualify as tax deductions.

If the seller takes back a second mortgage

Assume, for example, that in addition to a first mortgage at a bank, the seller holds a $10,000 second mortgage secured by the property that calls for monthly interest-only payments for three years and then a balloon payoff of the entire principal. All of your payments on the note during the three years would be deductible as interest.

If you pay the lender no interest

What about a "zero-interest" deal involving seller financing at the best of all interest rates: 0%? Although you might find such a deal, beware that the IRS does not believe such generosity exists. The law assumes the financing costs are actually built into the price of the home, so the buyer's basis is reduced by subtracting the value of interest-free financing from the purchase price.

The law also demands that the seller report as interest income each year an amount that reflects what would have been charged if the note carried a reasonable rate of inter-

Time Saver

Keep careful records as you go along. It's much simpler than trying to reconstruct your home's basis after you sell.

est (see Chapter 10). If you consider a zero-interest deal, be sure the price you pay reflects the tax consequences.

Special rules also apply to graduated-payment mortgages and other financing plans. The more you stray from conventional financing, the more you need to consult with an attorney or accountant to discuss the tax twists and turns involved in your home-buying pursuits.

Local Assessments

In addition to real estate taxes, it is not unusual for local governments to assess homeowners for services or benefits provided during the year. Depending on what the charge is for, it may be a deductible expense or an addition to basis.

In general, assessments for benefits that tend to increase the value of your property—sidewalks, for example—should be added to the basis of your property. Special charges for repairs or maintenance of local benefits, such as sewers or roads, however, can be deducted as additional local taxes. Fees for specific services, such as garbage collection, are neither deductible nor additions to basis.

Improvements and Repairs

Monthly payments are just the beginning of the costs of owning a home. You can count on spending plenty of money over the years maintaining, repairing and improving your property. Here, too, Uncle Sam gets involved.

For tax purposes, work around the house is divided between projects considered *repairs* and those qualifying as *capital improvements* that enhance rather than just maintain the home's value. The distinction is critical. The cost of repairs is a nondeductible personal expense. What you pay for improvements is nondeductible, too, but such expenses add to your basis. The idea here is that although you will use and enjoy the improvements, they also are likely to boost the amount a buyer will pay for the place. Since you add 100% of the cost of improvements to your basis, every $100 of such expenses will ultimately reduce by $100 the potentially taxable profit when you sell.

An improvement is something that adds value to your home, prolongs its life or adapts it to new uses. There is no laundry list of what the IRS considers an improvement. However, the box below lists items and projects that can qualify.

Repairs, on the other hand, merely maintain the home's condition. Fixing a gutter, painting a room or replacing a window pane are repairs rather than improvements. In some cases, though, the cost of projects that ordinarily fall in the repair category—such as painting a room—can be added to basis if the work is done as part of an extensive remodeling or restoration. Also, some major repairs—such as extensive patching of a roof—may qualify as basis-boosting improvements.

Basis-Boosting Improvements to Your Home

- **Addition or conversion of:** unfinished attic, basement or other space to living area.

- **Air-conditioning:** a central system or window units that you will sell with the house.

- **Heating and cooling:** attic fan, furnace, furnace humidifier, heat pump, thermostat, hot-water heater, radiators and radiator covers.

- **Bathroom:** bathtub, Jacuzzi, shower, shower enclosure, faucets, toilet, sauna, medicine cabinets, mirrors, towel racks.

- **Built-in bookcases.**

- **Safety features:** burglar- and fire-alarm system, smoke detector, intercom and telephone outlets, doorbell.

- **Electrical:** new or upgraded power lines, replacement of fuse box with circuit breakers, additional outlets or switches, floodlights.

- **Fireplace:** including mantle, chimney, built-in fireplace screen.

- **Weatherproofing:** insulation, weather stripping and caulking.

- **Kitchen:** refrigerator, freezer, dishwasher or stove sold with the house, cupboards, garbage disposal, countertops, exhaust fan.

- **Landscaping:** trees, shrubs and underground sprinkler systems.

- **Outdoors:** aluminum siding, skylight, deck, garage, garage-door opener, carport, shed, fences and gates, lamppost, walls, screen and storm doors, porch, new roof, gutters, termite-proofing, waterproofing, paving and resurfacing of a driveway or sidewalks, barbecue pit, birdbath, hot tub, swimming pool.

- **Plumbing:** new pipes, sump pump, septic system, solar-heating system.

- **Rooftop TV antenna and wiring.**

- **Washer and dryer sold with the house.**

- **Windows:** screens, storm windows, shutters, awnings, weather stripping.

Money Saver

Keep track of the cost of all home improvements. They reduce the taxable profit dollar for dollar when you sell.

Keep detailed records of any work done around the house, including receipts for items that might qualify as improvements. The pack-rat habit can pay off handsomely. It's better to save papers you might not need than to toss out evidence that could save you money. In addition to receipts and canceled checks, keep notes of exactly what was done, when and by whom.

When toting up the cost of improvements, be sure to include any incidental costs. If you pay to have your lot surveyed as part of installing a fence, for example, the cost of the survey can be added to your basis. Although you can count what you paid hired workers, you can't add anything for your own time and effort if you do the work yourself.

Home Equity Loans

This is an area of great opportunity and great confusion. To understand the rules so that you can take the maximum advantage of them, some background is necessary.

In 1986, Congress decided to outlaw the deduction of "personal interest." As discussed in Chapter 15, that category includes interest on car loans, credit card accounts, student loans, personal loans and about every other kind of personal borrowing most taxpayers do . . . except for home mortgage interest.

By creating different classes of interest—some deductible and some not—Congress immediately created problems. How would one type be distinguished from another and, more importantly, how could the law discourage ever-ingenious taxpayers from rearranging their financial affairs to sidestep the intent of the law? For example, if you use a second mortgage on a house to buy a car, would the interest be deductible mortgage interest or nondeductible personal interest? To answer such questions, Congress divided debt secured by a home—and your second home if you have one—into two categories:

Acquisition Debt

You can deduct all the interest you pay on up to $1

million of "acquisition debt." That's money you borrow to buy, build or substantially improve your principal residence or a second home. For the interest to be deductible, the loan must be secured by the house.

Yes, $1 million is an almost inconceivable amount of mortgage debt. (At 8% interest on a 30-year loan, the monthly payments would be over $7,000.) But the amount of debt on which *you* can deduct mortgage interest is likely to be far less.

Your personal ceiling is set by the size of the loans used to buy or build your first and second homes, plus amounts borrowed for major improvements. As you pay off those loans, the amount of tax-favored acquisition debt declines. And, of course, there's always a chance that Congress will lower the $1 million ceiling in the future.

"That's nothing . . . Listen to him explain this other deduction!"

From the Wall Street Journal; Permission, Cartoon Features Syndicate.

(There's an exception to the general definition of acquisition debt. If on October 13, 1987, the mortgage debt on your principal home and a second home exceeded the amount borrowed to buy, build or substantially improve the homes, you can count that higher amount as acquisition indebtedness.)

Home Equity Debt

This is the Congressionally sanctioned end run around the elimination of deductions for interest paid on personal loans. In addition to deducting interest on acquisition debt, homeowners can deduct interest on up to $100,000 of "home-equity debt." The interest on such debt is fully deductible—whether you tap your equity via refinancing, a second mortgage or a home-equity line of credit—as long as the loan is secured by your principal residence or a second home. Although you can deduct

Trade $10,000 of 18% nondeductible credit card debt for $10,000 of 7.5% deductible home-equity debt and slice after-tax carrying costs by $1,260 (if you're in the 28% bracket).

such interest almost regardless of how you spend the borrowed money, there are a couple of exceptions.

If you use the borrowed money to invest in tax-exempt bonds or single-premium life insurance, you can't deduct the interest no matter what kind of loan is involved. Also, if you are subject to the alternative minimum tax discussed in Chapter 4, you can't deduct interest on home-equity debt unless the mortgage was taken out before July 1, 1982, and secured by a home used by you or a family member. (Interest on acquisition debt is deductible for purposes of the AMT.)

Another restriction—likely to come into play only if home prices plunge in your area—blocks the deduction of interest if the combination of home-equity debt and acquisition debt exceeds the fair market value of the house. If the balance on your mortgage is $100,000 and your home value is just $105,000, then, interest would be deductible on no more than $5,000 worth of home equity debt.

Tax saving opportunities

The special status of home-equity debt offers great tax-saving opportunities. If you can exchange nondeductible personal borrowing for deductible home-equity borrowing, you get Uncle Sam's help paying the interest on your debts. This makes home-equity lines of credit the debt of choice for millions of homeowners. These loans offer a line of credit—which you can usually tap simply by writing checks—secured by your home. In addition to preserving the deductibility of interest charged, these loans often carry much lower interest rates than unsecured borrowing.

That makes a home-equity line of credit a powerful tool. Beyond considering this source for your future borrowing needs, you may want to tap a home-equity line to pay off higher-priced debt on credit cards, auto loans and personal notes. Trading $10,000 of 18% nondeductible debt for $10,000 of 7.5% deductible debt would slice the after-tax carrying costs from $1,800 to $540 a year for a taxpayer in the 28% bracket.

Although the tax law encourages consumers to borrow against their homes, a note of caution is necessary. To qualify for the tax deduction, these loans must be secured by your home, which means that if you find yourself unable to repay, your home is at stake. Don't let the siren song of deductible interest pull you into a deal if you don't fully understand the terms.

If you consider a home-equity loan, shop carefully. The cost of setting up the line of credit varies widely and can be stiff. Interest rates and repayment schedules also differ substantially.

When you buy a home, the rules on acquisition indebtedness may encourage you to hold down your down payment. Remember that the size of your tax-favored debt is based on your original mortgage—not the price of the house. The law can also encourage you to borrow to pay for a home improvement rather than to pay cash. As long as the debt is secured by the home, the amount that pays for the improvement counts as acquisition debt. The tax subsidy of the interest cost could make borrowing cheaper than the amount you'd lose by pulling cash out of an investment to pay for the improvement.

It's important to keep reliable records of your borrowing to back up the deductions you claim. If you use a home-equity line, carefully distinguish between borrowing that pays for major home improvements and loans used for other purposes. The amount that goes for improvements is added to your acquisition debt, rather than eating away at your $100,000 home-equity allowance.

Also, if you use money borrowed on a home-equity line of credit or second mortgage for investment or business purposes, you can choose whether to treat the interest as home-equity interest or deduct it as investment or business interest. If, for example, you opt to count it as investment interest—in which case the restrictions discussed in Chapter 10 would apply—the borrowing would not reduce your $100,000 home-equity allowance.

Refinancing

If you refinance a mortgage—as millions of homeowners have done to take advantage of lower interest rates in recent years—there are tax angles to consider.

Tax Treatment of Points

First of all, points you pay to get the new mortgage are *not* fully deductible in the year paid, except to the extent that you use the funds for home improvements.

Here's an example: A homeowner with a $100,000 mortgage refinances at $120,000 and uses $20,000 to build a swimming pool. Assume that two points (2% of $120,000, or $2,400) were charged. Because one-sixth of the money went for a home improvement, one-sixth of the points, or $400, may be deducted in the year paid. The rest must be deducted evenly over the life of the loan. On a 30-year mortgage, that would basically mean one-thirtieth of the remaining $2,000, or $66.66, would be deducted each year, assuming the homeowner remembers to do so. If the house is sold and the mortgage paid off before the end of the term, any remaining portion of the points could be deducted as interest at that time. (If the refinancing is part of the original purchase of your home—say you refinance to pay off a bridge loan or a short-term balloon note—the points can be fully deducted in the year paid.)

Better Rates Mean Higher Taxes?

Q: *I refinanced my mortgage to get a lower rate last summer, and now I hear that that's going to raise my tax bill. Is that possible?*

A: Yes. Homeowners who refinance to lower rates and lower monthly payments have to share their good fortune with the IRS. Unless you hiked the size of your loan, the lower rate means you're paying less interest. That translates to a smaller tax deduction and a larger tax bill. Refinancing during 1992 saved homeowners an estimated $9 billion in interest, for example, and increased their tax bills by about $2.5 billion.

Tax Status of Interest

Refinancing can affect the tax status of the interest you pay on the mortgage, too. The amount of the new loan qualifying as acquisition debt is limited to the debt outstanding on the old loan, plus any part of the new money used for major home improvements. Again, an illustration best tells this tale:

Assume that several years ago you bought a $150,000 home with $30,000 down and a $120,000 mortgage. The debt is now paid down to $90,000 and you decide to refinance for $150,000. What's the tax status of the new loan?

Interest on $90,000—the balance on the old loan—is sure to be deductible because that amount qualifies as acquisition indebtedness. The treatment of the other $60,000 depends on how the money is used.

Any part spent for major home improvements also earns the status of acquisition debt. Plunge $20,000 of the new loan into a swimming pool, for example, and your acquisition debt jumps from $90,000 to $110,000. Any part of the new loan that neither replaces the old mortgage nor pays for improvements—$40,000 in this example—is not acquisition debt.

The Reward for Prepaying Your Mortgage

Although the deduction for home mortgage interest is a great tax break, you might be better off paying off your home loan early. Prepaying your mortgage can be considered a risk-free investment that yields the same rate that you're paying on the loan.

The advantage of prepaying your mortgage—perhaps by adding $25 or $100 to each monthly payment—can be dramatic. On a $100,000 loan at 10%, for example, your $877.57 monthly payments would add up to $315,950 over 30 years. Add $100 a month to your payments and you'd retire the mortgage more than 10 years early and at a total cost of about $225,000. You'd avoid paying more than $90,000 in interest.

Even considering the loss of the tax break, you'd be more than $64,000 ahead, assuming you're in the 28% bracket.

We'll be happy to prepare a personalized Mortgage Prepayment Illustration for you, showing the impact of a single $1,000 prepayment or regular $100 monthly prepayments. If you're interested, drop us a note that includes your name, the current balance on your home mortgage, the interest rate and your monthly payment for principal and interest (don't include any amounts for property taxes or insurance). Send that note and a stamped, self-addressed business sized envelope to Kevin McCormally, Kiplinger Books, 1729 H Street NW, Washington, D.C., 20006.

That doesn't necessarily mean you can't deduct the interest, however. Because the debt is secured by your home, the interest may be deducted as home-equity interest, subject to the $100,000 cap. If the extra funds are used in a business, the interest can be written off as a business expense. If you use the cash for an investment, the interest may be deductible as investment interest, within the limits discussed in Chapter 10.

If none of those options protects you, however, the interest would be nondeductible personal interest.

Refinancing a Mortgage

Q: *We've paid our mortgage down to about $75,000 and we want to refinance for $125,000, using the extra money to add a swimming pool and to pay off some bills. Will all the interest on the new mortgage be deductible?*

A: It depends. The law permits the deduction of interest on up to $1 million of "acquisition indebtedness" plus up to $100,000 in home-equity loans secured by your principal residence or second home. When you refinance, acquisition indebtedness is the amount outstanding on the old mortgage—$75,000 in your case—plus any amount of the new loan used for substantial improvements—like your pool. If you spend $25,000 on your pool, then interest on $100,000 of the new mortgage would be deductible for sure. Interest on the other $25,000 could be deductible as interest on home-equity debt, if you're not over the $100,000 level.

Deductibility of Prepayment Penalties

Another tax issue rising out of some refinancings is how to treat prepayment penalties. If the lender holding the original loan slaps you with a penalty for paying it off early, the amount is considered interest and is fully deductible in the year you pay it.

When You Sell Your Home

You don't have to file any forms with the IRS when you buy a home or make improvements that add to the tax basis. When you sell, though, the government wants the details. After all, there may be a tax to collect. There's a good chance, though, that the sale won't add a dime to your tax bill.

When you sell, you will see how clever you have been to keep meticulous records of every improvement to your home over the years. To determine the tax consequences, you have to know the *adjusted basis* of your home, and that's where your well-kept files come in.

Your adjusted basis is what you paid for the house plus the cost of all improvements, minus any casualty losses on the property you claimed while living there—for fire or storm damage, for example. (Chapter 15 explains casualty-loss deductions.) The basis is also reduced by any gain from a previous home you rolled over into the house being sold, as discussed later.

Your profit or loss on the sale is the difference between that adjusted basis and the amount you realize on the sale. Since nothing involved with taxes is easy, the amount realized is not simply the selling price. That's just the beginning point. From it you subtract costs connected with the sale. Common selling expenses include real estate commissions, advertising and legal fees, points paid for a buyer, the cost of termite inspection and almost anything else you have to pay to sell the place. Not included, however, are amounts you spend for repairs or other efforts to make the place more attractive to buyers.

If your adjusted basis is more than the amount realized, your loss is not deductible. (Note that this may change. At our deadline, Congress was considering giving some sort of tax break to homebuyers who lose money when they sell.) In the more likely event that the bottom line shows a profit, the gain may be taxable in the year of the sale, sometime in the future, or perhaps never. The opportunity to put off or completely avoid tax on the profit is one of the most valuable tax benefits enjoyed by homeowners.

Rolling Over the Gain

Fortunately, it's easy to defer the tax bill almost indefinitely. To do so, all you have to do is buy—within a specified time period—a new principal residence that costs at least as much as you get from the sale of the one sold.

To qualify, you must buy or build *and* occupy the new home within two years—before or after—the sale of the old one. (If you are in the armed forces or living outside the United States when your home is sold, you may qualify for a longer replacement period allowing up to four years after the sale of your home to buy and occupy a new principal residence.)

Be warned that the IRS is inflexible about the replacement period. In a case in which a serious illness prevented a taxpayer from occupying the new home before the deadline, the IRS prohibited the rollover. What if you're building a new home and it burns down just before you're planning to move in? Again, the IRS says you forfeit the rollover privilege.

Here's an example of how the rollover works. Assume, for example, that the adjusted basis of your home is $70,000 and you sell it for $100,000. Within the replacement period, you buy and move into a new home that costs $125,000. The tax bill on your $30,000 profit is deferred. Rather than report it as income in the year of the sale, you reduce the basis of the new home by that amount. The basis of the new home becomes $95,000—the $125,000 purchase price minus the $30,000 of deferred gain.

If you later sell that house for $150,000, in the eyes of the IRS the profit would be $55,000, the combination of the $30,000 gain from the first house and $25,000 from the second. Of course, you could put off the tax bill again by buying a replacement home within two years that costs $150,000 or more. Its basis would be reduced by the $55,000 of rolled-over gain.

You don't have to invest the actual proceeds of the sale in the new home to qualify to defer tax on the gain. Say you sold a house for $200,000 and bought a new one for $210,000. You don't have to put $200,000 into the new

No Rollover

· ·

Q: *When my wife and I married, I sold my condo and moved into her house. Is there any way to put off paying tax on the profit I made on my apartment?*

A: Not unless you and your wife decide to buy a new home and you move into it within two years of the time you sold your condominium. To postpone the tax bill on the sale of a personal residence, you must buy a new home that costs at least as much as the one you sold. Since you haven't bought a new home, you don't qualify for the rollover. If you were at least 55 years old when you sold the condo and had owned and lived in it for at least three of the previous five years, however, you may qualify for the exclusion that lets qualifying taxpayers avoid the tax on up to $125,000 of home-sale profit.

house to defer the tax bill. You can defer the full amount even if you make a minimum down payment on the new house and use the remaining proceeds for some other purpose. The key is that the new home cost at least as much as the one you sold, not how you pay for the new house.

Marrying or divorcing?

What if you and your fiancé each own a home, sell both of them and together buy a new home? You can defer the gain on both of the old homes if the price of the new house exceeds the *combined* sales prices of the old ones. Any profit left out of the rollover, though, would be taxable in the year of sale. What if one taxpayer sells a home to move in with a new husband or wife in a home the spouse already owns? Sorry, there's no chance to defer tax in this situation. But if the seller is over age 55, he or she might qualify for the exclusion discussed beginning on page 171.

The law provides for the situation in which a jointly owned home is sold in connection with a divorce and each spouse buys a separate home. If each spouse invests his or her share of the proceeds of the sale in a new principal residence—within the rollover period—the tax bill on the profit is deferred.

Say that you and your spouse divorce and sell your jointly owned home for $150,000, including $40,000 profit. Assuming that each of you is entitled to half the proceeds of the sale, each has a $20,000 gain. Either of you can defer tax on the gain by buying a new home that costs at least $75,000, your half of the amount realized on the sale.

If your next house costs less . . .

In any situation, if you choose a replacement home that costs less than the one you sold, you will owe tax on the profit to the extent that the *adjusted sales price* of the old home exceeds the cost of the new one.

The adjusted sales price is usually the same as the amount realized on the sale, but it can be less if prior to the sale you incurred qualifying *fix-up expenses,* such as the cost of painting or repairs to make the home more attractive to buyers. Those are costs that can't qualify as improvements to boost your basis. And, they come into play for tax purposes only if your replacement home costs less than the one you sold. Although real estate agents encouraging you to spruce up the place may suggest that such costs are deductible, they are not. If you don't buy a replacement home, or if you buy one that costs enough that you can roll over all your profit, fix-up costs have no tax-saving power.

Consider this example: You sell your home for $100,000. Your adjusted basis is $70,000 and your new home costs $90,000. Of the $30,000 profit ($100,000 –$70,000) on the sale, you can roll $20,000 ($90,000 –$70,000) into the new house, giving it a basis of $70,000 ($90,000 –$20,000). The other $10,000 of profit would be subject to tax. However, if you had spent $1,000 on qualifying fix-up expenses, that amount is subtracted from the amount realized to arrive at the adjusted sales price. That lets you defer the tax on an extra $1,000. That also reduces the basis of the new home by $1,000, to $69,000. Reducing the basis assures that sometime in the future, Uncle Sam will get a shot at that $1,000.

To qualify, fix-up expenses must be for work done during the 90 days before you sign a contract to sell your house and must be paid for within 30 days afterward.

Trading down without tripping up. It's possible to buy a less expensive home without winding up with taxable profit in the year of the sale. Anything you spend on

---

Flat Tax and Mortgage Deductions

● ●

Q: *I'm thinking of buying my first home but am worried that a flat tax will eliminate the deduction for mortgage interest. Without the tax break, I might not be able to afford the mortgage payments. Maybe I'm better off renting. Should I worry?*

A: In its purest form, the flat tax proposal would eliminate all deductions, including the one for home mortgage interest. And losing that deduction would significantly increase the real cost of a home mortgage. Remember, though, that flat-tax proponents say that even without deductions, the lower tax rate they propose would result in most taxpayers paying less federal tax, not more. Also, it's unclear how the loss of the home mortgage interest deduction—and it's affect on the cost of homeownership—would affect rents. Finally, if a flat tax is approved (and that's a big if), it's likely to be several years in the future. It's a mistake to let the prospect of a flat tax weigh too heavily in your homebuying decision.

the new place that qualifies as an improvement—such as the cost of renovation, putting on an addition or adding a swimming pool—can serve to raise the new home's "price" for rollover purposes. The key here is that you must incur the expense and pay the bill within the two-year replacement period.

This provision can prove especially rewarding if you transfer from an area of the country with high home prices to an area of more modestly priced homes. Say the adjusted basis of your old house is $100,000. You sell it for $150,000, after expenses. Thanks to a transfer to a less expensive part of the country, your new home costs just $120,000—the amount that sets the ceiling for rolling over the proceeds of your home sale. That leaves $30,000 of profit out in the cold, taxable in the year of the sale. In the 28% bracket, the bill is $8,400.

You can hold down or eliminate that tax bill, though, by investing more in the new place. If you spend $30,000 or more on improvements within two years after the sale of the first house, you can roll over the entire profit.

The rollover provision applies only to your principal residence, not to a second home, say, or rental property. And if you use part of your principal home for business— by renting out a room, say, or having a home office for which you claim deductions—part of the profit from the sale will not qualify for rollover treatment. If you claim 10% of your home as a home office (under the rules described in Chapter 13), for example, 10% of the gain on the sale won't be eligible for the deferral.

There is no limit on the number of times or the amount of profit you can roll over from one home to the next. In fact, the profit from the first home you own is likely to affect the tax basis of the last place you live, a point that emphasizes the importance of detailed record keeping.

There is a restriction, however, that generally prevents you from using the rollover provision more than once every two years. If during a two year period you buy or build more than one new home, only the last one counts as your new home for figuring the rollover. Assume that you sell one house in January 1996 and defer the gain by buying another home the same month. Then in August 1996 you sell that house and buy another one. The rules prohibit postponing tax on appreciation of the intermediate house. Rather, the profit from the first home is considered to be rolled over into the third. Any profit that builds up during the time you owned the middle house is taxed.

That restriction doesn't apply if the sale of your home is connected with a job-related move that qualifies you to deduct moving expenses, as discussed later in this chapter. In that case, in the example above you could roll over the profit from house one to house two and then from house two to house three. (There are proposals in Congress to eliminate this confusing restriction in all cases.)

Reporting Home Sales

For the year of the sale, you must file a Form 2119, *Sale or Exchange of Principal Residence*, with your tax return—whether or not you owe tax on the sale. It's a relatively simple form, and it includes a section for determining the adjusted basis of your new home. Since each sale will affect the basis of your next home, you'll want to hang on to a copy of every Form 2119 you file throughout your home-owning career.

What if you plan to buy a replacement home but haven't closed the deal by the time your tax return is due for the year of the sale? You can still postpone the gain. Just file a Form 2119—reporting only the date your old home was sold—with your return. If the replacement home you buy costs enough to defer all of your gain, just notify the IRS Service Center where you filed your return and file a completed Form 2119 at that time. If the new house doesn't cost enough to permit a rollover of all the profit—or if the replacement period expires before you buy—you'll have to file an amended tax return (see Chapter 2) for the year of the sale. In addition to the tax on the profit, you'll have to pay interest.

If you follow the "trading down without tripping up" strategy discussed earlier, you handle things the same way. You report the sale of the first home for the year of the sale and, after you complete your major improvements on the new place, file a completed Form 2119 showing the replacement.

If you report the profit from the home sale—under the assumption that you won't replace the house—and later decide to buy a new home, you'll have to file an amended return. If you end up occupying the new place within the replacement period, you can retroactively defer the gain and reclaim the tax you paid on the original return.

The $125,000 Exclusion

So, over the years you keep hauling your profit with you from one home to another, holding the IRS at bay by purchasing more and more costly homes. But what happens when you finally decide to cash in on all that profit? When you decide not to buy another house, is the IRS going to swoop down and demand a healthy share of your nest egg?

Not if you qualify for the homeowners' icing on the cake: the right to escape tax entirely on up to $125,000 of profit. The same $125,000 exclusion is available whether you're married filing a joint return or single filing an individual one. If you are married filing separate returns, the limit is $62,500 for each spouse.

The value of this tax break is enhanced by the fact that it usually comes around retirement time, when extra cash often comes in particularly handy. Sheltering $125,000 of gain saves you $35,000 if it otherwise would have been taxed at 28%. Perhaps that's the real American dream! With such a rich reward at stake, it's essential that you know how to claim it.

How it works

To qualify, you must be at least 55 years old when you sell your home and you must have owned and lived in the home for at least three of the five years leading up to the sale. If you are married and the house is jointly owned, you can qualify as long as either you or your spouse meet all three requirements: age, ownership and residency.

Money Saver

The right to take up to $125,000 of profit tax-free is the icing on the homeowner's cake.

Unlike the rollover rule, which applies only if the house sold is your principal residence at the time of the sale, you don't have to be living in the house when it is sold to qualify for the exclusion. You can still dodge tax on the profit as long as the sale occurs before so much time has passed that you no longer meet the three-out-of-five-year residency test.

Assume, for example, that you are at least age 55 and have owned and lived in your home for at least three years. You retire and move to an apartment. As long as your home is sold within two years of the move, you will meet the three-out-of-five-year test and qualify for the exclusion. That applies whether you rent your old home or leave it vacant prior to the sale.

The $125,000 Exclusion

Q: *I know there's a special break that lets you avoid taxes on up to $125,000 of profit on the sale of your home. If I die before I sell the house, does that tax break disappear with me and therefore mean my children will have to pay tax on the $125,000?*

A: You can exclude from taxable income up to $125,000 of profit from the sale of your home if, at the time of the sale, you are at least 55 years old and have owned and lived in the house for at least three of the five year's leading up to the sale.

But don't feel rushed into selling your home. If you still own it when you die, another section of the law wipes out the income tax on all the profit that built up while you owned the place—even if it's far more than $125,000.

Marrying or divorcing?

Married couples are limited to a single $125,000 exclusion, and if one spouse used the exclusion before marriage, that scotches the other spouse's right to it as long as they are married. That restriction can give rise to tax-planning opportunities. Say that you own a home and plan to marry someone who also owns a home. Assume, too, that both of you meet the age, ownership and residency tests. If each of you sells your house before marriage, you each qualify for up to a $125,000 exclusion. Wait until after the ceremony, though, and together you can exclude only $125,000. Similarly, if you plan to marry someone who has already used the exclusion, selling your home before the wedding can protect your right to the exclusion.

The exclusion can also come into play in divorce. If you're planning a divorce, in some circumstances it may make sense to hold off selling the family home until after the split. If the profit will exceed $125,000, postponing the sale until you are both single co-owners of the place can permit each ex-spouse to exclude up to $125,000 of gain.

(Note this: At our deadline, Congress was considering a change that would allow you to claim the exclusion even if your spouse had excluded gain on an earlier home sale prior to your marriage. If a change is enacted, write or e-mail the author at the address in the front of this book for a free update.)

Save it for later

You don't necessarily want to use the exclusion the first time it's available to you. In fact, that can be a costly mistake. This is a once-in-a-lifetime opportunity. You can't use part of the exclusion to shelter $50,000 of profit on one home, for example, and later use the rest of it to avoid tax on the sale of another. Use any part of the exclusion and you use it all.

Your best bet will usually be to hold off using the exclusion until you sell what you expect to be your last home or until you can take advantage of the full $125,000. Don't worry about shortchanging your heirs by forfeiting the tax break if you die before using it. The tax on all profit that builds up during your life is excused when you die.

You claim the exclusion on Form 2119, the same form you use to report home sales and the deferral of gain.

Owner Financing

Sometimes, particularly when mortgage rates are high, the sale of a home goes through only because the seller helps finance the deal. If you wind up holding a note of some sort, your tax picture is immediately more complicated.

The selling price of your home—for purposes of determining the gain to be rolled over, excluded or taxed—includes the face value of any mortgage or note you receive, as well as cash. If you are deferring tax on the gain or using the exclusion to shelter it from the IRS, you basically report the sale just as you would if you received all cash.

Payments on the note may be a combination of return of your basis (nontaxable), part of your gain (deferred or excluded) and interest on the loan (taxable). You should report the interest as income on Schedule B, the same form you use to report interest on a bank account. There's even a special line for reporting interest on seller-financed mortgages, and you need to list the payer's social security number.

If gain is taxable in the year of the sale and you help finance the deal, you may report the profit on an installment basis. That permits you to pay tax on the profit as you receive it over the years. Installment sales are discussed in Chapter 10, as are the rules demanding that you charge a reasonable interest rate on the loan.

What If You Can't Sell?

It's a homeowner's nightmare: You move to a new home but can't find a buyer for the old homestead. Not only might you have to get a bridge loan to finance the new house, you also face the prospect of making two mortgage payments month after month. Few family budgets can handle that financial burden. One solution is to rent your former residence to generate cash to help pay the bills. But that can lead you into a maze of tax complications.

The rules that let homeowners defer tax on the profit from one house by rolling it over into a new home apply only to your principal residence. Can a house that's being rented to someone else when you finally sell it qualify as *your* home? If not, the vagaries of the housing market could force you to pay tax on the profit rather than roll it over.

The good news is that if you can show the rental was temporary, the house still qualifies as your principal residence and you can roll over the gain—as long as you sell the old house within two years of the time you buy the new home. If the old home hasn't sold within the rollover-replacement period, you're out of luck.

Things get complicated, though, when it comes to writing off your expenses on the temporary rental property.

Temporary or not, you become a landlord in the

eyes the IRS. And, as you would expect, the IRS demands that you treat the rent you receive as income, assuming you rent the place for more than 14 days during the year. You may be able to completely offset the tax bill on the rental income, however, with deductions for rental expenses including the continued mortgage interest and tax payments on the house, the cost of repairs and even depreciation.

The big question is whether the arrangement can produce a tax loss if expenses exceed rental income—as they often will under these circumstances. Such a loss, of course, could shelter other income—such as part of your salary—from tax, assuming you actively manage the rental and don't run afoul of the passive-loss rules explained in Chapter 10.

But the IRS says you can't have it both ways—you can't treat the house as a principal residence for rollover purposes and as a rental property for tax-loss purposes. According to the IRS position, you can deduct rental expenses up to the amount of your rental income, but no more.

The issue is up in the air, however, because courts have disagreed on that point. In a key case in which the taxpayers beat the IRS, the court ruled, basically, that because the taxpayers charged fair-market rent for their home they deserved the same write-offs available to other landlords, even if that meant they had a tax loss to shelter other income. At the same time, because the taxpayers continued their efforts to sell the place—and in fact did sell it before the replacement period ran out—the rollover provision also applied.

The IRS is sticking to its position, though. If you find yourself in this situation and claim a rental loss, the IRS may challenge your deductions if it audits your return.

Permanent rental

If you're unable to sell your old house within two years, you may want to consider making the rental arrangement permanent. After the replacement period ends, any profit on a sale—including gain from previous homes that had been rolled over into the house—will be taxed. Nei-

Money Saver

You can deduct losses from the temporary rental of a home before it's sold.

ther the rollover nor the $125,000 exclusion provision will protect you.

Some homeowners plan from the outset to hang on to their old homes, a move that can be among the easiest ways to become a real estate investor and latch on to the tax benefits discussed in Chapter 10.

There's a potential catch to converting your home to a rental property, however, beyond forfeiting the chance to roll over the profit into a new home. The value of the house for figuring depreciation deductions—a key write-off for real estate investors—is your adjusted basis or the fair market value of the house, whichever is less. The basis may be far less than what the house is worth when you convert it, particularly if you have pushed it down by rolling over profit from previous homes.

Assume, for example, that your house is worth $150,000. You bought it for $100,000 several years ago and, at that time rolled over $30,000 in profit from your previous home. If you convert the house to a rental property, your basis for depreciation purposes is a skimpy $70,000. Because you cannot depreciate the value of land, you must subtract its value to determine the amount on which to base your depreciation write-offs. (If someone else bought your home for $150,000 and turned it into a rental property, the new owner's basis for depreciation purposes would be $150,000—minus the value of the land—and he or she would enjoy depreciation deductions more than twice as large as you are allowed.)

Refund on an ARM Adjustment

Q: *During the summer, I got a check from my mortgage lender along with a note explaining that it was a refund for an overcharge on my adjustable-rate mortgage last year. Apparently they goofed when figuring the ARM adjustment. Do I have to pay tax on this refund?*

A: Perhaps. It depends on whether you itemized deductions on your federal return. If you didn't, the refund is tax-free. If you did itemize, however, the refund is probably taxable. The refund retroactively reduces the amount of mortgage interest you paid last year, and that means you deducted too much on your return. Although that's not your fault, the IRS demands that you even things up by reporting the refund as income on this year's return. In some cases, part of the refund may be tax-free even if you itemized. The same rules apply as to a state-tax refund. See Chapter 15.

Selling for a Loss

Although profits from the sale of your home are taxable—except to the extent that you can defer or exclude the gain—losses are not deductible. You may have heard, however, that there's a way to write off such losses. Often promoted as a great tax scheme, promoters say home-sale losses can be deducted if, prior to the sale, you convert your house to a rental property.

That's true, but there's a catch that makes the tactic worthless. The basis for figuring your loss begins as the *lower* of the adjusted basis or fair market value at the time of the conversion. (The basis is increased for any improvements after the conversion and reduced for any depreciation claimed.) In other words, any loss in fair market value that occurs while you're living in the house *still* can't be deducted.

As noted earlier, Congress may change the rules in this area to help homeowners hurt by falling home prices.

Six Percent Commission

● ●

Q: *When our home sold for $205,000, the agent's 6% commission claimed a whopping $12,300. Can we deduct that amount on our tax return?*

A: No, but the commission does reduce the amount realized on the sale and therefore cuts your profit by $12,300. That has no immediate tax benefit, however, if you are putting off the tax bill by rolling over the entire profit into a new home.

Vacation Homes

Taxes take no holiday at your vacation getaway. In fact, the rules that apply have been declared "exasperatingly convoluted" by no less than an authority in the U.S. Tax Court.

Strictly Personal

First, look at the bright side. If your home away from home is only that, a second residence that's never rented out, the tax benefits come with few complications. You can deduct mortgage interest on a second home just as you can

Money Saver

You can rent out your vacation home—or even your principal residence—up to 14 days a year and pay no taxes on the rental income.

on your principal residence. If you own a third house, however, you're out of luck. Congress apparently figures that anyone who can afford more than two homes can handle the mortgage interest without the help of a tax deduction. Also, if the mortgage debt on your first and second homes exceeds the $1 million, interest on the excess debt is considered nondeductible personal interest.

A motor home or boat can qualify as a second residence for purposes of this deduction. To meet the IRS definition of a home, the boat or recreational vehicle must have basic living accommodations, including cooking facilities, a place to sleep and a toilet. (However, if you are subject to the alternative minimum tax, discussed in Chapter 4, interest on a loan for a boat you use as a second home can't be deducted.)

Property taxes are deductible too, regardless of how many homes you own.

However, points paid to get a mortgage on a vacation home are not deductible in the year paid. Instead, the points are deducted proportionally over the life of the loan, as discussed on page 153.

Mixed Personal and Rental Use

It's when you start renting the vacation home—as many owners do to help pay the freight—that things get tricky.

In an uncharacteristic display of generosity, the IRS does not care about any rental income you receive if you rent the place for 14 or fewer days during the year. That nugget in the tax law leads some homeowners who find themselves in a temporarily hot rental market—say the Atlanta area during the 1996 Olympics—to rent their homes briefly when they can command especially high rents. (The rule offers the opportunity for tax-free income from a principal residence as well as a second home.)

There's no limit on how much you can charge for the use of your home. As long as your temporary tenants stay no more than two weeks during the year, the rent you receive is tax-free. (Note that this tax break is under attack in Congress. If it is eliminated, we'll included that fact in the free update you can get by following the instructions in the front of this book.) Rent for more than 14 days and you become a landlord in the eyes of the IRS. You have to report rental income and you qualify to deduct rental expenses.

The 14-day/10% rule

How much time tenants use the property versus how much time you enjoy it yourself controls whether the house is treated as a personal residence or a rental property. The distinction is the key to the tax ramifications.

If personal use accounts for more than 14 days during the year or more than 10% of the number of days the place is rented (26 or more personal days compared to 250 rental days, for example), the house is considered a personal residence. Hold personal use below the 14-day/10% threshold, however, and the house is considered a rental property.

Because the tax consequences turn on personal use, it's important to know that the IRS takes a broad view of what counts. It includes:

- **Any day the property is used by you or any part-owner** (unless it is rented as a principal residence to a part-owner under a shared-equity arrangement, as discussed on page 183).

- **Any day it is used by a member of your family, whether or not rent is paid.** For this test, a member of your family includes your spouse, brothers and sisters, parents and grandparents and children and grandchildren.

- **Any day it is rented for less than fair market rent.**

- **Any day the property is used by someone in connection with an arrangement that gives you the right to use another dwelling,** such as if you trade a week at your beach home for a week at a mountain resort.

- **Any day the property is used as a result of your donating its use.** If you donate use of your vacation home to a charitable organization—to be auctioned off at a fund-raising

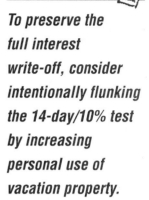

Money Saver

To preserve the full interest write-off, consider intentionally flunking the 14-day/10% test by increasing personal use of vacation property.

event, for example—the period the property is used under the arrangement counts as personal use.

Note that time you spend at the place doing repairs or general maintenance does not count as personal use. As long as that is the primary purpose of staying at the vacation home, the day is not counted as personal use. You must keep detailed records showing the dates of personal use, rental use and repair and maintenance days.

How to handle tax losses

The breakdown between personal and rental days is crucial because it controls whether or not the property can produce tax losses. You can use such losses—available only if personal use is limited so the property qualifies as a rental property rather than a residence—to trim your tax bill by sheltering other income, such as your salary.

These days, however, even limiting personal use no longer automatically opens the door to big tax losses. As discussed in Chapter 10, the law now limits the deduction of losses from "passive" activities, a category that includes all losses on rental property. There is an important exception, though, that protects many vacation homeowners. If your adjusted gross income is less than $100,000, you can deduct up to $25,000 of rental losses each year. The $25,000 allowance is gradually phased out as AGI rises to $150,000.

To sidestep the passive-loss rules, you must "actively" manage the property, a requirement you can meet as long as you're involved in such decisions as approving tenants, rental terms and repairs. One more rule: Your average rental period must be for more than seven days. So, if your normal rental is one week, make sure you get at least one two-week tenant so your average inches above seven days.

Expenses you can't deduct because of the passive-loss rules aren't lost forever. Unused losses are held over to future years when they can be used to offset income from the vacation home or other passive investments. Also, any passive losses unused when you sell the property can be deducted against the profit on the sale or any other income.

(See Chapter 10 for more details on the passive loss rules.)

Tax loss or mortgage interest deduction?

Even if the $25,000 exception protects your rental write-offs, there's another potential trap. Limiting personal use of your vacation home may mean giving up the right to some mortgage interest deductions.

Remember that the law now permits mortgage-interest deductions for loans secured by your first and second *residence*. If your vacation place is a business property, however, the mortgage isn't covered. Part of the interest would still be deductible—the portion attributable to the business use of the property—but the remainder falls in the category of personal interest and therefore is nondeductible.

That rule has led some tax advisers to recommend that taxpayers intentionally flunk the 14-day/10% test by increasing personal use of vacation property. That way, you preserve the full interest write-off. Part of the interest would be deducted as a rental expense and the rest as mortgage interest. What you give up, of course, is the opportunity to claim a tax loss.

If you're in a situation to choose whether to pass or flunk the 14-day/10% test, you'll have to do a lot of number crunching to figure out which one will produce the best overall result.

Family Loan

● ●

Q: *I want to loan my daughter and her husband the money for the down payment on a house. I've heard that the IRS demands that I charge them interest. Is that right?*

A: It depends on the size of the loan you have in mind. First, consider why Uncle Sam thinks this is any of his business. Congress was worried that parents in a high tax bracket could make an interest-free "loan" to a child, and income generated by the funds would be taxed at the child's lower tax rate. To prevent that, the IRS treats such loans as though the lender were charging a reasonable rate of interest and making a gift to the borrower of the amount necessary to pay it. The lender had to report that "phantom" interest as income.

There are exceptions to that rule, however, and one covers you. First, if the amount of the loan is $10,000 or less, the IRS doesn't care whether you charge interest or not. And, for loans up to $100,000, the government won't get involved as long as the borrower's investment income doesn't exceed $1,000. (For both the $10,000 loan limit and the $1,000 investment-income level, a husband and wife are treated as one person.)

Pinpointing Your Deductions

To figure your vacation-home deductions, you have to allocate expenses between personal and rental use. There are two ways to do this—the IRS method and another approach that has been approved in court cases. The one that's best for you depends on your circumstances.

According to the IRS, you begin by adding up the total number of days the house was used for personal and business purposes. Your deductible rental expenses are the same proportion of the total as the number of rental days is to the total number of days the place was used.

For example, assume you have a cabin in the mountains that you use for 30 days during the year and rent out for 100 days. The 100 days of rental use equals 77% of the total 130 days the cabin was used during the year. Using the IRS formula, 77% of your expenses—including interest, taxes, insurance, utilities, repairs and depreciation—would be rental expenses.

The IRS is particular about the order in which you deduct those expenses against your rental income. You deduct interest and taxes first, then expenses *other* than depreciation, and then depreciation. The sequence is important, and detrimental, because of the rule that limits rental deductions to the amount of rental income when personal use exceeds 14 days or 10% of total use. Remember that property taxes not assigned to rental use could be claimed as regular itemized deductions instead. But by requiring you to deduct those expenses against rental income—that

---

Hobby-Loss Worry

● ●

Q: *We own a vacation home that we rent out most of the year. Year after year we show a tax loss, and I'm worried about the hobby-loss rules. After a while will the IRS reject our loss deductions because we never make a profit on the place?*

A: Not necessarily. The hobby-loss rules presume you're in business to make a profit if you report a profit in at least three out of five years. If you fail that test, you may be called on to prove you're trying to make money. You'd need records showing that you charge a reasonable rent, for example, and make reasonable attempts to keep the place rented. Remember, too, that profit on real estate is often based significantly on the appreciation of the property, something that doesn't show up on annual tax returns.

might otherwise be offset by depreciation you *won't* get to claim—the law squeezes the write-off for taxes as an itemized deduction.

By using a different allocation formula, though, you can limit the interest and tax expenses used to offset rental income and thereby boost the write-off of other rental costs. Courts have allowed taxpayers to allocate taxes and interest over the entire year rather than over just the number of days a property is used. In the example above of 100 days of rental use, that method would allocate just 27% (100 ÷ 365) of the taxes and interest to rental income. That would leave more rental income against which other expenses can be deducted. The extra taxes and interest can be deducted as a regular itemized deduction.

Although the court-approved formula can pay off when the 14-day/10% test makes the property a personal residence, the IRS version can be more appealing if the place qualifies as a business property. You need to look at the specifics of your situation to determine the best method for you.

Equity Sharing

Despite all the advantages of homeownership, rising home prices can make it tough to afford a home, particularly that first house. Coming up with the cash for the down payment is often a family affair, with parents helping their children buy into the American dream of homeownership. The tax consequences of making a low- or no-interest loan to help your children buy a house are discussed in Chapter 8.

Here's a look at another path to the same goal that may make sense for you: equity sharing.

The parties in a shared-equity arrangement don't have to be related, but this discussion will focus on parents and children. Basically, rather than making a loan or gift to your child, equity sharing involves becoming his or her partner. You become part-owner and rent your share of the place to the child. As an investor, you share in the appreciation of the house. As a landlord you also get rental income and the tax deductions that go along with rental real estate.

Assume the equity is split 50/50, although the property does not have to be divided equally. You and your child each put up half of the down payment and agree that you will each pay half of the mortgage interest, property taxes and other expenses such as insurance and repairs. Your child would also have to agree to pay you fair market rent for your half of the house.

The child, as the owner-occupant of the house, gets the tax advantages of homeownership, on a scaled-down level. The mortgage interest and property taxes he pays are deductible, just as if he owned the house outright. (Of course, like any tenant, he can't deduct the rent he pays.)

You, as the owner-investor, get all the tax advantages of owning rental real estate. You report the rent you receive as income and deduct the mortgage interest and property taxes paid as a rental expense. You also deduct your share of the insurance bills, for example, and the cost of repairs. In addition, you can claim depreciation deductions based on the cost of your half of the house. Under current tax law, residential real estate is deductible over 27.5 years and straight-line depreciation is used. If your expenses outstrip the rent you receive, you may be able to qualify to deduct up to $25,000 of your losses against other income. See Chapter 10 for the details.

© 1991 Gorrell—Richmond News Leader

When the house is sold, you and your child will split the proceeds. As an investor, your profit is taxable in the year of the sale. Since the house is the child's principal residence, however, he or she may defer the tax bill by rolling the profit into a new home.

Dotting the I's, Crossing the T's

Setting a fair rent for your share of the house is a key to whether a shared-equity arrangement will pass muster with the IRS. Remember that the owner-occupant has to pay rent only on the part of the house you own. In a 50/50 deal, if similar homes in the area generally rent for around $1,000 a month, for example, you wouldn't need to set the rent above $500. You could probably set it somewhat lower, in fact, since you can count on the owner-occupant to be a particularly good tenant. Presented with such arguments a few years ago, the U.S. Tax Court said that "fair rent" for a relative can be as much as 20% lower than fair rent for a stranger.

Shared-equity deals have to be set up under a written agreement that spells out the conditions of the deal, including each partner's share, which one will make the house a home, how expenses will be split and the fact that the owner-occupant will pay rent to the other owner. Because of the complexities, if you're interested in equity sharing, you should find a lawyer, real estate agent or mortgage-company official who is familiar with these arrangements. It may take some effort, but the tax savings could be well worth the trouble.

Moving Expenses

Buying and selling a home are often connected with a job switch, and that can give rise to special write-offs for part of your moving expenses. See Chapter 14 for details.

Investment Income & Expenses

One of the key goals mentioned when pundits talk of tax reform is to get Uncle Sam out of your investment decisions, so that your choice of where to invest your money can turn on economic factors rather than tax consequences. Despite such intentions, though, changes always seem to bring confusion and complexity rather than simplicity. The continual shifting of the tax rules—taking incentives away from certain investments, adding them to others—adds currency to the old saying: Investors can live with a bad tax law, but they can't live with uncertain tax law.

Like it or not, though, that's exactly what you have to do. Nowhere is this more true than in the area of capital gains, which is what the tax law calls profits from the sale of assets such as stocks, bonds, mutual fund shares and real estate. Every year, political debate rages over just exactly how those profits should be taxed.

Proponents of treating gains more leniently than wages and other kinds of income argue that it's a fiscally savvy way to stimulate the economy; opponents brand it a financially irresponsible give-away to the rich. Everyone has studies to "prove" his or her point. The latest statistics show, for example, that just over 10% of all tax returns report capital gains, and fully half of those returns come from taxpayers with less than $50,000 of income. But 40% of the gains went to taxpayers with incomes of over $200,000.

Although the outcome of the battle is never certain,

this much seems clear: As long as there is an income tax, Uncle Sam will have an abiding pecuniary interest in your investments, and income from different investments will be treated differently by the taxman. That means after-tax return—what you get to keep in your pocket after April 15—is a critical element to consider as you weigh the increasing number of choices in the investment marketplace. Knowing how the IRS treats various investments and how to use the tax rules to your best advantage can be as valuable as a hot stock tip.

Capital Gains: Will They or Won't They?

All through 1995, investors were on tenderhooks. Would Congress finally come through with a big break for capital gains, as promised in the House Republicans' *Contract with America*? If so, would Democratic President Bill Clinton sign it? Within the first 100 days, the House approved legislation to make 50% of capital gains tax-free and to apply *indexing* to future gains, so any portion of a profit attributable to inflation would be tax-free, too. In other words, if you sold a stock for a 10% gain after owing it for three years during which inflation totaled 9%, you'd have only a 1% gain—and just half of that would be taxed.

But would the Senate and President Clinton go along? If so, would the change be retroactive to cover all sales since the beginning of 1995, or apply to sales only after the change was signed into law? Hundreds of thousands—no, *millions*—of dollars in tax savings hung in the balance.

Alas, at our deadline, this matter was still up in the air. For an update on this critical issue, write or e-mail the author at the addresses listed on page i. The remaining discussion here is based on the law at the time we went to press.

Long-Term and Short-Term Gains

The law divides investment profits into two classes

"We don't seem able to check crime, so why not legalize it and then tax it out of business."

—WILL ROGERS

determined by the calendar: Long-term gains and short-term gains. Just how long you have to own property for the profit to qualify as long-term is another matter on which Congress keeps changing its mind. For most of the last 50 years, one year has been the magic length, although at times six or nine months has sufficed.

Currently, one year is the dividing line, and the proposed changes in how gains are taxed would not alter that. Assets owned one year or less produce short-term gains or losses; those owned longer get long-term treatment. When figuring the holding period, the day you buy property does *not* count, but the day you sell it does.

What's the difference? For a few years leading up to 1991, almost nothing at all. Short- and long-term gains were both fully taxed, just like any other income. Now there is a difference—but only for higher-income taxpayers. Before reviewing today's specifics, take a quick glance back at the not-too-distant past.

Before 1987 the difference between long- and short-term gains was enormous: 100% of short-term profits were taxed; 60% of long-term gains were completely tax-free. Only the remaining 40% of the profit was taxed. When the top tax rate was 50%, the top rate on long-term gains was just 20%, because the IRS ignored 60% of the profits.

When Congress abolished the 60% exclusion, the IRS was given the go-ahead to tax 100% of capital gain profits. For those in the 15% or 28% bracket—where the vast majority of taxpayers fall—the gain is taxed in the top bracket. However, if you're in the 31% or higher bracket—with 1996 taxable income over $96,900 on a joint return, for example, or over $58,150 on an individual return—you get a break. The maximum tax rate on long-term gains is 28%.

Without this special rule, a $10,000 long-term gain would boost your tax bill by $3,960 in the 39.6% bracket. The 28% limit, however, caps the extra tax at $2,800, and saves you $1,160. (That's almost as good as getting to treat 30% of the gain as tax-free.) Although the law says the 28% cap applies to *net capital gains*, in this case that's defined as net long-term gains (that is, long-term gains minus long-term losses) minus any net short-term losses. It does not protect short-term gains.

Whether or not you benefit from the 28% cap, you have to watch the calendar when you sell stocks, bonds or other assets. You have to report short-term and long-term gains separately on your tax return. If you wind up with a net long-term loss and a net short-term gain—or vice versa—they offset one another dollar for dollar. If Congress reinstates an exclusion for long-term gains, it may take more than $1 of long term losses to offset $1 of more-heavily-taxed short-term gain.

Special breaks for small company stock

Regardless of the outcome of the 1995 capital gains debate, there is an exception to the rule that 100% of long-term gains are taxable. To encourage investment in small business, in 1993 Congress created a 50% exclusion for the gain from the sale of a special kind of stock. With the 28% capital gains cap, the 50% exclusion makes the top rate for qualifying profit just 14%.

Don't get too excited, though. The break applies only to "qualified small-business stock" that you buy when it is originally issued (after August 10, 1993) and own for at least five years before selling. To target small businesses, the break applies only if the company has gross assets under $50 million when the stock is issued and the stock of certain kinds of companies can't qualify at all, including financial, farming, professional service and health-related firms.

There's also a limit on how much gain any taxpayer can exclude under this provision. The exclusion is limited to ten times your basis in the stock or $10 million from the stock of a single issuer, whichever is greater. And if you are subject to the alternative minimum tax (see Chapter 4), half of the gain you exclude under this provision is subject to the AMT.

Even if you're still interested, you may have a tough time finding qualifying stock. Remember, it can't be traded on the exchanges because to qualify you must buy the

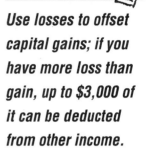

Money Saver

Use losses to offset capital gains; if you have more loss than gain, up to $3,000 of it can be deducted from other income.

stock at its original issue. Investments that qualify will generally be speculative, high-risk deals, and your broker may not even handle them. Remember, it never makes sense to make an investment primarily to get a tax break.

Another tax incentive to encourage investment in small businesses takes a page from the rule book that applies to the sale of homes (see Chapter 9). The law allows you to defer the tax due on gains from the sale of publicly traded securities if, within 60 days of the sale, you roll over the proceeds of the sale into a *specialized small business investment company.* A SSBIC is a company or partnership licensed by the Small Business Administration that steers investors' money into minority-owned businesses.

This provision lets you put off the tax on the gain from the sale of securities, not avoid it completely. When you ultimately sell the SSBIC stock, your taxable profit will include the gain from the previous sale.

In addition to having to complete the rollover within 60 days, the amount of gain you can defer is limited to $50,000 in any year and $500,000 over your lifetime. If you're interested in SSBIC stock, contact the Small Business Administration for a list of qualifying companies.

Capital losses

Since the government demands a share of your investment success, it's only fair that Uncle Sam also shoulder at least part of your losses. And yes, you can deduct capital losses … up to a point.

First, when figuring your net results in both the short- and long-term category, losses can offset gains dollar for dollar. If you wind up with a net loss in one category and a net gain in the other, the loss can offset the gain dollar for dollar. (As noted above, that might change if a long-term gain exclusion is restored.) And if your overall losses exceed your gains, you can deduct up to $3,000 of the excess loss from other income, such as your salary. If you have excess losses over the $3,000 limit, you can carry them over to future years to be deducted against capital gains or up to $3,000 of other income each year.

Know Your Basis

No matter what percentage of your capital gains is taxable and regardless of what tax rate applies, this is a given: the smaller the profit you report to the IRS, the lower your tax bill will be. That's why knowing your tax basis is critical. Your basis is, basically, your investment in the property. It is the amount you will compare to the sales proceeds to determine the size of your profit or loss. The higher your basis, the less gain there is to be taxed.

The higher you can prove your basis to be, the less gain there is to be taxed...and the lower your tax bill.

Although this sounds like a simple concept, it isn't necessarily so. For one thing, your basis depends on how you get the property in the first place, and it can change while you own it.

Purchase

The tax basis of assets you purchase is what you pay, including commissions or other costs associated with acquiring the property. Say you buy 100 shares of XYZ Inc. at $40 a share, and you pay a $100 commission. The total cost is $4,100, and the tax basis of each of your shares is $41. If you sell the 100 shares for same $40 each, and pay $100 commission on the sale, you have a $200 *loss*—your $4,100 basis minus the $3,900 proceeds of the sale. (See Chapter 9 for details on how to track the basis of your home.)

Gift

The basis of property you receive as a gift depends on whether your ultimate sale of the asset produces a profit or loss. If you sell for a profit, your basis is the same as the basis of the previous owner. In other words, the basis is transferred along with the property. If you sell for a loss, though, the basis is either the previous owner's basis or the value of the stock at the time of the gift, whichever is lower. Basically, this prevents shifting a tax loss from one taxpayer to another.

For example, say your aunt gives you 100 shares of a mutual fund for which she paid $5,000 but which are worth only $2,500 at the time of the gift. If the fund turns around and you sell for $6,000, your basis for determining gain is $5,000. If you sell for less than $2,500, however, the basis for figuring your loss is the $2,500 value at the time you received the gift. The loss in value while your aunt owned the stock is ignored. What if the selling price falls between $2,500 and $5,000? You have neither gain nor loss. (If the gift is big enough to require the donor to pay federal gift tax—see Chapter 18—that cost can increase the basis.)

If you use the donor's basis as your own, your holding period for figuring whether you have a short- or a long-term gain or loss includes the time the donor owned the property. If you use the fair market value at the time of the gift as your basis, your holding period starts the day after you get the gift.

Inheritance

When you inherit stock, mutual fund shares or other property, your basis is usually set at the value of the asset on the date of death of the previous owner. Assuming the asset had appreciated, the basis is "stepped up" to market value, so the income tax on any profit that built up while the previous owner was alive is forgiven. You are taxed only on appreciation after you inherit the stock. If the stock price falls before you sell it, you can claim a tax loss. (An exception to the general rule, which applies only when an estate is large enough for a federal estate-tax return to be filed, sets the basis of inherited property at its value six months after the owner died. If the executor of the estate chooses that value for estate-tax purposes, it becomes your basis in the stock.)

Joint ownership: If you own stock or other assets with a spouse as joint tenants or tenants by the entirety—forms of ownership that insure that on the death of one co-owner the survivor becomes the sole owner—the basis is adjusted upward on the death of the co-owner. Basically, the survivor is treated as though he or she inherited half of the asset, with that portion of the basis increased to current market value. For example, assume you and your spouse jointly own stock with a basis of $20 a share and your spouse dies when the shares are worth $40 each. Your basis in the shares would become $30: half of the original basis plus half of the fair market value at the time of your spouse's death.

Community property: If you live in a community-property state, the entire basis of community property—not just half—may be increased to date-of-death value upon the death of one spouse. Since that could have a major impact on the taxes due when the stock is sold, check this point carefully if you live in one of these states: Arizona, California, Idaho, Louisiana, Nevada, New Mexico, Texas, Washington or Wisconsin.

Unmarried partners: When unmarried individuals own property in joint tenancy, there's another twist. Each owner's share of the property—and therefore the part of the basis that's stepped up when that owner dies—is based on how much each owner contributed to the purchase price. Assume, for example, that you and your brother buy a cabin, with you contributing 20% of the cost and him paying the remaining 80%. If he dies first, 80% of the basis would be stepped up. Your basis would become your original investment, plus 80% of the cabin's value at the time of his death.

When a survivor can't prove his or her contribution, the IRS assumes the deceased owner provided all of it. This rule works in the IRS's favor as far as estate taxes are concerned because the full value of the property must be included in the estate of the first joint owner to die. But it backfires for the IRS when it comes to the basis because the entire amount is stepped up.

Capturing your tax advantage. The step up is enormously valuable, saving taxpayers an estimated $9 billion a year, compared to the taxes that would be due on the sale of inherited assets if the previous owner's basis were used to figure the profit. But some taxpayers may unknowingly forfeit it by selling highly appreciated assets late in life, perhaps in an attempt to simplify their affairs.

Even when the basis should be stepped up because property is held at the time of death, the savings might elude survivors. It's up to the heir to use the higher basis when the inherited property is sold. If you don't know the rules, you could wind up overpaying your taxes.

To protect yourself, review your holdings to ensure that the basis of any property you've inherited has been properly stepped up. How do you set the value? For publicly owned stocks, it's fairly easy to find the price on the date of death of the previous owner by visiting a library that has *The New York Times* or *The Wall Street Journal* on microfilm. For other kinds of property—such as real estate and antiques—it's more difficult. Such assets should have been valued at the time the estate was distributed. Ask the executor. If he or she can't help, ask an accountant or attorney experienced with estates for help establishing the proper basis.

What if you have already sold inherited property, figured the gain on an *unstepped-up* basis and overpaid your tax? If the return on which you reported the sale is still open to amendment—and it is if no more than three years have passed since the deadline for filing it—you can reclaim your money by filing an amended return using Form 1040X (see Chapter 2).

When it comes to the holding period, the sale of inherited property always produces a long-term gain or loss.

Divorce

Stocks, real estate and other assets received as part of a divorce settlement retain the same basis they had when owned by your ex-spouse. In other words, the paper gain or loss that built up while your spouse owned the property and any tax liability for it are transferred to you. See Chapter 8 for a discussion of how this should be taken into account when structuring the divorce settlement.

Shifting Basis

Your basis in an asset doesn't necessarily stay the same from the time you acquire it until the time you sell it. When a company in which you own stock declares a stock split, for example, your basis in the shares is spread across both the new and old shares. Say you own 100 shares with a basis of $10 each in a firm that declares a two-for-one split. Your total basis of $1,000 (100 x $10) would be spread among the 200 shares, giving each share a basis of $5. With real estate, the cost of capital improvements—such as a new roof—are added to basis; depreciation you claim is subtracted from it.

Money-Saving Strategies

Keeping track of the basis might sound like a hassle, but it's essential for successful tax planning. It's particularly important when you buy the stock of the same company or shares of the same mutual fund at different times and at different prices. When you decide to sell some of the shares, being able to identify which ones to part with will permit you to control the tax consequences of the deal.

Consider this example. You bought 100 shares of XYZ stock in January 1993 for $2,400, giving you a basis of $24 per share. In January 1994, you purchased 100 more shares, this time for $2,800. Your basis in each share is $28. In January 1995, you purchased another 100 shares for $3,000, giving each share a basis of $30.

When the stock hits $40 a share in mid-1996, you decide to sell 100 shares. If you simply tell your broker to sell 100 shares, the IRS FIFO rule—first in, first out—comes into play. It's assumed that the first shares you purchased— the 1993 group with the $24 basis—are the first ones sold. That would create a taxable profit of $16 a share or $1,600. But if you direct your broker to sell the shares purchased in 1995, with a $30 basis, the taxable profit will be $10 a share, or just $1,000.

In either case you would get $4,000 from the sale of the stock, but your tax bill would be significantly different. In most cases, you'll probably want to structure the sale to produce the smallest taxable profit. It's possible, though, that circumstances will warrant selling the asset with the lowest basis first—if you have sufficient losses to offset the larger gain, for example, or if you need higher investment income to permit you to write off investment expenses.

Also, if you want to make sure your profits qualify as long-term rather than short-term, you need to be sure the shares you sell have been owned for more than one year.

In any case, only if you have conscientiously maintained records do you have the flexibility to insure the best after-tax outcome. Records of what you own, your basis and the paper profit or loss are especially helpful at the end of the year when you review your portfolio for tax-motivated sales, as discussed in Chapter 17.

Mutual Funds

Mutual funds, those wonderful investments that let you buy a managed portfolio of stocks or bonds, or a mixture of both, are often an investor's first introduction to complex tax rules that go along with investing. And, with hundreds of thousands of novice investors pouring hundreds of billions of dollars into funds over the last few years, there's plenty of confusion. Unfortunately, that also means there's plenty of opportunity to overpay tax, too.

No less an authority than Fred Goldberg (who was head of the IRS from 1989 until 1992) is convinced that a lot of taxpayers pay too much tax on their mutual fund profits *simply because they don't understand the rules.* Don't be one of the victims. If you're new to mutual funds, take Goldberg's worry as a warning. If you're a veteran investor, take it as a reminder that the sometimes mysterious and often maddening tax rules are a constant threat. Paying more tax than you have to is a guaranteed way to undermine your investment success. Here's what you need to know to protect yourself.

Tracking Your Basis

Except for money-market funds—in which the value of shares remains constant at $1 per share—the price of mutual-fund shares fluctuates, just like the price of individual stocks and bonds. When you sell shares, you need to know exactly what your tax basis is to pinpoint the taxable gain or loss.

(continued on page 198)

Mutual Fund Worksheet

The better your records, the less risk you'll overpay the tax due on your mutual fund profits. For each fund, set up a worksheet like this one to record purchases, redemptions and the tax basis of your shares. The basis of shares you buy is what you pay for them (including commission). See the discussion on page 191 for figuring the basis of shares you acquire by other means, such as by gift or inheritance. Remember, too, that if you have dividends automatically reinvested, each reinvestment amounts to the purchase of additional shares, the basis of which is their purchase price.

This worksheet includes a column for tracking the average basis of your shares in a fund. Average basis is one of the methods the law allows shareholders to use when calculating whether the sale results in a profit or a loss. The example here assumes you're using the single-category, rather than the double-category, method. (See page 202 for a discussion of the difference.)

Figuring how average basis changes when new purchases occur is relatively straightforward. If you buy 100 shares for $1,000, your average basis is $10 per share (the $1,000 cost divided by 100 shares purchased). If you then buy 100 additional shares for $1,500, your average basis of your 200 shares is $12.50 (the total $2,500 invested divided by the total 200 shares owned).

Some taxpayers are confused, though, when it comes to figuring the average basis after a sale. Extending the example above, say that you redeem 50 shares for $600. That would result in a $25 loss, using the average basis method, because the basis of those 50 shares is $625 (50 times the $12.50 average share basis). But what is your average basis *after* the sale?

Do you subtract the $600 redemption from your $2,500 investment and divide the result by the 150 shares you still own? That would give you an average basis of $12.67 ($2,500 –$600 = $1,900 ÷ 150 = $12.67). But that's wrong. Your average basis before and after the sale remains identical, at $12.50 in this example.

After the first redemption, your average basis is no longer equal to total investment (purchases minus redemptions) divided by the number of shares you own. Instead, you reduce your total basis in the fund by the amount of basis—not the amount of cash—you pulled out of the fund. In this example, then, the total basis after the redemption is $1,875 ($2,500 –$625.) Dividing that by the 150 remaining shares sets the average basis at $12.50, exactly the same as it was before the sale.

The example in the worksheet is similar, but includes a dividend reinvestment. The share price column assumes the fund is a no-load; if commission was charged, it should be included in the cost.

Your Mutual Fund

Date	Buy or redeem	Dollar Amount	Number of shares	Share price	Share basis	Total Basis	Total Shares Owned	Average Basis	Dollar Gain or (Loss)
3-15-95	buy	$1,000.00	100	$10.00	$10.00	$1,000.00	100	$10.00	
6-15-95	buy	1,000.00	90.91	11.00	11.00	2,000.00	190.91	10.48	
12-28-95	buy	99.76[1]	8.56	11.65	11.65	2,099.76	199.47	10.53	
4-15-96	redeem	500.00	47.62	10.50	10.53	1,598.32	151.85	10.53	($1.44)[2]

[1]*Dividend reinvestment.* [2]*Assumes average basis is used to figure gain or loss. If first-in/first-out method were used, you would assume you sold shares from the first block of shares that you bought. Since the basis of those shares is $10 each, the transaction would result in a $23.80 gain. Alternatively, if you used the specific-identification method and directed the fund to sell shares from the group purchased 6-15-95 (with a basis of $11 each) you'd have a $23.82 loss.*

As noted earlier, your basis is basically how much you've invested in a fund. You compare that amount to what you get when you redeem shares to see if you have a profit or a loss. That doesn't seem too baffling. So what's the problem? *Here's* the problem:

If you invest $1,000 in a no-load fund whose price is $10 per share, your basis for each of your 100 shares is $10.

If you invest $1,000 in a fund with an 8.5% load whose price is $9.15 a share, your tax basis for each of your 100 shares is, again $10. (Although your shares are worth just $9.15 each, the tax law acknowledges that the commission was certainly part of their cost.)

If you inherit 100 shares from your grandmother who purchased them for $1 each but they were worth $10 each when she died, your basis is, yes, $10.

If Uncle Ed gives you 100 shares for which he paid $10 each but which were worth $25 each at the time of the gift, your basis is—you guessed it—$10.

Oh, one other thing: When you redeem mutual fund shares, the IRS gives you four options for figuring the basis of the ones you sell. Your tax bill could vary significantly depending on which one you choose. Your four choices are detailed in the section on Picking the Right Basis beginning page 201.

Since it's up to you to know the tax basis of your funds, you must keep thorough records. For each fund you invest in, set up a separate file—either on paper in a file folder or on a computer—and keep it up-to-date. You can use the worksheet on page 197 as a model. Record the date of each purchase, the amount invested, the number of shares purchased and the cost per share (including any sales fee). Your records should also reflect the average cost basis of your shares in each fund, in case you decide to use the average-basis method to figure your tax bill when you sell, as explained later in this chapter. If you acquire shares by some means other than purchase—as a gift or inheritance, for example, or as part of a divorce settlement—see the earlier discussion in this chapter for details on pinpointing your basis.

To see how important it is to keep track of all the details, including sales commissions, consider this example:

Fund A has no load, Fund B has an 8.5% load. Assume that when you invest, the shares in each fund have a net asset value of $20. If you put $1,000 in the no-load fund, you get 50 shares, each with a tax basis of $20. Invest in the load fund, however, and $85 of the $1,000 will go to pay the commission. The remaining $915 buys 45.75 shares, each with a basis of $21.86.

Now, assume you redeem the shares for $21 each. Your investment in Fund A will result in a $50 gain ($1,050 proceeds −$1,000 basis). The investment in Fund B leaves you with a $39.25 loss ($960.75 proceeds −$1,000 basis).

Reinvesting Dividends

It's also critically important to keep track of all your purchases. That might sound like common sense, but some investors forget that when they choose to have fund dividends automatically reinvested, they're actually buying additional shares. Say, for example, that you earn $87.50 in dividends that are reinvested in shares that, on the date of the distribution, are selling for $18.77 a share. You get 4.66 shares, each with an $18.77 basis.

Keep a running tally of your investment in the fund. If you liquidate your entire investment at once, your gain or loss will be determined by comparing how much you get with how much you paid for every share you own, whether purchased outright or via dividend reinvestment. By keeping track of all those dividend reinvestments, you'll be sure not to pay more tax than you owe.

Shifting Basis

Your basis in fund shares can change while you own them, too. On rare occasions, a fund decides not to distribute to shareholders part of the capital gains earned by selling stocks or bonds within the fund. Instead, the fund retains and pays tax on those profits. Such **undistributed capital gains** increase your basis in fund shares and complicate your tax return.

Money Saver

Keep track of reinvested dividends; it's critical to holding down the tax when you sell your shares.

If your fund does this, you'll receive a Form 2439 showing your share of the undistributed gain and your portion of the tax bill the fund paid on the gain. You have to report the undistributed gain as taxable income—even though you didn't get it—but you also get to claim a tax credit for the amount of tax paid by the fund on your behalf. You also increase the tax basis by the difference between the undistributed gain you report and the credit you claim.

For example, say you own 100 shares of a mutual fund that reports an undistributed gain of $100 and a tax paid of $34. You'd report the $100 of income, take a credit for the $34 of tax paid and increase your basis in the shares by $66. That might appear to be a hassle, but remember that hiking your basis will trim the tax bill due when you ultimately sell your shares.

Just as you may have to report mutual fund income you don't receive, it's possible to get a payment from the fund that's not taxable. Funds occasionally make a payment that doesn't come out of earnings or profits. Such **return of capital distributions** are sometimes called tax-free dividends or nontaxable distributions, but they should not be confused with tax-free income passed through to owners of tax-exempt bond funds. Instead, they are a return of your investment and reduce your basis in the mutual fund shares. Although you don't have to pay tax on these distributions, there is a place on Schedule B to report them, an exercise which should remind you to adjust your basis.

Another important way basis can change is if you own shares jointly with someone else, such as your husband or wife. Upon the death of the joint owner, the basis of the shares is stepped-up to effectively wipe out the tax on his or her portion of the profit that has built up. This can result in huge tax savings for the survivor, if he or she knows the rules.

Consider this simplified example: You and your husband bought $10,000 worth of shares in a mutual fund many years ago and never added a dime to your investment. When your husband dies and you become sole owner of the shares, they're worth $40,000. Your basis instantly becomes $25,000. Why? Because the law steps up your husband's part of the basis to the shares' value at the time he died. Since he is considered to have owned half the shares, the basis of those shares becomes $20,000 (half of the $40,000 date of death value of the investment). Adding that to your half of the original basis— $5,000—gives you your new, $25,000 basis. The tax on $15,000 worth of profit is forgiven. If you lived in a community property state, the new basis might be $40,000. (See the discussion of the basis of inherited property earlier in this chapter for details.)

Money Saver

When you sell mutual fund shares, specify which shares to part with—based on their basis. You'll control the tax consequences of the deal.

Selling the Right Shares

If you sell only some of your shares—rather than liquidating your entire position at once—your record keeping will pay off handsomely. In choosing which shares to sell, you can pick the ones with the basis that produces the best tax result. Assuming all your shares have appreciated, selling those with the highest basis will produce the lowest taxable gain. If your other investments have produced capital losses, however, you may want to sell low-basis shares to take a bigger profit for the losses to offset.

Picking the right basis

Since your shares are pooled in a single account by the mutual fund, who knows which shares are sold and which are retained? You do, if you keep good records. As noted earlier, you have four choices when it comes to fixing the basis of your fund shares.

- The **specific identification** method holds that if you direct the fund to sell specific shares—such as the 100 shares purchased on July 3, 1980, for $27.85 a share—it's the basis of those shares that determines the tax consequences of the sale. You should keep records of your sale order, including a copy of the letter to the fund identifying the shares to be sold by the date you acquired them and the price that you paid. You should also ask the fund for a letter confirming your directive, and keep that letter in your files, too. If you order the sale by phone, send a follow-up letter asking for written confirmation.

- If you simply call or write the fund and ask that a certain number of shares be redeemed without specifying which ones, the IRS's FIFO rule—**first in/first out**—comes into play. It is assumed that the first shares sold are the first ones you bought. So, the shares you have owned the longest, perhaps those with the lowest basis, are the ones considered to be sold.

- The IRS also permits mutual fund investors to use an **average basis** for figuring gain or loss on the sale of fund shares. Before long, this will be the method of choice for most mutual fund investors. It lacks the flexibility of specific identification, but it can't be beaten for simplicity.

There are really two average basis methods—single- and double-category.

With the *single-category method*, you add up your total investment in the fund (including all those bits and pieces of reinvested dividends), divide it by the number of shares you own and, *voila*, you know the average basis. That's the figure you use to calculate gain or loss on sale. If your investments over the years result in a $22.48 average basis and you redeem 100 shares at $25 a share, for example, you'd have a $252 gain ($2,500 minus $2,248). When it comes to determining whether a gain or loss is long- or short-term, you assume the shares sold are those you've owned the longest.

The *double-category method* is similar, but you divide the shares according to whether you've owned them long-term (more than one year) or short-term (one year or less). You find the average short-term basis and the average long-term basis. When you sell, you use the long-term average basis to figure the tax consequences of the sale, unless you specifically advise the fund that you want to sell shares from the short-term group.

The single-category method is gaining more and more converts because an increasing number of funds are actually doing the work for shareholders. The funds send out an extra statement each year—a copy of which does *not* go to the IRS—showing the average basis of shares redeemed during the year. Congress may soon pass a law requiring all funds to do so.

You can switch between specific identification and FIFO, but once you use the average basis method for a fund, you're stuck with it for as long as you own shares in that fund. IRS Publication 564, *Mutual Fund Distributions*, explains the average basis method in more detail.

Fund Switching and Wash Sales

Shareholders sometimes get an unpleasant surprise at tax time when they learn that switching among mutual funds—even within a family of funds—is a taxable transaction. Inside a fund family, for example, a telephone call can send your money from a stock fund focusing on a specific sector of the market to a bond fund invested heavily in low-grade securities. It's so easy that the tax consequences can be overlooked.

Remember, though, that such a switch means selling shares in the fund you're leaving. Unless you're moving funds out of a money-market fund, the switch usually produces a taxable capital gain or a tax-saving loss. The same thing goes if you write checks on a stock or bond fund account. To cash the check, the fund has to sell some of your shares. If you write one check each month, you'll have a dozen separate transactions to report to the IRS, and it's up to you to figure out the gain or loss on each one.

Beware, too, that the wash sale rule—discussed in more detail on page 209—applies to mutual funds.

Wash Sale Rule

Q: *I own stock that has taken a beating in the market. I'd like to sell to get the loss deduction but think the company has a lot of upside potential. Is it true that the tax rules say that if I sell I have to wait a certain amount of time before buying it back?*

A: You don't have to wait, but if you buy back too quickly you can be tripped up by the wash-sale rule. Basically, the loss on the sale is disallowed if within 30 days before or after you sell you buy back the same stock. The IRS figures you're really in the same position you were before the sale, so you don't deserve the tax break of a loss. To accomplish your purpose but get around the wash-sale rule, you could buy additional shares of the stock at the current, depressed price and then wait 30 days before selling the older block of shares for a loss. Or, you could sell now and wait 30 days to buy the shares back.

Basically, if you sell shares for a loss and within 30 days before or after the sale buy shares in the same fund, your loss is disallowed for tax purposes. The wash sale rule won't trip you up, though, if you switch between similar funds—say, from one family's international stock fund to another family's international stock fund.

Annual Fund Income

Even in years you don't sell shares, the IRS is interested in your fund investments, since they are likely to generate taxable income. In January you should receive a 1099–DIV form from each fund in which you own shares, showing income received during the year.

Income from money-market and taxable bond funds

This is considered dividend income for tax purposes, even though the source of the income is interest. The fact that it's being funneled through the fund changes its tax status. (If you goof and report this income as interest, you may hear from the IRS demanding tax on the dividends and a penalty for failing to report them. Straightening things out is a hassle you don't need.)

Losing with Tax-Frees

● ●

Q: *I invested in a tax-free municipal bond fund for three years, and when I sold it the shares were worth less than what I paid. Can I deduct the loss even though this was a tax-free investment?*

A: Yes. If you sold for less than your basis in the shares, you have a deductible capital loss. You can use it to offset any capital gains and up to $3,000 of other income. An exception to this basic rule won't affect you because you owned the shares for three years. When muni-bond fund shares are owned for six months or less, though, any loss must be reduced by the amount of any tax-free income received from the fund during the time you owned it.

Income from tax-free municipal bonds funds

Interest from muni bond funds retains its shield from federal income tax, but you do have to report it on your federal return. Although dodging Uncle Sam, the income may well be taxed by your state unless it comes from bonds issued within your state. In that case, the interest may be double-tax-free—or even triple-tax-free, if you face a local income tax. (See the discussion of municipal bonds later in this chapter.) Your fund should tell you what portion of the income you received was attributed to homegrown issues. Many tax-exempt funds also hold private-activity bonds, the interest from which can be hit by the alternative minimum tax, which is discussed in Chapter 4. If you're subject to the AMT, check the mutual fund's portfolio carefully. You may do better investing in a fund that spurns bonds potentially subject to the AMT.

Note this, too: Although income attributed to muni bond interest is tax-free, don't feel double-crossed if you get a notice from the fund that you received some taxable income, too. The fund may have parked some cash temporarily in taxable investments, or the managers may have taken some capital gains by trading bonds within the fund. Your share of such profits is taxable.

Income from funds invested in U.S. government securities

Interest from U.S. Treasury securities owned directly by taxpayers is exempt from *state* income taxes, and that tax freedom is generally maintained if you buy a fund that invests in those securities. If you own shares in this kind of fund, check this point carefully before reporting income you don't have to on your state return. Your fund should tell you what part, if any, of the income you receive qualifies for the state tax break.

Plain ol' dividends

Ordinary dividends—basically your share of the fund's dividend or interest income—are taxable in the year paid, whether you have the dividends paid out in cash or have them reinvested in new shares. Dividends are reported to you by the fund on a Form 1099–DIV.

Knowing when a stock fund declares dividends—the **ex-dividend** date—can give you a tax advantage. Generally, when the dividend is declared, the share value drops by about the same amount. If you invest in the fund just before the ex-dividend date, the dividend you receive amounts to a

Money Saver

Buy fund shares right after the ex-dividend date. You'll buy at a lower price and avoid an unnecessary tax bill.

refund of part of your purchase price. The problem is that you also get stuck with a tax bill on that dividend income. You'd be better off buying after the ex-dividend date, when you could buy the shares at their reduced price. Your out-of-pocket cost is the same, but your tax bill is lower.

A capital-gains distribution

A Form 1099–DIV may report this income to you, which is your share of the profits fund managers score by trading within the portfolio during the year. Regardless of how long you owned the mutual fund shares, this income is considered a long-term capital gain.

Even a tax-exempt municipal-bond fund can show a taxable capital-gains distribution, as noted above. That's not back-door taxation because the payout doesn't come from tax-free interest earned by the fund. Rather, it's your share of the profit realized when the fund manager sold bonds from the portfolio.

One thing you won't see is a short-term capital gains distribution. By law, short-term gains are reported to shareholders as ordinary dividends, which means they can't be offset by capital losses.

Foreign tax—payment and credit

In recent years, the top-performing mutual funds have included funds that invest in foreign securities. If you own shares in such a fund, you may be in line for a foreign tax credit. If so, your 1099–DIV will show the amount of foreign tax paid on your behalf. You have to include that amount with your taxable income for the year. But, to prevent you from paying tax twice on the same income—once to the foreign government and once to Uncle Sam—you may claim the amount as a deduction or a tax credit. In almost all cases, the credit is more valuable since it reduces your tax bill dollar for dollar. The deduction, on the other hand, reduces your taxable income. If you're in the 28% bracket, a $100 deduction saves you $28. Regardless of your tax bracket, a $100 credit saves you $100.

The catch is that while claiming the deduction is a breeze—you just report it along with other itemized deductions on your Schedule A—taking the foreign tax credit can be a mind-boggling hassle that demands filling out a Form 1116, Foreign Tax Credit for Individuals. Although wrestling with the form can be frustrating, it promises to be valuable.

Stocks

Whether or not you benefit from the current 28% cap on the tax on capital gains discussed earlier in this chapter—or the even bigger tax breaks Congress is considering bestowing on investment profits—stocks retain a special tax advantage. Profits are *not* taxed as they build up. The IRS gets a crack at share price appreciation only when you decide to sell your shares. Whether you're just getting your feet wet in the market or you're a seasoned investor, it's important to keep an eye on the tax angles so you share as little as possible of your portfolio success with Uncle Sam.

"It's not whether you win or lose. It's whether you can deduct your losses."

From the Wall Street Journal; Permission, Cartoon Features Syndicate

Unlike a savings account—in which someone else keeps track of exactly how much you earn and must pay tax on—investing in stocks demands that you be a meticulous bookkeeper. For one thing, you need to be able so show how long you own a stock before selling it. The special break for long-term capital gains applies only if you own the stock for more than one year before selling. It's also up to you to be able to pinpoint the tax basis of your investment.

It All Begins with Basis

Your tax basis, your investment in the shares, is the amount you subtract from the proceeds of a sale to see if

Money Saver

A short sale can let you lock in profit on a stock and postpone reporting that profit until the year you close the deal.

you have a taxable profit or a tax-saving loss. The higher your basis, the less tax you owe. When you buy stock, your basis is what you pay for it, including brokerage commissions. If you acquire your stock by some other method—from a gift or inheritance, for example, or as a result of a divorce—special rules apply. Your basis in shares purchased through a dividend-reinvestment plan is the stock's cost. Thus, if you have $100 in dividends reinvested and it buys you eight additional shares, your basis in each share would be $12.50 ($100 ÷ 8).

A special rule applies to **stock splits**. A split occurs when a company decides to reduce the market price of its shares—without reducing their value. A two-for-one split, for example, means that for each share you own, you'll get an extra share. But you're really no richer. When a company in which you own stock declares a split, your basis in the shares is spread across both the new and old shares. Say you own 100 shares with a basis of $10 each in a firm that declares a two-for-one split. Your total basis of $1,000 (100 x $10) would be spread among the 200 shares, giving each share a basis of $5.

When you sell stock, you report each individual transaction on Schedule D, *Capital Gains and Losses*. There, you must show the dates of purchase and sale, the sales price and your basis, and the gain or loss on the deal.

Short Sales

But what if you sell stock you don't own? That's exactly what happens in a short sale. An investor borrows stock from a broker in order to sell it, usually with the hope that the stock price will fall. If it does, the investor profits by repaying the loan with shares purchased at the lower price. If the stock price increases, the investor loses and has to repay the loan with shares that cost more than those sold.

As far as the IRS is concerned, the transaction doesn't count for tax purposes until the investor delivers the stock to the lender to close the sale. If you sell stock short in 1995 and close the deal in 1996, for example, the gain or loss will be reported on your 1996 tax return, the one filed in the spring of 1997. The premium you pay the broker to borrow the stock used in the short sale is considered investment interest, deductible to the extent of your investment income, as explained beginning on page 252.

Sometimes an investor who owns stock will sell the same stock short, a maneuver called selling **short against the box**. This technique can be attractive at year-end because it permits you to lock in profit on a stock in an uncertain market while postponing recognition of the taxable gain until the following year. You could sell borrowed stock in December at the current price, for example, but the transaction doesn't count for tax purposes until the following year when you deliver your shares to repay the loan. The short sale shields you from market risk in the meantime. As far as the holding period goes, however, this maneuver does not work to convert short-term gain to long-term gain. If you have owned the stock for one year or less at the time of the short sale, your profit will be short-term even if more than a year has passed at the time you close the sale.

Wash Sale

The IRS doesn't like being made the chump, which explains the existence of the **wash-sale rule**. It is most easily explained by outlining the stratagem it aims to prevent: Assume you own stock showing a substantial paper loss. Although you have every confidence the shares will recover their value, you sell the stock to realize the loss and trim your tax bill and then buy back the shares so that you can profit if the expected rebound occurs.

It will work, but only if you wait at least 30 days after the sale before you re-buy the shares. Otherwise, the IRS will ignore the sale and deny the tax loss. It sees the deal as a wash because you wind up with the same stock in your portfolio.

The wash-sale rule applies if within 30 days *before or after* the sale of stock or other securities showing a loss you buy *substantially identical* stock or securities. There's no precise definition of *substantially identical*, but the rule clearly puts the kibosh on buying and selling shares of the same company.

Although you can't claim the tax loss on a wash sale, it's really postponed rather than forfeited. You get to add the disallowed loss to the basis of your newly purchased shares. For example, say you bought 100 shares of XYZ stock for $1,000 and later sell them for $750. Within 30 days of that sale, however, you purchase 100 shares of the same stock for $800. Your $250 loss on the sale is disallowed, but you get to add that amount to the $800 cost of the new stock, giving it a basis of $1,050.

Note that the wash-sale rule applies only to losses. It's okay with the IRS if you want to sell securities to realize a taxable profit and then turn around immediately and reinvest in the same issues.

Dividends

Ordinary dividends are your share of the earnings and profits of the company whose stock you own. And, like interest on a savings account, such dividends are fully taxable. But not all dividends are considered *ordinary* and, therefore, different tax rules apply. As an investor, it's up to you to study the 1099–DIV form you receive reporting corporate distributions and make certain you pay tax on no more than you must.

If you're in a dividend-reinvestment plan, for example, your taxable income for the year includes dividends that are reinvested in additional shares even though you never put your hands on the cash. When a plan permits you to buy shares at a discount from current market value, the amount of the discount is included in your taxable dividend income for the year.

Assume that you use your dividends to buy 50 shares of stock at a $2.50-per-share discount. That would give you an extra $125 of dividend income. Your basis in the new shares would be their true market value, that is, what you paid plus the discount amount you had to include in your income.

Many reinvestment plans let shareholders buy extra shares, with cash, at a discount, too. If you take advantage of such an offer, the amount of the discount on the extra shares is considered dividend income in the year you make the purchase.

What if the corporation decides to pay dividends on its common stock with extra shares of common stock rather than in cash? Generally, such stock dividends are not taxable. Rather, as with the stock split discussed earlier, the new shares simply dilute your basis in the stock, meaning you'll wind up paying tax on the dividend when you ultimately sell the stock. Say you have 100 shares of stock with a basis of $5,000 and you get a stock dividend of ten shares. The $50-a-share basis in the stock ($5,000 ÷ 100) becomes a $45.45-a-share basis ($5,000 ÷ 110).

If shareholders are given the option of taking the dividend in stock or in cash, the dividend is taxable even if you take the shares. You are taxed on the market value of the stock you receive. In this case, however, the basis of your original shares does not change and your basis in the new shares is the amount you have to include in income.

Companies sometimes make cash payments to shareholders that don't come out of earnings and profits but rather represent a return of part of the investors' original investment. Such **return of capital distributions** are not taxable. Instead, they reduce your basis in the stock. That will hike your profit or reduce your loss when you eventually sell the shares but has no immediate effect on your tax bill.

Although taxpayers are often confused, dividends paid on life insurance policies are not dividends as far as the IRS is concerned. Rather, the payments are simply considered a refund of part of the premium you paid for the policy. Such dividends are not taxable, whether you receive them in cash or have them applied to reduce the premium the following year. (As usual, there's an exception: In the unlikely event the dividends surpass the total of premiums paid, the excess would be taxed.)

Bonds

These interest-bearing securities are issued by corporations and the federal, state or local government or their agencies. Depending on the issuer and the type of bond, different tax rules apply.

Corporate Bonds

On the face of it, the taxation of interest earned on corporate bonds is simple. These company-issued IOUs generally pay interest every six months, and it is taxable in the year you receive it. Fair enough. And it can work that way if you buy a bond at **par**—that is, at its face value—and hold it until maturity. Interest will be taxed as it is received, and when you redeem the bond for exactly what you paid for it, there will be no taxable gain, no taxable loss.

But things often don't work out so neatly.

For one thing, you can buy bonds at a **premium** (more than face value) or a **discount** (less than face value). Neither is necessarily a bargain, but both complicate your tax picture.

And the value of bonds can fluctuate wildly while you own them. Because the interest rate paid on the bond is set, the value of the bond rises and falls as market interest rates change. If interest rates spike after you've bought bonds, the value can plunge. No one wants to pay full price for a bond paying 5%, say, if the going rate on newly issued bonds is 10%. If you sell, you'll suffer a loss. Similarly, if in that same 10% environment you own 14% bonds, you can count on a hefty profit if you sell.

Only by understanding the government's take can bond investors choose the investment that gives the best after-tax return.

Bonds sold between interest dates

Because interest generally is paid every six months, the price of bonds sold between interest dates includes an amount for interest accrued since the last payment date. If you're the seller, that amount is considered interest income—and should be reported as such rather than as part of the price received for the bond—for purposes of figuring whether you have a gain or loss on the sale.

If you're the buyer, this "purchased interest" is not part

of your basis in the bond. Rather, when you receive your first payment on the bond, part of it is considered a nontaxable return of your investment rather than taxable interest.

For example, assume that you buy a $10,000, 10% bond midway between semiannual $500 interest payments. You pay $10,250 for the bond and its $250 of accrued interest. When you receive the $500 interest payment on the bond, half of it is considered return of your investment. Although you must report the full $500 on your tax return—on Schedule B—you also get to subtract the $250 "accrued interest." Your basis in the bond is $10,000.

Bonds purchased at discount

Generally, when you sell stocks or bonds for more than you paid for them, the difference is a capital gain. That rule doesn't always apply, however, to bonds purchased at a discount from face value. Different tax rules apply to different types of discounts and to bonds issued at different times.

Original-issue discount bonds: Some bonds are originally issued at a discount price, which basically means part of the interest won't be paid over the life of the bond but rather in a lump sum when the bond matures and is redeemed for more than the purchase price. On such original-issue-discount (OID) bonds, the IRS doesn't mind if you put off receipt of the interest, but it won't hold off on the tax bill. Each year that you own the bond you have to report—as interest income—a portion of the original discount amount. There are different methods for figuring how much to report, depending on when the bond was issued. Fortunately, the issuer should send you a 1099–OID form showing how much to include in your taxable income.

Keep careful records. The original-issue discount reported as income increases your basis in the bond, which will affect the taxable gain or loss when you dispose of the bond.

Market-discount bonds: Bonds issued at par—face value—often sell at a discount, too, due to market forces. As mentioned above, when interest rates rise, the value of bonds carrying yesterday's lower rates fall. Until a few years

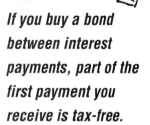

Money Saver

If you buy a bond between interest payments, part of the first payment you receive is tax-free.

As accrued interest is reported to the IRS, remember to increase your basis in zero-coupon bonds; otherwise you'll overpay your tax when you sell.

ago, gain on a market-discount bond held long-term was a capital gain. For bonds issued after July 18, 1984, however, at least part of the gain will be taxed as interest income. (Thanks to a change made in the 1993 tax law, the following rules also apply to discount bonds issued on or before July 18, 1984, and purchased after April 30, 1993.)

Basically, the difference between what you pay for the bond and its redemption value is considered to be interest that will accrue between the time you buy the bond and when it matures. Unlike the OID rules, you are not required to report the interest annually as it accrues. You can wait until you dispose of the bond—via sale or redemption—and figure what part of the proceeds is interest.

Although not required, you may choose to handle market-discount bonds the same way the law demands that OID bonds be treated. That is, you may report part of the market discount as interest each year as it accrues, paying the tax and increasing your basis as you go along. Beware, though, that you can't use the annual reporting method for some market-discount bonds and not for others. Once you use it for one bond, it applies to all other market-discount bonds you own.

Zero-coupon bonds

Take the idea behind original-issue discount to the extreme and, *voila*, you have the zero-coupon bond. These debt instruments pay no interest over their lifetime but overcome that handicap by being issued at steep discounts from their redemption value.

How steep? A 30-year zero-coupon bond—with a face value of $10,000 and a yield to maturity of 10%—would cost you just $535. That's $535 today for $10,000 thirty years down the road. The difference is interest that builds up along the way.

A key disadvantage, though, is that the IRS won't wait 30 years to get its cut. The interest is taxed as it accrues. Each year you own zeros, you must report and pay tax on the interest your investment is assumed to have earned that year. It's not as simple as dividing the discount by the number of years until maturity and reporting the result as your annual interest. If that were the case in the example above, you'd divide the $9,465 discount by 30 and report $315 interest a year.

The method required by the IRS is much more complicated but, believe it or not, more advantageous to the taxpayer. Basically, interest is taxed as it would actually accrue. In the example of a $535 investment yielding 10%, the first-year interest would be closer to $55 than the $315 figured under the simpler method. The rate of accrual accelerates over the life of the bonds, so each year you'll have more to report.

Fortunately, you don't need a computer to figure out how much to report. Each year you should receive from the bond issuer or your broker a 1099–OID showing how much interest you must report on your return. As usual, record keeping is essential. All zero-coupon-bond interest you report as income to the IRS increases your basis in the bond, which will affect the gain or loss if you sell it before maturity.

The taxability of zeros makes them particularly attractive for funding retirement accounts, such as IRAs and Keoghs, in which the tax bill is deferred. Investors can buy tax-free zeros issued by municipalities, an investment that dodges the annual federal tax liability. Because the interest would be tax-free if it were paid periodically, there's no tax problem in having the accruing income assigned to you annually. Even though you face no annual tax bill, the accruing interest does hike your basis in a zero-coupon municipal. You must keep track to hold down the tax bill when you dispose of the bond. (Beware that although the IRS doesn't tax accruing interest on municipal zeros, your state might.)

Bond premiums

The IRS has special rules, too, if you buy a bond for more than face value, as you might if the bond pays higher interest than current market rates. You get your choice of amortizing the premium over the life of the bond—claiming a tax-saving deduction each year—or dealing with the premium when you dispose of the bond.

Time Saver

Issuers of zero-coupon bonds should send you a report each year showing how much "imputed" interest to report to the IRS.

If you hold the bond to maturity and redeem it for face value, the extra amount you paid for it can be claimed as a deductible capital loss.

If you choose to amortize the premium, you have to figure how much to deduct each year. How you do that depends on when the bond was originally issued.

- **For those issued on or before September 27, 1985,** you can determine the annual deduction by dividing the premium amount by the number of years to maturity (or to the call date if that option would produce a smaller deduction).

- **For bonds issued after that date,** the amortization deduction must be based on your yield to maturity on the bond. The amount will change each year, and you may well need an accountant's help to figure out the annual deduction.

When you amortize, how you take advantage of the annual tax savings also depends on when you bought the premium bond.

- **For bonds acquired before October 23, 1986,** the amortized premiums are deducted on Schedule A as miscellaneous itemized deductions *not* subject to the 2% rule discussed in Chapter 15.

- **For bonds acquired starting in 1988,** you handle the amortized premium amount by simply subtracting it from the amount of bond interest you report as taxable income. With this method, even taxpayers who don't itemize deductions can get the benefit of amortizing the premium.

- **For bonds acquired between October 23, 1986 and December 31, 1987,** you have your choice of deducting the amortized premium as an interest expense on Schedule A, or of subtracting the amount from interest income earned by the bond.

As you amortize the premium, your basis in the bond decreases in step with the deductions you claim. (If you buy a tax-exempt bond at a premium, you *must* amortize the premium over the life of the bond, but you get no deduction. Your basis falls each year, though, in accordance with the amount of the premium allocable to the year.)

The alternative to amortizing your bond premium is to wait until you dispose of the bond to collect the tax savings you're due. If you don't amortize, you don't have to reduce your basis. If you redeem the bond at par, you'll have a capital loss to the tune of the premium. Basically, since you didn't write off the premium over the years, you get to deduct it all at once.

Convertible bonds

These are bonds that can be exchanged for a specified number of shares of stock in the same company. Promoters call them the best of both worlds because they let you lock in the steady income of a bond and still have the chance to enjoy the appreciation of a stock. The IRS is willing to go along. The bond interest you receive is taxable, just as on any bond. If you opt to convert to the stock, that transaction is not taxable. Your basis in the bonds simply shifts to the stock, so your basis in the shares is what you paid for the bonds plus any extra you shelled out to convert. Only when you later sell the stock will the tax bill come due.

U.S. Government Obligations

The tax treatment of Uncle Sam's IOUs is similar to that of corporate bonds. An important exception, though, is that interest on Treasury bills, notes and bonds is exempt from state and local income taxes—just as is interest on U.S. savings bonds.

Say, for example, that you live in a state with an 8% state income tax and can choose between investing $10,000 in a fully taxable corporate bond yielding 8% and a state tax-exempt Treasury note yielding 8%. Either investment will generate $800 of interest income, and if you're in the 28% federal tax bracket, the IRS will demand $224 of your earnings. On the T-note, that's all you'd have to pay. With the corporate bond, however, your state would get a

Money Saver

Interest on Treasury bills, notes and bonds is exempt from state and local income taxes—just as is interest on U.S. savings bonds.

bite of your income, claiming $64. (That state tax bill would be deductible on your federal return—if you itemize deductions. In the 28% bracket, that would save you about $18, so the advantage of the Treasury over the corporate bond would be $46.)

T-bills, which are issued with 13-week, 26-week and 52-week maturities, also offer investors the chance to defer income from one year to the next. The bills are issued at discount, with the interest paid when they are redeemed at face value. The tax isn't due until the year the bills mature.

If you sell a T-bill before maturity, part of the sales price is considered accrued interest and must be reported as interest income rather than taken into account when figuring capital gain or loss. The amount counted as interest is determined by dividing the number of days you owned the T-bill by the number of days in its term and multiplying the result by the discount. Assume you buy a six-month T-bill at a discount of $500 from face value and sell it after four months. Divide 120 (the number of days in four months) by 180 (days in six months). Multiply the result (0.66) by the $500 discount to find that $333 of the sales proceeds should be reported as interest.

Treasury notes and bonds

These are similar except that notes have maturities ranging from one to ten years and bonds are issued with maturities in excess of ten years. Both pay interest every six months, and it's taxable in the year you receive it. (As with Treasury bills, interest from notes and bonds is exempt from state and local income taxes.) Basically, when these obligations are purchased at a discount or premium price, the same rules apply as for corporate IOUs.

Ginnie Maes

Investors in Ginnie Maes buy into a pool of government-backed home mortgages. Although payment of both principal and interest is guaranteed by a federal agency—the Government National Mortgage Association (GNMA)—the income is not automatically exempt from state taxes. However, part of each payment will be totally tax-free. That's because you're just getting back some of your own money.

Remember, Ginnie Maes represent an investment in home mortgages. As homeowners make their monthly payments, your share of the interest and principal is passed on to you. The principal portion is a return of your investment and therefore is not taxable. With each payment, you should get a statement showing what part is taxable interest income and what part is nontaxable return of principal. Keep careful records to insure you don't pay tax on the return of your own money.

Municipal Bonds

It's not how much you make; it's how much you get to keep after expenses that matters. And, with Uncle Sam's levy being one of the biggest expenses you face as an investor, avoiding the tax bill can be a key to investment success. Enter municipal bonds.

Just as U.S. government securities are exempt from state and local income taxes, IOUs issued by states and municipalities escape the grasp of federal revenuers. Known generically as municipal bonds—or munis—these tax-exempt issues usually carry a lower interest rate than fully taxable bonds. Investors make up the difference—and sometimes more—via tax savings. Tax-free bonds became more attractive to higher-income earners in 1993 when Congress created the 36% and 39.6% tax brackets. The higher the rate you avoid, the more valuable avoiding tax becomes. Similarly, talk of a flat tax that would exempt all investment earnings from tax threatens municipals because they would lose their privileged status. Since it's likely to be many years before that happens—of it ever does—you need to know how to compare yields on taxable and tax-free securities.

Figuring taxable-equivalent yields

To know whether municipals make sense for you, you need to compute the **taxable-equivalent yield**—that is, how much you would have to earn on a taxable investment to

Money Saver

Muni bonds issued within your state may be triple-tax free, paying interest that avoids local, state and federal taxes.

have as much left over after taxes. The table on the next page shows the taxable equivalents for tax-free bonds issued at various interest rates. First, here's the formula for figuring the precise taxable-equivalent rate for any bond you consider:

$$\frac{tax\text{-}free\ rate}{1-federal\ tax\ bracket} = taxable\text{-}equivalent\ rate$$

For example, assume you are in the 31% tax bracket and are offered a 5.75% tax-free bond. You would divide 5.75 by 0.69 (1 −0.31) to find that the taxable-equivalent yield is 8.33%. In other words, you'd need a taxable investment paying more than 8.33% to beat the return on the 5.75% tax-exempt. In the 39.6% bracket, the divisor would be 0.604 (1 −0.396) and the taxable-equivalent yield would be 9.51%.

There's a similar formula for figuring things the other way, to find the tax-exempt equivalent of a taxable yield:

$$taxable\ rate\ x\ (1-federal\ tax\ bracket) = tax\text{-}free\ rate$$

Assume you are considering a taxable investment yielding 8%. If you are in the 31% tax bracket, multiply 8 by 0.69 (1 −0.31). The result is 5.52, telling you that a 5.52% tax-free yield will put the same amount in your pocket, *after tax*, as an 8% taxable yield. In the 39.6% bracket, the multiplier would be 0.604 (1 −0.396), so a tax-free yield of 4.83% will match a taxable yield of 8%.

Double- and triple-tax freedom

Taxable equivalents get a boost when you buy bonds issued within the boundaries of your own state if it, like most, exempts the income from state tax. If you happen to face a city income tax, municipals can brag of triple tax-free status—shielded from federal, state and local income tax.

Figuring taxable-equivalent yields gets more complicated if your investment dodges both state and federal tax. Because state income taxes paid are deductible on your federal return (if you itemize) you can't simply add the state rate to the federal rate and use the formulas above.

First, you must find the *effective* state tax rate—what

you pay minus the tax savings of deducting that amount. For example, if you pay an 8% state tax and deduct it in the 31% federal bracket, your effective state tax rate is 5.52% (the 8% state tax rate minus 31% of that rate). Thus, in the formula for figuring taxable equivalents, the tax rate used in the divisor would the combination of your federal rate (31%) and your effective state rate (5.52%), or 36.52%. So the divisor is 1 - 0.3652, or 0.6348. If you are considering a 6% municipal that is exempt from both state and local taxes, you would divide 6 by 0.6348 and find that the taxable equivalent is 9.45%.

Taxable tax-exempts

Call it an oxymoron if you want, but some tax-exempt bonds generate interest that can fall victim to the alterna-

1996 Taxable-Equivalent Yields

1996 Taxable Income	Tax Bracket	Tax-Free Yield						
		4%	5%	6%	7%	8%	9%	10%
Single Return								
Up to $24,000	15%	4.71	5.88	7.06	8.24	9.41	10.59	11.76
$24,001 to $58,150	28	5.56	6.94	8.33	9.72	11.11	12.50	13.89
$58,151 to $121,300	31	5.80	7.25	8.70	10.14	11.59	13.04	14.49
$121,301 to $263,750	36	6.25	7.81	9.38	10.94	12.50	14.06	15.63
More than $263,750	39.6	6.62	8.28	9.93	11.59	13.25	14.90	16.56
Joint Return								
Up to $40,100	15	4.71	5.88	7.06	8.24	9.41	10.59	11.76
$40,101 to $96,900	28	5.56	6.94	8.33	9.72	11.11	12.50	13.89
$96,901 to $147,700	31	5.80	7.25	8.70	10.14	11.59	13.04	14.49
$147,701 to $263,750	36	6.25	7.81	9.38	10.94	12.50	14.06	15.63
More than $263,750	39.6	6.62	8.28	9.93	11.59	13.25	14.90	16.56

This table shows the taxable-equivalent yields of tax-exempt investments for investors in various tax brackets in 1996. To use the table, find the point where your tax bracket and the tax-free yield intersect. If you are in the 28% bracket, for example, and are considering a 6% tax-free investment, the taxable-equivalent yield is 8.33%. You'd need a taxable yield of at least 8.33% to match the tax-free offering. For someone in the 31% bracket, that same 6% tax-free bond would be as valuable as an 8.70% taxable investment. As noted in the accompanying text, if the investment is free of state taxes, too, your taxable-equivalent yield would be higher.

tive minimum tax (AMT). Worried that some municipalities were taking unfair advantage of the federal tax exemption to raise "nonessential" funds at below-market rates, Congress made interest on "private purpose" bonds a preference item for the AMT, as discussed in Chapter 4.

Although interest from these bonds remains tax-free for the vast majority of taxpayers—those who are not subject to the AMT—the interest is hit by the 26% or 28% AMT rate when earned by investors subject to the AMT. Only certain bonds issued after August 7, 1986, are affected, and your bond dealer should be able to tell you whether bonds you are considering fall in the AMT shadow. This rule creates a potential benefit for some taxpayers. The AMT threat pushes up the yield slightly on affected

The Tax-Free Advantage—In-State, Out-of-State, or Both?

- If you live in one of the following states, there's an advantage to buying in-state municipals because these states tax the income on out-of-state bonds but give the tax-free nod to in-state obligations.

Alabama	Missouri
Arizona	Montana
Arkansas	Nebraska
California	New Hampshire
Colorado	New Jersey
Connecticut	New Mexico
Delaware	New York
Georgia	North Carolina
Hawaii	North Dakota
Idaho	Ohio
Kentucky	Oregon
Louisiana	Pennsylvania
Maine	Rhode Island
Maryland	South Carolina
Massachusetts	Tennessee
Michigan	Vermont
Minnesota	Virginia
Mississippi	West Virginia

- If you live in Iowa, Illinois, Oklahoma or Wisconsin, only certain in-state issues are exempt from the state income tax. Interest on other bonds is taxed at the state level. In Kansas, income from most homegrown municipal bonds issued before 1988 is subject to the state income tax; bonds issued in 1988 and later years are tax exempt.

- In the rest of the states and the District of Columbia, your after-tax yield will be the same on either in- or out-of-state bonds. In these states, interest is tax-free on both in- and out-of-state bonds:

  Alaska
  District of Columbia
  Florida
  Indiana
  Nevada
  South Dakota
  Texas
  Utah
  Washington
  Wyoming

private-activity bonds, and that's a bonus for investors who don't have to worry about the AMT.

Tax-free interest and social security

Taxpayers who receive social security benefits could argue that the alternative minimum tax threat isn't the first time Uncle Sam has decided to tax tax-exempt income. Since 1984, tax-free interest has been included in the calculation to determine what part, if any, of social security benefits are taxed. Since that could trigger a tax on otherwise tax-free benefits, many investors have seen this as a back-door way to tax their municipal bond income.

Social security benefits are taxable only if your modified adjusted gross income for the year exceeds a certain base amount—$25,000 if you file a single return, $32,000 if you file jointly. The catch in this case is that modified AGI includes tax-free bond interest. Basically, if your adjusted gross income for the year *plus* your tax-free income *plus* one-half of your social security benefits exceeds the base amount, up to 85% of your benefits can be taxed. See Chapter 12 for more details.

Whether or not your tax-free income may be nipped either by the tax on social security or the alternative minimum levy, the IRS wants to know just how much tax-exempt income you receive. There's a line on the tax forms to report this income. It's not only the IRS that's interested, either. Remember that municipal-bond interest might be taxable at the state level. Some states check what's reported on the federal return as tax-free in an attempt to catch taxpayers who ought to—but aren't—reporting that interest as *taxable* on their state returns.

Gains and losses on municipal bonds

Although interest from municipal bonds is exempt from the federal income tax, the IRS doesn't ignore the gain or loss that results when you sell the bonds. If you sell a bond for more than your basis, the profit is a capital gain; if you sell it for less, it's a deductible capital loss.

In general, your basis is figured the same way as for

taxable bonds. However, if you buy a tax-exempt bond at a premium, you must amortize the premium over the period you own the bond. This amortization reduces your basis in the bond, but unlike a taxable bond, you can't deduct the amortized amount. Because the interest you earn is tax-free—and you paid the premium to get a higher-than-current-market, tax-free rate—the premium amortization is not deductible.

If you buy a bond originally issued at a discount, you increase your basis each year as is required with taxable bonds, but you don't have to report the annual amortization of the discount as income. It, like interest paid on the bond, is tax-free.

Things are different, though, if you buy a municipal bond at a market discount. And, different rules apply depending on when you buy the bond. For those purchased before May 1, 1993, you don't amortize the market discount. Rather, your basis remains stable, and when you redeem the bond at face value, the difference between what you paid and what you receive is a taxable capital gain. When Congress hiked the top tax bracket to 39.6% while retaining the 28% cap on capital gains taxes, however, the lawmakers decided this rule was too generous.

Now, when you sell a market-discount tax-exempt acquired after April 30, 1993, any gain attributable to the discount is treated as ordinary income and taxed in your top bracket. Rather than report the full amount at the time you dispose of the bond, you have the same option available to taxable bondholders discussed earlier: to report a portion of the discount annually as it accrues.

Bond Swaps

If you own bonds showing a significant paper loss— say market interest rates have risen since you purchased the securities—you may want to consider a bond swap. With this maneuver, you simply sell the bonds to realize your loss and then reinvest the proceeds in other bonds. Depending on the quality and maturity of the replacement bonds, it's possible to wind up with bonds paying higher income than the ones you unloaded. In addition, you get the tax savings generated by deducting the capital loss. The wash-sale rule discussed on page 209 would disallow the tax savings if the replacement bonds are *substantially identical* to the ones you unloaded. Your broker should be able to help you select replacement bonds that don't run afoul of this rule. Bond swaps are often year-end moves and you should realize that the earlier you begin looking for a swap, the easier it will be to find a suitable issue to buy.

Bond Mutual Funds

You can avoid most of the tax headaches associated with bonds by investing in them via mutual funds or unit trusts that give you a share of a diversified portfolio of bonds. You get professional managers who not only choose the bonds for the portfolio but also worry about the tax ramifications. In most cases, you'll get a year-end report including the information you need to file your tax return. You must keep track of your basis in your investment in the mutual fund or trust but you don't have to worry about such details as amortizing bond discounts or premiums.

If the funds invest in tax-free issues, the income that is passed on to you retains its tax-exempt status. Residents of many states can choose from mutual funds and unit trusts that invest only in bonds issued by an individual state—insuring investors a double tax exemption.

For more information about mutual funds, see the discussion earlier in this chapter.

U.S. Savings Bonds

These used to be such lousy investments that the tax angles were among the least of the concerns of people who bought the bonds. Now, however, savings bonds have a lot to commend them. They have shed the fixed, well-below-market interest rate of the past. Series EE bonds are sold for half of their face value and newly issued bonds pay market-based rates from the beginning. (In the past, you had to hold bonds for five years to get these rates.)

That rate has reached as high as 11%. It was around 6% in the fall of 1995. A bank selling bonds can tell you the current rate.

Now for the tax breaks. Series EE bonds have two basic tax appeals:

- **The interest earned is exempt from state and local income taxes,** which means the earnings are worth somewhat more to you than interest that would be taxed. (If you face a state tax rate of 7%, for example, the tax-exempt status makes a 5% savings-bond yield worth about the same as a fully taxable 5.4% yield.)

- **You can put off the federal tax bill on the interest until you cash the bonds.** Such tax-deferred interest is advantageous because funds that otherwise would go to the IRS can remain invested for further growth. (Series HH savings bonds enjoy a similar freedom from state and local income taxes, but interest is paid out semiannually and is taxed in the year paid.)

A great way to save for kids

The tax-deferred nature of Series EE bonds has made them an attractive tool for a child's savings plan. You, or some other generous soul, can buy bonds for your children, and the investment will be permitted to grow unmolested by the IRS until the bonds are cashed. As long as the child is named owner of the bonds, he or she will be responsible for the tax bill, even if the parent or other purchaser is named the beneficiary. However, if you name yourself co-owner of the bond, you will be liable for the tax bill even if the child cashes the bond.

Because tax on the bonds is deferred until they are cashed, the annual earnings do not count for purposes of the "kiddie tax" discussed in Chapter 8. As long as the bonds are not cashed before the year the child reaches age 14, the interest will be taxed in the child's bracket rather than the parents'.

In some cases, though, it may make sense to skip the tax deferral and report the income each year as it builds up. If your child has a limited amount of income, this maneuver may effectively make part or all of the savings-bond interest completely tax-free. Annual reporting of the interest could be advantageous if the child's total income is so low that no tax would be due. In 1996, a child can have up to $650 of investment income tax-free, and an additional $650 is taxed at his or her own rate without triggering the kiddie tax.

To report the interest annually, simply file a tax return for the child for the first year he or she owns bonds and show the amount of interest that accrued during the year. Banks that sell bonds should have a table showing how much was earned by bonds purchased at different times during the year. You don't have to file another tax return until the child's income is high enough to require one.

> ## A 911 for Fund Investors
>
> •
>
> **Q:** *I sold fund shares for the first time last year and have discovered that my records are woefully incomplete. Is there any way I can protect myself from overpaying my taxes?*
>
> **A:** Don't despair. Call the fund and ask for help. Many funds have toll-free numbers—some operating 24-hours a day at tax time—to help shareholders. There may be a charge if you need several years' worth of records reconstructed, but it's better than overpaying your taxes by underestimating your cost basis. Good luck.

If you've been using the annual reporting method but are tripped up by the kiddie tax—because income you thought would be taxed in your child's low bracket is now being taxed in yours—you can switch back, deferring the tax bill until the bonds are cashed. To do so, you file Form 3115, *Application for Change in Accounting Method* with the IRS, and defer the tax on future earnings until the bonds are cashed.

When savings bonds are cashed, the owner will receive a 1099–INT form showing as income the difference between the purchase price and redemption value of the bonds. If you've reported some or all of the interest annually, however, you don't have to pay tax on that amount again. You do have to report the full amount of interest on your tax return but should also list the amount of "U.S. savings-bond interest previously reported" and subtract it from the interest total. Clearly, you must maintain careful records over the years to prevent you, or your child, from overpaying the tax bill.

Totally tax-free savings for college

Bonds purchased in 1990 and later years can be an even better vehicle for college savings. The interest can be totally tax-free if the money is used to pay tuition.

Assume, for example, that you redeem $10,000 worth of bonds, an amount that includes $5,000 in interest built up over the years. In the 28% bracket, that $5,000 would cost you $1,400 in added income tax. However, if you qualify for the break and spend the $10,000 on a child's college bills, you avoid that tax bill. Basically, the $1,400 is Uncle Sam's contribution to the tuition.

Unlike the basic savings bond strategy, to qualify for this break the student *cannot* own the bonds. They must be purchased and owned by the parents, who must be at least 24 years old when the bonds are purchased. The interest is tax-free if, in the year you redeem the bonds, you also pay qualifying educational expenses—basically, that's tuition and fees for a dependent child—equal to the amount you got from cashing in the bonds.

If you pay $10,000 in tuition and fees and redeem bonds worth $10,000 or less, for example, all interest would be tax-free. If you redeemed $10,000 worth of

---

Savings Bond Backfire

• •

Q: *Last fall our daughter cashed in her collection of savings bonds to pay college tuition. At the time, the bank gave her a 1099–INT form stating that she collected about $2,600 in interest. It's clear that the same information was sent to the IRS. We thought one of the main reasons for using savings bonds for a college fund was to get what amounted to tax-free interest. We followed the advice to file a tax return for the first year we purchased bonds in our daughter's name, to establish that she was reporting interest annually rather than letting it build up. Have we been doubled-crossed? Does our daughter have to pay taxes on all the interest?*

A: No. Although the IRS did receive a copy of the form, your daughter won't have to pay tax on the interest. She should report it, along with any other interest received during the year, on Schedule B if she files a Form 1040 or Schedule 1 of the 1040A short form. A couple of lines below the subtotal, she should write "U.S. savings bond interest previously reported" and enter the total interest reported over the years under the election to report annually. Subtract that to arrive at the taxable amount.

bonds and paid just $7,500 for a child's tuition and fees, however, just 75% of the interest would be tax-free.

The income qualifier

Note this: The tax break disappears at higher income levels. For 1995, for example, the right to exclude bond interest was phased out as adjusted gross income on a joint return rose between $63,450 and $93,450. For single parents, the 1995 phase-out range was $42,300 to $57,300. If your AGI on a 1995 joint return is $78,450, for example, just half of the savings bond interest would be tax-free, since $78,450 is halfway through the phase-out zone. If AGI is above $93,450, the interest would be fully taxable.

The phase-out ranges are supposed to increase each year to account for inflation. For 1996, for example, the range for joint returns will be $65,200 to $95,200 and for single returns, $43,450 to $58,450. The ranges could be slightly higher for both 1995 and 1996 , too, if Congress gets around to fixing a snafu in the way the law was written.

Remember that your eligibility for this tax break is determined by your income when you redeem the bonds— perhaps many years in the future—rather than when you buy them. And the income limits presumably will continue to rise to reflect inflation (and there has been talk in Congress of eliminating the income limit altogether). Assuming a 4% annual inflation rate, in 18 years—when today's newborn is ready to go to college—the phase-out range on joint returns would begin at approximately $130,000.

Some parents may discover an added benefit to registering bonds in their own names rather than the child's name, as required under the old tax-saving method. When the student owns the bonds, it's really up to him or her how to spend the money, be it on college bills, a new car or a "learning experience" in Paris. With the new rules, the parent controls the cash, and the tax break comes only if it's used to pay for college. You use Form 8815 to report the redemption of bonds that qualify for this break.

Inherited Bonds

What if you inherit Series E or EE bonds? The IRS demands that someone pay tax on the interest that's built up during the previous owner's life, but doesn't care whether you or the deceased owner foots the bill. Even if the bonds are not redeemed, the untaxed interest can be reported on the decedent's final tax return. In that case, you would be responsible for the tax only on the interest earned after you inherited the bonds.

If the interest isn't reported on the deceased's final tax return, you assume the tax liability along with ownership of the bonds. When you cash the bonds, you'll owe tax on all the interest. The choice turns on the tax rate that would apply if the interest were reported on the decedent's final return as opposed to yours and on how long you're likely to hold on to the bonds—and therefore how long you'll hold off the tax bill if you assume the liability.

Worthless Stock

Q: *I own 100 shares of stock in a company that went bankrupt earlier this year. Can I deduct what I paid for the stock as a capital loss?*

A: You can claim a loss for worthless stock, figured as though you sold it for $0 at the end of the year in which it became worthless. The question, though, is whether your shares are worthless. Some stock continues to trade even while a firm is in bankruptcy and, even if the shares are no longer traded, it's possible that they may have some value. Stock is considered worthless for tax purposes only when there is no realistic chance of recovering any part of its value. If you're sure the stock isn't coming back but uncertain you could convince the IRS of that fact, you may want to ask your broker if he or she can arrange for another client to buy your shares for a nominal amount—say $1. Then you can report a loss equal to your basis minus the $1.

Passive-Loss Rules

For years, Congress chipped away at tax shelters, those investments with more tax appeal than economic sense. In 1986, the lawmakers struck a powerful blow to deals that thrive on the seemingly daffy promise of huge losses. The weapon is tight restrictions on losses from *passive* activities, a classification that includes businesses in which the investor does not "materially" participate—including all **limited partnerships**. The material-participation test is a tough one, demanding that you be regularly and substantially involved in the business year-round. Practically all rental activities automatically fall in the passive category, too, regardless of how involved you may be. (A valuable exception applies to owners of rental real estate who are "actively" involved, as discussed later in this chapter.)

The killer is that losses from investments branded passive can be deducted only against *passive income*, that is, income from profitable passive activities. Passive losses can't be used to shelter income from other activities, such as your job or investments in stocks and bonds. The law prevents paper losses generated by a limited partnership—via the pass-through of oil depletion write-offs, perhaps, or real estate depreciation deductions—from wiping out part of the tax bill on your salary or portfolio income. Most passive losses come from limited partnerships and real estate, but the crackdown can affect businesses that generally aren't labeled tax shelters.

Consider the case of two brothers who jointly own a toy store. One brother actually runs the store, working 40 hours a week and making most of the purchasing and hiring decisions single-handedly. The other brother's interest is mostly financial, and although he has a voice in major decisions, he's seldom involved in the day-to-day operations. The brother who works in the store would pass the material-participation test and wouldn't have to worry about the passive-activity rule. His brother, however, would be tripped up by the rule and forbidden to use his share of the store's losses to shelter other income.

IRS regulations outline what's required to pass the material-participation test and thus qualify to write off business losses against nonbusiness income. You pass the test if:

- **You work in the business 500 or more hours during the year.** That's just ten hours a week;

- **You're the primary person involved,** virtually to the exclusion of everyone else, even if you put in less than 500 hours; or

- **You put in at least 100 hours during the year and it's more time than anyone else has put in,** including employees.

There's a special rule for some real estate professionals that can free them from the general rule that real estate is automatically a passive activity. To qualify, basically, more than half the time you spend working during the year (and a minimum of 750 hours) has to be in the real estate business—defined to include property development, rental, management and real estate brokerage businesses.

Despite the restrictions on passive losses, they are not stripped of all tax value. First of all, any deductions you deserve for passive-activity-related expenses—such as interest payments or depreciation—can still offset income from the investment. Any excess loss can be used to shelter income from other passive activities, such as a profitable rental or partnership.

Beyond that, any leftover loss will be suspended and carried forward until a future year when you have passive income to offset. When you dispose of an investment that has generated unused losses, those losses are unleashed to shelter any income, whether passive or not.

If you are tripped up by the passive-loss rules, you have several options. One is to ditch the investment that's throwing off suspended losses. That may be much easier said than done. You may have to take a distress-sale price that could be worse than the suspension of the tax benefits.

Another point to keep in mind: The passive loss rules create planning opportunities along with the headaches. Losses suspended now could wind up being worth more to you in the future when you get to use them—to shelter a big profit when you finally dispose of the passive investment, for example.

Rental Property

Investors in rental property know how slippery a tax landscape can be. Sometimes Congress seems to fall

all over itself to create new tax breaks for real estate. At other times, the lawmakers seem almost vengeful as they snatch away the breaks. Depreciation schedules are speeded up or slowed down, capital gains breaks for profits grow and shrink, disappear and reappear. The passive-loss rules discussed above were devised specifically to severely limit the opportunity to use losses on rental property to shelter income from other sources, such as your salary or investments.

Through it all, though, Uncle Sam is a partner in your business as a landlord, demanding to share the profits, willing to help shoulder at least some of the expenses. Whether you're a veteran investor in rental property or just considering your first real estate investment, the tax angles may well be pivotal to your success.

Depreciation

This is a noncash expense that can put money in your pocket. The law lets you depreciate rental property, claiming deductions that are supposed to reflect how the building is being "used up." You depreciate your tax *basis* in the building, which is basically what you paid for the property minus the value of the land. Depreciation is a key to many real estate investments because even if rental income fails to cover all out-of-pocket expenses, the tax savings from depreciation—by sheltering other income from the IRS—can make up much, if not all, of the difference.

The law sets how fast you can depreciate property and, therefore, how big your deductions will be. Before 1987, buildings could be depreciated over 19 years (never mind the fact that a building would probably last much longer) using a method called the Accelerated Cost Recovery System (ACRS). It was "accelerated" because the write-off schedule bunched bigger deductions in the earlier years. Now, only straight-line depreciation is allowed—meaning the same percentage of the basis is written off each year—and different rules apply for residential and commercial, non-residential real estate.

Money Saver

Even if rental income fails to cover all out-of-pocket expenses, the tax savings of depreciation can make up much, if not all, of the difference.

- Residential real estate put into service in 1987 and later years is depreciated over 27.5 years.

- For non-residential property put into service between January 1, 1987 and May 12, 1993, the depreciation period is 31.5 years. (If you had a binding contract to buy or build commercial property before May 13, 1993 and it was put into service before January 1, 1994, you use the 31.5 year recovery period.)

- For non-residential property put into service on or after May 13, 1993, it's 39 years.

- *Note this:* If you placed a building into service when a more generous depreciation schedule was allowed, you continue to use that schedule.

Depreciating a New Roof
. . . .

Q: *I own a commercial office building and recently paid $11,000 for a new roof. How do I depreciate that cost?*

A: Such improvements to property are treated the same as the property itself. Since it is a commercial building, the cost is depreciated over 39 years. Basically, you treat the roof as a separate piece of property.

How it works

For new investments, the first-year depreciation deduction depends on the month you put the property into service and is based on what accountants call the **midmonth convention**: Regardless of what day of the month you start depreciating the building, you get credit for half of the first month. Put a rental house into service on July 1, for example, and your first-year depreciation write-off would be for 5½ months—half of July plus the rest of the year.

To figure how much depreciation you can write off, begin with the depreciable basis—which is the cost of the building itself. (You can't depreciate the value of the land.) Divide the basis by either 27.5, 31.5, or 39—depending on the type of property and when it was put into service—to find the annual depreciation amount. Divide that by 12 to get the monthly figure, and multiply that amount by the number of months the property was available for rent, whether or not you actually had a tenant.

On a residential property with a $100,000 basis, a full year's depreciation would be $3,636 ($100,000 ÷ 27.5). One month's worth would be $303. Thanks to the midmonth convention, the first-year depreciation deduction for a property put into use anytime in July would be $1,667 ($303 x 5.5). If you put the property into service in December, the first-year write-off would be just $152.

After the first year, you deduct 3.64% of your basis for residential property each year until the final year when the write-off would be slightly smaller depending on the first-year deduction. For commercial property, a full-year write-off would be either 3.17% or 2.56% of basis, depending on whether you're depreciating the property over 31.5 or 39 years.

Remember this about depreciation: Each deduction you take reduces your *adjusted basis* in the property. When you sell the property, it's the adjusted basis that's compared to the sales proceeds to determine your profit on the sale. Thus every dollar you deduct as depreciation now can come back as a dollar of extra profit when you sell later.

If you make capital improvements to your rental property, the cost is added to your tax basis and will trim the taxable profit when you sell. Such improvements should be depreciated separately from the building. Say, for example, that four years after you begin renting a du-

Temporary Rental . . . .

Q: *I put my home on the market last October when I bought a new house. The old place didn't sell, though, and after several months I had to rent it out. After several months, I found a buyer. Now I'm told that because I rented it out I forfeited the right to defer the tax on the sale by rolling the profit into my new home. Is that true?*

A: Not necessarily. The deferral of tax applies only when you sell your principal residence and buy another home that costs at least as much within two years. Although that break isn't available for profit from the sale of a rental property, temporarily renting your home doesn't automatically deny you the chance to roll over the profit. The IRS permits such a rental as a matter of convenience if you can show that you continued to try to sell the house and indeed did sell it within the two-year rollover period.

plex you add a $20,000 addition. You would depreciate that $20,000 over its own 27.5-year tax life rather than simply including that amount when figuring future depreciation write-offs for the building.

Other Rental Expenses

You can still deduct the costs of producing rental income. Uncle Sam demands a share only of your *net* income, so it's clearly in your best interest to keep track of all the tax-saving expenses that can trim that figure. Be sure to count the following:

- **Mortgage interest**

- **Property taxes**

- **Insurance premiums you pay**

- **Fees paid to a management company**

- **Cost of newspaper ads** advertising the availability of the property

- **Legal or accounting costs** connected with drafting a lease or evicting tenants

- **Cost of repairs** to the property

- **Any utilities you pay** for your tenants or while the place is vacant between renters

- **Salary or wages you pay to others** to take care of the property, for cleaning or gardening, for example. This includes what you pay your child if he or she really works on the rental. The tax advantages of employing family members are discussed in Chapter 8.

- **The cost of travel to look after your properties.** This can include the cost of driving across town to repair a leaky faucet or the expenses—including travel, meals and lodging—of visiting out-of-town rental property. The principal purpose of such trips must be inspecting or working on your property. Taking a two-week vacation to Florida and spending an afternoon checking on a rental condo won't qualify. A week-long visit, five days of which are spent on painting and repairs to prepare the place for a new tenant, would qualify. (If you drive your own car, you can deduct actual expenses or the IRS standard mileage rate, which was 30 cents a mile in 1995, plus parking and tolls.)

Surviving the Passive-Loss Rules

As part of the crackdown on tax shelters, discussed earlier, Congress severely limited the ability of investors in "passive activities" to deduct losses from those investments against other kinds of income. Rental real estate is specifically labeled a passive activity.

That could have been a knockout blow for a lot of landlords who count on tax losses to make their real estate investments financially feasible. But the law includes a major exception to the passive-loss rules that makes rental real estate an oasis in the otherwise barren tax-shelter landscape. And special relief has been added for real estate professionals. First a look at the basic exception, then at the special rules for real estate pros.

If you qualify for exception, you can continue to deduct up to $25,000 of rental real estate losses against other income, such as your salary or interest and dividends.

To qualify, you must *actively participate* in the management of the property. Fortunately, the demands for passing that test aren't particularly onerous. You don't have to be on call for middle-of-the-night repairs, or to cut the grass and collect rents. The IRS rules don't say exactly what you do have to do, but even if you hire a management firm to handle day-to-day matters, you can be actively involved as long as you approve tenants, set the rent and okay capital improvements.

The $25,000 exception isn't for fat cats, though, no matter how actively they're involved. It is phased out as adjusted gross income (which is basically your income before subtracting itemized deductions, exemptions and rental losses) moves between $100,000 and $150,000. The $25,000 loss allowance is reduced by 50% of your AGI

Money Saver

An exception to the passive-loss rule could allow you to write off $25,000 of rental losses.

Money Saver

Store suspended passive losses for future years when you have passive income to shelter.

over $100,000. This is how the tax break evaporates as your income rises

You May Deduct

If AGI Is	Rental Losses Up To
Up to $100,000	$25,000
110,000	20,000
120,000	15,000
130,000	10,000
140,000	5,000
150,000	0

The $25,000 allowance and the phaseout schedule are the same whether you are married filing a joint return or single filing an individual return. If you are married filing separately, however, and you and your spouse lived together at any time during the year, neither spouse gets a loss allowance. In other words, although filing separately might pull AGI on one or both returns below the $150,000 level, the maneuver won't work to revitalize passive losses that would be denied on a joint return. If you are married and live apart from your spouse for the entire year, you can deduct up to $12,500 of otherwise disallowable losses if you file a separate return.

The $25,000 allowance doesn't protect losses generated by a limited partnership or any rental property in which you own less than 10%. But note this important point: Passive losses that you can't deduct immediately are not useless. They are suspended rather than obliterated. You can store the losses for future years and deduct them when you have passive income to shelter. And when you ultimately sell a rental property that generated passive losses, any unused losses are liberated to be deducted against any type of income, including your salary.

There's also a special break for real estate professionals that can free them from the general rule that rental real estate is *automatically* a passive activity. To qualify, basically, more than half the time you spend working during the year (and a minimum of 750 hours) has to be in the real estate business—defined to include property development, rental, management and real estate brokerage businesses. Of the 750 hours—that's 100 seven and a half hour days—at least 500 must be devoted to the rental activity, or only 100 hours if no one else spends more time on it than you do, to qualify. Thus, a builder or a real estate broker who spends only a few hours a month managing a rental would not qualify for this break. If you file a joint return, however, you can qualify if either you or your spouse passes the tests. The prize for passing, of course, is that rental losses aren't branded as passive and therefore can be deducted against other kinds of income.

Converting Your Home to a Rental Property

This is how many taxpayers get into the landlord business—by deciding to hold on to their house when they move to a new home. That may sound like an easy way to do it; after all, you know the property and the neighborhood and probably have a good idea of what would be a reasonable rent. If you can afford it, why not turn the old homestead into a rental property? That way you could enjoy the rental income and tax benefits, not to mention the continued appreciation on the place.

Uncle Sam has a few special twists for home-owners-turned-landlords. You do qualify to write off all the basic rental expenses, and if those expenses exceed your rental income, you can use the loss to shelter up to $25,000 of other income as long as you pass the active-participation and income tests outlined above. But you fall under a unique rule when it comes to figuring depreciation and calculating the gain or loss when you sell the property.

Although your home probably appreciated—perhaps quite significantly—while you lived in it, you don't get to use the higher value for depreciation purposes. Your tax basis in a converted residence is the *lower* of the house's value when you convert it to rental property or your adjusted basis. That means you're usually stuck with adjusted basis, which is generally what you originally paid for the place, plus the cost of improvements. If you rolled over the profit from a previous home—as discussed in Chapter 9— your basis is reduced by the amount of the profit on which you deferred the tax.

This rule can make a big difference in your depreciation write-offs. Say you bought your home several years ago for $50,000, $40,000 of which was the value of the building. Although you've made no improvements, it's now worth $120,000, $100,000 of which is the value of the building. If you convert it to rental use, your depreciation is based on the $40,000 basis.

Back in the days when the congressional penchant was to liberalize depreciation rules—that is, change the law to permit quicker write-offs—there was another rule to hold down depreciation on residences transformed to rentals. Basically, you had to use the depreciation rules in effect when you bought the property, not the possibly more liberal method in force when you converted.

Now that Congress has slowed down depreciation schedules, there's a new rule. If the depreciation method in effect when you bought the property would deliver bigger annual deductions—as it certainly would if you bought the house while ACRS was in effect from 1981 through 1986—you *can't* use it. Instead, you're stuck with current 27.5-year depreciation period. Heads you lose, tails the IRS wins.

Special vacation-home tax rules apply to a property you rent part-time and also use personally, and these are discussed in Chapter 9. *Also note this:* Converting a home to a rental property means forfeiting the right to roll over profit on the ultimate sale of the house into a new home. That tax break applies only when you're selling one principal residence to buy another principal home.

Tax myth debunked

One final point on the question of converting a home to a rental property. Some tax "experts" recommend this as a loophole to get around the law's prohibition of deducting a loss on the sale of a personal residence. If your home has lost value, they say, convert it to a rental and then sell it as a business property. The loss on a rental can be written off.

Sounds great, but it won't work. As noted above, when you convert a home to a rental property, the basis is either your basis or the current market value, *whichever is lower*. Since the goal of the maneuver is to deduct a loss, the value must be less than your basis. But it's that lower value that becomes the basis of the rental property. You would get to deduct a loss only if the house lost more value after the conversion…and that's probably not what you want.

Tax-Free Exchanges

You may have heard of a "tax-free exchange" of real estate, a concept that has definite appeal. This maneuver allows you to dispose of rental property without triggering an immediate tax bill on the gain. It's perfectly legal and can be much simpler than you might imagine—which explains why it's becoming an increasingly popular way for landlords to replace one rental property with another. If you're planning to sell one business or investment property and plow the proceeds back into a similar one, a tax-free exchange is worth a look. Although this isn't rocket science, you'll need professional help to make sure the deal passes muster with the IRS.

A tax-free exchange doesn't really make the profit on the first property tax-free. But it lets you put off the tax bill until the new property is sold. It's akin to the way homeowners are allowed to roll the profit from one principal residence into another. For an exchange to qualify, the properties involved have to be of a "like kind," but that term is liberally defined. Clearly, exchanging a rental house for another rental house is covered, but so is trading raw land for an apartment building. Only business and investment properties are covered, though, not vacation homes.

An exchange need not be a direct swap. You don't have to find someone who has a property you want and happens to want your property, too. That's allowed, but not likely…or necessary. The owner of the property you want

Money Saver

A tax-free exchange doesn't have to be a direct swap of one property for another.

doesn't have to wind up with your property. He or she can walk away from the deal with cash. In fact, an exchange can seem very much like selling one property and buying another. Although tax law is usually very clear that the substance of a deal is more important than its form, this is an exception. Even if a transaction looks a lot like a sale-and-purchase, if the proper *t*'s are crossed and *i*'s are dotted, it can be a tax-free exchange.

Typically, you contract with an independent third party to act as an intermediary who accepts cash for the property you're unloading and uses it to acquire the replacement. The law requires that the deal be set up so that

"You cannot deduct last year's taxes as a bad investment."

© Reprinted by Permission Tribune Media Services

you don't have "actual or constructive receipt" of the sales proceeds while the exchange is pending. Because you're to be kept at arm's length from the money while the deal is pending, the intermediary is supposed to be someone you can't control.

If all that sounds complicated, it is. But with the proper professional help—someone who has had experience with tax-free exchanges so you're not paying for their education—an exchange can pay off handsomely.

Consider an example. Say you have a rental house with an adjusted basis of $50,000 and that it is now worth $150,000. You'd like to expand your rental activities by buying a duplex with a price tag of $250,000. If you sell the first house, you'll owe tax on $100,000 of profit. That will cost you $28,000 if you're in the 28% bracket or protected by the 28% cap on long-term gains. Instead, assume you arrange for a tax-free exchange to acquire the duplex—for your $150,000 house plus $100,000 in cash. Properly structured, the deal lets you avoid that $28,000 tax tab.

Avoid is really too strong a term. Defer is more accurate. Your basis in the new building would not be its $250,000 price but rather your old $50,000 basis plus the $100,000 cash you had to put into the deal. When you later sell the duplex—assuming you don't work another tax-free exchange—the gain would be based on your $150,000 basis. That would give the IRS its delayed shot at the $100,000 of profit that built up in the first house.

Although holding off Uncle Sam is always an appealing prospect, like-kind exchanges have disadvantages. For one thing, your depreciation deductions on the new property will be held down because you carry over the basis from old property. Also, if you use a like-kind exchange instead of a sale in a year in which you have suspended passive losses, you can't use those losses to offset part of your profit on the property.

To qualify as tax-free, the exchange must take place within a specified time frame. You must identify the property you're going to receive within 45 days of transferring your property, and the trade must generally be completed within 180 days. Note, too, that the tax advantages can be lost if the exchange is with a related person (brother, sister, parent, grandparent, child, grandchild) and either property is disposed of within two years of the trade.

Installment Sales

Installment sales are a popular method for selling property, particularly rental real estate, because the seller can help grease the deal by providing at least part of the necessary financing for the buyer. Rather than demanding the full price up front, with an installment sale you agree to have the buyer pay at least part of the price in the future. And, wonder of wonders, the IRS doesn't tax your profit on the sale until you actually get the money.

If you will receive at least one payment in a year after the sale, you can use the installment method to report and pay tax on the profit as you receive it. Each year, the payments you receive will have three components:

- **Return of your basis,** which is nontaxable;

Money Saver

An installment sale lets you put off tax on your profit until the year you actually get the money.

- **Profit,** which is taxable; and

- **Interest on the "loan"** you made by financing the sale, and the IRS demands that you charge interest. This, too, is taxable.

The interest portion should be easy to identify and segregate. To determine how much of the rest of the payments is taxable, you must first figure the "gross profit percentage" on the sale.

If the sale isn't plagued by depreciation recapture, discussed next, the gross profit percentage is determined by dividing gain on the sale (proceeds minus basis) by the contract price. Assume that you sell for $150,000 a rental house that had a tax basis of $75,000. You receive a $25,000 down payment and the contract calls for $25,000 payments (plus interest) for each of the next five years. The gross profit percentage on this sale would be 50%: $75,000 profit ÷ $150,000 contract price. That means 50% of the down payment and of each subsequent payment you receive is taxable gain. The other half is the nontaxable return of your basis.

Depreciation Recapture

This is a complication—one of many—that may make you wonder whether the benefit of delaying the tax bill is worth the hassle. As mentioned earlier in this chapter, because depreciation reduces your basis, it translates into higher gain when you sell. And if you used an accelerated depreciation method—as most residential real estate investors who bought their property before 1987 do—you claimed more depreciation over the years than you would have been allowed under straight-line depreciation. Although the law encourages that, it also calls for that extra depreciation to be "recaptured" when you sell. The part of the profit that results from that extra depreciation is taxed as ordinary income rather than as capital gain. That can be painful if it means you're taxed in the 31%, 36% or 39.6% bracket instead of enjoying the 28%

cap that applies to long-term gains.

And, no matter what your tax bracket, the law demands that all depreciation recapture be taxed in the year of the sale, regardless of when the income is received. When considering an installment sale, consider the impact of depreciation recapture. You'll probably want the down payment to be at least enough to cover the tax bill due on the sale.

Depreciation recapture also affects the gross profit percentage on the deal. When figuring that ratio, you reduce your gross profit on the sale by the amount of depreciation recapture taxed in the year of the sale.

In the example above, if the seller had to report $5,000 of depreciation recapture, the gross profit percentage would be 46.6% ($70,000 ÷ $150,000) rather than 50%. Because some of the profit has to be reported up front, there's less of it to be taxed as the installment payments are received.

Minimum Interest

The law requires that you charge an adequate amount of interest on the installment sale, and it's not because the IRS is worried that you'd otherwise have an unfair advantage over banks and other lenders. The rationale is to prevent the price from being set artificially high to make up for interest-free or below-market financing. The IRS cares about the price of the sale, of course, because it affects the seller's gain or loss and the buyer's basis for depreciation.

You can meet the IRS definition of adequate and still give the buyer a break on the interest rate. The law demands that you charge a rate at least equal to the "applicable federal rate" (AFR) at the time of the sale. The AFR is set by the IRS and is basically what it costs the government to borrow money. Regardless of the AFR, however, you don't have to charge more than 9%, compounded semiannually. If the AFR at the time of the sale is less than 9%—it was just under 7% in late 1995—you can use the lower rate.

Money Saver

Life insurance loans let you get a built-up cash value tax-free.

If the contract fails to provide for adequate stated interest, the IRS has ways—very complicated ways—for figuring what part of each payment is "imputed" interest. That's the part treated as interest no matter what you call it. This affects your gain or loss and the buyer's basis. You have to report the imputed interest as income, and the buyer gets to count it as interest paid, which may be deductible by him or her. It's much easier to check with the IRS before finalizing a deal to be sure you include an adequate interest rate.

Life Insurance

As Congress has squeezed the tax benefits out of many investments, life insurance has taken on a special glow. Policies that combine investments with insurance—including whole life, universal life, variable life and single-premium life policies—enjoy tax-favored status. Part, and sometimes a very substantial part, of the premiums go not to pay for insurance but for investments that build cash value. Earnings on that cash value are protected from the IRS. The tax bill is deferred until you cash in the policy or, if it is in force when you die, the proceeds go to your beneficiary completely free of any federal income tax.

There are even ways to get at those earnings tax-free without dying for the privilege. Policyholders are permitted to borrow against the cash value in their policies. They are very special loans, too, since they never have to be paid back. Any outstanding loan at the time of death is simply deducted from the proceeds paid to beneficiaries. Although borrowers have to pay interest on the loan, in the sweetest deals the cash value in the policy earns just as much as the interest charged.

Single-Premium Policies

Insurance companies are always working to create policies that exploit the tax benefits of life insurance. And sometimes they're too successful. Consider, for example, a type of policy that was widely promoted as the last great tax shelter after Congress passed the Tax Reform Act of 1986: Single-premium life insurance policies.

These policies are mostly investment, with barely enough insurance veneer to qualify for the tax breaks. As the name implies, you pay the premium only once and that buys you a paid-up policy. The death benefit is small, but the key here is the investment. With most policies, the entire premium immediately starts earning interest—or may be invested in your choice of various stock and bond mutual funds—and starts building cash value. The cost of insurance comes out of your earnings.

Because the investment is wrapped inside an insurance policy, the earnings accumulate tax-free, just as money in an individual retirement account grows without annual interruption from the IRS. A $100,000 investment in a single-premium policy yielding 8% annually, for example, would grow to more than $466,000 in 20 years. The same amount in a taxable investment would reach just over $271,000 in two decades, if annual taxes in the 36% bracket were paid out of investment earnings.

The sweetest thing about a single-premium policy—before the congressional crackdown discussed below—was that the earnings could be completely tax-free. Although the earnings would be taxed if the policy were cashed in, investors could dance around the tax bill by borrowing against the policy. Many policies were designed so that there was effectively no charge for the loan. Interest on the loan was offset by earnings that continued to be credited to your cash value. Although structured as a loan, it worked like a withdrawal since such loans didn't have to be repaid.

If that sounds too good to be true, your hearing is good. Congress has closed the door on tax-free loans from single-premium policies. Basically, unless you pay premiums for at least seven years, policy loans are considered taxable withdrawals. In addition to the tax, there's a 10% penalty unless you're at least 59½ years old or disabled.

There's an important exception for single-premium policies purchased before June 21, 1988. Those older policies retain the tax- and penalty-free loan feature.

Despite the crackdown on single-premium policies, other cash-value life insurance policies still sport the tax advantage of tax-free buildup of cash value and the loan privilege. Insurers were quick to create "seven-pay" policies to stretch premiums over a long enough period to maintain the policyholder's right to tax-free loans.

Some policies allow partial withdrawals of cash value, too. As long as the policy isn't caught up in the single-premium life rules, such withdrawals can be tax-free. The IRS assumes that the first money pulled out is a return of your premiums rather than the earnings. When withdrawals exceed your total investment in the policy, however, additional withdrawals are considered taxable income.

Annuities

These are also life insurance products sporting tax advantages. But there's really almost no life insurance involved. The hint of insurance—just enough to earn the tax break—guarantees that if you die before beginning withdrawals, and the annuity is worth less at that time than the total of your investments, the insurance company will pay your beneficiary an amount equal to your investments.

Annuities come in two basic flavors: fixed and variable. With a *fixed annuity,* your investment earns interest at a rate set by the insurance company, a rate that can change periodically in line with market interest rates. A *variable annuity* gives you investment options much like a family of mutual funds. The insurance company offers you the choice of several funds—stock, bond, money-market, and so on—and your return depends on the success of the investments you choose.

Unlike bank CDs and mutual funds, however, the annuity contract serves as an impenetrable wrapper that keeps the tax collector's hands off your earnings. No tax is due until you pull funds out of the contract, presumably in retirement, either in a lump sum or by annuitizing the contract and having the company make payments to you for life.

Such tax-deferred growth gives funds invested in an annuity the same advantage as cash stashed in an individual retirement account, discussed in Chapter 11. Unlike an IRA, though, you can't deduct amounts put into an annuity.

If you cash in the annuity before retirement, you'll pay dearly. For one thing, most contracts impose surrender charges during the first several years. Any *earnings* pulled out of the annuity are taxable, and if you're under age 59 ½ you'll be hit with a 10% penalty tax. But what portion of a withdrawal is earnings? That's easy—if you cash in the annuity and pull out all the funds. You are taxed—and possibly penalized—on the difference between your original investment and what you get.

It's trickier, though, if you pull out only part of the money, and it depends on when you made the annuity investment. If it was purchased on or before August 13, 1982, the IRS considers the first money pulled out of the annuity to be a tax-free return of your investment. Only after you have recovered your full investment is any further withdrawal taxed. For investments after that date, however, the rule is turned around. The first money out is considered earnings—taxable and potentially subject to the 10% penalty.

Say, for example, that you invest $10,000 in an annuity today and its value grows to $25,000 in ten years. If you were to cash in the contract, $15,000 would be taxed, and if you were under age 59 ½, the 10% early-withdrawal penalty would apply to that $15,000. The other $10,000 would be a return of your original investment—untaxed and penalty-free. If you simply withdrew $10,000 from the contract, it would all be taxed and penalized. If this investment had been made on or before August 13, 1982, however, that $10,000 withdrawal would be a nontaxable return of your investment. (If you choose to receive lifetime payments, a portion of each one is tax-free, as discussed in Chapter 12.)

The 10% penalty does not apply to payouts to taxpayers under age 59 ½ who are disabled. Nor does it apply to any payment that is part of a series of periodic payments based on your life expectancy. If you decide to annuitize a

Money Saver

When you shop for an annuity, be sure that the fees charged by the insurance company don't devour a good portion of the tax breaks.

contract at age 50 and receive equal payments over the rest of your life, for example, you would dodge the early-withdrawal penalty.

A key to shopping for an annuity is to watch that the fees charged by the insurance company don't devour a good portion of the tax breaks. And, generally, investing in an annuity makes sense only after you've taken full advantage of other tax-deferred retirement plans, such as IRAs and company 401(k) retirement plans, that give you more bang for your buck.

Savings Accounts and CDs

Ho, hum. Boring old savings accounts and certificates of deposit. Not much opportunity for tax savings here. But on the bright side, the tax treatment is fairly simple and straightforward: The interest you earn is fully taxable. There are a few twists, though.

Interest earned by a savings account is taxable in the year it's credited to your account, whether or not you withdraw the money. Even if a savings and loan or credit union labels the income on your account as dividends, the IRS says it's interest, and that's how you should report it.

With certificates of deposit that mature in a year or less, the interest income is taxable in the year the deposit matures. This rule permits you to shift taxable income from one year to the next and hold off Uncle Sam from one April 15 to the next. If you invest in a six-month CD in July 1996, for example, the interest will not be taxable until 1997, when the certificate matures. You'd report the interest on your 1997 return filed in the spring of 1998.

Interest paid on time deposits with maturities of more than a year is taxable as it's credited each year. The institution where you invest should send you a notice of how much to report on your return.

If you withdraw funds early from a CD, the bank or s&l is likely to exact an early-withdrawal penalty. You can deduct that charge even if you don't itemize your deductions. It's an "adjustment to income" claimed on the front of the Form 1040.

What about "gifts," such as the ubiquitous toasters offered by savings institutions to induce you to make a deposit? The value of the gift is included in the amount the bank tells the IRS it paid you during the year. The extra tax would be insignificant if a toaster is involved. But if you receive a pricey inducement—cars have been offered on multiyear, jumbo deposits—you could face a hefty tax bill.

Children's Accounts

If you set up custodial accounts for your minor children, the interest earned should be reported on the child's tax return if the child's total income for the year exceeds $650, unless you report the income on your own return, as discussed in Chapter 8. (The $650 threshold applies in 1995 and 1996. It will rise in the future with inflation.) Worries that parents were dumping funds into kids' accounts so the interest would be taxed in the child's low tax bracket rather than the parents' higher one prompted the enactment of the "kiddie tax," which is also discussed in Chapter 8.

Joint Accounts

When married couples who file joint returns own joint accounts, there's no tax problem. All the interest is simply reported on the joint return. When unmarried taxpayers share an account, though, things can be complicated.

If you have a joint account with your sister, for example, the s&l will report income to the IRS in the name of the owner whose social security number is listed first on the account. That means you could be paying tax on interest that really went to your sibling. You can avoid that, but it will take some effort.

Here's how to do it: Assume you receive a Form 1099–INT from the s&l showing $1,500 of interest but

Time Saver

With a joint account, be sure to list first the social security number of the owner who's supposed to report the interest to the IRS.

that you and your sister have agreed to share the income in proportion to the amount invested in the account. You each have deposited half the funds, so $750 of the interest is yours, $750 hers. Because it was all reported to you, you're considered the "nominee recipient" of your sister's $750.

To shift the tax bill where it belongs, you need a blank 1099–INT form, which you can get at a local IRS office or by calling 800–TAX–FORM. Fill it out, showing $750 of interest income for your sister. Give your sister a copy of the form—by January 31 after the year for which the income was reported—and file another copy, along with a Form 1096 (also available from the IRS), with the IRS service center for your area by February 28. With those forms, you show yourself to be the payer of the interest and your sister to be the recipient. When you file your own tax return, you report the full $1,500 of interest as income on Schedule B, but also subtract the $750, labeling it as a "nominee distribution." It's much easier to maintain separate accounts.

But what if you have signed on as a joint owner of a savings account (or interest-bearing checking account) belonging to a parent, for example, simply as a convenience so you can withdraw funds for them if necessary? The key is to be sure that the real owner of the account—your mother or father in this example—is the one whose social security number is listed first. The interest will be reported in her or his name, not yours. If things get fouled up and the income is reported in your name, you'll have to go through the nominee-distribution rigmarole.

Investment Interest and Expenses

Although Congress has made many kinds of interest paid on loans nondeductible, carrying charges on a loan used to make an investment can be written off—*in most cases*. As usual, the law includes exceptions and limitations to keep you on your toes.

First, the exceptions. For the interest to be deductible, the investment has to be designed to produce taxable income. Interest on a margin loan from your broker to invest in stocks or taxable bonds qualifies. But if the borrowed money is used to invest in tax-exempt securities, the interest is not deductible. Ditto if you borrow to buy a single-premium life insurance policy or annuity. Congress doesn't want the IRS subsidizing loans to help you purchase tax-favored investments.

If you borrow to invest in a passive activity, the interest is an expense of the passive activity—and thus is deductible only to the extent of passive income.

There's a limit to how much investment interest you can deduct. The write-off is restricted to the amount of taxable investment income you report. But what is *investment income?* Before 1993, it included interest, dividends and capital gains. Now, however, if you benefit from the 28% tax cap on long-term capital gains discussed at the beginning of this chapter, you can't include your capital gains when figuring your investment interest limit. This affects only taxpayers in the 31%, 36% or 39.6% bracket, and is designed to prevent them from deducting interest in those brackets if capital gains from the assets they borrow to invest in are taxed at just 28%. (If you're affected, you do have the option of foregoing the 28% cap on long-term gains. If you pay tax on those profits in your top tax bracket, you can include the capital gains when setting your investment interest limit. Although it's difficult to construct a scenario where this would make sense, it might if, for example, the bigger investment interest deduction pulled you down into a lower tax bracket.)

Any interest you're unable to deduct because of the cap is not lost forever. It may be carried over to future years and deducted as soon as there's sufficient investment income to offset it, or on the final tax return after your death.

What if you borrow money on a home-equity line of credit and use the funds for an investment? Is the interest deducted as home mortgage interest or as investment interest? It's up to you. If you opt to treat it as investment interest, the deduction is controlled by these restrictions. If

Money Saver

You can still deduct interest on loans used to make taxable investments.

The cost of computer software and on-line services used to track your investments is a deductible expense.

you treat it as home-equity debt, the interest is deductible up to the limits discussed in Chapter 9.

Investment interest is deducted on Schedule A with your other itemized deductions. But in almost all cases you must also file Form 4952, on which you compute the allowable deduction and, if necessary, what part of your expense must be carried over to future years.

Other Investment Expenses

Even if you don't borrow to help finance your investment portfolio, there are plenty of expenses associated with trying to make money with your money. Generally, the most important costs are those that affect your basis in the property. The importance of maintaining meticulous records to verify your basis cannot be overemphasized. Record keeping is the key to insuring that you're not overtaxed when you sell the investment.

Some expenses can be written off in the year you pay them, including the following:

- **Rental of a safe-deposit box** used to store taxable securities

- **Investment counselor** or management fees

- **Subscriptions** to investment-advisory newsletters

- **Cost of books** and magazines purchased for investment advice

- **Cost of computer software and on-line services** used to track your investments

- **State and local transfer taxes** on the sale of securities

- **Fees paid to a broker or other agent to collect bond interest or stock dividends.** (Unlike commissions paid to brokers on the purchase of stock—a cost which is added to basis—this type of fee is deductible.)

- **Cost of travel to see your broker to discuss investments.** (This does not include simply dropping by the broker's office to check on the general condition of the market or to watch the ticker tape.) If you drive your own car, you can deduct the actual cost (see Chapter 13) or the IRS standard rate, which was 30 cents a mile in 1995. The 1996 rate may be higher. To the standard rate, you can add what you pay for parking or tolls.

If some of those expenses seem to fall in the nickel-and-dime category, you may appreciate what Congress has done to relieve you of the burden of keeping track. In a move to "simplify" your tax life, the law now allows such expenses to be deducted only to the extent that they—when added to all your other "miscellaneous" expenses— exceed 2% of your adjusted gross income. Chapter 15 pinpoints other expenses that fall in the miscellaneous cauldron for purposes of passing the 2% threshold.

This is supposed to simplify matters because if you're sure you're not going to rack up

"His last request is to call up the Internal Revenue Service and tell them to go to hell!"

From the Wall Street Journal; Permission, Cartoon Features Syndicate.

enough expenses to garner any tax benefit, you theoretically don't need to keep track of any of the costs. The flaw in the logic, of course, is that you won't know whether you'll pass the 2% barrier unless you keep track of qualifying expenses throughout the year.

There is no such uncertainty about one kind of investment expense that used to be deductible: The cost of attending an investment convention, seminar or similar meeting. As discussed in Chapter 13, such write-offs are now forbidden.

Retirement Plans: Do It Yourself

Note: At our deadline, Congress was considering significant changes for individual retirement accounts, including allowing taxpayers with higher incomes to deduct contributions, increasing the amount that can be set aside for a non-working spouse and even creating a brand new type of IRA from which all withdrawals would be tax-free. The changes would likely apply to 1996 and future years. When Congress makes up its mind, we'll prepare a free update for you. You can get it by contacting the author at the address on page i. The rules described here are those in effect in late 1995.

The promise of longer life spans brings with it the guarantee that you'll need more money to sustain a comfortable lifestyle in retirement. The tax law is filled with incentives to encourage and help you save for your golden years. This chapter focuses on do-it-yourself plans: individual retirement accounts (IRAs), Keogh plans and Simplified Employee Pensions. Chapter 12 addresses plans that must be set up by your employer: pension and profit sharing plans, 401(k) and 403(b) plans, as well as social security.

Individual Retirement Accounts

It's no wonder IRAs are so attractive. They strike a blow for two of our most cherished goals: avoiding taxes and providing for a financially secure retirement. When

IRAs first became widely available in 1981, the accounts were immediately dubbed "everybody's tax shelter." Money deposited in an IRA could be deducted on your tax return, and earnings inside the account were protected from the IRS.

With those advantages, the decision of whether or not to use an IRA was a cinch—the epitome of a "no-brainer" investment decision. You put $2,000 into an IRA and, in the days of the 50% tax bracket, could automatically knock as much as $1,000 off your tax bill: an immediate return as high as 50%. You didn't have to be a financial wizard—or pay one for advice—to understand the value of an IRA deduction or the power of tax-deferred earnings inside the tax shelter. Promoters promised us the chance to retire as IRA millionaires, and millions of us believed. The threat of a penalty if you tap your IRA before age 59½ seemed a small price to pay.

Unfortunately, Congress couldn't leave well enough alone and, in 1986, added restrictions that destroyed the beautiful simplicity of the IRA. Although everyone who qualified for an old IRA can still make contributions, some taxpayers don't get to deduct those deposits. The restrictions are explained in detail after a review of the basic IRA rules.

"I have always felt that tax reform is a change in the tax law that I favor, or if it is the other man defining tax reform, it is a change in the tax law that he favors."

—SENATOR RUSSELL LONG

The IRA Basics

The IRA tax shelter is open to anyone under age 70½ who receives compensation, which is earnings from a job rather than income from investments. Income that counts for IRA purposes includes:

- **Wages, salaries and tips;**

- **Sales commissions;**

- **Professional fees;**

- **Bonuses;**

- **Self-employment income; and**

- **Alimony.**

Money Saver

There's no minimum age for having an IRA. A single $2,000 deposit at age 10 could grow to $375,000 by age 65.

Income that doesn't count as compensation includes:

- **Interest and dividends;**

- **Profit from the sale of stocks or other property;**

- **Rental income;**

- **Pension or annuity income; and**

- **Deferred compensation.**

The annual limit on IRA contributions is $2,000 or 100% of your compensation, whichever is less. Thus, if you earn just $1,000, your maximum IRA contribution for the year is $1,000.

There is no minimum age for IRA participation. If your 10-year-old has compensation—from a paper route, say, or from working in a family business, as discussed in Chapter 8—he or she can stash up to $2,000 of that pay in an IRA. (The extended period of time such a contribution would have to grow inside an IRA accentuates the power of this tax shelter. A single, $2,000 investment at age 10 would grow to more than $375,000 by age 65, assuming an average 10% annual yield, and to more than $1 million with a 12% average yield.)

As explained later, the law demands that you begin withdrawing from your IRA by April 1 of the year after you reach age 70½. That age also brings an end to your IRA deposits. Starting with the year you reach age 70½, you can no longer contribute to your account. By that time you're supposed to be enjoying your retirement nest egg, not continuing to use tax breaks to build it up. For taxpayers born between July 1, 1925, and June 30, 1926, for example, 1995 was the final year for IRA contributions. (Those deposits would be written off on returns filed in the Spring of 1996.) The following table shows the last year of IRA eligibility for taxpayers with certain birthdays.

Birthday Between	*Last Year for IRA Contribution*
July 1, 1925 to June 30, 1926	1995
July 1, 1926 to June 30, 1927	1996
July 1, 1927 to June 30, 1928	1997
July 1, 1928 to June 30, 1929	1998
July 1, 1929 to June 30, 1930	1999
July 1, 1930 to June 30, 1931	2000

Spousal IRAs

There's an exception to the $2,000 annual limit for couples in which one spouse does not have a job. In addition to your own IRA, you can open an account for a non-working spouse and contribute a total of $2,250 to the two accounts. The money can be split however you wish, as long as neither account gets more than $2,000. Also, you may continue contributing up to $2,000 of your compensation to a non-working spouse's account even after you reach age 70½, assuming he or she is under that age.

When both spouses have jobs, each may have his or her own IRA with a $2,000 contribution limit. That means a working couple can sock away as much as $4,000 in IRAs each year, as long as each spouse has at least $2,000 in compensation. (As noted earlier, one change Congress is considering is to boost the amount that can go into an IRA for a non-working spouse.)

IRA Custodial Fee

• •

Q: *Each year my broker takes $25 out of my IRA account to pay his custodial fee. Is that cost deductible?*

A: No. If you paid the fee separately, however, it might have a tax benefit. The cost would be included with your other miscellaneous expenses and you can deduct the amount by which the total exceeds 2% of your adjusted gross income. Even if you don't earn a deduction, there's an advantage to paying the fee separately rather than having your broker dip into your IRA. The money stays in your account and continues to grow tax-deferred. Once you near the age when you'll begin withdrawing from the IRA, however, it's probably better to let the broker take the fee out of the account. Basically, that lets you pay the fee with pre-tax dollars, since money paid out of the account is taxable to you.

Putting in too much

The government is serious about the annual limits. Excess contributions are hit with a 6% penalty tax. Assume, for example, that you work part-time and, expecting to earn more than $2,000 for the year, you deposit $2,000 in your IRA at the beginning of the year. Because you have a bad year, though, your earnings total just $1,500. Your deduction is limited to $1,500, and the extra $500 is subject to the 6% penalty. That will cost you $30. The penalty applies each year until the excess is either withdrawn or absorbed by the unused portion of a future year's contribution. If you qualify for a $2,000 contribution the following year, for example, depositing just $1,500 would absorb the $500 excess contribution and avoid another 6% penalty. You'd get to deduct the extra $500 in the second year.

It's possible to dodge the first-year penalty, too, by withdrawing the extra money before you file your tax return for the year involved. Because you had not yet deducted the IRA deposit, you don't have to report the withdrawal as income. Any earnings on the extra $500 should be withdrawn from the account, too. That amount would be taxed, and if you are under age 59½ at the time, the earnings would also be hit with a 10% early-withdrawal penalty, discussed later.

A matter of timing

The deadline for making your IRA contribution each year is the day your tax return is due for that year. That's usually April 15, of course, but it can be a day or two later if the 15th falls on a weekend. If you mail your IRA contribution, you meet the deadline if it's postmarked on the due date.

Although you may be tempted to hold off as long as possible to make your deposit, making it sooner rather than later can pay off handsomely. The earlier you make your contribution, the sooner your money begins earning in the supercharged environment of the IRA, as the following table indicates. In each case, an annual deposit of $2,000 and a yield of 10% is assumed.

Total at End of	If Annual Deposit Made at:	
	End of Year	Beginning of Year
year 5	$12,210	$13,431
10	31,875	35,062
15	63,545	69,899
20	114,550	126,005
25	196,694	216,364
30	328,988	361,887
35	542,049	596,254
40	885,185	973,703

Restricted Write Offs

Here's the fly in the ointment, which, because of the confusion it has caused, has led an untold number of taxpayers to stop adding to their IRAs. As one of many ways Congress has concocted to raise taxes without raising tax rates, the law now restricts the right of millions of taxpayers to deduct IRA contributions. There are two tests for determining whether you're among the losers.

First, are you an "active participant" in a company pension plan? You are, as far as the law is concerned, if you are eligible to participate in any of the following types of plans, whether or not your benefits are vested:

- **Pension, profit-sharing or stock-bonus plan**

- **401(k) plan**

- **Simplified employee pension plan (SEP)**

- **Qualified annuity plan**

- **Retirement plan for state and federal employees, including civil service and the Federal Employees Retirement System**

- **Keogh plan**

- **Tax-sheltered annuity (403(b) plan)**

If you're eligible for such a plan during any part of the year, you're considered covered for the entire year as far as the IRA test goes. (If you are in a profit-sharing plan but no contribution is made to your account for the year, however, you are not considered covered for that year.) The Form W–2 you receive from your employer should indicate to you—and the IRS—whether you are an active participant in a company plan.

Note this: If you are married and either you or your spouse is covered by an employer-sponsored plan, both of you are regarded as covered for purposes of this test and your IRA deductions are in jeopardy.

If you are not tripped up by the company-plan test, you can continue to deduct your IRA contributions regardless of how high your income is.

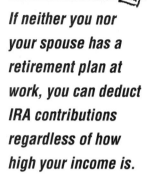

Money Saver

If neither you nor your spouse has a retirement plan at work, you can deduct IRA contributions regardless of how high your income is.

The income test

If you are covered by a plan, however, a second test will determine whether you can write off your contributions. The IRA deduction is phased out for active participants in company plans whose "modified" adjusted gross income (AGI)—which is basically AGI before subtracting IRA contributions—exceeds $25,000 on an individual or head-of-household return or $40,000 on a joint return. *If your AGI is below the threshold, you can deduct your full IRA contribution.* As AGI passes the $25,000 or $40,000 level, however, the maximum deduction is reduced by $10 for each $50 of additional AGI. (If you exclude from income any interest on U.S. savings bonds used to pay college costs, as discussed in Chapter 10, that amount is included when figuring modified AGI for this test.)

For example, AGI of $5,000 over the threshold would cut the maximum annual deduction to $1,000. You could still contribute up to $2,000, but whether you deposited $1,000, $2,000 or any amount in between, only $1,000 would be deductible. On a joint return reporting AGI of $45,000, each spouse could write off up to $1,000 of IRA contributions, assuming husband and wife each had compensation of at least $1,000 during the year.

There is a $200 floor under the deductible IRA. When your AGI is between $9,000 and $10,000 over the

---

IRA for Children

Q: *I've heard of something called the "kid IRA." Can I put money in an IRA for my child?*

A: Technically, no. But as soon as your child has any earned income—from baby sitting or a paper route, perhaps—he or she can contribute up to $2,000 of that income to an IRA. Sure, it's doubtful that your teenager will want to put earnings away for retirement. But you can encourage that by offering to replace funds he or she stashes in an IRA. (It doesn't really matter whether the child's actual earnings, or a gift from you, goes into the account.) For added encouragement, remember the power of long-term compounding in an IRA. Assume a 14-year-old earns $200 a year baby sitting for three years in a row and makes three $200 contributions to an IRA. And, assume she never adds another dime to the account and the investments earn an average of 10% a year. By the time she turns 65, the IRA will hold over $70,000.

threshold, the permissible deduction stays at $200, rather than sliding to a laughably low $10 before disappearing. The table below shows how rising AGI diminishes the allowable IRA deduction.

Adjusted Gross Income		Top IRA Deduction
Single Return	Joint Return	
Up to $25,000	Up to $40,000	$2,000
25,500	40,500	1,900
26,000	41,000	1,800
26,500	41,500	1,700
27,000	42,000	1,600
27,500	42,500	1,500
28,000	43,000	1,400
28,500	43,500	1,300
29,000	44,000	1,200
29,500	44,500	1,100
30,000	45,000	1,000
30,500	45,500	900
31,000	46,000	800
31,500	46,500	700
32,000	47,000	600
32,500	47,500	500
33,000	48,000	400
33,500	48,500	300
34,000	49,000	200
34,500	49,500	200
35,000	50,000	0

Note: On a joint return, each spouse who earns at least the equivalent of the top IRA deduction corresponding to his or her adjusted gross income may deduct that amount.

When you contribute to a spousal account—so the top unrestricted deduction is $2,250 instead of $2,000—the deduction is also phased out as your AGI exceeds the $40,000 threshold for a joint return. Here's an example of how it works: When AGI is $45,000, the $5,000 of excess AGI is 50% of the $10,000 phase-out range. Your combined deduction for regular and spousal accounts would be limited to 50% of $2,250, or $1,125. You could split that amount however you wish, as long as neither account receives more than $1,000— half of the customary $2,000 limit.

What if your spouse is covered by a pension plan at work but you're not? Does filing separate returns preserve your right to an IRA deduction? The answer is no. The law is clear that if you and your spouse live together during any part of the year and one of you is covered by a retirement plan at work, you're both considered covered for the purposes of this rule. And the deduction phase-out range for married taxpayers who file separate returns is $0 to $10,000; the right to any IRA deduction disappears when AGI on the separate return hits $10,000. However, if you are married but you and your spouse didn't live together during the year, you are considered single as far as the IRA rule goes. If you're not covered by a company plan, you can deduct IRA contributions regardless of how much you earn. If you are covered, the phase-out begins at $25,000.

By Geoffrey Moss © 1986. Washington Post Writers Group. Reprinted with permission.

(One plan before Congress would gradually raise the phase-out ranges to $85,000 to $95,000 for single filers and $100,000 to $110,000 for joint filers.)

Do non-deductible contributions make sense?

That's the big question if your write-offs are restricted, and expert opinion runs the gamut from an emphatic yes to an absolute no.

One thing is certain: Without the write-off, the IRA's appeal is tarnished. But don't sell the wounded shelter short. Indeed, if you were planning to retire a millionaire based on annual $2,000 contributions, the same $2,000 deposits will still make you a millionaire. The money will grow just as fast in a nondeductible IRA as in a deductible one. The difference is that each contribution will cost you more because Uncle Sam will no longer subsidize your retirement savings with the instant gratification of a tax deduction.

Accounting headaches

The creation of nondeductible IRAs brings new accounting headaches. Before they arrived, the rules were straightforward. Just as every dime you put into an IRA was deductible, every dime withdrawn was taxed as ordinary income. That's still the way it is for taxpayers who make only deductible contributions. However, if you make nondeductible deposits, part of each withdrawal will be a return of your already-taxed investment. Congress doesn't want to tax you twice on that money, so that part will be tax-free.

But the lawmakers didn't make it easy. Rather than let taxpayers set up separate accounts—and then choose whether to withdraw taxable funds from a deductible IRA or tax-free money from a nondeductible account—the law says that an ever-changing percentage of each withdrawal will be taxed. You have to determine what's what. Here is how you do that:

1. Find the total amount in all of your IRA accounts at the end of the year.

2. Find the total that you withdrew from the accounts during the year.

3. Add (1) and (2).

4. Find your *basis* in your IRAs—the total of your nondeductible contributions over the years minus any tax-free withdrawals made in previous years.

5. Divide (4) by (3). That's the percentage of your year that is tax-free. The rest is taxable.

Here's an example: Assume your IRAs hold $50,000 at year end. Your basis is $10,000, reflecting your nondeductible contributions. During the year, you withdrew $10,000 from your accounts. Adding that amount to the year-end balance brings the total to $60,000. Dividing

Time Saver

When you begin withdrawing IRA funds, skipping nondeductible contributions lets you avoid maddening paperwork.

$10,000 by $60,000 pinpoints your basis at 16.66% of the total. That means 16.66% of your $10,000 in withdrawals ($1,666) would be tax-free. The other $8,334 would be taxed in your top bracket.

In the following year, your basis would be $8,334—the original $10,000 minus the $1,666 you recovered tax-free.

Investors who make nondeductible IRA contributions must file Form 8606 with their tax returns—showing the nondeductible amount. You have to keep copies of the annual forms for as long as you have an IRA (perhaps for the rest of your life) so you can prove what part of your distributions are a tax-free return of those nondeductible investments.

The aggravation of aggregation

The demand that taxpayers aggregate deductible and nondeductible IRAs—for purposes of determining what part of a withdrawal is taxable—has convinced some advisers that investors should shun the nondeductible variety. Although getting to treat at least part of a withdrawal as tax-free may appear to be an advantage, consider the potential problems.

Say you have $98,000 in an IRA made up of deductible contributions and earnings. Caught by the new restrictions, you make a $2,000 nondeductible contribution, and shortly after you report it on your tax return you decide to withdraw the $2,000. Thanks to the aggregation rule, you can't treat the $2,000 as a return of that nondeductible investment. Rather, you would have to pay tax on 98% of it. In the 28% bracket, that would cost you $549. The taxable part would also be hit with the 10% early-withdrawal penalty if you were under 59½. Had you invested the $2,000 outside the IRA, you could have retrieved it without being taxed or worrying about that penalty.

Just how significant this potential problem is to you depends on several factors, including the size of your IRA and how soon you'll want to get at your money. It's something to keep in mind, though, when you choose between nondeductible IRA contributions and alternative investments.

Should you open a separate account for any nondeductible contributions? The aggregation rule would seem to make separate accounts superfluous, but keeping the money separate may simplify your bookkeeping chores. Your choice may turn on whether using an additional account will involve extra costs.

The hindsight rule

If your income is close to the new IRA thresholds, you may not know until the end of the year whether your contribution will earn you a deduction. If your decision on whether to continue using an IRA turns on its deductibility, should you wait until you're certain? Remember, it's best to put your cash in early in the year. The deductible-nondeductible twist to the equation doesn't alter that.

Fortunately, you don't have to make an irreversible decision. You can put your contribution in at the beginning of the year and start earning tax-deferred income. If it turns out that your AGI is so high that you can't deduct the contribution—or you discover a better investment for the money—you can withdraw the funds. As long as the contribution and any earnings on it are out of the IRA by the time your tax return is due, there will be little or no penalty. If you are under 59½ when you pull the funds out, the IRS will impose the 10% early-withdrawal penalty to the earnings on the now-withdrawn deposit. If you contribute $2,000 in January and it earns $200 by the time you change your mind, for example, you would withdraw $2,200. The $200 of earnings would be taxable in your top bracket and the 10% penalty would add $20 to your tax bill. If you are at least 59½, there's no penalty.

The Power of the IRA

Despite the restrictions, the tax incentives to sign up for an IRA are compelling. Remember, most taxpayers aren't affected by the limits. If you're among the lucky group, every dollar you deposit can be deducted on your tax return. In the 28% bracket, a $2,000 deduction saves you $560 immediately—money that would otherwise go to the IRS. (You get this write-off even if you don't itemize other deductions.) An added bonus is that most states bestow similar tax benefits on IRAs. If you live in a state with an 8% income tax and you get to deduct the $2,000 IRA deposit on your state return, you save another $160.

You get an advantage even if you can't deduct your contributions. As long as funds are tucked inside the IRA tax shelter, earnings accumulate tax-free. Holding off the IRS gives the power of compound interest added magic.

Consider this example: You put $2,000 aside each year in a taxable investment yielding 10%. Each year, the IRS demands 28% of the earnings and, at the end of 20 years, your account holds a total of $89,838.

Now put that same $2,000 a year in an IRA where growth won't be interrupted annually by Uncle Sam. Assuming the same 10% yield, at the end of 20 years your account will total $125,005. The $35,000-plus difference is the power of the IRA tax shelter. Although all the IRA earnings would be taxable when withdrawn—while the tax bill has already been paid on the non-IRA investment—you still come out well ahead.

The following table shows how a series of $2,000 annual contributions made at the beginning of each year will grow inside an IRA, assuming various investment results.

IF $2,000 ANNUAL CONTRIBUTIONS

Balance at End of	Assuming Compound Annual Yield of				
	6%	8%	10%	12%	15%
year 5	$ 11,951	$ 12,672	$ 13,431	$ 14,230	$ 15,507
10	27,943	31,291	35,062	39,309	46,699
15	49,345	58,649	69,899	83,507	109,435
20	77,985	98,846	126,005	161,397	235,620
25	116,313	157,909	216,364	298,668	489,424
30	167,603	244,692	361,887	540,585	999,914
35	236,242	372,204	596,254	966,926	2,026,691
40	328,095	559,562	973,703	1,718,285	4,091,908

Early Withdrawal Penalty

If the tax breaks are the carrots Congress uses to encourage you to save for your retirement, penalties for early withdrawal are the sticks that make sure you keep at it. Make no mistake: IRA money is different from funds you are saving on your own for, say, a child's college education or a retirement cushion. You may think of those accounts as sacrosanct, but you know you can put your hands on the cash in an emergency.

It's different with an IRA. When you accept the tax breaks, you sign the government on as a partner—and a stern one at that. Dip into the account early—as far as the law is concerned, generally anytime before you're 59 ½ is early—and you'll be hit with a 10% penalty for premature distribution. Take $5,000 out at age 50, for example, and you probably will be slapped with a $500 penalty. In addition, the full $5,000 will be included in your income for the year and taxed in your top tax bracket. (If part of the withdrawal is attributed to nondeductible IRA contributions that part is neither taxed nor subject to the 10% penalty.)

IRA and Divorce

• •

Q: *My wife and I are getting a divorce, and one of our major assets is her IRA. Can I get that IRA as part of the divorce settlement, or would it have to be cashed in and taxes and penalties paid?*

A: This is the one instance—other than death of the owner—that the law allows the ownership of an IRA to be transferred. If the IRA is transferred by a written divorce decree, or a document related to the decree, the transfer is tax-free. The IRA would then be yours, so withdrawals would be taxed to you and, if you are under 59½, subject to the 10% early-withdrawal penalty.

The premature-distribution penalty is waived if you become permanently disabled. To qualify for this exception, the IRS says you must be unable to do any substantial gainful activity and that the mental or physical disability must be expected to last longer than a year or lead to death. The 10% penalty also does not apply if an IRA is distributed after the death of the owner, regardless of how old he or she is at the time of death or the age of the beneficiary.

In addition to those exceptions, there's another way to get at your IRA money early without penalty. It's explained beginning on page 278. (One proposal before Congress would allow penalty-free early withdrawals if the money is used for specific purposes, such as buying a home or paying college bills. If such exceptions are okayed, we'll provide the details in the free update you can order by contacting the author at the address on page i.

Investment Options

You have almost unlimited choices of where to invest, and as the table on page 268 demonstrates, a slight difference in investment performance can make a major difference in how comfortable your retirement will be.

You can choose a bland—but predictable—investment, such as a bank account, or go for spicy, speculative stock in a new company. You can buy high-grade corporate bonds, zero-coupon bonds or junk bonds. You can choose all sorts of mutual funds, buy into a shopping center or sign up for an annuity contract. About the only place you can't put your money is in collectibles, which the law defines to include art work, antiques, gems, stamps and precious metals. An exception to the precious metals ban, however, permits IRA investments in gold and silver American Eagle coins issued by the federal government.

Where you put your money depends in part on your temperament or, put another way, how much risk you can take and still sleep at night. Another factor is how the IRA fits into your overall retirement planning. If you're counting on it to provide a significant portion of your retirement income, you may be more conservative than someone whose IRA is relatively less important thanks to expected benefits from social security, company retirement plans or outside investments.

Your age comes into play, too. Someone with decades to go before retirement may choose more volatile investments, figuring there's plenty of time to make up any loss in the early years. (Losses inside an IRA are almost never deductible; the one exception is if cashing in all your IRAs would produce less money than you've invested via nondeductible contributions.) One nearing retirement, on the other hand, may be drawn to investments with guaranteed yields.

Choosing your trustee

However you decide to invest your IRA money, you must do it through a trustee or custodian approved by the IRS. Although you can't be the trustee of your own IRA, you can retain complete total control over the investments inside the account.

There's no shortage of qualified trustees:

- **You can set up your IRA at a bank, savings and loan or credit union,** where your funds are likely to be invested in certificates of deposit or money-market deposit accounts.

- **You can choose** a mutual fund where your retirement cash will go into a professionally managed portfolio of stocks or bonds or into a money-market fund.

- **Insurance companies offer IRAs, too,** with funds invested in either fixed or variable annuities. Some advisers shun annuities for IRAs because earnings on an annuity are sheltered from the IRS whether they're in an IRA or not. However, others point out that if earnings outstrip those on alternative IRA investments, you can ignore tax peculiarities outside the IRA and focus only on the performance inside.

- **Brokerage firms offer the ultimate in IRA investment flexibility** with a self-directed account. Offered by full-service and discount brokers, these IRAs let you pick the exact stocks, bonds, mutual funds and other investments you want in your account. The brokerage firm serves as the trustee, but you're the boss. You have to use a self-directed account to invest in gold or silver coins, real estate investment trusts and limited partnerships.

When choosing a trustee for your IRA, pay particular attention to the fees charged. Some IRA sponsors offer IRA accounts free, others impose annual fees. Such charges are considered miscellaneous itemized expenses, which means you might get to deduct them. But, as discussed in Chapter 15, such expenses can be written off only to the extent that your total costs in that category exceed 2% of your adjusted gross income. To earn a chance at the deduction, you have to pay the fee directly, rather than allowing the sponsor to deduct it from your IRA.

You can have as many IRA accounts as you want. You can use a single IRA for all your contributions over the years, open a different account with each year's deposit or split each year's contribution among several accounts. Although the IRS doesn't care how many IRAs you open, trustee fees and bookkeeping chores put a damper on having too many.

Moving Your Money Around

Although a key trade-off for the IRA tax breaks is the threat of the 10% early-withdrawal penalty, you are not locked into the same investment from the time you put your money in the tax shelter until you retire. You may move your money around freely to take advantage of changes in market conditions or your investment philosophy. There are, of course, rules to be followed. And you don't want to switch your IRA around willy-nilly. Some investments, such as CDs and annuities, can carry early-withdrawal penalties that have nothing to do with the IRS.

When you decide to transfer your retirement funds from one trustee to another, you have two ways to do it.

Direct transfer

This involves telling your current IRA sponsor to transfer the funds to a new account. The sponsor you are *switching to* should be able and willing to help expedite the move. The first step is to set up a new account for your money to go *to*. You may have to stay on top of the transfer because institutions giving up IRAs are sometimes less than speedy. Before you begin the process, be sure you know how long it's likely to take and that you understand any exit or setup fees involved.

You can use the direct-transfer method as frequently as you wish, and it is usually the most convenient way to go.

Rollover

The alternative is to use a rollover. This choice may be quicker, which could be important if you're trying to lock in a certain investment.

With a rollover, you actually cash in one account and personally serve as the go-between, shepherding the funds to the new IRA. Within 60 days of the date you receive the money, it must be reinvested in the new IRA. Miss the deadline and you forfeit the right to a rollover; as far as the IRS is concerned, you have liquidated the IRA and the full amount is taxable. If you are under 59½, the 10% early-withdrawal fine will be due, too.

If you use a rollover, be sure to tell the sponsor you are leaving not to withhold any part of your money for income taxes. Otherwise, 10% of the amount withdrawn will be withheld and sent to the IRS, as though a taxable distribution rather than a tax-free rollover was involved. You won't be able to get your money back until you file your tax return for the year and get a refund of the amount overpaid.

The rollover method can be used only once every 12 months for each account you have. If you have three separate IRAs, for example, you may roll over each of them once a year.

A temporary loan. Although the law forbids borrowing against your IRA—doing so is considered a taxable distribution—the rollover provision offers an opportunity to use IRA money temporarily. You can withdraw funds from the account and use them for whatever purpose you choose—such as a bridge loan when buying a new home, for example. As long as the same amount you withdrew is safely tucked back into an IRA within 60 days, there is no adverse tax consequence. (The money can be rolled back into the same account from which it came.)

Getting the Money Out

Sooner or later, you will want to get at the money you have squirreled away in your IRAs. There are three basic sets of rules for IRA withdrawals, each tied to the owner's age.

- **Until you reach age 59½,** withdrawals are usually subject to the 10% penalty. (A penalty-free way to tap an IRA at an earlier age is discussed beginning on page 278.)

Money Saver

If you use an IRA rollover, tell the sponsor you're leaving not to withhold any part of your money for income taxes.

- **Between the day you reach age 59½ and the year in which you reach age 70½,** you may withdraw as much or as little from the account as you like, penalty-free.

- **Once you reach age 70½,** you must take a minimum amount out of your IRAs each year or face a stiff penalty.

At any time, money coming out of the IRA is taxable, except to the extent that it represents a return of nondeductible contributions. The tax deduction you take when you put money in really just puts off the tax bill on the deposit until the money comes out. Also, when the tax-deferred earnings are withdrawn, the IRS finally gets a crack at them.

You can cash in your IRA all at once, but doing so could subject you to an enormous tax bill. You'll probably do better *tax-wise* by taking out as little as necessary each year during the 59½-to-70½ period. Not only does that hold down the tax bill you owe each year, but it also leaves more money in the tax shelter to enjoy continued tax-deferred growth.

IRA Rollover

• •

Q: *Last summer I gave up on the mutual fund where I had my IRA, withdrew the $4,700 and rolled it over into a new IRA. I got a Form 1099-R from the mutual fund that lists the $4,700 as a distribution. I assume the IRS got a copy of the form and expects me to include the payout in taxable income. I know that, because I made the rollover, the money is not taxable, but how do I let the IRS know the money is still in an IRA so they don't hassle me?*

A: The tax form makes provisions for your situation. Whether you file a Form 1040 or Form 1040A, you'll find a line to report the full distribution—that's the amount the IRS compares to the reports it receives from IRA trustees—and another line to report the taxable part. That's where you'll show $0. To qualify as a rollover, the funds must have been deposited in the new IRA within 60 days after you received the money.

Your minimum withdrawal schedule

The IRA shelter, however, does not last forever. These tax-favored accounts were created to help you accumulate money for your retirement—not build up a pile of money for your heirs to inherit. That's why the law demands that you begin pulling money out when you reach age 70½. The minimum withdrawal schedule is designed to get all your money out—and taxed—by the time you die, or at least by the time your designated IRA beneficiary dies. If you don't take out the minimum required each year, the IRS will claim 50% of the amount you fail to withdraw.

- **The first mandatory distribution must be made by April 1 following the year you reach age 70½.**

- **If your 70th birthday falls in January through June,** you will be 70½ before the end of that year and must begin tapping your IRA by the following April.

- **If your 70th birthday is July 1 or later,** the first required distribution would be for the next year and you could put it off until April 1 of the following year.

Minimum IRA Withdrawals

To determine how much you must withdraw from your individual retirement account after age 70½ to avoid the 50% penalty tax, divide your IRA balance at the end of the previous year by a life expectancy figure from the table below. If you have not named a beneficiary for your account, use the figure in the single-life column. If you have a beneficiary, find the joint-life figure at the point where your age intersects with the age of your beneficiary. For example, if you are 72 on your birthday in 1996 and your beneficiary is 65, the joint life expectancy is 22.5 years. To determine the minimum mandatory IRA withdrawal for 1996 you would divide the account balance at the end of 1995 by 22.5. For life expectancies not shown here, see IRS Publication 590, *Individual Retirement Arrangements*.

LIFE EXPECTANCY

Your Age	Single	Joint Beneficiary's Age										
		60	61	62	63	64	65	66	67	68	69	70
70	16.0	26.2	25.6	24.9	24.3	23.7	23.1	22.5	22.0	21.5	21.1	20.6
71	15.3	26.0	25.3	24.7	24.0	23.4	22.8	22.2	21.7	21.2	20.7	20.2
72	14.6	25.8	25.1	24.4	23.8	23.1	22.5	21.9	21.3	20.8	20.3	19.8
73	13.9	25.6	24.9	24.2	23.5	22.9	22.2	21.6	21.0	20.5	20.0	19.4
74	13.2	25.5	24.7	24.0	23.3	22.7	22.0	21.4	20.8	20.2	19.6	19.1
75	12.5	25.3	24.6	23.8	23.1	22.4	21.8	21.1	20.5	19.9	19.3	18.8
76	11.9	25.2	24.4	23.7	23.0	22.3	21.6	20.9	20.3	19.7	19.1	18.5
77	11.2	25.1	24.3	23.6	22.8	22.1	21.4	20.7	20.1	19.4	18.8	18.3
78	10.6	25.0	24.2	23.4	22.7	21.9	21.2	20.5	19.9	19.2	18.6	18.0
79	10.0	24.9	24.1	23.3	22.6	21.8	21.1	20.4	19.7	19.0	18.4	17.8
80	9.5	24.8	24.0	23.2	22.4	21.7	21.0	20.2	19.5	18.9	18.2	17.6

Money Saver

You can use the IRA rollover provision to borrow money from your account without penalty—as long as the same amount you withdrew is safely tucked back within 60 days.

Minimum withdrawals are based on your life expectancy, as estimated in tables published by the IRS. To find the required IRA distribution each year, you divide the amount in your IRA at the end of the previous year by the number of years you are expected to live. A 70-year-old, for example, has a life expectancy of 16 years, according to the IRS tables. If you had $200,000 in an IRA, the first required withdrawal would be one-sixteenth of that amount, or $12,500. If you have named a beneficiary for your IRA, your minimum withdrawal would be based on the longer joint life expectancy of you and your beneficiary. (Life expectancies for various ages are shown on the previous page. For your age, use your age on your birthday in the year of the withdrawal.)

That may not sound bad, but here's the kicker: *The IRS demands that you figure the minimum distribution for each IRA you own.* If you have several accounts and have named beneficiaries of different ages, the life expectancy divisors will mean a different percentage has to come out of each account.

Once you determine the minimum withdrawal demanded from each account, add them together to find the total you need to withdraw for the year. You may then decide which account or accounts to tap into to meet the minimum distribution requirement. Say, for example, that you have five accounts and you determine you need to withdraw a total of $15,000. If you want to take the full amount out of a single IRA—say the one returning the lowest return on your investment—that's okay. You don't have to take money out of every IRA you own.

Stretching it out

When you're figuring minimum withdrawals, you are permitted to recompute your life expectancy each year, a move that will let you stretch IRA distributions—and therefore extend the tax shelter—over a longer period of time.

Consider again someone who is 70 years old at year-end. Assuming no beneficiary, the IRA owner's life expectancy is 16 years and one-sixteenth of the account must be withdrawn. If life expectancy is not recomputed, the following year one-fifteenth of the remainder of the account would have to be withdrawn, then one-fourteenth, one-thirteenth and so on.

However, the longer you live, the longer the actuaries expect you to live. Notice in the table on page 275, for example, that although a 70-year-old is expected to live 16 years—to age 86—a 75-year-old is given a life expectancy of 12.5 years—to age 87½. The minimum withdrawal rules let you take advantage of that fact of life by recalculating your life expectancy. Rather than base the payouts on a steady one-sixteenth–one-fifteenth–one-fourteenth stream, you can figure it using your extended life expectancy each year. The first payout would still have to be one-sixteenth of the amount in the account. But the next year the divisor would be 15.3 rather than 15, the following year 14.6 rather than 14, and so on. You can also recalculate joint life expectancy.

If your goal is to keep as much as possible in your IRA for as long as possible, you might consider naming the youngest beneficiary possible and giving yourself the longest life expectancy. But it won't work. If your beneficiary is someone who is other than your spouse, special rules come into play. Basically, regardless of the age of your beneficiary—unless it is your spouse—he or she won't be considered to be more than ten years younger than you for purposes of figuring joint life expectancy. You can use your spouse's actual age, no matter how young. In any case, remember that the key when naming a beneficiary should not be how his or her age will affect the minimum payout schedule but rather that the beneficiary will get what's left in the account when you die.

As sweet as the IRA shelter is, it doesn't always make sense to hold down withdrawals. You may simply need more money than the IRS says you have to take. Also, if a future Congress raises tax rates, pulling out funds early may let you dodge a bigger tax bill.

Deadlines and penalties

As noted earlier, in the year you reach age 70½, you have until April 1 of the following year to actually make the first mandatory withdrawal. If your 70th birthday falls in the first half of 1996, for example, you will be required to make a withdrawal for 1996. But you have until April 1 of 1997 to do it. Putting off the withdrawal would let you postpone reporting the amount on a tax return until you file your 1997 return in 1998.

After the first year, required withdrawals must be made by December 31. If you delay your first withdrawal until April 1, you will be required to take two distributions during that calendar year.

If you have a good reason for failing to make the mandatory withdrawal—say the IRA sponsor provided you with incorrect balance information or you didn't understand the life-expectancy method—the IRS can (but doesn't have to) excuse the 50% penalty on the amount you should have withdrawn. You figure any penalty due on Form 5329, *Return for Individual Retirement Arrangement and Qualified Retirement Plan Taxes.* If you think you have a good enough excuse to get the IRS to waive the penalty, attach your explanation to the form.

Getting your money early

The life-expectancy tables also play a key role in a valuable exception to the 10% penalty for withdrawals prior to age 59½. The penalty is waived if the withdrawal is part of a series of roughly equal payments tied to your life expectancy. If you have a substantial amount in your IRA accounts, this rule may permit you to claim penalty-free withdrawals of thousands of dollars a year.

To use this loophole to get at your IRA early, you must stick with the lifetime payout schedule for at least five consecutive years *and* until you're at least 59½. Violate either of those requirements and the 10% penalty would be applied retroactively to your pre-59½ withdrawals.

Dipping into an IRA Early

• •

Q: *Is it true there is a way to get money out of an IRA without penalty before age 59½?*

A: Yes. The 10% early-withdrawal penalty is waived if you arrange to take the money out evenly over your life expectancy, even if the first payment comes before you are 59½.

Here's an example: If you are 55, your life expectancy is 28.6 years. Assume you have a total of $100,000 in your IRA accounts. Spreading that amount over almost 29 years would put your annual withdrawal at a relatively paltry $3,500. Fortunately, the IRS allows you to take a reasonable investment return into account when figuring your penalty-free payouts. This acknowledges that the money you don't withdraw will continue to grow inside the IRA tax shelter. In this example, if you project that your IRA investments will earn 9% a year, the annual penalty-free payout would rise to nearly $10,000.

If you start such life-expectancy-based withdrawals at age 55, by the time you reach 60 you will be free to change the withdrawal schedule—you will have met both the five-year and the age 59½ requirements. From then on you can take out more or less money without worrying about the recapture rule.

While such pre-59½ withdrawals dodge the 10% penalty, the money pulled out of the IRA would be taxed, except to the extent it is a return of nondeductible contributions.

Although the IRS publishes life expectancy tables, the agency does not set a "reasonable" interest rate for use in this computation. It has approved the use of the federal long-term interest rate—a rate that the IRS publishes monthly and in late 1995 was around 7%. Different rates could be acceptable, too, such as the rate being paid by insurance companies on immediate-pay annuities or perhaps the average annual return of a mutual fund where your IRA has been invested over the last ten years.

To illustrate how this rule can help you beat the IRA clock, the table on the next page shows approximately how much can be withdrawn each year penalty-free by taxpayers of various ages, based on every $10,000 in the IRA when withdrawals begin and various interest rate assumptions. If the withdrawals were based on longer joint-life expectancies for you and your IRA beneficiary, less could be withdrawn each year.

Money Saver

You can tap into your IRA before age 59½ without penalty by setting up a withdrawal schedule based on your life expectancy.

BEATING THE IRA CLOCK

Age	Life Expectancy In Years	Annual Penalty-Free Withdrawal Per $10,000			
		6%	8%	10%	12%
45	37.7	$635	$785	$935	$1,085
47	35.9	645	790	940	1,090
49	34	660	800	945	1,095
51	32.2	670	810	950	1,100
53	30.4	680	820	960	1,105
55	28.6	700	835	975	1,115
57	26.8	715	850	985	1,125

If your aim is to hold down how much you withdraw under the life-expectancy exception, note that when figuring how much to withdraw you do *not* have to consolidate all your IRAs. Say, for example, that at age 55 you have a total of $500,000 in your IRAs. Assuming an 8% yield and your life expectancy of 28.6 years, your annual penalty-free withdrawals would be about $42,000. But what if you needed only $20,000 a year? You could transfer $250,000 to a separate IRA and begin early withdrawals from it.

You can find life expectancies for other ages in IRS Publication 575, *Pension and Annuity Income.* To figure the annual penalty-free withdrawals for your specific situation, use a financial calculator or ask an accountant or financial planner.

Death and the IRA

What if the IRA owner dies while there's still money in the tax shelter?

First, the 10% early-withdrawal penalty does not apply to distributions. The beneficiary of the account can cash in the IRA without worrying about that penalty, regardless of how old the owner was at the time of death or how old the beneficiary is when he or she claims the cash.

The potential problem, however, is that the money pulled out of the IRA is taxable to the beneficiary (except to the extent that it represents nondeductible contributions). That could create a substantial tax bill. You may be better off leaving the money in the IRA to continue taking advantage of the tax shelter. Of course, the IRS has something to say about that, too. The rules for inherited IRAs depend on the age of the owner at the time of death and who the beneficiary is:

- **If the owner was old enough to have begun making required withdrawals**—at least 70½—distributions must continue to the beneficiary at least as fast as if the original owner were still alive. That's the rule *unless* the beneficiary is the owner's widow or widower. If you are the surviving spouse, you can simply treat the IRA as your own so that no further payout would be required until you are 70½.

- **If the owner was younger than 70½,** the payout rules also depend on the beneficiary's relationship to the IRA owner:

    Surviving spouse. A widow or widower has the greatest latitude. You may treat the IRA as your own or, if you choose not to, the funds can remain in the deceased spouse's account until the year he or she would have reached age 70½, at which time withdrawals would have to begin, based on the life expectancy of the beneficiary.

    Other beneficiary. If the beneficiary is not the surviving spouse, the new owner has two basic choices: To withdraw everything from the IRA within five years of the death of the owner or to begin withdrawals within one year of the death of the owner, based on the life expectancy of the beneficiary. The second choice could permit you to extend the tax shelter far longer than five years, depending on your age.

    No beneficiary. If you are not the named beneficiary of the IRA—but inherit it under the original owner's will, for example—your only choice is to cash in the entire IRA within five years.

Keogh Plans

Long before individual retirement accounts became the darlings of taxpayers, Congress provided an array of tax incentives for setting aside today's income for tomorrow's

---

Money Saver

If you're beneficiary of your spouse's IRA, you can claim it as your own and postpone withdrawals until you're 70½.

needs. Keogh plans and Simplified Employee Pensions are additional do-it-yourself plans for folks with income from self-employment, whether it's your own full-time business, a sideline business or free-lance or consulting work. First, consider the Keogh.

Keoghs are sometimes called H.R. 10 plans, and often misspelled with a "u" in the middle. (The first appellation credits the congressman who sponsored the legislation creating the plans; the second refers to the number of the legislation that authorized them.) Money you contribute to a Keogh is deductible, and earnings inside the account grow without interruption from the IRS until you withdraw the money, presumably in retirement. In these ways, Keoghs are like IRAs, but there are many differences and most benefit the taxpayer.

For example, rather than an annual $2,000 limit on contributions, the most popular Keogh plans permit deposits of up to $30,000 a year. Payouts are taxable, but there are special methods to ease the tax bite. Also, Keogh plans are not affected by the restrictions on IRA deductions. You can deduct every dollar you are permitted to put in a Keogh, regardless of how high your income is or whether you or your spouse is covered by another retirement plan.

If you have employees, establishing a Keogh plan requires that you make contributions for them as well as yourself. The discussion here, however, focuses on taxpayers who don't have employees and who therefore are the only participants in the retirement plan.

To qualify for a Keogh, you must have self-employment income. That means money you earn working for yourself rather than someone else. Investment income doesn't count.

Different Kinds of Keoghs

How much money you can sock away in a Keogh and write off on your tax return depends on which kind of plan you choose.

Profit-sharing defined-contribution Keogh

This is the most flexible plan that lets you decide each year how much to contribute. You can even forgo deposits altogether if you decide to skip a year. The maximum annual contribution to a profit-sharing plan is 15% of *net* self-employment income, up to a top pay-in of just under $20,000.

Unfortunately, when figuring the top contribution you can make, you don't just find 15% of net income reported on your Schedule C business return. For this purpose, net income is income reduced by the Keogh contribution itself. Until recently, that twist meant the top contribution was really 13.0435% of net self-employment income. Here's why: Say your self-employment income for the year is $20,000. Fifteen percent of that would give you an annual contribution of $3,000. However, $3,000 works out to a *too-high* 17.65% of $17,000—your income minus the $3,000 Keogh deposit. However, if you multiply $20,000 income by that strange factor—13.0435%—you get $2,609. That's the maximum Keogh pay-in because it's 15% of $17,391, which is $20,000 minus the $2,609 contribution itself. Whew!

You think that's complicated? Well, things get worse thanks to the change that allows taxpayers to deduct 50% of the self-employment tax they pay (see Chapter 3). That deduction also reduces "net" self-employment income for purposes of figuring the top Keogh contribution. So, to find the maximum contribution to a defined contribution Keogh, you will reduce self-employment income by the self-employment tax deduction and multiply the remainder by 13.0435%.

Say, for example, that your net business income is $20,000 and your self-employment tax deduction is $1,413. The maximum Keogh contribution would be $2,424—13.0435% of $18,587 ($20,000 –$1,413).

Fortunately, the IRS has prepared a special table for calculating maximum Keogh pay-ins. It appears in Publication 560. (See the Appendix for instructions on how to get free copies of IRS publications.)

Brace yourself for another complication if you'd like to contribute more than $20,000 to your Keogh. Besides

Time Saver

Figuring your maximum Keogh contribution can be difficult; fortunately, the IRS has prepared a table that does the work for you.

limiting a Keogh contribution to a certain percentage of self-income, the law also sets a dollar cap of $30,000 a year. But for profit-sharing Keoghs, the dollar limit is really less. Here's why:

The law now sets $150,000 as the maximum amount of compensation that can be taken into account when calculating contributions to a retirement plan—whether it's a Keogh, a company pension plan or some other plan. And, 13.0435% of $150,000 is just $19,565. (The $150,000 limit applies for both 1995 and 1996; it may rise in the future to keep up with inflation.) As noted below, there is a way around this squeeze if you want to contribute up to $30,000 to a Keogh.

Money-purchase defined-contribution Keogh

This plan really does have a $30,000 annual limit because you're allowed to sock away up to 20% of your self-employment income toward that goal. (And, 20% of the $150,000 compensation cap is $30,000.) Actually, the law permits contributions of up to 25% of net self-employment income, but 25% of after-contribution income is the same as 20% of precontribution income. As with the profit-sharing variety, net self-employment income is reduced by the amount of the self-employment tax deduction before applying the 20% factor.

Although that gives you the potential of a bigger deduction, it comes at a price: You're *required* to make the fixed-percentage-of-income contribution each year. If your plan calls for a 20% annual contribution, you have to deposit that much even if things are tight.

One way to boost the percentage of your earnings eligible for a Keogh without locking yourself into a 20% money-purchase plan is to set up both kinds of defined-contribution plans. You could commit 7% of earnings to a money-purchase plan, say, and use a profit-sharing plan to shelter up to 13% more of your self-employment income.

Defined-benefit Keogh

This third variety is the most demanding plan, but it also offers the greatest potential tax shelter. With it, you decide how much you want to receive from the plan each year after you retire. Your contributions—up to 100% of your self-employment earnings—are based on how much you must set aside each year before retirement to build a fund sufficient to pay the desired level of benefits.

There is a restriction on how big the Keogh retirement benefit you're shooting for can be, though. In 1996, the limit is the average of your self-employment earnings during your three highest-earning years or $120,000, whichever is less. That limit may rise in the future to keep up with inflation.

Defined-benefit plans are particularly attractive to older taxpayers—age 50 and older, say—who want and can afford to build up a big retirement fund quickly. Because this type of plan involves complicated actuarial computations, you'll probably need a lawyer or an accountant to help you set it up and figure the required contribution each year.

Keoghs and IRAs

You can have a Keogh plan in addition to an IRA. However, a Keogh counts as an employer-provided retirement plan for purposes of the IRA restrictions that are discussed earlier in the chapter. Basically, if you have a Keogh plan and your adjusted gross income for the year is more than $35,000 on a single or head-of-household return or $50,000 on a joint return, you can't deduct IRA contributions.

Keogh plans are offered by the same types of sponsors that handle IRAs—banks, savings and loans, mutual funds, insurance companies and brokerage firms—and the same kinds of investments are available. Unlike trustee fees for IRAs, which are deductible only if you pass the 2%-of-AGI threshold for miscellaneous deductions, trustee fees for a Keogh plan are deductible as a business expense, assuming you pay the expense separately rather than have it deducted from the account.

As with IRAs, your Keogh contribution can be made as late as April 15 of the following year. (Keogh contributions can be made even later, in fact, if you get an extension for filing your tax return, as discussed in Chapter 1.)

Money Saver

You may be allowed to cash in your Keogh as early as age 55 without penalty.

There is an important difference on the issue of timing, however. The Keogh plan to which the contribution is made must be set up by year-end for you to claim a deduction. Even if you're not certain exactly how much you can put in the Keogh, the plan must be established by December 31. Any contributions made as late as the filing deadline could then be deducted on your return. With an IRA, you can set up a new account as late as April 15 and still get a deduction on the return for the previous year.

Penalties and Payouts

Tapping a Keogh before age 59½ will generally trigger a 10% early-withdrawal penalty, but there are more exceptions than there are with IRAs:

- **There is no penalty if the owner is disabled or if the funds are distributed after the owner's death.**

- **The penalty is waived if funds are withdrawn periodically over your life expectancy,** as under the IRA rules discussed earlier in this Chapter.

- **The penalty does not apply to funds withdrawn to pay catastrophic medical bills,** defined as those that exceed 7.5% of your adjusted gross income.

- **And, if you close the business that generated the self-employment income going into the Keogh,** you can get at your money without penalty as early as age 55.

- **You can get at your money at any age, without penalty, if withdrawals are part of a series of roughly equal payments tied to your life expectancy.** This exception is the same as the one for IRAs discussed beginning on page 278.

The threat of the penalty does not mean your Keogh funds are locked in a single investment until you retire. As with an IRA, you can have more than one Keogh plan and you can move your money around using the direct trustee-to-trustee transfer or rollover methods discussed earlier. You can use the direct transfer method as often as you want but you can use the rollover just once during any 12-month period. Also, beware that using the rollover method might result in 20% of your money being withheld for the IRS even if you complete the tax-free rollover so that no tax is due. Your Keogh could be caught up in the "pension payout trap" rules discussed in Chapter 7.

When you reach age 59½, you can withdraw funds from your account without penalty. Between that time and the year you reach age 70½, you can withdraw as much or as little as you want from your Keogh. Once you reach 70½, though, the law demands that the Keogh tax shelter begin disappearing—just as with an IRA. At that time, the law demands annual payouts based on your life expectancy or the joint life expectancy of you and your beneficiary. (See the life expectancy table on page 275.) Failure to withdraw funds fast enough subjects you to a 50% penalty: The IRS will relieve you of half the amount you should have pulled out of the Keogh.

Note this additional difference between IRAs and Keoghs. With an IRA, not only are withdrawals required to begin after age 70½, but that age also brings an end to your right to contribute to the account. With a Keogh plan, however, there is no prohibition against continuing tax-deductible contributions. Regardless of your age, if you continue to have self-employment income, you can stash part of it in your Keogh tax shelter.

Lump-sum distribution

There is a special, often favorable, taxing method available to Keogh investors. If you have had the plan for at least five years and cash in the entire account at once, the withdrawal may qualify as a lump-sum distribution. If you were born before 1936 or are over age 59½ at the time of the distribution, part of the payout could be totally tax-free and the rest taxed under the special five- or ten-year averaging method. The details of those methods—which are also available to trim the tax on lump-sum distributions from company plans—are discussed in the next chapter. In brief, if you qualify for five-year averaging, the tax is figured as though you were receiving the Keogh money over five years rather than all at once. That, plus

Money Saver

Keogh contributions —and deductions— can continue after age 70.

the potentially tax-free portion, can hold Uncle Sam's take to far less than it would be if the payout was simply taxed in your top tax bracket.

Beware, though, that the averaging method can be used only once in your lifetime. You wouldn't want to "waste" the tax benefits by applying averaging to a relatively small Keogh payout, for example, if it is likely you would want to apply it later to a larger company-plan distribution.

When the owner dies

What happens to money in a Keogh plan when the owner dies? First of all, if the money is paid out in a lump sum, the beneficiary may treat up to $5,000 as a tax-free death benefit. (Congress is considering ending this break, though.) Otherwise, if the Keogh owner has begun receiving benefits from the plan, the remaining funds must be paid to the beneficiaries at least as rapidly as under the schedule used by the Keogh owner. If the owner dies before distributions begin, the general rule calls for the money in the plan to be paid out within five years.

There are exceptions, of course. If the only beneficiary is the widow or widower of the Keogh owner, the money can remain in the Keogh tax shelter until the year the owner would have reached age 70½. At that time, the beneficiary must begin pulling funds out of the plan at a rate that will deplete distributions over his or her life expectancy. If the beneficiary is someone other than the surviving spouse, the five-year rule can be skirted if, by the end of the year following the year the Keogh owner dies, distributions begin on a schedule that will deplete the account over the beneficiary's life expectancy. Whether a surviving spouse or another beneficiary is involved, you can withdraw more than the minimum if you wish. Withdrawals are fully taxable.

Reporting Requirements

Just as the tax benefits can be greater, there's more paperwork involved with a Keogh plan than with an IRA. The general rule demands that you must file an intimidating Form 5500 each year, but there's an exception for owners of small Keoghs. You don't have to file at all if your account balance is $100,000 or less. This break applies only if you qualify for the 5500EZ, which you do if your plan covers only you or only you and your spouse. If you have more money in your account, or if you can't use the 5500EZ because your plan covers employees other than you and your spouse, you must file a 5500 annually. And if you have a defined-benefit plan, you must also file a Form 5500 Schedule B, a complicated two-page form showing how you arrived at the required contribution. That schedule must be signed by an actuary attesting to the accuracy of the information.

One bright spot: The Keogh report for the year isn't due April 15. The deadline is generally July 31.

Time Saver

The deadline for filing the annual Keogh report isn't April 15; it's generally July 31.

Simplified Employee Pensions

Although designed as an easy-to-administer retirement plan for small businesses, you can can also open a SEP if you have self-employment income from a sideline business or free-lance work. As with a Keogh plan, if you have full-time employees, you must make contributions for them as well as yourself. This discussion, assumes no employees are involved.

Sometimes called SEP-IRAs or Super IRAs, these plans are a hybrid between Keogh plans and individual retirement accounts. You must have self-employment income to use an SEP, and the annual contribution limit is the same as for profit-sharing Keoghs: 13.0435% of net self-employment income (reduced by the self-employment tax deduction as discussed on page 283) up to a top deposit of just under $20,000. In the past, SEP contributions could be as high as $30,000. But as noted earlier in the section about Keogh plans, $150,000 is now the most compensation that can be considered when figuring a plan contribution. And, 13.0435% of $150,000 is $19,565.

With a SEP you can change the percentage of income deposited in the SEP each year or skip contributions altogether some years.

Contributions go into a special individual retirement

account at a bank, mutual fund, brokerage or other sponsor. You have the same investment and transfer options as with a regular IRA. When you set up the account, be sure the trustee knows it is a SEP instead of a garden-variety IRA. Otherwise you might run into resistance if you try to deposit more than $2,000 a year.

SEPs are covered by many of the same rules that apply to IRAs. Your contributions are deductible, and earnings compound tax-deferred. The 10% early-withdrawal penalty hits payouts before age 59 ½—with the same exceptions that apply to IRAs discussed earlier in this chapter— and distributions are required starting the year you reach age 70 ½. The big differences are that you can sock much more in a SEP and you can write off SEP contributions without regard to the new restriction on IRA deductions for high-income taxpayers who are covered by company retirement plans.

SEPs are not burdened by the annual reporting requirements that apply to Keogh plans. All you have to do is claim the deduction for your contribution. Another advantage is that, unlike the December 31 deadline for opening a Keogh plan, taxpayers who choose this plan can open the account as late as April 15 and still deduct contributions for the previous year. If you miss the deadline for opening a Keogh, you can use the SEP as a last-minute tax shelter.

Note this, too: The SEP is considered an employer-provided plan for purposes of the IRA-deduction restriction. If you have such a plan and your AGI for the year is over the IRA income thresholds, you won't be able to write off contributions to a regular IRA.

Retirement Plans: With Help from the Boss

While do-it-yourself IRAs, Keoghs and Simplified Employee Pensions will clearly be an important source of retirement income for coming generations, company retirement plans and social security are still the mainstay for most Americans. Undoubtedly, the more you know about how the plans work—and how payments from them are taxed—the better off you'll be in retirement. First, consider 401(k) plans, the fastest growing company-sponsored plan, and their close cousins, 403(b)s, then review the rules for traditional pension and profit-sharing plans and social security.

401(k) Plans

A 401(k) plan—imaginatively named after the section of the tax law that authorizes it—must be set up by your employer. This isn't a do-it-yourself tax shelter. But that's not necessarily bad. When the employer is involved, some of the company's cash—rather than just your own—is usually set aside for your golden years.

With 401(k) plans, there's some volunteerism on your behalf, too. In fact, these plans involve employees volunteering for a pay cut in order to cut their tax bills. What's going on here? Has the obsession to beat the IRS added financial hara-kiri to the arsenal of tax-saving strategies?

Not at all. Also known as "salary reduction plans" and "cash or deferred arrangements," 401(k)s give employees the option to divert a portion of salary to a tax-sheltered savings account set up by the employer. The IRS agrees to postpone taxing the portion of the pay you agree to postpone receiving.

Say, for example, that you earn $50,000 a year and your company's plan permits you to divert as much as 10% of your salary to the 401(k). That means you could request a $5,000 pay cut, with the cash that would otherwise be in your paycheck going into the 401(k). The advantage is that only the remaining $45,000 would be taxed—saving $1,400 in the 28% bracket. The result is that for an after-tax cost of $3,600, you have set aside $5,000 in a tax-sheltered retirement account. The 401(k) has even more appeal if you're in a higher tax bracket.

As with an IRA, earnings accumulate tax-free, so you have the power of compounding working on 100% of your earnings. The tax bill doesn't come due until you tap the account.

There is a limit on how much you can sock away in a 401(k) each year, but the limit is far above the $2,000 IRA cap. For 1996, the cap is $9,500, an amount that will increase to keep up with inflation. (The 1995 limit was $9,240.) Your personal limit depends on your salary and what percentage the company permits you to put into the retirement plan. Most firms allow contributions of between 2% and 15% of compensation.

The Company Match

A special attraction of 401(k) plans is that most firms sweeten the pot by matching part of the employee's contribution. Companies often kick in 50 cents for each dollar an employee sets aside. Some firms match 25% or less and others match dollar for dollar. Matching contributions do not count toward the annual contribution cap.

If your firm offers matching contributions, learn how the company funds are vested, that is, when the money is yours to take if you leave the firm. Your own money is automatically 100% vested, so no matter when you leave, you can take it with you. The company's contributions, however, may be progressively vested over the years. If you quit after just a few years you may forfeit part or all of the matching deposits. This point is controlled by the blueprints of your employer's plan. The vesting rules are discussed in more detail beginning on page 296.

Getting Your Money Out

Like IRAs, the aim of 401(k) plans is to encourage saving for retirement. So along with the tax breaks come restrictions aimed at keeping you away from your nest egg until you enter retirement. Basically, salary funneled to a 401(k) account is locked up until you leave the company, unless you die or become disabled first.

You may be able to get at your money early if you face financial hardship, though you have to be in pretty bad shape to qualify. Basically, you must prove an immediate and heavy financial need—to pay medical bills, cover a down payment on a home or avoid being evicted, for example—to qualify for a hardship withdrawal. You also have to show that you don't have another source for the cash—that your savings are depleted and you're unable to borrow from a bank. The IRS imposes other restrictions, too, and it's up to your company to decide whether or not to permit hardship withdrawals and, if so, under what circumstances.

Even if your plan provides for such withdrawals, you're

Forbidden Forms

Q: *For the past few years, I have filed the 1040A short form, which is so much easier than the 1040. I retired last year and began to draw a small pension. Is it true I have to switch to the long tax form because I'm retired?*

A: Not any more. The 1040A short form has been revised to allow its use by taxpayers who receive pension income. Before the change, the short form could not accommodate pension, annuity or IRA income, or taxable social security benefits. That forced most retired taxpayers to use the long form. Thanks to the change, you can continue to use the short form.

"The art of taxation consists in so plucking the goose as to obtain the largest possible amount of feathers with the smallest possible amount of hissing."

—*Jean Baptiste Colbert*

not home free. Hardship withdrawals are subject to the 20% withholding rule discussed on page 298 and those made before age 59½ are subject to a 10% early-distribution penalty. The money will also be taxed in your top bracket. The most you can pull out for hardship expenses is the total of your personal contributions to the account. You are not allowed to touch company deposits or earnings.

Note that a key difference between IRAs and 401(k)s is that, except in limited circumstances, you *can't* get money out of a 401(k) early—even if you're willing to pay the 10% penalty. Plan rules control whether you can tap the account early.

You can get your money when you leave the job, but if that's before the year you reach age 55, you have to worry about the 10% early withdrawal penalty. Note, however, that the penalty is waived if the distribution is made:

- **After your death;**

- **Because of your disability;**

- **As part of a series of roughly equal payments** based on your life expectancy or the joint life expectancy of you and a beneficiary;

- **To pay deductible medical expenses** that exceed 7.5% of your adjusted gross income.

At any age, you can avoid the penalty on a 401(k) payout by rolling the funds into an IRA.

401(k) loans

There may be a way to tap your account early without being burned by the 10% penalty. Company plans can permit employees to borrow from their accounts. Government restrictions on such loans are detailed beginning on page 300. Basically, you can borrow no more than half of your account, up to a maximum loan of $50,000, and the loan must be repaid within five years, unless the money is used to buy a principal residence. Although the law permits such loan provisions, it's up to your company whether you can borrow from the plan. About half of the 401(k)s offered by firms include the right for employees to borrow from their accounts.

Taxation of Benefits

Since pre-tax money goes into a 401(k), the IRS gets a shot at the money when it comes out. If you receive a lump-sum distribution from your 401(k) when you leave the company, that amount might qualify for the averaging method to trim the tax due, as discussed beginning on page 306. In most cases, your best option at retirement will probably be to have the money transferred to an IRA from which you can make withdrawals. See Chapter 11 for how IRA distributions are taxed.

A 401(k) counts as a company plan for purposes of the restriction on deducting IRA contributions, but deferring salary into a 401(k) may boost the size of your allowable IRA deduction. Because 401(k) contributions reduce your taxable salary, they may pull your AGI down to a level that permits IRA deductions.

A section at the end of this chapter discusses how 401(k) benefits are taxed after the death of the participant.

403(b) Plans

Continuing in the alphanumeric soup, 403(b) plans (also named after the section of the tax code that authorizes them) are tax-sheltered retirement programs for public-school teachers and employees of nonprofit organizations. Also known as tax-sheltered annuities or tax-deferred annuities, 403(b) plans are similar to 401(k)s in that they are generally funded through salary deferral. Earnings that are diverted to this type of savings plan don't show up in your taxable pay.

The percentage of salary that can be contributed annually to a 403(b) plan is limited by a complicated formula that involves how long you have been employed and how much you have contributed in previous years. Your plan administrator should be able to pinpoint your limit.

The rules for early withdrawals—including the 10% penalty on distributions prior to age 59½—are also similar to those that apply to 401(k) plans. These plans can also include provisions for hardship withdrawals and loans. But a lump-sum payout from a 403(b) can *not* qualify for the five- or ten-year averaging tax computation methods discussed starting on page 306.

Although called tax-sheltered annuities, you really don't have to invest your money in an annuity. Instead, you have almost unlimited choices of where to stash your retirement cash, although that fact may come as a surprise to many participants and even some plan administrators.

Your employer may require that payroll deductions to go to a limited number of choices, such as fixed or variable annuities. But, if you are not happy with the choices, you can transfer your retirement money to a *403(b)(7) custodial account* at a mutual fund or brokerage firm. There may be some obstacles—watch out for surrender charges—but you could be well rewarded for your efforts.

Company Pension and Profit-Sharing Plans

These retirement programs don't require employee contributions. Qualified plans—so called because they must adhere to government standards—let the employer claim an immediate tax deduction for funds set aside for the employees, although employees aren't taxed until they actually get their hands on the retirement benefits. Just how those benefits are taxed is discussed beginning on page 301.

Vesting

First consider how you earn nonforfeitable rights to the money that is being set aside for you—a process called *vesting.* Companies usually require you to work for a certain number of years before you are guaranteed retirement benefits. Quit or get laid off before putting in the required time and you can kiss part or all of your benefits good-bye.

When you have worked long enough to have an unqualified right to your benefits, you are considered fully vested. To protect employees, the law sets limits on how long employers can make you wait before you're fully vested. Companies have two options. Under one, known as cliff vesting, you will lock in benefits after five years in the retirement plan. Leave before five years, though, and you forfeit all your benefits. The other option lets you gradually earn nonforfeitable rights to benefits over a series of years. If the gradual method is used, the *slowest* allowed vesting schedule earns you a nonforfeitable right to 20% of your benefits after three years and an additional 20% each year until you are 100% vested after seven years. The table below shows how the schedules work.

	Percent Vested	
Year in Plan	**Cliff**	**Gradual**
1	0%	0%
2	0	0
3	0	20
4	0	40
5	100	60
6		80
7		100

Employers can provide for speedier vesting if they wish, and if you're on the job at the normal retirement age—usually 65—you're fully vested no matter how long you've been on the job.

Early-Distribution Penalties

The same 10% penalty that hits early withdrawals from individual retirement accounts applies if you receive money from a company plan early. Although *early* is defined in the law as before you reach age 59½, an exception to the penalty means most employees can take penalty-free payouts starting the year they reach age 55. The age 55 exception applies if you get the payout because you leave the job—which, of course, is usually the case. The penalty stretches to age 59½ only for unusual payouts taken while you're still on the job.

Since the point of retirement plans is to help make sure you'll have money to live on in retirement, the 10%

Money Saver

Even if you want to spend part of a pension payout right away, have it transferred first to an IRA. You can then tap the IRA without worrying about withholding.

penalty is designed to encourage you to roll over early payouts into an IRA. Such a rollover lets you dodge the 10% penalty but, once inside the IRA, the money is still tied up until you're at least 59½.

There are, of course, other exceptions to the early-withdrawal penalty. At any age, it does not apply if:

- **You are disabled.**

- **The distribution is made to your beneficiary** after your death.

- **The payments are made in roughly equal installments over your life expectancy** or the life expectancy of you and your beneficiary. (This exception is the same as the one that applies to IRAs discussed in the previous chapter.)

- **The money is used to pay medical expenses** in excess of 7.5% of your adjusted gross income.

Even if you avoid the penalty, the money you receive will be taxed as ordinary income in the year you receive it.

Avoid a Pension Payout Trap

The IRA rollover has almost irresistible appeal because it allows you to both avoid the early-withdrawal penalty and continue to postpone paying tax on the benefits. To add even more encouragement, the law now demands that if you don't have the money sent directly to an IRA (or to a new employer's retirement plan, if it accepts such rollovers), 20% of the payout will be withheld for the IRS. This applies to plan distributions that go to employees who retire, quit or lose their jobs.

This is not an extra new tax, but rather a forced *pre-*payment of a tax bill you may or may not owe. If you do roll over the payout yourself, no tax would be due. Even if tax is due on the payout, the 20% rule may send too much to the IRS. In either case, you couldn't get your money back until you file your tax return for the year of the payout.

Although you can still legally handle the rollover yourself—by taking the payout and depositing it in an IRA within 60 days—the withholding rule might make that impossible to do. After all, unless you agree to a direct IRA rollover, 20% of your money will be shipped off to the IRS. Unless you can come up with an equal amount from another source, you won't have enough to put the full payout amount into an IRA. Any part of the payout that's not in an IRA within 60 days will be taxed and, possibly, penalized.

Fortunately, there's an easy way around the withholding trap, and employers are required to tell departing employees about it. Just have your employer send the money directly to the IRA—or a number of IRAs—of your choice. Or, if you're taking a new job and the new employer's retirement plan accepts rollovers from other qualified plans, you can ask your employer to make a direct rollover to that plan. In either case, as long as the money never passes through your hands, there is no withholding. (In practice, you may be the go-between even with a direct transfer. Many firms write the check *payable to the IRA* and have the employee see that it gets where it's going.)

Even if you want to spend part of the money right away, have it transferred first to an IRA. You can then tap the IRA without worrying about withholding.

In some circumstances, however, rolling the money into an IRA could be a costly mistake. If you were born before 1936 or are at least 59½, you may qualify to use five- or ten-year averaging to reduce the tax on your payout (see page 306). But if you roll the money into an IRA, you forfeit the right to use averaging. If averaging makes sense for you, you'll have to put up with the new withholding rule.

A direct transfer could also be a mistake for someone leaving a job between age 55 and age 59½. If you plan to spend some of the money, it will be taxed regardless of your age. But age plays a role in whether you'll be hit with the 10% penalty for early withdrawal. As noted above, that penalty applies if you're under age 55 when money comes out of a company plan (after you leave the job) but it applies up to age 59½ when money comes out of an IRA.

If you're over 55 but not yet 59½ when you get the payout, using a direct rollover to put the money in an IRA would extend the threat of the early-withdrawal penalty. If you're in this situation and know you'll need part of the money before age 59½, ask your employer to split the payout so that part goes directly to an IRA and the rest goes to you. Although the money you receive will be subject to withholding, you'll avoid the penalty.

Withholding applies to almost all payouts from company retirement plans. *Not* covered are distributions in the form of an annuity or a series of payments spread over ten years or more, or required distributions made because you're over age 70½. Because such payments can *not* be rolled over into an IRA, there's no mandatory 20% withholding for failing to do so.

Plan Loans

Although you usually can't withdraw funds from a company plan early without penalty, you may be able to borrow from the plan—with *no tax, no penalty and no withholding.* Check with company officials to see if your pension or profit-sharing plan permits you to borrow against your vested benefits.

To make sure loans aren't used as a loophole around the early-distribution rules, there are restrictions:

- **You have to pay interest on the loan.** But since it is secured by your interest in the plan, the rate may be below what you would have to pay on other borrowing.

- **If the loan is for any purpose other than to buy a principal residence, it must be repaid within five years.**

- **There's no time limit for repaying home loans, but these must include a regular repayment schedule with payments required at least quarterly.** (Note this: Although the interest paid on a mortgage secured by your home remains deductible—as discussed in Chapter 9—interest on a home loan secured by your retirement account would not qualify for that deduction. It would be considered nondeductible personal interest, as discussed in Chapter 15.)

- **There's also a limit on how much you can borrow.** Basically, the loan can't be more than half of your vested benefit in the plan, up to a maximum loan of $50,000.

Taxation of Benefits

When you begin receiving benefits, the IRS will be standing by to tax all the money that has built up in your retirement tax shelters. Benefits under a company retirement plan are usually paid out either as a lump sum or as an annuity, with regular payments for a set number of years or for the rest of your life.

Annuities

If the company fully funds the annuity, every dime you receive is taxable. When you have contributed after-tax funds to the plan, however, part of the annuity payments will be tax-free because they are simply a return of your already taxed investment.

Figuring out what's what is quite complicated. The tax-free portion depends on how much after-tax money you have invested and the total you are expected to receive in retirement payments. Because annuities usually guarantee payment for the rest of your life, the amount you are expected to receive depends on how long you're expected to live after payments begin (see the table on the next page.)

If you choose a joint-and-survivor annuity—with payments guaranteed during your life and, if you die before your beneficiary, through his or her life, too—the expected return would be based on your joint life expectancy.

Say, for example, that you have contributed $10,000 to a company retirement plan that beginning at age 65 will pay you $200 a month for the rest of your life. According to the IRS, a 65-year-old is expected to live for 20 years. Assuming you receive $200 a month for 20 years, you will re-

"And if she doesn't file?"

Drawing by Shanahan; © 1991 The New Yorker Magazine, Inc.

ceive payments totaling $48,000. Your $10,000 investment is 21% of that total, so 21% of each payment you receive would be tax-free.

A simpler—and better—way

Credit where credit is due: The IRS has a simplified method for figuring the tax-free portion of annuity payments. Even better news, for most taxpayers the easier method will also produce a smaller tax bill. To save you the trouble of rummaging through pages of life-expectancy tables and struggling with the calculations demanded for some annuity payouts, the optional method groups taxpayers into five age categories. Based on your age when you begin receiving payments, the table on the next page shows the number of payments to use to find the tax-free portion.

IRS Life-Expectancy Tables

This table shows the life expectancies that the IRS uses for determining the expected return from annuities for taxpayers of various ages. If you have contributed to a company plan, get help to determine what part of the payments you receive is tax-free. Life expectancies for other ages and other age combinations can be found in IRS Publication 575, *Pension and Annuity Income.*

Life Expectancy in Years

| Your Age | Single | Joint Beneficiary's Age | | | | | | | | | | |
		60	61	62	63	64	65	66	67	68	69	70
60	24.2	29.7	29.2	28.8	28.4	28.0	27.6	27.3	27.0	26.7	26.3	26.2
61	23.3	29.2	28.7	28.3	27.8	27.4	27.1	26.7	26.4	26.1	25.8	25.6
62	22.5	28.8	28.3	27.8	27.3	26.9	26.5	26.1	25.8	25.5	25.2	24.9
63	21.6	28.4	27.8	27.3	26.9	26.4	26.0	25.6	25.2	24.9	24.6	24.3
64	20.8	28.0	27.9	26.9	26.4	25.9	25.2	25.1	24.7	24.3	24.0	23.7
65	20.0	27.6	27.1	26.5	26.0	25.5	25.0	24.6	24.2	23.8	23.4	23.1
66	19.2	27.3	26.7	26.1	25.6	25.1	24.6	24.1	23.7	23.3	22.9	22.5
67	18.4	27.0	26.4	25.8	25.2	24.7	24.2	23.7	23.2	22.8	22.4	22.0
68	17.6	26.7	26.1	25.5	24.9	24.3	23.8	23.3	22.8	22.3	21.9	21.5
69	16.8	26.5	25.8	25.2	24.6	24.0	23.4	22.9	22.4	21.9	21.5	21.1
70	16.0	26.2	25.6	24.9	24.3	23.7	23.1	22.5	22.0	21.5	21.1	20.6

Age	Number of Payments
55 and younger	300
56 to 60	260
61 to 65	240
66 to 70	170
71 and older	120

If you begin receiving payments at age 65, for example, you would divide your total investment by 240 to find out how much of each payment is tax-free. Beyond the simplicity, the real advantage of the new system is that it lets you ignore the tax-hiking effect of choosing a joint-and-survivor annuity. Since two beneficiaries have a longer life expectancy—and thus more payments over which to recover the investment—using the regular IRS method means that a smaller portion of each payment would be tax-free.

How it compares: To see how the optional method can hold down the tax bill, consider the case of a taxpayer who contributes $24,000 to a company pension plan. At age 65, he chooses a joint annuity that will pay $1,000 a month for his life and that of his 59-year-old wife. The couple has a joint life expectancy of 28.2 years, and, according to the regular IRS method, about $70 of each $1,000 payment would be tax-free.

With the optional method, however, the choice of a joint annuity has no impact. Dividing the $24,000 investment by 240 tells you that $100 of each payment is tax-free. That lets you recover your investment faster, but it does not boost the total amount you'll receive tax-free. With either method, you'll get the full $24,000 tax-free, but it will take an extra 8.2 years to get it using the regular method.

The optional method can be used for payments from annuities that began payments after July 1, 1986. With older annuities, you're stuck with the old method.

Playing the grinch

In the past, if you outlived your life expectancy, you could continue to exclude part of each payment even though you had already recovered your entire investment in the contract. Now, once you have recovered your

Money Saver

*Before you figure
your tax on a
lump-sum
distribution, subtract
any after-tax
contributions you
made to the plan.
That money
is tax-free.*

investment—the $24,000 of after-tax contributions in our example above—100% of all future payments is taxed.

To be fair, the law also allows a tax deduction on your final tax return if you die before recovering all of your contributions. That won't help you, but it may be important to your heirs if you are receiving partially tax-free annuity payments and die before the age assumed by the life-expectancy tables.

Commercial annuities

If you buy a commercial annuity—perhaps to supplement your company pension—the optional method for figuring the tax-free portion of each payment is not available. You must calculate the tax-free part based on the ratio of your cost to your total expected return.

When figuring your tax-free portion, you can't count as part of your investment funds from an IRA or Keogh plan or pretax contributions you made to a 401(k) or other tax-sheltered retirement plan. Because those funds and the earnings on them have not yet been taxed, they will be taxable when they are withdrawn—whether directly or via annuity payments.

Lump-Sum Distributions

When you retire, you may be offered a chance to take your retirement benefits in a lump sum. Temper your excitement about the prospect of getting a big hunk of cash with the thought of the huge tax bill it will trigger. The tax law gives you several options on how to handle such a payout, and the choice you make can have a lot to do with how financially comfortable you are in retirement.

When you receive a lump-sum payment, the first thing you should do is subtract from the distribution any after-tax contributions that you made to the plan. That's your money, and it's tax-free. As for the taxable part:

• **You can simply take the cash and pay tax on it in your top bracket.** That's sure to be the worst choice taxwise.

- **You can roll over the funds into an IRA,** a move that postpones the tax bill until you later withdraw the funds from that tax shelter. This choice is attractive if you won't need the bulk of the money for at least a few years.

- **You may be able to apply a special computation formula**—there are two versions, five- or ten-year forward averaging—to the payout and perhaps treat part of the distribution as tax-favored capital gains. This could be your best bet if you plan to spend a substantial part of the payout fairly soon.

Beware: The new withholding rules discussed earlier in this chapter must be taken into account as you consider how to handle a payout from your company retirement plan.

The rollover

In the past, there was a slew of rules to wade through to make sure a company-plan payout qualified to be rolled over. Now, basically any lump-sum payout qualifies. (Any part that represents your own after-tax contributions to the plan can't be rolled over. You get that money tax-free.)

If you want to use the rollover option, your best bet will be to have your employer ship the money directly to the IRA—or IRAs—of your choice. The direct rollover lets you avoid the 20% withholding discussed earlier. If you handle the rollover yourself, you have 60 days from the time you get the money to have it safely ensconced in an IRA. Once the money is here, you can move it around as often as you like, using the procedures discussed in the previous chapter. If you want to diversify your investment, you can roll the money into several IRA accounts.

The advantage of the rollover route is that you continue to hold the IRS at bay. Funds that otherwise would go to pay taxes remain in the account and continue to enjoy tax-sheltered growth.

Choosing an IRA rollover does prevent you from using the special averaging methods discussed next. Whether that's a significant loss would depend on how quickly you'll need access to your funds. Holding off the tax bill by using an IRA for just a few years could more than compensate for skipping the chance to pay a reduced tax bill now.

If you have a Keogh plan—set up with self-employment income—you can hold off the IRS *and* retain the right to averaging. The company-plan distribution can be rolled over tax-free into the Keogh. If you later take a lump-sum distribution from the Keogh, it could qualify for averaging.

Five- or ten-year averaging

These special computation methods tax the distribution all at once, but the bill is figured as though you received the money over a number of years. Although you must actually pay the tax right away, the amount due will be significantly less than if the full amount was heaped on top of your other taxable income.

This is one of the many areas complicated by recent changes. In 1986, Congress decided to abolish the ten-year averaging method and replace it with a five-year version. However, the lawmakers decided to preserve the option of ten-year averaging for taxpayers born before 1936. If your age gives you the right to choose between five- and ten-year averaging, prepare for some hair-raising calculations. (Congress is now threatening to abolish five-year averaging, and keep the ten-year version only for those born before 1936. If a change is made, we'll cover it in the free update you can order by writing the author at the address on page i.)

To use either type of averaging, your lump-sum distribution must:

- **Come from a qualified plan in which you have participated for at least five years before the distribution;**

- **Represent your entire interest in the plan and be paid to you within a single tax year;**

- **Be paid after you leave your job; and**

- **Be paid after you reach age 59½.**

If your payout passes the test, what's the prize?

First, consider five-year averaging. If the distribution is less than $70,000, part of it is absolutely tax-free, thanks to the *minimum-distribution allowance*. This break can exempt from tax 50% of the first $20,000 of a lump-sum distribution. As the payout rises above $20,000, the tax-free portion shrinks. The maximum allowance of $10,000 is reduced by 20% of the amount by which the distribution exceeds $20,000. This table shows how the minimum-distribution allowance is phased out:

Distribution	Tax-Free Amount
$10,000	$5,000
20,000	10,000
30,000	8,000
40,000	6,000
50,000	4,000
60,000	2,000
70,000 and more	0

The tax on the rest of the distribution is figured this way:

- **Divide the total by 5.**

- **Find the tax on the resulting amount** using the current rates for single taxpayers (1996 rates are on page 65, 1995 rates are in the appendix). Your actual filing status and your other income for the year don't matter.

- **Multiply that tax by 5** to find the tax bill on your lump-sum distribution.

Consider this example. Say you receive a lump-sum distribution of $200,000. That's too big to benefit from the minimum-distribution allowance. But you benefit from averaging. One-fifth of $200,000 is $40,000. The 1996 tax bill on that amount is $8,080. Multiplying that by 5 gives you a tax bill on the lump sum of $40,400.

A stiff bill to be sure, but without averaging, the tax on a $200,000 lump sum could be as high as $79,200, depending on your other income. A key privilege of averaging is that you get to take quintuple advantage of the lower tax brackets. Each fifth is treated as though it were your only income for the year.

Born before 1936? If you were born before 1936, you have the option of using ten-year averaging. It works in basically the same way. You first subtract any after-tax contributions—your tax-free portion of the payout. If the remainder is less than $70,000, you get the advantage of the minimum-distribution allowance. Divide the remainder by ten and find the tax on that amount, using the rates for single taxpayers, and multiply it by ten.

Sounds great, but there's a catch. To use the ten-year version, you must apply the tax rates that applied in *1986*—regardless of when you actually receive the distribution. Those rates, shown in the table on the next page, are much higher and the tax brackets much more steeply graduated than current rates.

Consider the effect on a $200,000 lump-sum distribution, which, using five-year averaging and 1996 rates produced a tax bill of $40,400.

The payout is too big to benefit from the minimum-distribution allowance, so divide the full amount by ten. The tax on $20,000, using the special 1986 rates, is $3,692.20. Multiply that by ten and your tax on the $200,000 payout is $36,922.

That's $3,478 less than the bill using five-year averaging—a bonus due to your age.

The tax might be even lower if you qualify to treat part of the payout as a capital gain and pay a flat 20% tax on that portion. Basically, benefits earned before 1974 can qualify for this treatment, and your employer should tell you how much qualifies. As long as you were born before January 1, 1936, you can build this capital-gain twist into either five- or ten-year averaging. Whether doing so makes sense, however, depends on the size of your distribution. You need to crunch the numbers both ways to see if electing capital-gains treatment can save you money. It's up to you whether to carve out pre-1974 benefits or apply averaging to your full distribution.

Considering how complex this is, and how important it is that you make the right choice, you may well need professional help in sorting through your options.

Too Much of a Good Thing

Although Congress has been more than happy to help taxpayers save for their retirement, there is a limit on that generosity. Most taxpayers have nothing to worry about, though.

For one thing, there's a limit on how much of your compensation during your working years can be taken into account by your employer when figuring how much to set aside for your retirement. Currently, that cap is $150,000. Even if you make $1 million a year, only $150,000 can be considered when toting up your benefits under a qualified retirement plan.

There's also a limit on the annual retirement benefit that can be paid under a qualified plan. For 1996, the cap is $120,000, and it will rise in the future with inflation. If you retire before age 65, the maximum benefit is reduced, and it can also be trimmed if you participate in the plan for fewer than ten years before retiring.

The law also includes a 15% penalty tax if you receive *too much* in retirement benefits in any year. As far as

1986 Tax Rates for Use with Ten-Year-Averaging

These are the rates applied to one-tenth of your taxable distribution when applying ten-year averaging.

Taxable Income		Tax
Up to	$ 1,190	11% of total
$ 1,191 to	2,270	$ 130.90 plus 12% of amount over $ 1,190
2,271 to	4,530	260.50 plus 14% of amount over 2,270
4,531 to	6,690	576.90 plus 15% of amount over 4,530
6,691 to	9,170	900.90 plus 16% of amount over 6,690
9,171 to	11,440	1,297.70 plus 18% of amount over 9,170
11,441 to	13,710	1,706.30 plus 20% of amount over 11,440
13,711 to	17,160	2,160.30 plus 23% of amount over 13,711
17,161 to	22,880	2,953.80 plus 26% of amount over 17,161
22,881 to	28,600	4,441.00 plus 30% of amount over 22,880
28,601 to	34,320	6,157.00 plus 34% of amount over 28,600
34,321 to	42,300	8,101.80 plus 38% of amount over 34,321
42,301 to	57,190	11,134.20 plus 42% of amount over 42,301
57,191 to	85,790	17,388.00 plus 48% of amount over 57,190
Over 85,790		31,116.00 plus 50% of amount over 85,790

Congress is concerned, too much is anything over $155,000 in 1996.

That's not $155,000 from any single plan. It's $155,000 in total taxable retirement benefits (social security benefits don't count). If you held several jobs during your career and enjoy several pensions, the limit applies to the combined amount you receive, *plus* any IRA or Keogh withdrawals during the year. The 15% tax applies to any excess over $155,000, and it's in addition to the regular income tax you must pay on the benefits.

There is an exception if you receive a lump-sum distribution and elect to use five- or ten-year averaging. In that case, your annual limit jumps to $775,000 for the year of the distribution. (If you elected a special "grandfathering" provision on your 1987 or 1988 tax return, benefits accrued before August 1, 1986, are protected from this penalty.)

When figuring whether you are threatened by the $155,000 annual limit, don't count benefits that are rolled over tax-free into an IRA. Only when you pull that money out of the IRA does it fall under the rule.

If there's "too much" in your retirement plans when you die, your estate can be hit with a surtax equal to 15% of the excess amount. When figuring how much is too much here, you basically find how much it would cost someone at your age to buy an annuity that would pay $155,000 for the rest of his or her life expectancy. For someone age 65, that's about $1 million. So, if you die at age 65 with more than that amount in qualified plans and IRA accounts, the excess would be hit by the extra 15% tax. The trigger point drops as you get older. For someone age 75, for example, it's about $850,000. (If your surviving spouse is the beneficiary of your plans, this extra estate tax can be delayed until he or she dies, and perhaps reduced or eliminated if the amount in the accounts is drawn down by that time.)

A section at the end of this chapter discusses how benefits from these plans are taxed after the death of the plan participant.

Social Security Benefits

Congress seems determined to make this issue more and more complicated.

Not so long ago, the tax rules for social security benefits were the epitome of simplicity: Benefits were tax-free. Period.

Now beneficiaries fall into one of three categories:

1. Those whose benefits remain totally tax-free.

2. Those who can have up to 50% of their benefits taxed.

3. Those who can have up to 85% of their benefits taxed.

If you're among the 10 million or so retirees whose benefits are hit, you need to know the rules.

The first step in determining whether or not your benefits are vulnerable is to find your "provisional income." That's basically your adjusted gross income *plus* any tax-exempt interest *plus* 50% of your social security benefits.

Your benefits are totally tax free if your provisional income is less than $25,000 if you file a single or head-of-household return or less than $32,000 if you file a joint return. (Unlike many other thresholds in the tax law, these figures are *not* indexed to rise with inflation. That's not an oversight, either. Congress did it deliberately so that, over time, more and more beneficiaries would be subject to this tax.)

If your provisional income exceeds the threshold for your filing status, what portion of your benefits can be taxed depends on how high your income is.

If it is between $25,000 and $34,000 on a single or head-of-household return or between $32,000 and $44,000 on a joint return no more than half of your benefits can be taxed. The amount included in taxable income is the lesser of half of your benefits or half of the amount by which provisional income exceeds the trigger point.

Assume you and your spouse file a joint return. Your AGI for the year is $30,000, and you have an extra $4,000 of tax-free interest from municipal bonds and $5,000 of social security benefits. Adding your AGI ($30,000), your tax-exempt interest ($4,000) and half of your benefits ($2,500) gives you $36,500. That's $4,500 over the $32,000 threshold for joint returns. Since half of that amount ($2,250) is less than half your benefits ($2,500), the smaller amount is the part of your social security that is taxed. In the 28% bracket, the extra $2,250 of taxable income will cost $630.

The 85% Rule

When provisional income *exceeds* $34,000 on a single return or $44,000 on a joint return, things get more complicated, but the bottom line is this: In almost all cases, 85% of your benefits are taxed. The IRS has devised an 18-line worksheet for figuring how much of your benefits are taxable. You'll find it in the instructions for your tax return.

What about married couples who file separate returns? They can forget the $25,000/$32,000 and the $34,000/$44,000 thresholds. Their threshold is $0—and they can be certain that 85% of their social security benefits are taxable.

Note this: At our deadline, Congress was considering repealing the rules that allow up to 85% of benefits to be taxed and restoring the cap that allows no more than half of one's benefits to be taxed. If this change is made, we'll include details in the free update you can get by writing the author at the address in the front of this book.

Strategies

If part of your benefits are threatened, some planning can help limit the bite. If your AGI will include amounts withdrawn from an IRA, for example, you may be able to stagger your withdrawals and vary your income so that your social security benefits are taxed only in alternate years. The same goes for the sale of stocks or other appreciated property. By timing your sales, you may be able to boost your income in years when 85% of your benefits will be taxed anyway and limit income in intervening years to reduce the amount of your benefits that fall prey to the IRS.

If you have municipal bonds, you may consider unloading them since this "tax-free" income can trigger a tax on your social security benefits. That could backfire, however, because switching to a comparable taxable investment would probably give you a higher yield that could push even more of your benefits into the taxable range. Even though tax-exempt income is taken into account in the social security formula, the income itself is still not taxed.

Death, Taxes and Retirement Benefits

What if you inherit retirement-plan benefits from a spouse, say, or someone else? First, such benefits are a major league exception to the general rule that inherited assets are tax-free. Basically, the retirement income will be taxed to you just as it would have been taxed to the employee if he or she had lived to enjoy it. (An exception to the exception, though, allows $5,000 of death benefits to be tax-free in some cases. Check with the plan administrator on this point.)

By Geoffrey Moss © 1987, Washington Post Writers Group. Reprinted with Permission.

On the bright side, you don't have to worry about the 10% early-withdrawal penalty that usually applies to withdrawals before age 59½. That penalty is waived if the distribution is made on account of the employee's death, regardless of the employee's age or the age of the beneficiary who gets the money.

How quickly you withdraw the funds, though, will determine how quickly you pay the taxes. Of course, the law has something to say about the speed of the withdrawals:

- **If the owner was old enough to have begun making required withdrawals—at least age 70½**—distributions must continue at least as fast as if she or he were still alive.

- **If the owner was younger than 70½,** the payout rules depend on the beneficiary's relationship to the employee, and widows and widowers have the most latitude. If you are a surviving spouse and get a lump-sum distribution—as you might from a profit sharing plan or a 401(k)—you can roll the amount into an IRA. In that case, the basic IRA rules, detailed in the previous chapter, would apply. Basically, you would be penalized if you withdrew funds before you were 59½, and you could put off withdrawals until the year you turn 70½. Another choice available only to a surviving spouse is to put off withdrawals—and the tax bill—until the year the employee would have reached age 70½ and, at that time, begin withdrawals based on the beneficiary's life expectancy. (You'll find life-expectancy tables on page 302.)

Additional choices are available whether or not the beneficiary is the surviving spouse.

If, for example, the owner would have qualified to use five- or ten-year averaging to hold down the tax bill on a lump-sum distribution, the beneficiary can use those methods, too. The other basic choices are to withdraw all the funds—and pay the taxes—by the end of the fifth year following the death of the employee; or to begin withdrawals within one year of the death of the owner, based on the life expectancy of the beneficiary. That final choice could permit a non-spouse beneficiary to extend the tax shelter far longer than five years, depending on that beneficiary's age.

Note this: These choices are the ones allowed by tax law; the deceased employee's plan may have additional restrictions.

What about social security survivor's benefits? The same rules apply as those for regular social security retirement benefits: Although most are tax-free, up to 85% can be taxed, depending on the recipient's other income.

Finally, what if you and your spouse were receiving benefits under a joint-and-survivor annuity, under which payments continue after the death of your spouse? The same portion (if any) of the benefits that was tax-free before the joint-beneficiary's death remains tax-free.

Business & Employee Expenses

It takes money to make money. That axiom is normally associated with investments, but you often have to spend money to earn money on the job, too, whether as an employee or in your own business. And, believe it or not, the IRS is reasonable enough not to tax you on the *outgo* necessary to produce taxable *income*.

This chapter is devoted to ways to make those expenses pay off in tax savings. Every $100 worth of deductible expenses trims $28 off your income tax bill if you're in the 28% bracket and can save you an *extra* $15.30 if you're subject to the self-employment tax. Total savings: $43.30 per $100 of deductions...not counting any state income tax savings.

To be sure, people who have their own businesses have more opportunities to shift their expenses to Uncle Sam than do those who work for others. But employees make a costly mistake if they *assume* they're out of luck. Yes, the notorious *2% rule* creates a high hurdle: Most employee business expenses are considered miscellaneous expenses and are deductible only to the extent that all your miscellaneous expenses exceeds 2% of adjusted gross income. If your AGI is $75,000, for example, the first $1,500 of miscellaneous expenses are not deductible. But don't mope. Whether you are an employee or self-employed, your chore is to make the most of the write-offs left open to you.

Automobile Expenses

If you use your car on business, either as an employee whose job requires it or in your own business, the cost is a deductible expense. Sounds simple enough. But the IRS is so worried about taxpayers inappropriately writing off the cost of personal driving, and so intent on thwarting those who try, that business use of a car drives you smack into a Pandora's box of rules.

The first step to protecting the deductions you have coming is to maintain thorough records of your business driving to pinpoint what portion of your costs qualify as business expenses rather than nondeductible personal expenses. Keep track of all your business mileage and compare it to the total mileage driven during the year.

It's almost impossible to use a car 100% of the time for business because commuting to and from the office is considered personal driving. If you have more than one office, either for the same employer or for more than one job, trips between offices do count as business mileage.

Standard-Mileage Rate

Once you have determined your business use of your car, you may choose between two methods of calculating your deduction. One—the standard-mileage rate—is by far the simpler. And, as you would expect, it may be the less valuable.

Each year, the IRS announces its standard business mileage rate for the year. This is the fixed per-mile rate you can use to find your deduction. For 1995, the IRS standard rate was 30 cents a mile. (The 1996 rate had not been announced at press time, but may be a penny or so higher.) If you drove 20,000 business miles during 1995, the standard rate delivered a $6,000 deduction.

If you use the standard rate, add to your deduction all parking fees and tolls paid in connection with your business use of the car. Also, if you are self-employed, you can deduct as a business expense the interest on a car loan to the extent you use the car in your business. If you use the car 50% of the time in business, for example, you can deduct 50% of the interest on the loan. This break doesn't apply to employees who use their cars on the job. Their car loan interest is not deductible.

To use the standard-mileage rate, you must choose it for the first year you use the car for business.

Actual-Cost Method

This system also requires you to keep track of business and personal mileage, and it demands a whole lot more. To complicate things, different rules apply depending on whether the car is used predominately for business or personal driving.

As the name suggests, this method requires that you keep track of the actual expenses of owning and operating your car, including the cost of gas and oil, lubrication, tune-ups, repairs, tires, washing and waxing, auto-club memberships, license tags and auto insurance.

© 1988 Carlson—Milwaukee Sentinel

What about interest on an auto loan? The same rule applies as if you were using the standard mileage rate: For employees, none of the interest is deductible; for self-employeds, the business portion is deductible.

To determine how much of your expenses are deductible, you figure what percentage of the mileage driven during the year qualifies as business mileage. If you drove 15,000 miles during the year, with 10,000 being on business and 5,000 personal, for example, 66.7% of your expenses would be deductible.

Don't shy away from the actual-cost method because of the paperwork and calculations involved. Thanks to congressional crackdowns aimed at blocking undeserved auto deductions, a lot of record keeping is required for any deductions. In any event, the rewards for your efforts can be high.

Depreciation

In addition to out-of-pocket expenses, your deduction includes an amount for depreciation. That's how you recover the cost of the car. Depreciation could easily produce the largest of all your auto write-offs.

Find the basis

The first step in determining your depreciation deduction is to find the car's *basis*. That is its value for tax purposes and it starts out, easily enough, at what you pay for the car, including state sales tax. Finding the basis is more complicated if you trade in one business car for another, particularly if you use the auto for personal as well as business driving, as is almost always the case.

First, consider the simpler calculation: trading in a car used 100% of the time for business for another used 100% of the time for business. The tax basis of the new car is the adjusted basis of the old one—generally that's what you paid for it minus the depreciation deductions you claimed in previous years—plus the extra money you had to pay on top of the trade-in. Say you bought a car for $20,000, claimed depreciation deductions totaling $8,835 over the first three years, and traded it in on a new car. If the new car cost $10,000 more than the trade-in value of the first car, its basis would be $21,165, which is the $10,000 cash you put into the deal plus the $11,165 adjusted basis ($20,000 - $8,835) of the old car.

Now consider the more prevalent scenario: trading in one mixed-use car for another. The basis of the new car would be the adjusted basis of the old one—it's cost minus whatever depreciation deductions you have claimed—*plus* the amount you paid in addition to the trade-in, *minus* the difference between the depreciation claimed and what you could have claimed if the old car had been used 100% for business. The result of this convoluted calculation is to pull down the starting basis of the new car to the same level as if you had used the trade-in 100% for business.

Figuring your deduction

Once you know your basis, you can calculate your depreciation deduction. Business autos have a five-year depreciation life, but the write-offs actually stretch over six years. Generally, no matter when during the year you purchase depreciable property, the law gives you credit for half a year's worth of depreciation. Because you can't get more than half a year's worth the first year, you are forced to extend write-offs into the sixth year to depreciate the full business cost.

Here's the schedule for writing off the cost of an auto, assuming the vehicle is used more than 50% of the time for business:

Year	Deduction
1	20.00%
2	32.00
3	19.20
4	11.52
5	11.52
6	5.76

The car would be depreciated even more slowly if it was not used more than 50% for business, as discussed later.

A first-year write-off reducer

There is also an exception to the general rule that permits a half-year's depreciation for the first year. If more than 40% of all the depreciable property you buy during the year is purchased in the final three months, the write-off for each asset is figured assuming it was put into service in the middle of the quarter in which it was purchased. If you buy a new business car in October, November or December and its depreciable basis is more than 40% of the total basis of all the property purchased during the year, for example, your write-off would be greatly reduced. You would qualify for just six weeks' worth of depreciation for the first year. In the example of the $12,000, 80% business-use car, the first-year write-off would fall from $1,920 to $480. Keep that in mind if you consider buying a new

Money Saver

Buying a new business car before October 1 could mean a much larger first-year depreciation deduction.

car late in the year. Buying before October 1 could mean a much larger depreciation deduction for the year.

Getting Too Personal

If the car is primarily a personal vehicle—that is, business use does *not* account for more than 50% of total use—your deductions are crimped. Instead of using the accelerated method of depreciation available for business cars, you must write off primarily personal vehicles over five years using the straight-line method.

Here's a side-by-side comparison of the depreciation allowed for business cars, depending on whether they pass the 50% test:

Year	Depreciation Allowed If Business Use	
	Exceeds 50%	Is 50% Or Less
1	20.00%	10%
2	32.00	20
3	19.20	20
4	11.52	20
5	11.52	20
6	5.76	10

Recapture of the write-off

What if you start out using the car more than 50% for business but later drop below the threshold? The law "recaptures" part of the depreciation write-offs you claimed in earlier years. You have to report as taxable income—for the year business use fails the 50% test—the amount by which your deductions using the accelerated write-off schedule exceeded what you would have claimed had you used the straight-line method all along.

The Luxury-Car Rule

A part of the law that allows taxpayers to *expense* up to $17,500 worth of otherwise depreciable property seems to offer business-car buyers a real bonus. But it's an illusion. Also known as the Section 179 deduction, after the part of the tax law that permits it, expensing lets you treat up to

$17,500 of expenditures that normally would be depreciated over a number of years as current expenses that you can write off immediately.

Sounds great: Buy a new car with a depreciable basis of $17,500 and automatically deduct $17,500. But there's a hitch. Another section of the tax law—known as the luxury-car rule—short-circuits the potential advantage of expensing for business cars and clamps down on depreciation deductions for "expensive" autos. This rule grew out of Congressional concern that the tax law was being exploited by some businesspeople to subsidize opulent vehicles. Although getting from point A to point B on business is certainly a legitimate deductible expense, the argument went, it really isn't *necessary* to do the traveling in a Rolls or a Ferrari—or, considering how low Congress has set the threshold, even a nice Chevy.

To make their point, the lawmakers enacted the luxury-car rule. It sets a dollar limit on the annual depreciation deductions for a business auto. For a car purchased in 1995, for example, the first-year write-off is limited to $3,060. (The 1996 limit had not been announced at our deadline.) That's the same deduction you'd rack up with the basic first-year 20% depreciation of a $15,300 car. Regardless of the cost of the car you buy, you can't claim more than $3,060 of depreciation for the first year. The annual depreciation limits for a car put into service in 1995 are presented in the following table. (The amounts may increase each year to reflect increases in car prices. However, the limits in effect when you buy your business car apply for as long as you own it.)

Year	Depreciation Gap
1	$3,060
2	4,900
3	2,950
Succeeding years	1,775

Despite the five-year tax life for cars, the luxury-car restriction means it will take 11 years to fully depreciate a $25,000 business car.

Because this rule thwarts the use of expensing, it affects cars that cost even less than $15,300. If it weren't for the luxury-car rule, for example, the buyer of a $7,500 business car could use expensing to deduct the full cost in the first year. The luxury-car rule, though, puts a $3,060 first-year cap on the combination of expensing and first-year depreciation.

If you use your car for both business and personal driving, the luxury-car cap is reduced to reflect your personal use. Say the business/personal split is 75%/25%. Your first-year depreciation deduction would be limited to $2,295, which is 75% of $3,060.

Leasing

Nothing should be simpler, right? You lease a business car and you can deduct the total of your monthly payments multiplied by the percent of business use. If the payments total $3,600 and you use the car 80% of the time for business, you deduct $2,880 (80% of $3,600). You still have to maintain careful records of your associated expenses, such as gas, oil, maintenance and repairs, but you escape the hassle of figuring depreciation allowances.

Indeed, that's how the tax rules work. But there's a significant *but.* To prevent you from sneaking around the luxury-car rules, you may have to report as *income* an amount to offset part of the tax savings generated by writing off your lease payments. This extra income is assigned to you if the value of the car when it is leased is more than $15,500. (That's the 1995 trigger point; it should be slightly higher in 1996.) Just how much you must include depends on the value of the car at the beginning of the lease, when during the year the car is leased and the percentage of business use of the car. The amount also increases each year of the lease.

The IRS publishes a table of income-inclusion amounts in IRS Publication 917, *Business Use of a Car.* Here are a few examples from the 1995 table:

Value Of Leased Car	Income Inclusion to Offset Lease Deduction				
	Year				
	1	2	3	4	5
$20,000	$ 46	$102	$ 150	$ 179	$ 207
25,000	96	210	311	373	429
30,000	148	324	481	575	665
50,000	357	781	1,158	1,388	1,603

The taxable amount for the first and last years of a lease depends on how much of the year you had the car. Also, in the year the lease expires, you use the income amount for the preceding year.

Assume, for example, that on April 1, 1995, you lease for three years a car worth $30,000. For 1995 and 1996 you use the car exclusively for business, but business use falls to 45% in 1997 and for the months in 1998 before the lease expires.

- For 1995, you may deduct 100% of your lease payments. To know how much offsetting income to include, find the line in the preceding table for a $30,000 car. The first-year income amount is $148. However, since you had the car for only part of the year—75% in this example—you report only part of that amount. The first-year amount is $111 (75% of $148).

- In 1996 your exclusive business use again earns you the right to deduct all of your lease payments but you offset part of the break by reporting as income the full second-year income amount: $324.

- In 1997, when business use falls to 45%, you deduct just 45% of the lease payments, and the offsetting amount to include in income is 45% of the third-year amount: $216 (45% of $481).

- In 1998, the last year of the lease, you again base the income amount on the third-year figure: $481. But you report offsetting income of only $54: $481 x 45% business use x the 25% of the year you had the car.

In addition to deducting part or all of your lease payments, you also write off the business cost of operating the car—gas, oil, repairs, insurance, and so on, but not depreciation. You can't use the standard-mileage rate.

Record Keeping

It has always made sense to keep an up-to-date log of business trips, including notes about who you visited, where and why and the mileage involved, as well as saving receipts for gas, oil, maintenance and all other costs if you use the actual-cost method for figuring your car write-offs. But until a few years ago, the IRS could accept less, such as your word and some corroborating evidence. You even had the "Cohan rule" working for you. That dates back to a 1930 court case that pitted entertainer George M. *"I'm a Yankee Doodle Dandy"* Cohan against the IRS. Cohan won deductions the IRS wanted to deny when the court ruled that the lack of evidence didn't automatically obliterate the right to a tax deduction. If it was clear you incurred deductible expenses but you couldn't prove the exact amount, the court might allow an estimated write-off rather than none at all.

But Congress decided that rule was too lenient and said it can't be used when it comes to auto deductions. The IRS has also been directed by the lawmakers to be extremely skeptical of any deductions that aren't supported by written records. The IRS has added questions to the tax return, questions aimed at unnerving taxpayers who might be tempted to claim higher deductions than they're due. The IRS wants to know:

- **Total miles driven during the year,** broken down by business mileage, commuting mileage and other personal mileage.

- **If the car was employer-provided,** was it available for personal use in off-duty hours?

- **Is another vehicle available for personal use?**

- **Do you have evidence to back up your deduction** and, if yes, is it written evidence?

Although Congress clearly hopes those questions will

put the brakes on creative tax-return preparation, the lawmakers have also called on the IRS and the courts to stop being pussycats about slapping negligence and fraud penalties on taxpayers caught claiming auto write-offs they don't deserve.

The message is clear: Get in the habit of keeping the records and saving all the receipts that can successfully withstand any IRS assault on your deductions. In addition, keep a logbook in the glove compartment. Record the distance driven on business each day, with notes on the business purpose of each trip and any expenses incurred for which you did not get a receipt, such as parking fees or tolls.

If your business use of the car is fairly standard throughout the year, the IRS will permit you to use a "sampling method" to substantiate your business mileage. You may need only to keep a detailed log of business trips for the first week of each month, for example, if you can show that you followed the same routine throughout the month.

Remember that you need solid evidence of your business mileage even if you base your deduction on the IRS standard rate. With a good record of the business use of your car, it's easy at year-end to figure the business/personal breakdown by comparing the business mileage with the total number of miles racked up on the odometer.

Claiming Your Deductions

If you are self-employed, you claim your automobile-expense deductions along with other business expenses on Schedule C. If you use the actual-cost method, you also have to file Form 4562, where you figure the allowable depreciation.

Employees claim their unreimbursed car expenses along with other employee business expenses on Form 2106. Remember, though, that these unreimbursed business costs are miscellaneous expenses, deductible only as itemized deductions and only to the extent that the total exceeds 2% of your adjusted gross income.

Time Saver

If your business driving is fairly standard, use a "sampler method" to back up your deductions rather than writing down every trip.

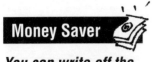

Computers and Other Business Equipment

Computers have a five-year tax life, just like cars. And, as with business autos, it takes six years to deduct your full business costs, thanks to an accounting procedure that basically gives you half a year's worth of depreciation the first year, regardless of when during the year you put the machine into use. Since you get only half a year's depreciation the first year, you need to tack an extra year on at the end to recover your full cost. (There's an exception to this "midyear convention" that comes into play if you put more than 40% of new business property into use during the last quarter of the year. In that case, the first year write-off for each piece of property is figured as though it was put into use in the middle of the quarter in which it was purchased.)

Special rules apply to computers, too, apparently growing out of congressional concern that the tax law was too heavily subsidizing the purchase of many home computers. If you use your home computer in connection with your job, for example, it's almost impossible to write off its cost. To qualify for an employee business-expense deduction, the computer must be *required* by your employer. If you're simply encouraged to take work home from the office, that's not enough.

If you pass that test or have your own business, your depreciation deductions turn on the business/personal breakdown of use. Here are the write-off schedules depending on whether the machine is primarily a business tool or a personal one:

| | Depreciation Allowed If Business Use | |
Year	Exceeds 50%	Is 50% or Less
1	20.00%	10%
2	32.00	20
3	19.20	20
4	11.52	20
5	11.52	20
6	5.76	10

If business use does not exceed 50%, you relinquish the accelerated schedule shown on the left and are stuck with the straight-line timetable shown on the right. Slipping below the more-than-50% threshold knocks your depreciation deductions during the first two years down from 52% to 30% of the business cost. Whether or not you pass the 50% test, of course, your depreciation is based on the business proportion of the computer's cost.

Assume you buy a $3,000 computer and, once you've calculated all the kids' time on the machine for homework and games, business use is just 40%. Your first-year depreciation deduction would be just $120 (40% *business use* x $3,000 *cost* x 10% *depreciation*).

When figuring whether you meet the 50% requirement, don't count time spent using your computer to keep track of your personal investments. Only time spent on your business counts. If business use surpasses 50%, though, you can then add in investment time for purposes of determining what percentage of your cost is deductible.

If business use exceeds 50% when you first buy the computer but later falls below the threshold, the tax law "recaptures" some of your earlier depreciation. In the year personal use predominates, you have to report as income the difference between the depreciation you claimed in earlier years and what you would have been due using the slower straight-line schedule designed for mostly personal machines.

Depreciating software

The rules for depreciating business software differ depending on whether it is bought as part of a package with computer hardware or purchased separately. In the first case, the value of the software is depreciated at the same rate as the hardware—over six years. When purchased separately, however, the cost is usually written off over three years, and the mid-year convention does not apply. Thus, if you buy software in December, you would deduct one-thirty-sixth (2.78%) of the cost that year, one third of the cost in each of the two succeeding years, and the remainder of the cost in the fourth year. Another exception: If you can

Money Saver

Computer time you rack up tracking your investments can hike the percentage of the machine's cost that's deductible.

show that the software has a useful life of one year or less, you can deduct the full cost in the year you buy it.

Other office equipment

Office equipment like typewriters and copy machines have the same five-year tax life as computers. However, office furniture, such as chairs, desks and file cabinets, have a seven-year tax life. And it takes eight years to deduct your full business costs, because the same accounting procedures apply as with computers. The 50% rule that can squeeze computer write-offs doesn't apply here. Regardless of the business/personal breakdown, here's the write-off schedule:

Year	Percent Of Business Cost That Is Deductible
1	14.29%
2	24.49
3	17.49
4	12.49
5	8.93
6	8.93
7	8.93
8	4.46

Cellular phones

If you use a cellular telephone in your business, it has a seven-year tax life but it *is* covered by the 50% business-use requirement that stands between computers and rapid depreciation. If business use of the phone does not exceed 50%, your depreciation write-offs are stunted—you're stuck with a ten-year depreciation schedule compared with the seven-year schedule for mostly-business phones.

More important than sluggish depreciation, though, is that failure to use your computer or phone mostly for business means forfeiting the chance to "expense" part or all of the business cost, as discussed next.

Expensing

As discussed in the section on business cars, this provision of the tax law offers the chance for super-accelerated depreciation. Expensing permits you to write off in one year up to $17,500 of business costs that would otherwise be depreciated over five or more years. You basically treat those costs as current expenses—fully deductible in the year incurred—just like what you pay out for salaries, office supplies or utilities.

Consider a $3,000 computer used 75% of the time for business. By passing the 50% threshold, you qualify for expensing and can deduct the entire business cost of $2,250 (75% of $3,000) on the tax return for the year you bought the computer, rather than in bits and pieces over six years.

When you consider expensing, remember that it gives you the greatest tax-saving boost when applied to property that would otherwise have the longest depreciable life. If you have your choice between applying expensing to seven-year property, such as furniture, or five-year property, such as a computer, choosing the furniture will maximize your write-offs.

In the past, the expensing deduction could not exceed profit from your business. If it would push you

© 1991 Gorrell—Richmond News Leader

into the red, any excess deduction was carried forward to future years. Now, however, if you have a job in addition to your business, an expensing deduction that exceeds business profit can offset salary income. If you put more than $200,000 of equipment into service in any one year, you gradually lose the right to use expensing. The $17,500 limit is reduced dollar for dollar as expenditures exceed $200,000. If you buy more than $217,500 of equipment in a year, you can't use expensing.

Money Saver

Keep a log book near your computer to document business use to safeguard your deductions.

Record Keeping

You need to keep records establishing the cost of the property you depreciate and, if there is a split between business and personal use, evidence supporting the business percentage you claim. When figuring the depreciable business cost—or basis—include any sales tax paid.

Because the IRS has a special eye on computers and cellular telephones, your records of business and personal use must be particularly good. Keep a log book near the computer, for example, and have every user sign in, noting the date, the time use begins and ends, and the reason for using the computer. If the reason is not personal, cite the specific business or investment project. When you file your return, you will be asked flat out, on Form 4562, whether you have written evidence to support your write-off.

Home-Office Expenses

If you qualify to deduct home-office expenses, the IRS will help pay bills that are normally considered personal. These include part of what you pay to light and heat your home, a share of the rent if you are a tenant or depreciation on your house if you own it, a portion of your homeowners insurance and part of your maintenance and repair expenses. Not surprisingly, the rules are strict.

Although home-office deductions are open to both employees and self-employed taxpayers, as a practical matter it's almost impossible for employees to qualify. In addition to meeting all the other tests discussed below, for an employee to claim these tax-savers, the office has to be maintained for the convenience of the employer. Basically, that means you have to be required to work at home, not just choose to do so. Furthermore, employees who do qualify for home-office deductions must claim them as miscellaneous deductions, which subjects them to the 2%-of-AGI floor detailed in Chapter 15.

If you have a sideline business in addition to your job and run your business out of your home, you aren't tripped up by the convenience-of-your-employer test. This type of moonlighting is, in fact, the basis of many home-office deductions.

Exclusive Use

The biggest roadblock to qualifying for these deductions is that you must use a portion of your home *exclusively* and *regularly* for your business. The office is generally in a separate room or group of rooms, but it can be a section of a room if the division is clear—thanks to a partition, perhaps—and you can show that personal activities are excluded from the business section.

The law is clear and the IRS is serious about the exclusive-use requirement. Say you set aside a room in your home for a full-time business and you work in it at least ten hours a day, seven days a week. Let your children use the office to do their homework, though, and you violate the exclusive-use requirement and forfeit the chance for home-office deductions.

The rule doesn't mean you're forbidden to make a personal phone call from the office or that you have to rush outside whenever a family member needs a moment of your time. Although individual IRS auditors may be more or less strict on this point, some advisors say you meet the spirit of the exclusive-use test as long as personal activities invade the home office no more than they would be permitted at an office building. (Two exceptions to the exclusive-use test are discussed later in this section.)

There's no arbitrary definition of what constitutes regular use. Clearly, if you use an otherwise empty room only occasionally and its use is incidental to your business, you'd fail this test. But if you work in the home office a few hours or so each day, you'd probably pass. This test is applied to the facts and circumstances of each case that is challenged by the IRS.

Principal Place of Business

In addition to passing the exclusive- and regular-use tests, your home office must be either the principal loca-

Money Saver

To qualify for home-office deductions, the office must be your principal place of business, not just your principal office.

tion of that business or a place where you regularly meet with customers or clients. If you are an employee and have a part-time business based in your home, you can pass this test even if you spend much more time at the office where you work as an employee.

There is, though, the question of what constitutes a business. Making money from your efforts is a prerequisite, but for purposes of this tax break, profit alone isn't necessarily enough. If you use your den solely to take care of your personal investment portfolio, you can't claim home-office deductions because your activities as an investor don't qualify as a business.

Taxpayers who use a home office exclusively to actively manage several rental properties they own, though, may qualify for home-office tax status—as property managers rather than investors. As with the regular-use test, whether your endeavors qualify as a business depends on the circumstances. The more substantial the activities, in terms of time and effort invested and income generated, the more likely you'll pass this test.

What if your business has just one office—in your home—but you do most of your work elsewhere? First, remember that the requirement is that the office be the principal *place* of business, not your principal *office*. In an important Supreme Court case a few years ago, a doctor lost his attempt to claim home-office expenses even though his home office was his only office. The court denied the write-offs because it said his principal place of business was the hospital where he cared for patients.

Even if your business has more than one office and the away-from-home location is where you spend the most time, you can qualify for home-office write-offs if you meet with customers, patients or clients in the business part of your house. That provision can prove helpful, for example, to doctors, accountants and salespeople who have a business location elsewhere but maintain a home office for meeting with clients in the evenings or on weekends. Such at-home dealings must be an important, rather than an incidental, part of the business.

If your home office is in a separate, unattached

structure—a loft over a detached garage, for example—you don't have to meet the principal-place-of-business or the deal-with-customers test. As long as you pass the exclusive- and regular-use tests, you can qualify for home-business write-offs.

Day-Care Facilities and Storage

The exclusive-use test does not apply if you use part of your house to provide day-care services for children, the elderly or handicapped individuals. If you care for children in your home between 7 A.M. and 6 P.M. each day, for exam- ple, you can use that part of the house for personal activi- ties the rest of the time and still claim business deductions. To qualify for the tax break, your day-care business must meet any applicable state and local licensing requirements.

Another exception to the exclusive-use test applies to a portion of your home used to store inventory you sell in your business. Assume your home-based business is the retail sale of home-cleaning products and that you regularly use half of your basement to store inventory. Occasionally using that part of the basement to store personal items would not cancel your home-office deduction. To qualify for this excep- tion, your home must be the only location of your business.

Business Percentage of House

Your business deductions are based on the percent- age of your home used for the business. The most exact way to figure this proportion is to measure the square footage devoted to your home office and find what per- centage it is of the total area of your home. If the office measures 150 square feet, for example, and the total area of the house is 1,200 square feet, your business percentage would be 12.5% (150 ÷ 1,200).

An easier way is acceptable if the rooms in your home are all about the same size. In that case, you can figure the business percentage by dividing the number of rooms used in your business by the total number of rooms in the house.

Special rules apply if you qualify for home-office deduc-

Money Saver

If your home office takes up 20% of the house, you can deduct 20% of your utility bills, house insurance bills and overall home repairs and maintenance costs.

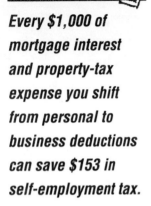

Every $1,000 of mortgage interest and property-tax expense you shift from personal to business deductions can save $153 in self-employment tax.

tions under the day-care exception to the exclusive-use test. Your business-use percentage must be discounted because the space is available for personal use part of the time. To do that, you compare the number of hours the day-care business is operated, including preparation and clean-up time, to the total number of hours in the year (8,760).

Assume you use 40% of your house for a day-care business that operates 12 hours a day, five days a week for 50 weeks of the year. That's 3,000 hours out of the total of 8,760 hours in the year. That's 34% of the available hours, so your business write-off percentage is 13.6% (40% of 34%).

The Payoff

Although this is a complicated area, the tax savings can be well worth the hassles involved. Here's what you can write off.

Direct expenses

Money spent to repair or maintain the business space is deductible. If you paint the room that is your home office, for example, the entire cost can be deducted.

Indirect expenses

These will probably be your most fruitful home-office deductions. Because part of your home qualifies as business property, part of the costs of running it can be converted from nondeductible personal expenses to business write-offs. If your office space takes up 20% of the house, you can deduct 20% of your utility bills, house insurance bills and overall home repairs and maintenance costs. (In a nickel-and-dime crackdown, Congress says no part of the cost of the first telephone line in your home can be deducted. The full cost of a special line for your business and other direct expenses—such as the cost of long-distance calls—can be written off.)

Interest and property taxes

Mortgage interest and property taxes are deductible expenses whether or not you qualify for home-office deductions. But with a home office you convert part of those expenses from personal itemized deductions to business write-offs. Because business expenses reduce self-employment income, they can also trim what you owe in social security taxes. For 1996, the self-employment tax claims 15.3% of the first $62,700 of self-employment and wage income. Every $1,000 of mortgage interest and property-tax expense you shift to the category of business deductions can save $153 in self-employment tax. (For details on social security taxes owed by self-employed individuals, see Chapter 3.)

Deducting rent, or depreciating

If you rent the home where your office is located, this computation is easy: You deduct the same percentage of your rent as the percentage of your home devoted to your business. If you own your home, you depreciate the business part of the house.

- **Commercial real estate—which is how that part of your home is categorized—put in service between January 1, 1987, and May 12, 1993,** is depreciated over 31.5 years, so a full year's depreciation would be just 3.17% of the business area.

- **If you put your home office into service on or after May 13, 1993,** the depreciation stretches over 39 years, making a full-year's depreciation 2.56% of the value of the business area.

- **If you established your home office before January 1, 1987,** you continue to base your write-offs on the speedier schedule in effect at that time. (Depreciation of real estate is discussed in Chapter 10.)

The first step in determining your depreciation deduction is to know the tax basis of your house. That's basically what you paid for the place, plus the cost of any improvements. You depreciate only the cost of the house, not the land, so you must make allowances for the value of your lot.

Assume your depreciable basis is $100,000 and you used 20% of the house all year for your home business. If your home office was put into service on or after May 13, 1993, your depreciation would be 20% of 2.56% of

$100,000, or $512.

Although that may seem like a lot of work to go through for a rather piddling deduction, remember that you exert most of the effort only once, when you set up your depreciation schedule, but get to claim the depreciation write-off year after year as long as you have the home office. Also, as with other home-office deductions, depreciation trims not only your income tax bill but may also limit the amount of social security tax owed on your self-employment income.

You can also claim depreciation deductions on furniture and equipment used in your business, as discussed later. You earn those write-offs whether or not you pass the home-office tests.

Limit on Write-Offs

The law puts a cap on how much you can deduct for the business use of the home. Basically, your home-office deductions can't exceed your home-based business income. In other words, home-office expenses can't create a tax loss to shelter other income. There are even rules on the order in which you should deduct expenses from your business income.

You first deduct the business portion of your mortgage interest and property taxes, for example. Then come expenses such as the cost of secretarial help and office equipment and supplies. Those costs could be deducted whether or not you qualify for home-office deductions. By making you deduct them first, this rule reduces the amount of business income left over to be offset by home-

---

Business Trip

● ●

Q: *I drove to a business convention in Chicago last spring. My wife went along, and while I attended meetings she went sight-seeing and visited relatives. Since there was no business purpose for her trip, are we limited to deducting only half of our expenses?*

A: There's no arbitrary 50% rule, and you can probably claim more. If you qualify to write off your costs as a business expense, you can deduct the full cost of driving your car to and from Chicago. After all, it costs the same whether you go alone or take a passenger. (If you and your wife had taken a plane, of course, only your fare would be deductible.) On the hotel bill, you can deduct the amount it would have cost you to stay in a single room, which is often close to or the same as the double-room rate. Fifty percent of the cost of business meals can be deducted but your wife's meal expenses are personal, nondeductible costs.

office expenses such as utility bills. The last thing you deduct is depreciation.

Dodging a Bullet

One problem with taking advantage of home-office tax benefits is that doing so can trip up some of the benefits written into the law for homeowners. As discussed in Chapter 9, when you move from one home to another, the tax on the profit is generally put off and, if you're 55 or older, the tax may be forgiven altogether. But the part of the house that is designated as business property does not enjoy that benefit, so a portion of your profit—the percentage you've been claiming as a home office—may be taxed in the year of the sale.

There's an easy way around this trap, though: Don't qualify to claim the home office in the year that you sell your house. By reconverting the space to personal use, you can defer tax on all the profit if you buy a more expensive home. If you plan to take advantage of the special break that lets older taxpayers exclude from tax up to $125,000 of profit on the sale of a home, you should eliminate the home office at least three years before you plan to sell. To qualify for the exclusion, you must have owned and lived in the house for at least three of the five years prior to the sale. If part of the house was business property during that three-year period, that part doesn't qualify as part of your residence.

(At our deadline, Congress was considering a change that would demand that part of the profit on the sale of a home—an amount equal to home-office depreciation deductions claimed over the years—would be taxed in the year of the sale. If this change is made, it will be covered in the free update you can get by contacting the author at the address on page i.)

Record Keeping

Employees claim home-office expenses as miscellaneous itemized deductions on Schedule A. Self-employed taxpayers use a special form that the IRS figures will take a little over an hour to complete. If that sounds ominous, you're correct in thinking the IRS takes a hard look at home-office deductions. You have to be prepared to back up your deductions if challenged.

That demands careful records to prove your write-offs are legitimate. Photographs of the office will be helpful. Take pictures showing the desk, file cabinets, typewriter and other business equipment. Keep a sketch of your home to back up calculations of the business percentage of total space. Have your home address and the number of your home-office phone printed on business cards and stationery. Keep a running log that shows when you use the office, what you work on and with whom you meet. This doesn't have to be fancy; notes on a desk calendar will do.

Travel and Entertainment

Ah, the expense-account life! The chance to get the IRS to help pay for your meals, your nights on the town, your travel to wondrous and exotic places. That's the image often associated with tax write-offs for travel and entertainment expenses. And it's accurate, as long as you can show that the costs involved are necessary to conduct your business.

Crackdowns

Things aren't as sweet as they once were, however. Just 50% of the cost of your business meals and entertainment can now be written off. In theory, you get at least some personal benefit from those business meals and good times. So, the argument goes, you should bear at least part of the cost. If you're self-employed, you tote up what you spent during the year on qualifying meals and entertainment and cut the total in half to arrive at your business deduction. Employees who are *not* reimbursed for their business meals and entertainment expenses are hit with a double whammy. Not only is 50% of the cost nondeductible, but even the deductible portion is treated as a miscellaneous itemized deduction. Such expenses are deductible only to the extent that all your miscellaneous expenses exceed 2% of your adjusted gross income.

You gotta talk business

Congress has also called a halt to the so-called quiet business meal. In the past, the cost of taking a customer or other business contact out to eat could be deducted even if not a word of business was discussed. Say you took a client out to dinner to maintain a relationship that might pay off in business down the road but didn't have any specific deal in mind at the time. The cost could still qualify as a deduction as long as it was associated with your business. Now to earn a deduction business must be discussed during or immediately before or after the meal.

This is the same rule that used to—and still does—apply to business entertainment expenses, such as a night at the theater or a sports event. Although you don't have to try to close a specific business deal in the midst of a sudden-death overtime, the law requires you to talk turkey before or after the game to establish that the entertainment was associated with the conduct of your business.

What about club dues?

What about annual dues you pay to belong to a country club or athletic club, for example, where you entertain business contacts? In the past, if you passed a series of tests, such costs could be deducted as business expenses. No more. Congress has put the kibosh on such write-offs, specifically banning deductions for dues for athletic and country clubs, business lunch clubs or hotel and airline clubs.

However, you can still deduct dues paid to professional service organizations such as business leagues, trade associations, Chambers of Commerce, medical and bar associations and public service outfits such as the Kiwanis, Lions and Rotary. You get the write-off, that is, if you belong for business reasons and the primary purpose of the organization is *not* entertainment.

More crackdowns

The IRS won't support ticket scalpers. The law limits

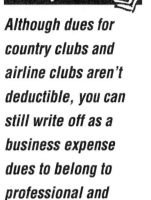

Money Saver

Although dues for country clubs and airline clubs aren't deductible, you can still write off as a business expense dues to belong to professional and service organizations.

Money Saver

If business takes you away from home overnight, the cost of food, lodging—even dry cleaning—can become deductible expenses.

the deduction for tickets to entertainment events, including plays, sports events and concerts, to 50% of the *face value* of the tickets. If you have to pay extra for the choice seats needed to impress a client, for example, the added cost is a nondeductible personal expense.

To put more teeth in the general requirement that only "ordinary and necessary" business expenses be deducted, the law lowers the boom on taxpayers who lease skyboxes or other luxury seats at sports arenas. If you use a skybox for business entertainment, you can deduct only 50% of the cost of the highest-priced nonluxury seats available. This crackdown applies only if you lease the skybox for more than one event. The full cost—subject to the 50% rule—can survive as a business write-off if you rent the box only once a year.

Travel Away from Home

Special tax benefits are available if your job or business takes you away from home. Suddenly, expenses that are nondeductible at home—including the cost of meals, commuting costs between your temporary residence (a motel or hotel) and your temporary work site, and laundry and dry-cleaning costs—become tax write-offs.

To qualify for this alchemy, you must be away from home on business at least overnight but not so long that the IRS figures you've really moved to the new location. The IRS assumes your away-from-home assignment is temporary if it lasts less than a year. Go beyond one year, though, and you're out of luck when it comes to these deductions. The law says more than one year is *not* temporary.

Whether you're on a business trip that keeps you away from home for just one night or on assignment for several months, the major deductible travel expenses can include:

- **The cost of getting to the new location,** whether in your own car or via plane, bus or train;

- **The cost of getting around on business while there,** via your own car, a rental car or public transportation (including the cost of what would be nondeductible commuting at home); and

- **The cost of meals and lodging while away from home,** whether or not there is any specific business purpose for the meal. Only 50% of the cost of your meals is deductible, though.

Mixing Business with Pleasure

What if you tack a personal vacation on to the end of your business trip? The tax consequences turn mainly on whether business or pleasure was the primary reason for the trip. That can be a tough call, but an important factor is the amount of time spent on business compared to the amount spent on pleasure. If more than half your time is spent pursuing good times instead of business, you're going to have a difficult time showing the primary purpose was business.

When business is the primary purpose and the travel is within the United States, you can deduct the full cost of your transportation to and from the business site, including the cost of any meals and lodging en route. What you spend while vacationing in the area would be nondeductible. Say you fly to Honolulu for a five-day business meeting, then extend your stay for four days of swimming, sight-seeing and luaus. The cost of the flight to Hawaii would be deductible, as would the cost of your lodging and 50% of the cost of your meals during the business part of your trip. None of the cost of food or lodging on the personal days could be written off.

When wife or husband joins you

What if your spouse goes along? That does not obliterate your right to business write-offs, but it's now almost impossible to deduct any of his or her expenses. Before 1994, you could include a spouse's expenses as business deductions if you could show a significant business reason for your spouse's presence. To put an end to disputes over what constituted a *significant* business reason, Congress banned such write-offs unless your spouse is an employee of the business and has a bona fide business reason for accompanying you.

Although you normally can't write off the extra costs incurred because your spouse is along, your husband or wife may still enjoy a tax-subsidized holiday. The reason: When your spouse accompanies you, your costs are likely to be less—perhaps significantly less—than twice what it would have cost you to go alone. The cost of a double room in a hotel may be the same as for a single, for example. You get to deduct the full single-room rate. Also, if you drive to the business meeting, the cost of operating your car or a rental are the same whether you go alone or have company—and so is your deduction.

Getting too personal

When you mix too much pleasure with your business, you risk losing the write-off for transportation costs. If the primary purpose of the trip is personal, you cannot write off any of the cost of getting to and from the site of the business meeting, although you may still deduct business-related expenses at the destination. Clearly, this is an area where careful planning can pay off in handsome tax savings and some personal pleasure to boot.

Travel overseas

The rules are different if your business takes you out of the country—in some ways more strict, in others more lenient.

As with domestic travel, your costs, including transportation, food and lodging en route, are deductible if the primary purpose of the trip is business. But unlike the all-or-nothing rule for domestic travel, it's possible to qualify to deduct part of your foreign travel expenses.

You can pass the primarily business threshold—and write off all your travel expenses—if the foreign trip takes you out of the United States for a week or less. If the primary purpose of a trip to Paris was an important one-day business meeting, for example, you could spend six extra days sight-seeing without forfeiting your travel-expense write-offs. Your sight-seeing expenses would be nondeductible, of course, but the full cost of getting to and from France could be written off.

For trips that are longer than a week, more stringent rules apply. At least 75% of the time you are out of the country must be devoted to business. If so, your travel expenses are fully deductible. But if you fail the 75% test, you have to split travel costs between business and personal purposes according to the number of days spent on each. If your breakdown shows a 60% business/40% personal split, for example, you would deduct just $1,200 of a $2,000 airfare. If the trip is primarily a vacation, though, none of the travel costs are deductible.

When counting up business days, include:

- Any day or part of a day when your presence is required at a particular place for a specific business purpose;

- Any day when you spend more than four hours on business;

- Weekend or holiday days that fall between business days; and

- Days spent traveling to and from the business location.

Conventions

Because sponsors expend loads of time, energy and money to make sure business convention programs offer plenty of appealing diversions, it's no surprise that the IRS applies special rules to convention-cost write-offs.

When the convention is held within the "North American area" (including the United States; Canada; Mexico; Puerto Rico; U.S. Virgin Islands; Guam; Jamaica; the Trust Territory of the Pacific Islands, including American Samoa; and Barbados), your expenses of attending are deductible so long as you can show that the convention agenda is connected with your business or job. For your traveling expenses to be deductible, of course, the primary purpose of the trip must be business related.

What if it's overseas?

Foreign conventions are a different matter. In fact, it's difficult for any convention outside the North American area to qualify for tax deductions. For expenses to be deductible, the convention must be *directly related* to your business; domestic meetings must be of only *general benefit* to your job or business. The tougher hurdle for a foreign convention is that it must be as reasonable to choose the foreign site as it would be to hold the convention within the favored North American area. Why hold the Sunbelt Widgetmaker's Annual Convention in Budapest rather than Phoenix? That is the question that must be answered to the satisfaction of a skeptical IRS.

Ships, ahoy!

What if the ingenious convention planners choose a cruise ship as the site of the seminar? The cost can still be written off if you can show the meeting is directly related to your business. But there is a $2,000 limit on how much you can write off for cruise conventions each year. Also, to qualify, the ship must be registered in the U.S., and all ports of call during the convention must be located in the United States or its possessions.

There's another special requirement for cruise conventions: To claim the deduction, you must include with your tax return a signed note from the convention sponsors listing the business meetings scheduled each day aboard the ship and certifying just how many hours you spent attending those activities.

Forbidden conventions

And, deductions for a couple of types of conventions are outlawed entirely: Those focusing on personal investments or financial planning and those where the primary activity is the distribution of videotapes for participants to watch at their convenience. No matter how vital the videotape to your business, you can't deduct the cost of going to the convention to pick it up.

Record Keeping

Be prepared for serious IRS scrutiny if you deduct business travel, entertainment or convention expenses. That's not to say you should steer away from any legitimate write-offs, only that careful record keeping is demanded if you want to preserve the deductions in the face of an IRS audit.

As with any deduction, it's up to you to maintain adequate records to justify the write-off. But in this area, Congress keeps reminding the IRS that it expects the revenuers to be rigorous when enforcing the substantiation rules. The lawmakers have stressed that neither the IRS nor the courts are to permit approximations of these expenses. The message: Either have proof or don't take a deduction.

- **For business meals and entertainment, you must have a receipt for any expense of $75 or more.** The $75 trigger point is for expenses on or after October 1, 1995. Before then, the receipt requirement kicked it at $25. You also need a record—perhaps in a daily diary or business log—of:

- **All expenses under the $75 threshold,** including taxi fares, telephone calls and other incidental expenses;

- **The date of the business meal or entertainment;**

- **The name and address of the restaurant or entertainment facility** and the type of entertainment—a play, baseball game, and so on;

- **The business relationship of the people entertained and the specific business reason** for the meal or entertainment.

- **To deduct the costs of traveling away from home overnight on business,** you must have a receipt for all lodging expenses. Your records must also show the day you left home, the date of your return and the business purpose of the trip.

An easy out—the standard allowance

For those who don't want to bother keeping track of daily meal expenses, the IRS offers a standard allowance that can be claimed in lieu of actual expenses. It's usually $28 a day but can be as high as $36 a day if the business trip takes you to certain high cost areas, such as Boston, Chicago, New York City, San Francisco and many other localities. You can claim a larger deduction if you have proof of higher expenses. Your best bet is to jot down the

Time Saver

The trigger point for demanding a receipt for business meals and entertainment is now $75, up from $25.

amounts in a business log and keep receipts.

When you're combining a vacation with a business trip, keep careful records of how much you spend each day so you can show that you pass the primarily business test necessary to convert your travel expenses into tax deductions. If a convention is involved, keep the program, with notations on which sessions you attended. When a cruise-ship convention is involved, you'll also need the signed statement mentioned earlier.

Thanks to the 50% deductibility rule on meals and entertainment, you must segregate such costs from travel expenses—transportation and lodging, for example—which remain fully deductible. When you take a client out to lunch, for instance, the cost of the meal is only 50% deductible, but the cab fare retains its 100% deductibility.

Job-Hunting Expenses

When you look for a new job, the IRS might pick up some of your costs—via tax savings. The key to tax deductions is to seek a new position in the same line of work, rather than try to switch careers. Perhaps our lawmakers worry that someone changing occupations might be willing to take a pay cut to make the change, while a job hunter looking for a different job in the same field is likely to do better financially, and in the process produce more income for the government to tax. Whatever the reason, job-hunting expenses are deductible when you confine your search to the same line of work you're in—whether or not you wind up changing jobs. The cost of seeking a job in a different occupation is not deductible, nor are expenses connected with landing your first job—or of reentering the work force after a lengthy absence.

If you qualify for job-hunting deductions, your write-offs can include travel expenses if your search takes you away from home overnight, including the cost of food, lodging and transportation. Your meal expenses are covered by the rule that limits the deduction to 50% of the cost. In addition, deductible job-hunting costs encompass what you spend for employment-agency fees, want ads, telephone calls connected with the job hunt, and the cost of printing and mailing resumes.

The 2% rule

There's a catch, though. Job-hunting expenses are miscellaneous itemized deductions, which means they're subject to the 2% rule: You may claim a deduction only for the amount by which the total of your miscellaneous expenses exceeds 2% of your adjusted gross income. If your AGI is $30,000, for example, only miscellaneous expenses in excess of $600 would be deductible. Keep careful records of all your job-hunting expenses to determine whether you have a tax deduction. If travel expenses are involved, it may be easy to pass the 2% text.

Education Expenses

The tax law will subsidize your pursuit of knowledge—if the schooling passes several tests. Just as the cost of hunting for your first job or a career switch is *non*deductible, so is the cost of education that prepares you for your first job or for a position in a different business or profession. To qualify for education deductions, you must already be working—either as an employee or self-employed—and the training must either be designed to maintain or improve the skills needed for your present job or be required by your employer or the law to keep that job.

You can't deduct the cost of courses taken to meet the minimum requirements of a job, and even if you could argue that a class improves the skills used on your present job, you can flunk the deductibility test if the education is also a step toward entering a new trade or profession.

What constitutes a new occupation? Clearly, if you sour on ditch-digging and sign on for night law-school classes, you're preparing for a new profession, and the costs would not be deductible. But if you're an attorney, the cost of continuing-education courses could be written off. What if you're a real estate agent who takes courses necessary to get a real estate bro-

Money Saver

If you're looking for a new job in the same field, your job-hunting expenses may be deductible.

ker's license? The Tax Court rejected such a deduction on the grounds that the broker's job was significantly different than the agent's. The IRS also says "no" to deductions for bar-review courses, even if you're already an attorney preparing for admission to the bar in an additional state.

Depreciate a Gift

• •

Q: *My kids got together and bought new furniture for my office as a Christmas gift. I don't want to play Scrooge, but if I had purchased the furniture myself I could have depreciated it as a business expense. Does the fact that I received it as a gift deny me the opportunity to write off the cost?*

A: No. If you could depreciate the furniture if you bought it yourself, you can write it off even though you received it as a gift. Your basis—the amount to be depreciated—is either the fair market value of the furniture when you received it or what your children paid for it, whichever is less. You can not, however, use the expensing provision to write off the full cost at once. To use that tax break, you must have purchased the property yourself.

Teachers required to take summer courses to keep their jobs can deduct the cost, and as far as the IRS is concerned, all teaching and related duties are considered the same general kind of work. Deductions are permitted for the cost of courses needed to switch from elementary education to secondary teaching, for example, as are those connected with a move from a job as a classroom teacher to a principal.

In general, to qualify to write off education expenses you need to mix work with schooling. But if you go to school during your vacation or during a temporary absence from work, you can still qualify. The IRS will consider up to one year off the job temporary for these purposes, and in some cases the courts have permitted even longer absences. You needn't go back to the same job to qualify to deduct educational expenses, just to the same line of work.

If you qualify, your write-offs include the cost of tuition, books, supplies, tutoring and any travel and transportation related to your studies. Whether you're temporarily a full-time student at a major university, attending a week-long continuing-education seminar or taking a correspondence course, keep careful records of your expenses.

If you have to go out of town for the course and you're away overnight, you can deduct travel expenses as long as the primary purpose of the trip is the educational activity. Basically, that means you write off the cost of getting to and from the site of the course or seminar, including what you pay for meals (subject to the 50% rule discussed previously) and lodging en route and while there.

Say you're a tax practitioner who travels 1,000 miles for a five-day course on the ramifications of yet another new tax law. After the seminar you stick around for a couple of days of sight-seeing. Your travel costs as well as tuition and any other fees connected with the course are deductible as job-related educational expenses. If you spend three weeks on vacation instead of just a couple of days, though, the primary purpose of the trip would be considered personal, and you would get no deduction for travel expenses.

What you deduct for transportation to and from your classes depends in part on where the courses are held vis-a-vis where you work. If you have to travel beyond the general area where you work, you can deduct the full cost. When the schooling is within that general work area—the IRS offers no specific distance—you write off only the cost of going from your workplace to the school and back to the workplace. If you drive your own car, you can deduct either the standard rate (30 cents a mile in 1995) or your actual expenses. The cost of getting to and from classes on a nonwork day is not deductible.

Travel as education

Congress has brought an end to an education write-off that had the aura of an awfully sweet deal. In the past, it was possible for a French teacher to deduct the cost of a trip to France to maintain general familiarity with the language and culture, for example, or for a social studies teacher to write off the cost of a trip to another state to learn about and photograph its people and geography for use in the classroom. No more. The law now bars the deduction for the cost of travel when the travel itself is the educational activity.

Money Saver

If you make a profit in three out of five years, the IRS will give you the benefit of the doubt that your endeavor is a business, not a hobby.

Self-employed taxpayers deduct qualifying educational expenses in full on Schedule C. Employees have to struggle past the 2% threshold to win their deductions. These costs are miscellaneous expenses deductible only if you itemize and only to the extent that your total in this category exceeds 2% of your adjusted gross income.

Hobby-Loss Rules

You've heard plenty about it: Play your cards right and you can convert your hobby into a sideline business and transform the cost of your avocation into tax deductions. An inviting idea, to be sure, and it *can* work. But the IRS isn't in the business of subsidizing your fun, which is why the hobby-loss rules are lurking in the tax law.

The best way to understand these rules is to think of the government as your partner in any business venture—willing to share the costs via tax-saving write-offs in exchange for the share of the profits it takes by taxing your earnings. Just as you wouldn't want to go into business with a ne'er-do-well nephew with a cavalier attitude toward the business, neither does Uncle Sam. You have to show that you're really out to make money, and at least occasionally show a profit, or the IRS will have nothing to do with the cost-sharing end of the arrangement.

Jumping the Hurdles

Recognizing that profits are not automatic in any business venture, regardless of how hard you're trying to make money, the law does not demand that you show a profit every year for your endeavor to be classified as a business rather than a hobby. But you do have to make money in three out of five years to get the benefit of the doubt and deduct losses in the two profitless years. (If your enterprise consists primarily of breeding, training, showing or racing horses, you don't have to be as successful. Turn a profit two years out of seven to dodge the hobby-loss rules and you'll qualify for business deductions.)

If you pass the test, the IRS can still audit your return and try to deny deductions, but it has to prove that you're not in business for a profit. If you fail the test and are audited, the burden of proof is on you to show that you really are trying to make money. And, the cards are stacked in the government's favor. Profit from a hobby is always taxed; loss is never deductible. That does not mean none of your hobby expenses can be written off; just that the deductions are limited to the amount of income your hobby generates.

Staying away from the hobby-loss trap is particularly important because, here again, the 2% rule limiting miscellaneous itemized deductions rears its head. If your activity qualifies as a business, you deduct your expenses in full on Schedule C, even if your costs exceed income. If it is classified as a hobby, though, not only are write-offs limited to the amount of income earned, but those allowed are deductible only as miscellaneous expenses on Schedule A. That means you get the benefit only to the extent that all your miscellaneous deductions exceed 2% of your adjusted gross income.

"We're disallowing some of the mileage you've declared… your entry for March 10 indicates you took a SCENIC route, not the most direct."

© *Copley News Service, Daytona Beach News Journal*

How it works in practice

Don't let the restrictions discourage you from trying to blend money-making efforts into your avocation. The types of activities that often draw scrutiny from the IRS can be viewed as a list of opportunities as well as risks: freelance writing; photography; painting; dog and cat breeding; stamp and coin collecting; raising flowers; boat chartering; and raising, showing or racing horses. If you are involved in those or any other activities that produce goods or services you could sell, consider mixing pleasure with profit, with the help of tax-saving deductions.

Say you're an amateur photographer, and you decide to try to capitalize on your skills by hiring yourself out to photograph weddings, birthday parties, award ceremonies, etc. You have business cards printed and buy ads in the local paper. You show your landscape photos at a gallery and sell several prints.

Your hobby has been transformed into a business. You have to report the income you earn, but you also earn deductions: for the cost of your film and processing, frames and mats, ads and business cards; the cost of getting to and from assignments, including food and lodging if you're away from home overnight; the cost of attending a photography seminar; and depreciation of your cameras and other equipment.

But what if, despite your best intentions and efforts, your costs exceed your income? Assuming you expect to turn a profit in the future and are running your activity in a businesslike manner, you can deduct the expenses even if you show a loss. If the IRS challenges your write-offs before you've had a chance to meet the three-of-five year profit test, you can ask the government to postpone its hobby/business decision until the end of the five-year period. If at that time the decision goes against you, you'd owe back taxes and interest.

Even if you lose on the three-of-five-year test, you can win the right to deduct losses if you can convince the IRS that you're really trying to make money. Among the factors that will be considered:

- **Whether you're managing the activity in a businesslike manner**—keeping good books, trying to drum up business, holding down costs where possible, charging reasonable prices;

- **How much time and effort you devote to the business**;

- **Whether you or your advisers have the expertise** needed for the type of business you've chosen;

- **Whether following a loss one year you make changes** in an effort to turn a profit in the future; and

- **Whether your profit expectation is based in part on expected appreciation** of assets used in the business.

Thorough records are essential. If you are challenged, it's up to you to prove that your endeavor is a profit-motivated enterprise worthy of the tax deductions you have claimed rather than a hobby masquerading as a business.

Child-Care Credit

Often, one of the biggest expenses associated with working is paying someone to care for your children while you're on the job. And here, too, the law is willing to lend a hand to help you earn money for the IRS to tax. The child- and dependent-care tax credit can serve as an annual rebate of as much as $1,440 of what you pay for child-care. The details are in Chapter 16.

Health Insurance for Self-Employeds

If you're self-employed, you may get to deduct 30% of the cost of health insurance for yourself and your family as an *adjustment to income.* That's valuable because, other-wise, that cost is added to other medical expenses and is deductible only to the extent that your total medical costs exceed 7.5% of adjusted gross income.

If you qualify and paid $3,000 for a family health poli-cy, for example, this rule allows you to write off $900 with-out worrying about the 7.5% floor. The remaining $2,100 counts toward that threshold.

There are restrictions, of course. Your medical-insur-ance deduction can't exceed the net income of your busi-ness. Also, you can't claim this deduction if you are eligible for health coverage offered by your employer—if you have a job as well as your own business—or by your spouse's em-ployer. For more on this write off, see Chapter 14.

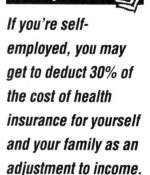

Money Saver

If you're self-employed, you may get to deduct 30% of the cost of health insurance for yourself and your family as an adjustment to income.

Miscellaneous Expenses

There are plenty of other ways you spend money in connection with your job, whether you're an employee or self-employed. And many of those costs can translate into tax deductions. The often-repeated bad news in this chapter—about the 2% threshold for deducting employee business expenses—applies to the expenses discussed in this section, too. One reason Congress built the 2% obstacle was ostensibly to simplify your life: If it's unlikely you will surpass the threshold, the argument goes, you'll no longer have to keep track of these expenses. There's a Catch-22 here, though. You'll never know if you will make it to the threshold unless you keep track of your expenses. The key difference is that in the past, you knew your record keeping would pay off in tax savings; now you can't be sure until you tote up all your expenses at year-end. If you are self-employed and write off business expenses on Schedule C, of course, you don't have to worry about the 2% barrier.

In addition to the types of expenses discussed earlier, here are others that can mean tax-saving deductions for you:

Special work clothes

You might be able to deduct the cost of your work wardrobe. To qualify, the clothes must be required by your job *and* not suitable for everyday use. Hard hats, work gloves and safety glasses qualify, for example, as do uniforms you must wear if you're a nurse, letter carrier, jockey, ballplayer, etc. Entertainers can deduct the cost of their theatrical wardrobe, assuming it's not fitting garb off the stage. What if you have to wear a suit to work but wouldn't be caught dead in such formal attire away from the office? No deduction because, regardless of your personal opinion, the IRS says the suit is suitable for everyday use.

If you can deduct the cost of your work clothes, you can also write off the cost of keeping them clean, including laundry and dry-cleaning bills. In one case an airline pilot was permitted to claim the cost of his shoeshines. The shoes were part of the uniform and not worn off the job.

Small tools

You don't have to spend thousands on cars, computers or office furniture to get Uncle Sam to help with the cost via a tax deduction. The cost of tools and equipment required in your work—a carpenter's saws, a lawyer's briefcase, a nurse's medical equipment, for example—all can qualify as tax-deductible business expenses. If the item is likely to last for more than a year, you have to depreciate it or use the expensing deduction discussed earlier in this chapter.

A physical exam required by your employer

By claiming this expense as an employee business expense rather than a medical expense, it becomes a miscellaneous itemized deduction subject to the 2% threshold instead of the tougher 7.5%-of-AGI threshold for medical expenses.

Professional expenses

The IRS permits deduction of such professional expenses as dues to professional societies, union dues and initiation fees, and subscriptions to professional journals and trade magazines.

Gifts

The cost of gifts you give in connection with your business is deductible, but Uncle Sam is something of a Scrooge here. You can't deduct more than $25 for the items you give to any one person during the year, regardless of how generous you actually are.

Job-security insurance

If you buy insurance to protect yourself against being ousted from your job for reasons other than poor performance—in the aftermath of a hostile takeover, say—the cost of the policy is a deductible employee business expense.

Write-Offs: Adjustments to Income

You don't have to itemize deductions to trim your taxable income. And that's good, since about seven out of ten taxpayers don't itemize. Instead, they claim the standard deduction on their returns. The standard deduction and itemized deductions are discussed in the next chapter.

Here, we want to highlight a group of write-offs that's available to itemizers and non-itemizers alike. Officially, they're called adjustments to income, but they sometimes go by the alias "above the line deductions" because you get to subtract them to arrive at your adjusted gross income (AGI). Other deductions, as well as exemptions, are subtracted from AGI.

Adjustments to income have special power for some taxpayers because restrictions on other tax-savers are based on AGI. The more you can pull down AGI, the less likely you'll be hurt by the limitation that can cut IRA deductions (Chapter 11), for example, squeeze the value of exemptions (Chapter 8), take away part of your itemized deductions (Chapter 15) or deny you the right to deduct passive losses from real estate (Chapter 10).

Except for the deduction for IRA contributions (which can be claimed on the 1040A short form), you must file the full-fledged Form 1040 to claim adjustments to income. Don't let that put you off. If you deserve an adjustment to income, use the 1040. You can skip all the lines that don't apply to you.

IRA Contributions

As discussed in Chapter 11, this is one of the few retroactive tax breaks around. If you qualify to deduct contributions to an individual retirement account—as most taxpayers do—you can make your deposit as late as April 15 and still deduct the amount on the return for the previous year.

If you and your spouse both work, you can each deposit up to $2,000 in an IRA. If your spouse doesn't work, you can contribute a total of $2,250, split between you and your spouse however you wish, as long as neither gets more than $2,000.

You don't file any extra forms when you claim a deductible IRA contribution. But if you make nondeductible contributions, you must report them on Form 8606. See Chapter 11 for details about who can deduct IRA contributions.

Moving Expenses

The cost of a job-related move used to be an itemized deduction, which was a bummer for the 70% of taxpayers who don't itemize. They got no help at all from Uncle Sam. Now, however, these costs are adjustments to income, open to itemizers and non-itemizers alike. This change could be especially important to college graduates who move to take their first job. They're often among the majority of taxpayers who *don't* itemize, so in the past they've been blocked from deducting moving expenses. There are two basic tests you must pass to get this tax-saver:

- **Your move must be connected with taking a new job that is at least 50 miles farther from your old home than your old job was.** If your former job was 10 miles away from your old home, for example, the new job has to be at least 60 miles away from that old home. Note that it does not matter how far the new home is away from your new job. If you are moving to take your first job, the 50-mile test applies to the distance

Money Saver

Need a retroactive tax break? If you qualify to deduct contributions to an IRA, you can make your deposit as late as April 15 and still deduct the amount on the return for the previous year.

Money Saver

Did you have to move to take a job? Take the cost of the move as an adjustment to income.

from your old home to your new job location.

- **You must work full time for at least 39 weeks during the 12 months after the move.** If you're self-employed, in addition to working 39 weeks in the first 12 months, you also have to work full time at the new location for at least 78 weeks out of the first 24 months. (To pass these tests you must work in the new area, not necessarily at the same job for the required time.) You claim the deductions on your tax return for the year of the move even if you haven't yet met the 39- or 78-week test by the time you file. If it turns out you are not eligible, you should either file an amended return for the year (see Chapter 2) or report as income on your next tax return the amount previously deducted as moving expenses.

What You Can Deduct

Fewer expenses are deductible now than in the past. Until a few years ago, for example, you could deduct the cost of pre-move househunting trips and even some of the costs of selling your old home and buying a new one. Those write-offs are gone. But the law still allows what are probably the most common and the most valuable write-offs:

- **The cost of moving your household goods** to the new location; and

- **The cost of moving yourself** and your family—travel and lodging expenses but not the cost of meals—to the new hometown.

When toting up the cost of the move, include what you pay for packing your belongings and charges for connecting or disconnecting utilities to move appliances. You can also include the cost of moving household goods and personal effects from a place other than your own home—say from your college student's dorm—up to the amount it would have cost to move them from your old home. You can even deduct the cost of moving your pets from the old home to the new one. If you drive your own car, you can deduct 9 cents a mile, as well as any parking fees and tolls incurred along the way.

You figure your moving expense deduction on Form 3903.

If your employer reimburses you for the move, you don't have to go through the rigmarole required in the past of reporting the reimbursement as taxable income and then offsetting it by claiming moving expense deductions. When your employer just pays expenses that qualify for the deduction—so there's no tax to collect—the IRS doesn't want to hear about it.

Self-Employment Tax

The self-employment tax can take a grueling toll, claiming 15.3% of your self-employment income. You do get part of it back, though, by deducting 50% of what you pay with the Schedule SE as an adjustment to income on your Form 1040. If you pay $2,000 in self-employment taxes, the $1,000 write-off here will save you $280 in income taxes, if you're in the 28% bracket.

Self-Employed Health Insurance Deduction

This on-again/off-again write-off is on again and Congress says it's permanent this time. In the past, the lawmakers allowed this deduction to disappear and reappear (sometimes retroactively).

If you are self-employed, this break lets you deduct 30% of what you pay for medical insurance for yourself and your family. (Before 1995, the deduction was for 25% of the cost of insurance.) Because this is an adjustment to income, you are guaranteed tax savings. Other medical costs (including the 70% of your premiums not deducted here) can be written off as itemized deductions only to the extent your medical costs exceed 7.5% of your adjusted gross income. (See Chapter 15 for details.)

If you qualify and pay $3,000 for a family health policy, for example, this rule allows you to write off $900 without worrying about the 7.5% floor. The remaining

Time Saver

If your employer pays expenses that would qualify for the moving-expense deduction, don't bother reporting it. There's no tax to collect, so the IRS doesn't want to hear about it.

$2,100 counts toward that threshold.

There are restrictions, of course. Your medical-insurance write-off can't exceed the net income of your business. Also, you can't claim this deduction if you are eligible for health coverage offered by your employer—if you have a job as well as your own business—or by your spouse's employer. You apply that "other insurance" test month by month. If your spouse gets a job in July that offers family medical insurance, for example, health insurance premiums you paid during the first six months of the year when that coverage was not available would still be eligible for this break.

And, note this: There may be a way to make 100% of your family's health premiums deductible. The IRS has okayed a plan in which a self-employed person hired his spouse and offered her comprehensive medical coverage at no cost as a fringe benefit. The spouse opted for family coverage, so the full cost of the family's insurance was deductible as a business expense (not an adjustment to income).

If you have other employees, you must offer them the same deal. But if your spouse is your only employee, this arrangement magnifies your tax deductions without raising your costs. For it to pass muster with the IRS, your spouse must be a bona fide employee, of course, and you need a "plan" under which the health care benefits are offered. It doesn't have to be an elaborate document, though. Ask a tax accountant or insurance agent to suggest appropriate language.

Self-Employed Medical Insurance

• •

Q: *I have my own business and am never sure whether I get to deduct part of my medical insurance premiums. What's the rule for 1996?*

A: The write-off that allows the self-employed to deduct 30% of the premiums paid for medical coverage is now permanent. Restrictions are discussed elsewhere in this chapter. If you made qualifying payments in 1994, you may deserve a retroactive refund. Although the break expired at the end of 1993, when Congress revived it in 1995 the decision was retroactive—covering 1994. If you qualify for a 1994 deduction, file an amended return to claim your refund. See Chapter 2 for details.

Keogh and SEP Contributions

The self-employed have a chance for a huge deduction here. As much as $30,000 a year can be stashed in a Keogh retirement plan. The limit if you use a simplified employee pension is nearly $20,000. Every dime you put in the plan can be written off as an adjustment to income. See Chapter 11 for the details.

Deduction of Penalty for Early Withdrawal of Savings

If you cash a certificate of deposit early, you'll be nicked with an early withdrawal penalty. Especially maddening is that although these penalties often offset much or even all of the interest earned on the CD, the bank still reports the full amount of interest earned as taxable income.

This adjustment to income lets you even things out by deducting that penalty. Even though you have to report interest you didn't really get, you offset that income by deducting the penalty here. You should get a Form 1099 from the bank showing not only the interest to report but also the penalty you get to deduct. You should deduct the full penalty, even if it's more than the interest earned.

Alimony Paid

As discussed in Chapter 8, alimony you pay under a divorce decree is deductible as an adjustment to income. You have to show on your tax return the social security number of your ex spouse who gets the money. The reason: the IRS wants to be able to check to make sure he or she is reporting the same amount as taxable income. Failure to include that social security number can trigger a $50 fine, and the IRS can reject your write-off, too.

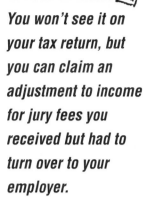

Money Saver

You won't see it on your tax return, but you can claim an adjustment to income for jury fees you received but had to turn over to your employer.

Jury Fees

Although you won't see this entry on your tax return, you can claim an adjustment to income for jury fees you received but had to turn over to your employer. Some employers continue to pay employees' full salary while they are doing their civic duty, but ask that they turn over their jury fees to the corporate treasury. The only problem is that the IRS demands that you report those fees as taxable income. Claiming an adjustment to income for the amount sets things straight. Since there's no special line for this write-off, write it in on the line where you total your other adjustments.

Moving Expenses

Q: *My daughter graduated from college last spring and moved cross country to take a new job. Can she deduct the cost of the move?*

A: Yes. Such expenses are now an adjustment to income, so they can be deducted even by taxpayers who don't itemize. Basically, she can write off the cost of getting herself and her household goods to her new home. If she drove her own car, she can deduct 9 cents a mile.

Write-Offs: Itemized Deductions

This is the fun part of taxes, if you'll forgive the use of that word in this context. Think of it as a treasure hunt. The more booty you discover, the lower your tax bill will be.

Over the years Congress has packed the tax law with goodies. It's the lawmakers' way of inviting you to let Uncle Sam pick up part of your expenses by reducing your tax bill. If you spend money for specifically sanctioned expenses, the IRS will ignore that part of your income. Every $1,000 of deductions knocks $1,000 off your taxable income, shaving $280 off your tax bill if you're in the 28% bracket. That effectively reduces your $1,000 out-of-pocket cost to $720.

First, the Bad News

A few years back, Congress decided that higher-income taxpayers shouldn't get credit for all their deductions. The squeeze was supposed to be temporary, ending in 1995. (Oh, sure.) But the lawmakers decided to extend it a bit—like forever. The crackdown is now permanent and it affects you if your 1996 adjusted gross income (AGI) exceeds $117,950. That threshold applies whether you file a joint, single or head-of-household return. If you're married and file separately, the threshold is cut in half, to $58,975. (The trigger points will rise in the future with inflation; for 1995 they were $114,700 and $57,350.)

If your AGI punctures the level, the tax-saving power of itemized deductions is eroded. You lose deductions equal to 3% of the amount by which your AGI exceeds the threshold. If your AGI is $150,000 in 1996, for example, you lose $962 (3% of the $32,050 excess) in itemized deductions. Reducing your deductions raises your taxable income by the same amount and, in the 31% bracket, the extra income boosts your tax bill by $298.

The deduction squeeze amounts to a not-too-cleverly disguised tax hike for taxpayers whose AGI is over the threshold. Taking away deductions in this way is exactly the same as adding 0.93% to your tax rate if you're in the 31% bracket—making the effective rate 31.93%. The impact

Who Deducts How Much?

Nobody's average, but it doesn't hurt to have an idea of how much your fellow taxpayers (and your President) are deducting on their returns. Here are the average amounts claimed on returns filed for 1994. In each case, the amount shown is the average deduction for taxpayers within each income group who claimed the specific type of deduction. Most returns don't claim a deduction for medical expenses, for example, but of those that do, the average amounts are shown.

Your own write-offs must be based on your records, of course. But if your totals fall far below the averages, take another look at your files and the tax rules. You may be missing something. Don't worry if your deductions are higher than the amounts listed. Claim every dime you're entitled to.

Adjusted gross income (AGI) is taxable income before subtracting deductions and exemptions. The column labeled "gifts" shows deductions for charitable contributions. We include a look at Bill and Hillary Clinton's deductions solely for voyeuristic purposes. The President and First Lady reported 1994 AGI of $263,900.

AGI	Average Deduction			
	Medical	**Taxes Paid**	**Interest Paid**	**Gifts**
$20,000 - $25,000	$2,865	$2,057	$4,920	$1,250
$25,000 - $30,000	2,924	2,351	5,134	1,195
$30,000 - $40,000	4,078	2,808	5,069	1,375
$40,000 - $50,000	4,531	3,372	5,678	1,520
$50,000 - $75,000	5,583	4,415	6,384	1,616
$75,000 - $100,000	7,788	6,208	7,626	2,380
$100,000 - $200,000	8,061	10,031	10,049	4,017
Over $200,000	17,200	29,842	18,074	11,444
Bill & Hillary Clinton	0	18,827	4,669	30,125

pushes the 36% rate to 37.08% and the 39.6% rate to 40.79%. (See Chapter 5 for a discussion of this and other "bubble brackets.")

This take-away does not hit all deductions. It spares write-offs for medical expenses, casualty and theft losses, gambling losses and investment interest. You get the full power of those deductions, notwithstanding your AGI. (As noted later in this chapter, medical expenses, gambling losses and casualty and theft losses are already subject to tough restrictions. The limit on investment interest deductions is discussed in Chapter 10.) And, regardless of how high your AGI goes, no more than 80% of your other itemized deductions can be taken away by this rule.

Don't think the new restriction makes your search for itemized deductions less important. In fact, the way it works gives you more incentive than ever to claim every possible deduction. Since the law sets a floor for itemized deductions—only those expenses that exceed the 3%-of-excess-AGI amount count—it takes away the first dollars of your itemized deductions, not the last. Once your deductions pass the floor, every *extra* dollar you write-off has full, tax-saving power.

Bigger Standard Deductions

Of course, the squeeze on deductions means nothing to you if you don't itemize. And for a growing army of taxpayers, itemizing doesn't make sense. In fact, millions who found itemizing profitable in recent years reject it now that beefed-up standard deductions are available.

All taxpayers are permitted to reduce their taxable income by the standard deduction for their filing status. This is a no-questions-asked write-off. You don't need any records to prove that you deserve the deduction. Even if you somehow made it through a year without incurring any of the deductible expenses detailed in this chapter, you still may claim the full standard deduction on your return. You itemize deductions only if the total of your allowable expenses exceeds your standard deduction. The standard deduction amounts for 1995 and 1996 are shown in the

Once your deductions pass the 3% AGI floor, every extra dollar you write-off has full, tax-saving power.

Money Saver

Even if you made it through a year without incurring any of the deductible expenses detailed in this chapter, you still may claim the full standard deduction on your return.

following table. (The amounts rise each year automatically to keep up with inflation.) If you're unsure of your filing status, see Chapter 8.

Filing Status	Standard Deduction 1995	1996
Single,		
under age 65	$3,900	$4,000
65 or older	4,850	5,000
Married filing jointly,		
under age 65	6,550	6,700
one spouse 65 or older	7,300	7,500
both 65 or older	8,050	8,300
Married filing separately,		
under age 65	3,275	3,350
65 or older	4,025	4,150
Head of Household,		
under age 65	5,750	5,900
65 or older	6,700	6,900
Surviving spouse,		
under age 65	6,550	6,700
65 or older	7,300	7,500

More for Some

As the preceding table indicates, senior citizens get a higher standard deduction. This makes up, in part, for Congress's decision a few years ago to eliminate their right to claim an extra personal exemption.

The standard deduction is also increased for taxpayers who are legally blind. If you are totally blind, you must attach a statement to your return saying so; if you are partly blind, you must attach a statement from an eye physician or registered optometrist certifying that you cannot see better than 20/200 in the better eye with glasses, or the field of vision is not more than 20 degrees.

- On a 1996 joint return, add to the amounts listed above $800 if one spouse is legally blind or $1,600 if both are.

- On married-filing-separately and surviving-spouse returns, add $800 if the taxpayer is blind.

- On single and head-of-household returns, add $1,000. (The additional amounts were $50 less per person for 1995 returns.)

Less for Others

Taxpayers who can be claimed as a dependent on someone else's return—a scenario that applies primarily to children claimed on their parents' return—are often stuck with a stunted standard deduction. For dependents, the standard deduction is the greater of $650 (in both 1995 and 1996) or the total of earned income, up to the regular standard deduction amount. (Earned income is basically earnings from a job rather than investment income. See the discussion of the "kiddie tax" in Chapter 8.) This rule basically prevents a dependent from using the standard deduction to shelter more than $650 of unearned income, such as interest and dividends. The limit is increased for taxpayers who qualify for the age or blindness addition. Thus, for example, in 1996 a single taxpayer age 65 or older who is claimed as a dependent by a son or daughter would have a minimum standard deduction of $1,650—$650 plus the extra $1,000 allotted because of age.

The standard deduction amounts for all taxpayers will continue to increase in the future to keep up with inflation.

Making the Most of Your Write-Offs

The bigger standard deduction focuses additional attention on "bunching" write-offs. This is the practice of alternating between claiming the standard deduction one year and itemizing the next. It can pay off if your deductible expenses routinely fall close to the standard

Hair Transplant

Q: *I've given up waiting for a product to grow hair and have decided to have a hair transplant. Is the cost of that kind of operation deductible?*

A: Probably not. Until 1991, such a cost was considered a qualifying medical expense. Now, the expense of cosmetic surgery directed at improving appearance—rather than ameliorating a deformity arising from a congenital abnormality, injury or disease—is not deductible.

deduction amount. Bunching is accomplished by accelerating the payment of deductible expenses in the year you'll itemize. This effectively depletes the following year's supply of deductions. It defers such payments in the year you'll use the standard deduction, thus pushing otherwise worthless deductions into the following year when they'll be valuable because you'll itemize. See Chapter 17 for details.

Medical Expenses

The list of medical costs that can be deducted stretches to the Mayo Clinic and back, but few taxpayers get any tax benefit. The reason for the seeming contradiction is that Congress keeps raising the ante for getting into the game. To deduct any medical expenses, your total outlay for qualifying costs during the year must exceed 7.5% of your adjusted gross income. (AGI is basically all your taxable income minus certain items, the most common of which are IRA and Keogh contributions and alimony you paid.)

To see the impact of this rule, consider a taxpayer with AGI of $50,000. The 7.5% test blocks the deduction of the first $3,750 of medical expenses. If you had $4,000 in unreimbursed medical expenses, for example, the deductible amount would be a skimpy $250. (An important, and increasingly available, loophole around the 7.5% rule are medical reimbursement accounts that many employers offer employees as a fringe benefit. These allow employees to divert part of their salary to an account that reimburses them for medical expenses. Since the money that goes through the account is not taxed, the effect is the same as allowing you to deduct medical costs without worrying about the 7.5% limit. Really, it's even better, because funds run through a reimbursement account also avoid social security taxes. See Chapter 6 for more on reimbursement accounts, and take advantage of one if your employer offers it.)

A basic definition

The tougher Congress makes it to get any medical deductions, the more important it is to know what can qualify for this tax saver. The basic definition of medical care is extremely broad. Qualifying expenses include what you pay for the diagnosis, treatment or prevention of disease or for treatment affecting any structure or function of the body. You also count the cost of transportation to and from the place you receive the care and the premiums you pay for medical insurance.

Clearly, what you pay in doctors' and dentists' bills qualifies, as do hospital bills and what you pay for prescription drugs. (The cost of over-the-counter medicines doesn't count.) Plenty of other expenses are accepted by the IRS, too, including many that are less likely to be covered by insurance, such as some nursing home fees and what you pay for medically necessary improvements to your home. Before looking in detail at what you can claim, consider whose expenses you are permitted to deduct on your return.

Whose expenses can you deduct?

In addition to what you pay for your own medical care, include what you pay for your spouse and anyone you claim as a dependent (see Chapter 8). If you were divorced during the year but paid medical bills incurred by your spouse while you were married, you can deduct those costs even though you file a separate return. Also count medical expenses you pay for someone who would qualify as your dependent (either individually or under a multiple-support agreement) except that he or she earned more than the personal exemption amount ($2,550 in 1996 and $2,500 in 1995) or filed a joint return.

If you are divorced, you can include in your deductible medical expenses any qualifying bills you pay for your child, even if he or she is claimed as a dependent by your ex-spouse.

Now, what's deductible?

Insurance

Qualifying costs include premiums you pay for policies that either pay for or reimburse you for:

Money Saver

The money that goes through a medical reimbursement account isn't taxed; the effect is the same as allowing you to deduct medical costs without worrying about the 7.5% limit.

Money Saver

When figuring your medical expenses, include the cost of transportation to and from the place you receive the care and insurance premiums you pay.

- **Doctor, hospital and surgical fees and other medical and dental expenses,** including the cost of membership in an HMO or similar plan;

- **Prescription drugs;** and

- **Replacement of lost or damaged contact lenses.**

You may also deduct what you pay for Medicare B supplemental insurance and, if you're not covered by social security but choose to enroll in the program, your Medicare A premiums as well.

You can't deduct premiums you pay for any policy that promises to pay you a set amount—$100 a day, say—for time you're in the hospital, insurance that pays you for lost earnings, or a policy that pays a flat amount for the loss of a limb, for example, or sight. To be deductible, the insurance benefits must be tied to the actual cost of medical care. On the bright side, benefits you receive under a nondeductible policy are tax-free.

Break for self-employed?

If you're self-employed, you may be able to deduct 30% of what you pay for medical insurance for yourself and your family without worrying about the 7.5% test. See Chapter 14 for details.

Swimming Pools and Other Home Improvements

You've probably heard stories about taxpayers writing off the cost of swimming pools as medical expenses. What quicker way to meet the 7.5% of AGI test than to spend $25,000 or so on a backyard pool?

There's a catch, of course. First of all, the pool—or whatever improvement—must be primarily for medical care. The improvement should be recommended by a doctor to treat a specific ailment. Putting in a pool for regular exercise to improve your general health doesn't cut it even if your doctor suggests it. In the cases in which courts have okayed medical deductions for the cost of pool construction, the pools were recommended for therapy for patients with such diseases as polio and severe osteoarthritis. To qualify for a tax deduction, the capital improvement must also pass the "reasonableness" test the IRS applies to all expenditures. It could be tough for a private pool to pass that test, for example, if you have ready access to another pool.

Still, medical deductions for pools have been approved. So have write-offs for the cost of installing home elevators for heart patients unable to walk up and down stairs, central air-conditioning systems for people with breathing problems, and special plumbing fixtures for the handicapped. If an improvement qualifies as a medical expense, so does what you pay for its operation and maintenance.

You don't necessarily get to deduct the full cost of medically required improvements. Your write-off is limited to the difference between what you pay and any increase in the value of your home. If you spend $25,000 on a pool, for example, and it boosts the value of your property by $15,000, the qualifying medical expense would be $10,000.

To claim a capital improvement as a medical expense, you should have a written statement from a doctor recommending that you make the improvement and evidence, such as before-and-after appraisals, showing how much, if any, the value of your property increased due to the improvement.

Fully deductible improvements

The cost of certain improvements made for handicapped individuals is fully deductible, even if the improvements increase the value of your home. These include:

- **Constructing entrance and exit ramps;**

- **Widening doorways and hallways to accommodate wheelchairs;**

- **Installing railings, support bars and other modifications in bathrooms;**

- **Lowering or otherwise modifying kitchen cabinets and equipment;** and

- **Adjusting electrical outlets and fixtures.**

Although capital improvements usually increase the

basis of your home for tax purposes (see Chapter 9), the portion of the cost you write off as a medical expense is not an addition to basis.

Quit-Smoking Course

• •

Q: *I finally beat my smoking habit by taking an expensive stop-smoking course. Can I write off the cost?*

A: The IRS is reconsidering its long-standing answer of "no" to this question. Despite the Surgeon General's warnings that smoking contributes to cancer and other diseases, the tax agency's position on medical deductions has been that courses aimed at kicking the habit generally don't meet the law's requirement that the medical care must treat or prevent disease. It's likely that the IRS will reverse field and okay the deduction, but it's unclear when the decision will be made. Of course, as with other medical expenses, the cost is deductible only to the extent that your total medical expenses exceed 7.5% of your adjusted gross income.

Travel Expenses

The cost of getting where you have to go for medical care is deductible, too. Count what you pay for cab, bus or subway fare, or ambulance hire. If you drive your own car to the doctor's office or hospital, tote up the deduction at 9 cents a mile, plus parking and tolls.

Trips to a local doctor are nickel-and-dime expenses that won't help much toward the 7.5% threshold. But out-of-town travel counts, too, and those costs can mount up quickly. Say, for example, that your local doctor recommends you go to the Mayo Clinic to see a specialist because the needed treatment is not available locally. The cost of travel to Minnesota would be deductible. What if the care is available locally but you choose to travel to a nicer clime—such as going to Hawaii for cataract surgery? No surprise here: The cost of the travel would not be deductible (but the cost of the surgery still would be).

In addition to the cost of trips to a distant hospital or clinic, you may be able to deduct the cost of travel that's recommended by a doctor as part of the treatment for a specific ailment. Taxpayers have won deductions for the cost of traveling to spend the winter in Florida, for example, when their doctors recommended that they avoid cold weather as part of their treatment. If you make such a trip for general health purposes, however, the cost is not deductible.

What about food and lodging costs connected with your medical care? The basic rule is that such expenses are not deductible unless they are part of the cost of a stay in a hospital or similar institution.

However, you may deduct the cost of lodging (but still not food) associated with deductible medical care. If you stay in a hotel while you are receiving treatment in an outpatient clinic, you can include the cost in your deductible medical expenses up to $50 a day. The daily dollar limit is per person. If you travel with a sick child to get medical care, for example, you could deduct up to $100 a day for your lodging expenses. And if you have to stay in a nearby hotel while a child is hospitalized, you may deduct up to $50 a day of your costs.

Here's a handful of less-than-obvious situations in which travel expenses have been permitted as medical deductions:

- **Plane fare to and from the hospital paid by a prospective kidney donor.**

- **Cost of transportation to and from Alcoholics Anonymous meetings** recommended by a doctor.

- **Fare for parent or nurse** who accompanies a patient on medically required trip.

- **Cost of a trip to Florida,** on the recommendation of a physician, to aid recuperation from a stroke.

- **Cost of parents' transportation to visit mentally ill child,** when doctor recommended visits as part of the child's treatment.

Nursing Homes and Special Schools

Include in your medical expenses wages and other amounts you pay for nursing services, including social security taxes you pay on the caregiver's wages. The person providing care does not have to be a registered or licensed nurse for the cost to be deductible, but you must be able to show that the services provided were for the medical care or treat-

Money Saver

If you stay in a hotel while you're receiving treatment in an outpatient clinic, include the cost in your deductible medical expenses—up to $50 a day.

ment of a patient. If the person also performed nonmedical chores, such as housekeeping, only the part of the expense attributable to medical care is deductible. The rest is a nondeductible personal expense. To back up your deduction, you or the attendant should keep a log showing the breakdown of time spent on personal versus medical duties.

Nursing home fees can quickly mount up to 7.5% of almost anyone's income. Such costs may be fully deductible, partially deductible or not deductible at all, depending on why someone is in the institution:

- **If the availability of medical care is the primary reason, the full cost can be deductible,** even though much of the cost is actually for otherwise nondeductible expenses such as food and lodging.

- **When someone chooses to live in a rest home or retirement center** primarily for personal rather than medical reasons the cost is generally nondeductible.

- **If part of the monthly fee is specifically for medical facilities** available at the institution, however, that segment of the charge can qualify as a medical expense.

The key to deductibility is the level of medical services provided at the institution and the condition of the resident.

What about advance payments, such as life-care or founder's fees, required by some institutions? The portion of such required charges allocated to medical care is deductible in the year paid as long as the fee is required as a condition of the institution's promise to provide future medical care.

Your medical deduction can also include costs for a special school or training for a physically or mentally handicapped person if the main reason for the expense is the school's resources for relieving the handicap. The IRS has approved deductions for the cost of a school that teaches Braille to a blind child or lip reading to a deaf child or that gives remedial language training to correct a condition caused by a birth defect. If the primary reason the person is at the school is for medically related treatment, the cost of food and lodging can also be included in the deduction.

Sometimes, colleges and private schools include in

their tuition charges a fee for student medical care. If you can get a breakdown of the bill showing what part of the total goes to those fees, you can include that amount in your deductible medical expenses.

Timing Deductions

Medical bills are deductible in the year you pay them. If you pay by check, the day you mail or deliver the check is the date of payment, even if the check isn't cashed until the following year. If you charge a medical expense to a credit card, payment is considered made the day you make the charge regardless of when you actually pay the credit card bill.

The 7.5% threshold for medical deductions gives added importance to the issue of timing. If you incur heavy expenses one year and it's clear that you'll pass the 7.5% test, you may want to try to cram in other medical expenses before year-end. Buy that new pair of contact lenses, for example, or give extra thought to scheduling that elective surgery before December 31. By paying the bills before the end of the year, you can guarantee their deductibility. Pushed into the following year, such expenses might not tip the 7.5%-of-AGI scale.

On the other hand, if you will fall short of the 7.5% threshold one year, try to hold off paying medical bills until after New Year's Eve. By pushing payment into a new year, you have at least a chance that the expense will be deductible.

Reimbursement

When figuring your medical-expense deduction, you must subtract any reimbursement you received from your medical insurance, of course. What if you pay a doctor's bill or other qualifying expense one year and get the check from your insurance company the next? The answer depends on whether you received any tax benefit from the expense in the year you paid the bill. If not—because your total costs fell below the 7.5% threshold so you didn't get to claim medical expenses—you can just pocket the reimbursement. If the reimbursement is for an expense that

(continued on page 378)

Money Saver

Medical bills charged to a credit card are deductible this year, even if you don't pay until next year.

Other Medical Deductions

Here's a rundown of some of the other expenses you may be able to include when figuring your medical-expense deduction:

- **Abortion.** You can include the expenses of a legal abortion.

- **Acupuncture.** The cost for such treatment is deductible.

- **Alcoholism.** Payments to a treatment center qualify, including the cost of room and board.

- **Artificial limb.** The cost of the prosthesis and associated expenses are deductible.

- **Birth control pills.** As with other prescribed medicines, the cost is deductible.

- **Braille books and magazines.** The amount by which the cost exceeds that of regular reading material may be written off.

- **Car.** The cost of outfitting an auto with special controls needed by a handicapped person may be included with your medical expenses.

- **Childbirth preparation classes.** The IRS says fees for the mother qualify but fees for the father/coach do not.

- **Chiropractors.** Their fees qualify.

- **Christian Science practitioners.** Their fees are deductible.

- **Contact lenses.** The cost qualifies, as does the cost of insurance against their loss.

- **Cosmetic surgery.** In the past, the cost of a face-lift or any other cosmetic surgery qualified as a medical expense. It didn't matter whether the operation was done to correct a physical defect or simply to serve your vanity. Now, though, different rules apply. The cost of surgery necessary to ameliorate a deformity arising from a congenital abnormality, injury or disease remains deductible. But there's no deduction for the cost of surgery directed at improving appearance rather than meaningfully promoting proper function of the body.

- **Crutches.** What you pay to buy or rent crutches or other medically necessary equipment is deductible.

- **Dental treatment.** The cost of everything from diagnostic x-rays to orthodontic treatment to dentures qualifies.

- **Doctor's fees.** When adding them up, count payments to anesthesiologists, dermatologists, gynecologists, neurologists, obstetricians, ophthalmologists, osteopaths, pediatricians, podiatrists, psychiatrists, surgeons and any other recognized medical practitioners.

- **Drug addiction.** As with treatment for alcoholism, treatment for drug addiction is deductible.

- **Eyeglasses.** Include in the deductible amount the fees for eye exams as well as the cost of the glasses.

- **Guide dog.** Medical expenses can include the cost of a guide dog for the blind or deaf, including the cost of the dog's care.

- **Health club dues.** As efforts to improve your general health aren't deductible, it's highly unlikely that you could persuade the IRS to let you write off these costs. However, if your doctor recommended that you join a health club as part of necessary therapy for a specific medical condition, the cost may be deductible.

- **Hearing aid.** The cost of the device itself and associated fees are deductible.

- **Lead-based paint removal.** This is one of the stranger examples of the way the IRS views qualifying medical expenses. You can count as a deductible expense the cost of removing lead-based paint if the paint is within the reach of a child who has suffered from lead poisoning. The cost of removing paint out of the reach of the child doesn't count toward the medical deduction, nor does the cost of repainting the scraped area.

- **Medicine.** Include in your deductible medical expenses what you pay for any *prescription* medicines and insulin. The cost of over-the-counter medicines is not deductible.

- **Oxygen.** The costs of oxygen equipment and oxygen to relieve breathing problems that are caused by a medical condition are deductible.

- **Psychoanalysis.** Fees paid for psychoanalysis are deductible.

- **Psychologist.** Also count what you pay a psychologist for care.

- **Stop-smoking program.** Despite the Surgeon General's long-standing campaign against smoking, the IRS has held that the cost of a program designed to kick the habit does not

qualify as a medical expense. However, the agency is reconsidering its position. Also, if you take such a course on your doctor's orders to relieve the symptoms of an existing disease—say, emphysema—the cost would be deductible.

- **Sterilization.** The cost of such an operation, including a vasectomy, is deductible.

- **Telephone.** What you pay for special equipment to permit the deaf to communicate over the phone is deductible.

- **Television.** The cost of a decoder so that a TV picks up closed-caption signals for the hearing impaired can be included with your medical expenses.

- **Weight-loss program.** As with stop-smoking courses, what you pay for a weight-loss program to improve your general health is not deductible. However, you may write off the cost of such a program recommended by your doctor as part of the treatment for a specific medical problem, such as hypertension.

- **Wheelchair.** The cost of a wheelchair, whether manual or motorized, is deductible.

was deducted in an earlier year, however, all or part of the reimbursement is considered income. The taxable amount is either the full reimbursement or the amount of your medical deduction write-off for the year in question (total expenses minus 7.5% of AGI)—whichever is less.

What if insurance pays you more than your medical expenses? Whether the excess reimbursement is considered taxable income depends on who paid for the insurance. If you did, the extra cash is nontaxable. But if your employer paid for the medical insurance, the "profit" is considered taxable income to you. And if you and your employer shared the cost of the insurance, the tax status of the excess reimbursement turns on the portion of the premiums each of you paid. If the premiums were split 50/50, for example, half the excess reimbursement would be taxable and half tax-free.

Damages

If you receive a settlement in a damage suit that includes money for medical expenses you deducted in an earlier year, that amount is considered taxable in the year you receive it, but only to the extent that the deduction actually reduced your taxable income for the year you wrote off the expenses. If a settlement includes funds for future medical expenses, the amount is not taxable, but neither are those future medical expenses deductible until they exceed the amount of the award allocated to future medical care.

Taxes

Before looking at the taxes you can deduct, remember that what could well be your biggest tax bill—what you pay Uncle Sam in income taxes—cannot be written off on your federal return. Nor can you deduct what you pay in social security (FICA) tax, which claims 7.65% of the first $62,700 of wage income in 1996, and which for a growing number of workers costs more than the income tax. State and local sales taxes are also on the nondeductible list.

Note, however, that those subject to the self-employment

tax can deduct 50% of what they pay. In 1996, that levy claims 15.3% of up to $62,700 of income and 2.9% of income over that amount. This write-off is an adjustment to income, which means you can deduct it whether or not you itemize other deductions (see Chapter 14).

State and Local Income Taxes

If you don't own a home and don't deduct mortgage interest, your state income-tax bill is likely to be your largest single itemized deduction. It's fairly easy to keep track of this deduction. Amounts withheld from your paychecks will show up on the Form W-2 you get from your employer; any income tax you pay via estimated payments will be recorded on your copies of estimated tax forms; and if you pay an extra amount when you file your state return, that amount will be on the return.

As with other expenses, you deduct state and local income taxes on the return for the year in which you made the payment, which may be a different year than that for which you owe the tax. Say, for example, that when you complete your 1995 state return in the spring of 1996 you discover that you owe an extra $500, which you pay when you file the return. Although the tax was assessed against your 1995 income, the fact that you paid it in 1996 means it should be deducted on your 1996 federal return. That's the one you'll file in 1997.

Timing your fourth-quarter estimated state-tax payment

If you owe estimated taxes on self-employment or investment income, the state tax bill offers some planning opportunities. In most states, the final estimated tax payment is due in January of the following year. If you make your final 1996 payment in January 1997, it would be deductible on your 1997 federal return. Make that payment by December 31, 1996, however, and you can include the amount in your 1996 deductions. (The payment is considered to have been made in 1996 as long as your check is in the mail by the end of the year, even if it's not cashed until

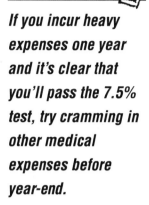

Money Saver

If you incur heavy expenses one year and it's clear that you'll pass the 7.5% test, try cramming in other medical expenses before year-end.

the following year.) For the deduction of such a payment to withstand IRS scrutiny, it must be a reasonable estimate of the tax you owe for the year involved. You may not, for example, make a huge fourth-quarter estimated payment to beef up your federal deductions if the outlay is actually a deliberate overpayment of your state taxes that you'll soon get back in the form of a state tax refund.

In some cases, it's better not to accelerate the tax payment. If you're not itemizing deductions—because your total expenses won't pass the standard deduction amount—holding off the fourth-quarter payment until January has a double benefit. It lets you hold on to your money a little longer and preserves the possibility that you'll get to write off the payment the next year. Also, if you expect to be in a higher tax bracket the following year, the value of the deduction would escalate. Finally, if you are subject to the alternative minimum tax (AMT, which is discussed in Chapter 4), don't prepay your taxes. State income taxes aren't deductible at all under the AMT.

© 1991 Carlson—Milwaukee Sentinel

State tax refunds

This is a confusing issue for many people, particularly now that state governments send out 1099-G forms reporting the refunds to taxpayers and the IRS. But don't let that form persuade you that the refund is automatically taxable.

If you did not itemize on your federal return for the previous year, the refund is tax-free. Even if you did itemize, part or all of the refund may be tax-free. You report taxable income only to the extent your earlier write-off resulted in a real tax benefit for you. To know whether part of your refund is tax-free, subtract the standard deduction amount for your filing status ($4,000 for singles, $6,700 for marrieds in 1996; $3,900/$6,550 in 1995) from the total of your itemized deductions for the year. If the difference is less than your state refund, part of the refund is tax-free. Report as taxable income only the amount by which your itemized deductions exceeded the standard deduction amount.

Consider an example: You file a joint return for 1995 and claim itemized deductions of $7,500, including $2,000 of state income taxes paid. In 1996, you receive a $500 state income-tax refund based on your 1995 state return.

Is it taxable? Yes, the entire $500 should be reported as taxable income on your 1996 federal return. The standard deduction on 1995 joint returns—for filers under 65—was $6,550. By itemizing $7,500 worth of deductions you knocked an extra $950 off your taxable income. Even if you had paid your state taxes on the button and claimed $500 less in that category, you still would have itemized rather than claiming the standard deduction. In this example, every dollar of the $500 state tax overpayment pushed down your federal taxable income in 1995. Uncle Sam evens things up by demanding that you report the $500 refund as taxable income in 1996.

If, in this example, your 1995 itemized deductions totaled just $7,000—instead of $7,500—only $450 of the $500 state tax refund would be taxable. Why? Because the itemized deductions reduced taxable income by just $450 more than if you had taken the $6,550 standard deduction. In other words, only $450 of the state tax deduction really reduced your taxable income in 1995, so you report only that part of the refund as taxable income to even the score.

State disability insurance

Residents of four states—California, New Jersey, New York and Rhode Island—can include in their state tax deduction required contributions to state disability-benefit funds.

Real Estate Taxes

State and local real estate taxes you pay on your

Money Saver

Make your final estimated state-tax estimated payment by December 31, 1996, and you can include the amount in your 1996 deductions.

If you didn't itemize on your federal return for last year, any state refund you received is tax-free.

home or other property are deductible. If you pay your property taxes through an escrow account funded via your monthly mortgage payments, you don't actually earn the deduction until funds are transferred out of the account to pay the tax bill. Your lender should send you a statement showing how much real estate tax was paid for you during the year. If you don't receive such a statement from the lender, ask for one.

If you're a renter, you may not claim a deduction for the part of your rent you figure goes to cover the landlord's property taxes. Even if a rent increase is specifically tied to a property-tax increase, you don't get a deduction. The law allows a write-off only for the person on whom the tax is directly imposed.

Municipal assessments

What about special municipal assessments imposed on homeowners for widening roads or adding sidewalks or street lights? As discussed in Chapter 9, such levies generally are not deductible but rather are added to the tax basis of their homes. The distinction between deductible real estate taxes and nondeductible assessments is that the tax-favored levies are for the general public welfare and assessments primarily benefit and add to the value of the specific properties involved.

When general revenues pay for such services as trash pickup, the cost is part of your deductible real estate taxes. However, if your community imposes a separate fee for such services, that charge is nondeductible.

Homes sold during the year

If you buy or sell property during the year, your real estate tax deduction may be more or less than you actually paid the taxing authority. The deduction is allocated between buyer and seller, based on the part of the property-tax year (which may not be the same as the calendar year) each owned the property. The settlement sheet should show the allocation. If you can deduct more or less property tax than you actually paid, the selling price of the house is adjusted—in the eyes of the

IRS—to reflect the difference, as discussed in Chapter 9.

Personal Property Taxes and Auto License Tags

State and local personal property taxes are deductible if the tax is imposed annually and based on the value of the property being taxed. Although only a few states and municipalities have a levy that's specifically called a personal property tax, in many states at least part of what you pay annually to register or license your car fits the definition and can be deducted.

The key to deductibility is that the annual license fee be based—at least in part—on the value of your car. Any part of the charge based on the auto's age or weight, for example, isn't deductible. To know whether you can deduct any part of the tag fees you pay, check with local officials.

Interest

In the good old days, interest was pretty much interest, and when you paid it on a debt for which you were legally responsible you could almost always write it off. Uncle Sam stood by to subsidize your borrowing. When the cost of carrying debt came up, the pertinent issue was the after-tax cost. If you were in the

Good Deed Goes Unpunished

• •

Q: *Last spring my alma mater invited me to return to campus for a "career day" talk with graduating seniors about my profession and job prospects in the field. The college agreed to pay $150 of what turned out to be $250 in expenses. When I got the check, however, the payment was labeled an honorarium rather than expenses. I'm concerned that now I'll have to report the $150 and pay taxes on it as well as being out the unreimbursed $100. Is this what they mean when they say no good deed goes unpunished?*

A: Don't worry. The trip will wind up cutting your tax bill rather than adding to it. How you handle matters on your return depends on whether the college sent you a Form 1099 listing the $150 as income received by you. If so, the school sent a duplicate to the IRS, and the agency expects the amount to show up somewhere on your return. Show the $150 as "other income" on the Form 1040 and then deduct the entire $250 in expenses as a charitable contribution on Schedule A. If you didn't get a 1099 from the college, treat the money as what it really was—reimbursement of expenses. That means you don't report the $150 as income. And you can still squeeze a charitable contribution out of the remaining $100 in unreimbursed expenses.

50% tax bracket—back when there was one—you knew the IRS would effectively pay half of the interest. On a 12% loan, that pulled the real, after-tax cost down to 6%.

No more. In place of that simple system, Congress concocted a complicated set of new rules to limit interest deductions. The restrictions demand that you separate interest expenses into five categories, with each one having its own tax status:

- **Qualified mortgage interest.** As every homeowner knows, mortgage interest survived the crackdown and remains deductible, as does interest on home-equity loans, as long as the debt doesn't exceed the limits detailed in Chapter 9.

- **Personal interest.** This category probably encompasses most of the interest you pay beyond that due on a mortgage. It includes interest on car loans, vacation loans, student loans, debt-consolidation loans and, of course, the ubiquitous credit card. It is not deductible.

- **Business interest.** This remains fully deductible. Although interest on a loan to buy a personal automobile is no longer deductible, for example, interest on a loan to buy a car for your business can be written off on your business tax return.

- **Investment interest.** The interest on money borrowed for investment purposes—on a margin account, for example—is deductible to the extent you have investment interest to offset, as discussed in Chapter 10.

- **Passive-activity interest.** If you borrow to invest in a passive activity, as discussed in Chapter 10, the interest has a special tax status rather than being added to

---

Scoutmaster's Uniforms

Q: *I'm a scoutmaster and had to spend nearly $100 on the uniform and associated paraphernalia I need to wear to meetings. Is there any tax break for that kind of expense?*

A: You can deduct, as a charitable expense, the cost and the cost of upkeep of such special uniforms needed when you donate your services. The key to the deduction is that the clothes be necessary and not suitable for everyday use.

other investment interest. It is deductible only against passive-activity income.

Tracing

Before looking at your interest deductions in detail, consider this zinger: It's up to you to trace the use of debt to prove which type of interest you pay during the year. The IRS has made it clear that in most cases it is how borrowed money is used—not the source of the loan or how it is secured—that determines the tax status of the interest paid.

The tracing rules are best illustrated with an example. Assume you borrow $100,000 on January 1 and put the proceeds in a checking account. On April 1, you withdraw $20,000 to invest in a limited partnership—a passive activity. On September 1, you use $40,000 from the account for a trip to Europe that includes the purchase of a new car—two major personal expenses.

Assuming no other expenditures from the account and no repayment of the debt, here's how the IRS sees things:

- **All the interest charges that accrued between January 1 and March 31** are considered investment interest (whether or not you earned interest on the checking-account balance).

- **From April 1 through August 31,** 20% of the interest is considered passive-activity interest and 80% investment interest.

- **From September 1 to year-end,** 40% is investment interest, 20% is assigned to the passive activity and 40% is personal interest.

There is a major exception to the IRS commandment that how borrowed money is used determines the tax status of the interest. When home-equity debt is involved (see Chapter 9), the fact that the loan is secured by your home generally makes the interest deductible regardless of how the money is used.

Managing commingling

Now, consider the issue of commingling. Mixing borrowed and unborrowed money begs trouble. Consider this example:

You borrow $10,000 and put it temporarily in an account with $10,000 of unborrowed funds. A month later, you withdraw $10,000 to pay for a vacation, and when you return from your trip two weeks later, you use the $10,000 left in the account to buy mutual fund shares.

Don't assume it's up to you to say which funds went where. The IRS applies a handy-dandy "first-out" rule: The first money out of the account is considered to be the borrowed money. In the example, the vacation was paid for before the investment was made, so it's assumed you used the borrowed money for the vacation and your own money for the investment. Thus, the interest on the loan is nondeductible.

An exception short-circuits the first-out rule if funds are withdrawn from the commingled account within 15 days of the time the borrowed money was deposited. During this "window," you get to decide whether the funds coming out of the account are the proceeds of the loan or the unborrowed money.

These are rules only an accountant could love, but you have to play by them to maximize your interest deductions. Your best bet is to avoid mixing borrowed and unborrowed funds.

Basic Rules for Deductibility

To deduct any interest you must be legally liable for the debt involved. Although it's doubtful that you go out of your way to pay someone else's debts, it can happen. Perhaps a down-on-his-luck relative asks that you make a mortgage payment or two while he's looking for a new job. If you do, don't expect Uncle Sam to join in your generosity. You can't deduct the interest part of the mortgage payment and neither can your relative. The better move would be to give him the money and let him make the house payment himself. By doing so, at least he preserves the deduction.

You write off interest on the return for the year you pay it. If you make an interest payment by check, it is considered paid on the day you mail or deliver the check. Drop your December mortgage payment in the mail December 31, for example, and you include the interest in the deduction claimed on your return for that year, even though the check won't be cashed until the following year.

Note that a mortgage lender might not include such a year-end payment in the statement sent to you—and the IRS—listing the amount of interest paid during the year. You may still include it with your deduction, however. If you are uncertain exactly what part of the payment was interest, ask the lender. Claiming a deduction larger than the amount shown on the report to the IRS is perfectly legal, but will probably prompt an inquiry from the IRS. You may want to attach a statement to your tax return explaining the discrepancy or, better yet, make the payment early enough so it is included on your year-end statement.

More Nondeductible Interest

Even before the deduction for personal interest was outlawed, the carrying charge on certain debts was nondeductible. Interest on money borrowed to buy or carry tax-exempt investments, such as municipal bonds, isn't deductible. If you're not going to be taxed on the fruits of your investment, the government doesn't want to be subsidizing your purchase.

The word *carry* is used above because the IRS can deny an interest deduction even if you don't directly invest borrowed funds in tax-exempts. If you buy tax-free securities with unborrowed money and then pledge the bonds as security for a loan, the IRS says "no" to the deduction of interest on that loan. The connection doesn't have to be so blatant, either. If you have substantial investments in tax-free municipals and are claiming big interest deductions, the IRS may contend that only because of the debt are you able to afford to keep, or carry, the tax-free investment. That could lead to the denial of a deduction.

Money Saver

Drop your December mortgage payment in the mail December 31, and include the interest in this year's deduction, even though the check won't be cashed until next year.

That doesn't mean all of your interest deductions are at risk if you own tax-exempt securities. Borrowing for personal purposes—such as a home or a car—is safe. But if you have a substantial position in tax-exempts and take out a large loan to invest in a real estate deal, for example, don't be surprised if the IRS comes knocking.

Also nondeductible is interest on a loan used to buy single-premium life insurance. As discussed in Chapter 10, single-premium life is a tax-advantaged investment. Denying the deduction for interest on loans to buy it is a way to prevent double-dipping for tax benefits. Also, if you own a life insurance policy that relies on systematic borrowing against the policy's cash value to pay the premiums, the interest on the loans is not deductible.

The Allure of Home-Equity Loans

The evaporation of personal interest deductions puts the borrower's spotlight on home-equity loans. As discussed in detail in Chapter 9, homeowners have an opportunity to skirt the crackdown on personal interest deductions. To the extent that you can convert personal interest to fully deductible home-equity interest, you can reduce the real cost of borrowing. Keep a close eye on the price tag on making the change, though. Home-equity loans sometimes carry heavy up-front costs, and you must never forget that your home is at risk if you fail to repay the debt.

Charitable Contributions

Give and you shall receive...a tax deduction. Uncle Sam encourages generosity by subsidizing it. Your gifts to qualified organizations reduce your taxable income dollar for dollar via an itemized deduction. That, in turn, reduces the true cost of your gift. Every $1,000 someone in the 31% bracket gives away to a qualified cause saves the donor $310 in federal taxes. The bottom line: Giving away $1,000 really costs just $690.

Qualified Organization

To be deductible, your gift has to go to a nonprofit religious, educational or charitable group that meets IRS standards. There's no shortage of qualified groups, ranging from the U.S. government itself to a volunteer nonprofit fire company. Almost all churches and other religious organizations qualify, of course, as do schools and hospitals, government agencies, veteran's groups, the Salvation Army, the United Way, the U.S. Olympic Committee, the Boy Scouts, the Girl Scouts and on and on.

If you're not certain whether the object of your generosity is approved by the IRS, ask an official of the group. If you're still uneasy, check with the IRS. It has a master list of qualified organizations: Publication 78.

Nondeductible donations

Note that the gift has to go to an organization. If you give money to needy individuals, no one will question your generosity, but neither will the government subsidize it. Such gifts don't count as charitable contributions.

It's possible, too, that donations to a qualified group can lose deductible status. There's no charitable write-off for contributions used by an organization in an attempt to influence legislation. If a group you support is involved in lobbying Congress, for example, contributions you make that are ear-marked for that effort are not deductible. The organization should tell you if part of your contribution is not deductible.

Too Much of a Good Thing?

There is a limit to how much you can deduct in any single year, but few taxpayers have to worry about reaching the ceiling. The rules are complicated, but basically your deductions for gifts to public charities, colleges and religious organizations can't exceed 50% of your adjusted gross income (AGI). Within that overall limit, gifts of appreciated property—discussed starting on page 396—can't total more than 30% of your AGI. Stricter limits apply to gifts to certain types of organizations. Contributions to veterans' groups, for example, come under an overall 30%-of-AGI limit, with a 20%-of-AGI cap on gifts of certain appreciated property.

The key to remember is that you can claim charitable-contribution deductions against up to 20% of your AGI without worrying about the twists and turns of the IRS limits. If your generosity exceeds that level, you may need professional advice to structure the gift for the best tax outcome. If you give more than you can deduct on a single year's return, the excess can be written off in future years. Any leftover deduction not used within five years, however, is lost for good.

Keeping Track

When figuring your deduction, you can include what you contributed in cash, property and out-of-pocket costs incurred in your volunteer work.

Cash is the easiest to keep track of and the easiest to value. Keep your canceled checks and a receipt from the organization or some other written record of your gift, including how much was given to whom and when. As noted later, when you contribute $250 or more, you must have a written receipt from the charity. When a receipt is impractical—say you regularly put a $5 bill in the collection plate at church or make it a habit never to pass a Salvation Army bell ringer without dropping a buck or two in the bucket— make notes of the contributions for your tax records. The better your records, the less likely an IRS agent will deny your write-off for such cash contributions if you're audited.

As with other itemized deductions, you write off your gifts for the year you make them. A check delivered or mailed by December 31, for example, is deducted on your return for that year. If you charge a contribution to your bank credit card—yes, fund-raisers are ingenious at finding ways to simplify your gift giving—you get the deduction for the year of the charge regardless of when you pay the bill. You have to make the contribution to earn the deduction, however. A pledge to make gifts in the future has no tax value; you get the deduction only when you fulfill the pledge by making the donation.

Something in Return

If you get something in return for your gift, you can't write off the full amount. Say, for example, that a local public television station offers a compact disc player in exchange for a donation of $1,000 to the annual fund drive. If the value of the CD player is $200, your deduction is limited to the $800 difference between what you gave and what you got. The law now requires that, if you get something in return for a donation over $75, the charity must set a value on what you receive and remind you to subtract that amount when figuring your deduction. This same rule applies if you buy something at a fundraising auction. The charity must value what you buy and you get a deduction only to the extent you pay more than the item is worth.

When low-cost items are involved, however, the IRS is willing to let you write off the full value of your contribution. But the government doesn't go overboard with its generosity on this issue. It applies only when the value of benefits received by the donor is 2% of the gift or $67, whichever is lower. If you gave $1,000, for example, the 2%-or-$67 rule would limit the value of an incentive to $20 (2% of $1,000). A more valuable benefit would reduce the amount you can deduct.

Charity or chance?

Charities often raise money through raffles or lotteries. Who hasn't been asked to buy chances on a new car, television or basket of cheer? Regardless of how generous the motives behind your purchase, however, you get the chance to win something. That means you're gambling, not giving, as far as the IRS is concerned. You can deduct what you pay for raffle and lottery tickets up to the amount of gambling winnings you report. (Yes, if you win a raffle, you're supposed to report the fair market value of the prize as taxable income.)

Money Saver

Keep track of what you spend for lottery tickets. That expense can offset the winnings you report as income.

Doing Good Work

In addition to funds you give directly to charity, you can deduct money you spend doing volunteer work for a qualified organization. If you drive your car—to volunteer at your church, a hospital or a school, for example—you can include in your charitable deductions an amount based on 12 cents a mile, plus parking and tolls. If you use taxicabs or public transportation, you can count the fares as charitable donations.

Other deductible out-of-pocket expenses may include the cost and care of any special uniform you're required to wear while performing services for the charity and materials and supplies you pay for—such as stationery and stamps—that are used in your volunteer efforts. If you pay a babysitter to take care of your children while you perform volunteer services, however, you can't deduct the cost. The IRS sees that as a personal expense regardless of what takes you away from home.

No write-off for your time or skill

You can't write off the value of services you donate. Assume, for example, that a carpenter who usually charges $35 an hour spends 20 hours helping build a wing on his church. He can't deduct $700—or any other amount—for his time (although his transportation to and from the work site and the cost of any supplies he paid for can be deducted).

Forbidding the deduction may appear unfair, but consider this: If the carpenter had charged for his time and then donated the $700 to the church, he would have earned a $700 deduction. But the tax-savings would have been wiped out by the extra $700 of taxable income he would have had to report. The tax result is identical to blocking the deduction for the value of donated services.

This rationale also works to prevent a deduction if you give a qualified organization reduced-rent or rent-free use of property you own.

Nor for blood

The same thinking is also behind the IRS's position that you may not claim a deduction for the value of blood you donate. If you sold your blood, you'd have taxable income to report. By donating it, this argument goes, you avoid that tax bill so there's no need for a deduction.

The cost of foster care

If you are a foster parent, you may deduct as a charitable contribution the cost of providing for your foster children that exceeds reimbursement you receive.

Hosting visiting students

You can also earn a charitable deduction if a student lives in your home under a program sponsored by a qualified organization. To qualify for this deduction, the student may be American or foreign and must be a full-time elementary or high school student. You can deduct up to $50 a month of what you spend for the student, including the cost of books, tuition, food, clothing and entertainment. When toting up the deduction, you can't include anything for the value of the housing you provide. For purposes of figuring how many $50 allotments you can claim, count any month that the student lives with you 15 or more days. (You lose the right to this write-off if the student is staying in your home as part of a program that will involve your child living with a family in a foreign country.)

Travel Expenses

Beyond local transportation expenses—and potentially far more valuable in terms of tax savings—you can write off the cost of travel when your charitable services take you away from home overnight. That includes the cost of transportation and food and lodging while you're away from home.

If you are chosen as an official delegate to your church's national convention, for example, the costs of attending can be deducted as a charitable contribution. If you attend such a convention on your own, however, your costs are considered nondeductible personal expenses.

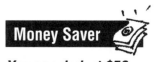

Money Saver

You can deduct $50 a month of the expenses of hosting a student in your home.

More work than vacation

Congress has lowered the boom on certain charitable-travel deductions, however, in response to a proliferation of highly publicized trips—sometimes called tax-deductible vacations. The idea was that taxpayers would travel to appealing locations and write off their costs on the grounds that they were performing services to assist the charities. Congress worried, though, that the amount of time spent benefiting the charitable organizations was relatively small compared to the time reserved for recreation. The solution the lawmakers came up with was to forbid a charitable deduction if the travel involves a "significant element" of personal pleasure, recreation or vacation.

That doesn't mean you have to have a miserable time doing your volunteer work to qualify for a tax deduction. Consider these examples:

- **As a troop leader, you take your Girl Scout troop on a camping trip.** You can deduct your travel expenses, assuming you are on duty in a substantial sense during the trip, even if you have a great time. If you have only nominal duties or for much of the trip aren't required to render services, you don't get a charitable deduction for your expenses.

- **You work for several hours each morning on an archaeological excavation sponsored by a charitable organization.** The rest of the day is free for recreation and sight-seeing. The IRS says no charitable deduction is allowed for your travel expenses, regardless of how hard you work during the morning hours.

- **You spend an entire day attending a charitable organization's regional meeting.** In the evening you go to the theater. Going to the show doesn't cost you the right to deduct your travel expenses as a charitable contribution.

Donating Property

Whether it's old clothes or Old Masters' paintings, donating property can earn you a tax deduction just like donating cash. Admittedly, giving anything but greenbacks makes it tougher to know just how big a deduction to claim and is more likely to raise eyebrows at the IRS. The law adds to the confusion, too, because the type of property donated, how long you've owned it, who you give it to and how they will use it all can come into play in setting the amount you can deduct.

Begin with what are probably the most typical property donations: used clothing and household goods. Your write-off for such gifts is the fair market value of the property at the time you give it. That's usually far less than you paid for it. To set a reasonable value—that is, one the IRS will accept—you have to consider anything that can affect the item's worth.

For relatively inexpensive items, this is a do-it-yourself job. If you give away an old car, for instance, you can start with used-car value guides available at banks and car dealerships. Don't assume prices listed in such guides pinpoint the value of your car, however. You've probably heard stories about owners of old clunkers who decided the tax deduction for giving them away would be worth more than what they could get by selling them. As you undoubtedly suspect, the IRS frowns on that approach. If the vehicle you plan to bestow on a qualified organization—a high school shop class, for example—is a pile of junk, the allowable deduction is probably closer to salvage value than the average retail price shown in used-car guides. On the other hand, if you plan to give away a cream puff, you may deserve a larger deduction. You may need to visit used-car lots and talk with dealers or mechanics to arrive at a fair figure.

You don't need an expert's opinion to set the value of used, everyday clothes you donated to Goodwill Industries, the Salvation Army or similar organizations. For that, a trip to a secondhand clothing shop will tell you what people are paying for similar items. The same kind of research is sufficient for household goods that you donate, such as furniture and appliances. The IRS has a helpful booklet—Publication 561, *Determining the Value of Donated Property*—that can be a valuable aid in setting the deductible amount for your gifts.

Money Saver

Write off the fair market value of the property you donate—including used clothing and household goods.

Money Saver

Donate appreciated property and your deduction can be much more than what you originally paid for it.

More than $500 worth

When the deduction you claim for donated property exceeds $500—in total, not per item—you need to file an extra form with your tax return: Form 8283, *Noncash Charitable Contributions.* The information required on the form is basically the same as you need to substantiate any charitable gift—what you gave, when and to whom and, for items valued at over $500 each, when and how you acquired the property and your cost or adjusted basis. (Your basis is the property's value for tax purposes. It's usually what you paid for the property—the cost of stock, including brokerage commissions, for example—but if real estate or other depreciable property is involved, the basis is the cost minus any depreciation claimed while you have owned the property.) Rather than just keeping the information with your records in case you're audited, the IRS demands that you send it in with your return when your write-off for gifts of property exceeds $500.

Appreciated property

When your philanthropic urge prompts you to give away appreciated property—such as stocks, real estate, art or antiques—the tax-saving potential can be much greater. And the rules are much more complicated.

First of all, your deduction depends in part on whether the property donated is considered *capital-gain or ordinary-income* property. Basically, capital-gain property is any that, if sold, would produce a long-term capital gain. To qualify as capital-gain property, you must have owned it for more than one year before giving it away. When you donate capital-gain property, your deduction is the fair market value of the property. This can be a major advantage because you get to write off the current value of the property without having to pay tax on the appreciation that built up while you owned it.

Say you own stock now worth $10,000 that you purchased many years ago for just $2,000. If you give the stock to your alma mater, church or other qualified organization, you earn a $10,000 deduction. In the 31% tax bracket, that would save you $3,100 in taxes. But your tax benefit is actually bigger than that. If you sold the stock rather than giving it away, you'd owe tax on the $8,000 profit on the deal. That would cost you $2,480, a bill you avoid by giving the stock away.

When you contribute tangible personal property—such as antique furniture, jewelry or a painting—how the organization uses it can affect your write-off. If your gift is sold for cash, for example, or used for a purpose unrelated to the organization's charitable function, your deduction is limited to your cost. You don't get to write off the appreciation. For example, say you give your alma mater a valuable painting that you've owned more than one year. If it is put on display for study by art students—a related use—you may deduct the full market value of the painting. However, if the painting is sold and the proceeds used by the school, your deduction is limited to what you paid for the painting.

Ordinary-income property includes assets owned one year or less, business inventory and works of art or manuscripts donated by the creator. The deduction for such gifts generally is limited to the donor's cost. An artist who gives away a painting, for example, is limited to deducting the cost of the canvas, paint and frame, regardless of how much the painting would sell for.

The distinction between capital-gain and ordinary-income property is probably most important when it comes to stocks and other assets for which the deduction is controlled by the holding period. In the earlier example of stock purchased for $2,000 and worth $10,000 at the time

---

Giving One's Time

● ●

Q: *Last year my church had a major fund-raising drive. I was asked to donate my services as a photographer in lieu of cash. Billed at my standard rate, the time I spent would have brought me $2,000. An accountant tells me that all I can deduct is the cost of the film and other supplies I used. I think he's being too conservative. Can I claim the full $2,000 as a charitable contribution?*

A: Your accountant is correct. The law doesn't permit a deduction for the value of your services. Here's why: If you had charged $2,000 for your services, that would have been taxable income. Turning around and donating the cash to the church would have earned you a $2,000 write-off. The result would be no change in your taxable income. Similarly, donating your time means you don't have the extra income to report in the first place, so there's no need for a deduction to offset it.

of the gift, if the donor had owned the property for one year or less, the deduction would have been limited to $2,000. Watch the calendar if you consider such gifts.

Bargain sales

What if rather than giving property away outright, you decide to sell it—100 shares of stock, two acres of prime land, or whatever—at a bargain-basement price? Can you deduct as a contribution the difference between what you charge the charity and what you could have made on the open market? As logical as that might seem, it's not necessarily so.

First of all, if ordinary-income property is involved, you get no charitable contribution if the bargain price is as much or more than your cost or other basis in the property—regardless of how big a discount is involved. Say, for example, that you own stock worth $10,000 that you purchased less than one year ago for $5,000. If you sell the stock to a charity for your original cost of $5,000, you get no deduction even though you are effectively giving the charity $5,000. You earn a deduction only if you sell it to the charity for less than your cost. In this example, if you sold the stock for $6,000—still $4,000 under its value—you not only are denied a charitable deduction, but also have to report $1,000 as a taxable gain.

What if you sell it for $4,000? Can you at least deduct the $1,000 discount below your cost? You get the tax benefit of a $1,000 deduction, but you must travel a twisted road to get it.

In the eyes of the IRS, this kind of transaction combines a sale with a charitable contribution. The first thing you have to do is allocate your basis ($5,000 in this example) between the sale and the donation. Since the $4,000 selling price is 40% of the $10,000 fair market value in this illustration, 40% of the basis would be allocated to the sale. Subtracting your $2,000 basis (40% of $5,000) from the $4,000 proceeds of the sale leaves you with a $2,000 taxable gain. Yes, the gain when you sell for $4,000 in this illustration is *more* than when you sell at $6,000. But the gain is more than offset because you get to claim a charitable deduction for the other 60% of your basis—or $3,000.

Remember that the discussion so far applies to bargain sales of ordinary-income property.

Different, more beneficial rules apply to capital-gain property. You still must allocate your basis between the sale and the contribution, but your deductible amount is based on the fair market value of the property sold rather than your basis. Again, consider stock now worth $10,000 that you purchased for $5,000—and that you've owned for more than a year so it qualifies as capital-gain property. If you gave the stock away outright, your deduction would be the full $10,000 fair market value. Here's how things work if you sell it to charity at the bargain price of $4,000:

Forty percent of the basis (the ratio of sales price to fair market value) is applied to the sales price; the other 60% to the contribution. Your taxable gain would be 40% of the $4,000 sales price, or $1,600. Your charitable contribution would be 60% of the $10,000 fair market value, or $6,000. It's no coincidence that that's the same as the difference between the bargain price and the fair market value.

Appraisals

When property you give is publicly traded stock or other securities, it's easy to pinpoint the fair market value. It's what the securities are trading for on the day of your gift. For other types of gifts, however, you may well need an outside appraisal. When your generosity passes a certain dollar threshold, in fact, the IRS demands that you get a written appraisal from a "qualified appraiser." Such appraisals are required when any single item of property, or a group of similar items, has a claimed value greater than $5,000. For stock that is not traded publicly, the triggering point is $10,000. The appraisal must be made by someone skilled in evaluating the specific kind of property you are giving away.

Beware that the IRS, worried that it has been burned often by charitable deductions based on inflated appraisals, casts a particularly skeptical eye on such write-offs. The agency has its own panel of experts to review the appraised value of art and other high-ticket property donations. Also,

Money Saver

If your gift is worth more than $5,000 you need an appraisal to back up your deduction.

the agency demands illustrated tax returns from taxpayers claiming large deductions based on the donation of works of art. When such art is valued at $20,000 or more, a color photo or transparency showing the gift must accompany the tax return.

The importance of an accurate appraisal is emphasized by the penalty the IRS imposes if the value of the donated property is significantly overstated. If the value on which your deduction is based is determined to be more than 150% of the property's actual worth and the deduction resulted in understating your tax bill by $1,000 or more, the penalty is 30% of the underpayment.

The cost of the required appraisal can't be folded into your charitable contribution. Instead, it can be deducted only as a miscellaneous itemized expense, which—as discussed later in this Chapter—makes it impossible for most taxpayers to get any tax benefit.

Life Insurance

Here's a way to get a tax deduction now for a gift the charity won't benefit from until after your death: Give the charity a life insurance policy on your life. The organization must be named both owner and beneficiary of the policy and you must irrevocably give up the right to change your mind. Folks often give paid-up whole life policies they no longer need or universal life policies that can be paid up in just a few years. Such gifts are frequently promoted by charities as an affordable way to make a substantial contribution.

Your tax deduction is the value of the policy when you give it away, which is generally a little more than the cash-surrender value, or the replacement value. Your insurance agent should be able to help set the value of your gift. If you make contributions to cover future premiums, you can deduct those gifts, too.

Giving Away the House

You can give away your home, claim an immediate tax deduction for your generosity and still get to live in the house for the rest of your life. This type of gift is often most attractive to single people with no close relatives to whom to leave the property. The provision of the law that allows an immediate deduction for the delayed gift of your home applies to vacation homes and farms, too.

Here's how it works: The property is deeded over to the charitable organization, but you retain the right to live on or work on the property for the rest of your life (and, if you wish, the lifetime of a survivor) or for a specific number of years. Your deduction is based on the current value of the property and your life expectancy. The older you are when you make the gift—and therefore the shorter the anticipated length (and consequentially the lower value) of your retained interest—the less you have to reduce the current value to arrive at your deduction. The charity to which you consider giving your property should be able—and quite willing—to help you get the necessary assistance to set the size of your deduction.

Get a Receipt

Congress has ordered the IRS not to accept a canceled check as proof of charitable contributions of $250 or more. To deduct such gifts, you must have a receipt. The $250 trigger point is for individual gifts, not the total you give a charity during the year. If you give $100 a month to your church, for example, you don't need a receipt even though the total donation is $1,200. If you give property rather than cash, the receipt has to describe the donation but the charity is not required to put a price tag on it. Estimating the value is still up to you.

What if you make charitable gifts via payroll deductions at work? If any single gift is $250 or more, you need pledge cards or some other proof of your gift. Notations on your check stubs are not enough.

The point of this rule, of course, is that Congress thinks our tax returns make us out to be more generous than we really are. The lawmakers hope the receipt rule will put the brakes on inflated deductions enough to raise about $100 million in extra taxes each year.

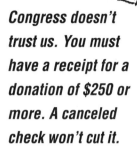

Money Saver

Congress doesn't trust us. You must have a receipt for a donation of $250 or more. A canceled check won't cut it.

By the way, the law says you must have the receipt at the time you file your tax return. You can't wait to see if you're audited and then ask the organization to provide you with a receipt.

Casualty and Theft Losses

This is another category of itemized deductions that, for most taxpayers, is more illusory than real. It's held out as Uncle Sam's helping hand to ease the financial pain when you suffer from misfortunes such as accidents, storms or theft. But Congress has erected a grueling gauntlet between you and the write-off. For all intents and purposes, casualty- and theft-loss deductions are available only to those of modest income—who may not benefit anyway because they may not be itemizing deductions—or to those who are hit by catastrophic losses. Here's why:

- **The amount of any uninsured loss must be reduced by $100.** If you suffer more than one loss during the year, the first $100 of each is ignored by the tax law.

- **Much tougher is a restriction that permits a deduction only when your remaining losses exceed 10% of your adjusted gross income (AGI).** You get a deduction only for the amount above the threshold. Unlike the $100 rule, the 10% threshold does not apply to each separate casualty or theft. It applies to the total of your losses during the year, after each one has been trimmed by $100.

Assume you are mugged and the thief gets away with $200 in cash and $3,500 worth of jewelry, and this is the only casualty or theft you suffer during the year. For tax purposes, you first reduce your loss by $100 and then subtract

No Receipt, No Proof

• •

Q: *I heard that canceled checks can no longer be used as proof that I made a charitable contribution. Is that true?*

A: Yes. You must have a written receipt to back up any contribution of $250 or more. When it passed that rule, Congress specifically told the IRS that it cannot accept a canceled check as evidence that a contribution was made.

10% of your AGI from the remaining $3,600. If your AGI is $30,000, the $3,000 reduction would leave you with a $600 loss deduction. If AGI is $36,000 or more, the 10% rule would bar the deduction altogether.

Although it's unlikely that you'll ever benefit from a casualty- or theft-loss deduction, it's important to be aware of the rules in case you are unfortunate enough to qualify for this write-off.

What's a Casualty?

According to the law, it is damage to or destruction of property caused by an identifiable event that is *sudden, unexpected or unusual*. As you may assume, taxpayers and the IRS often disagree over what fits the bill.

Clearly, damage from these "identifiable events" count: earthquakes, lightning, hurricanes, tornadoes, floods, storms, volcanic eruptions, sonic booms, vandalism, riots, fires, car accidents and, oh yes, shipwrecks. What if you accidentally knock a vase off its pedestal and into a million pieces? The IRS says that's not a casualty. How about when Rover romps through the house, knocking down the cabinet that holds your television, VCR and stereo? Again, the IRS says there's no tax deduction to help pay for the damage. What if you're driving along and your car's engine suddenly freezes up, resulting in thousands of dollars worth of damage? You guessed it: no deduction. The IRS figures the damage was due to normal wear and tear on the engine over a lengthy period of time.

What if you lose something valuable, like a diamond ring? That's not a casualty in the eyes of the tax law. However, if the ring falls into a garbage disposal, the damage would qualify for a casualty-loss deduction. So would the

The Value of Labor

• •

Q: *My sons and I spent most of the summer building a garage. It cost us $8,000, but if I had hired people to do the work, I'm sure the price would have been at least twice as much. When figuring the addition to the basis of the property, how do I calculate the value of our labor?*

A: You don't. The addition to the basis is the actual cost of the improvement to you. If you hire workers, you include the wages you pay them, but you get no credit for your own time and skills.

loss of a diamond if you can show it happened because the setting was damaged when the owner's hand was slammed in a car door.

Damage caused by termites or moths doesn't qualify as a casualty. It lacks the suddenness requirement. But even when the *cause* of damage can be laid to progressive deterioration, you may still have a deductible loss. If your hot-water heater bursts, for example, any resulting water damage qualifies even though the cost of repairing or replacing the heater does not.

And even if the damage is *your* fault, you can earn a casualty-loss deduction—unless willful negligence is involved. If you're responsible for a car crash, for example, or accidentally apply a chemical that kills your lawn and shrubs, the damage can qualify as a casualty loss.

You also qualify for a deduction if you lose money because a bank or other financial institution goes under and your deposits aren't insured. You actually have a choice of how to deduct such a loss: either as a casualty loss or as a nonbusiness bad debt, which is treated as a short-term capital loss. There are restrictions either way. The casualty loss is subject to both the $100 reduction and the 10% test. The nonbusiness bad debt, as other short-term losses, is deductible first against capital gains and then against up to $3,000 of other income. (Any leftover bad-debt loss would be deductible in future years.) Although you may claim a casualty loss in the year you can reasonably estimate your loss—probably the year the bank goes under—you can't claim a bad-debt deduction until the actual amount of the loss is determined, which may well be in a later year.

What Is a Theft?

The answer here is much easier than when determining what qualifies as a casualty. You have a theft loss when property you own is taken illegally. The key here is to show that the property was stolen rather than lost or mislaid. Be certain the theft is reported to authorities. If you are the victim of an investment scam or other swindle, whether or not your loss qualifies for a deduction turns on whether the venture that separated you from your money was illegal under federal, state or local law.

Pinpointing Your Loss

The amount of your loss is generally the decrease in fair market value of the property or your adjusted basis in the property, whichever is *less*. The decrease in market value is the difference between what the property was worth before and after a casualty or the full market value in the case of a theft. The question of value turns on what a disinterested person would pay for the property. You don't get any credit for sentimental value. The adjusted basis is usually your original cost plus the cost of any improvements you've made. You may need appraisals to set the before and after values, although what you will have to pay for repairs—after an automobile accident, for example—can serve as evidence of your loss. If you are restoring landscaping after a storm, you can base your casualty loss on what you pay to remove or prune damaged trees and shrubs and for the replanting necessary to restore your property to its value before the storm.

© *Jim Borgman—Reprinted with Special Permission of King Features Syndicate.*

Note that your loss doesn't depend on the replacement value of the damaged or stolen property. Say that you bought a chair for $400 and that four years later it is destroyed by fire. At the time, you could have sold the used chair for $100, but to replace it with a comparable new chair would cost you $700. What's your casualty loss? The decline in fair market value—$100—caused by the fire.

When your loss involves several separate items, as would be the case if your home burns or thieves clean out your apartment, you are expected to calculate the loss on each item rather than come up with an overall estimate.

The IRS offers a free booklet—Publication 584, *Nonbusiness Disaster, Casualty, and Theft Loss Workbook*—to help you inventory lost, damaged or stolen items and determine your deductible loss. (Even if you don't suffer a loss, the booklet is helpful as a handy tool for keeping a household inventory.)

Proving your case

As with any deduction, if you are audited you'll need evidence to back up your write-off. For starters, keep any newspaper articles reporting on the calamity that caused your loss, whether it was a fire, major storm, auto accident or robbery. Also make copies for your tax file of any pertinent police or fire reports. You'll also need to show that you owned the property at issue. You can't claim a casualty-loss deduction for damage to an auto registered in your daughter's name, for example, even if you're the one who winds up paying for the repairs.

Proving the size of your loss is tougher. In addition to receipts for repairs, you may need appraisals of the property's value before and after the loss. Before and after photographs can also serve to back up your deduction. Although it may be impossible to take such pictures after the casualty or theft, it's still a good idea to maintain a regularly updated photo file or perhaps a videotape of your belongings. Such pictures may also serve to jog your memory after a fire or theft when you're putting together a list of your losses. The cost of photos and what you pay for appraisals cannot be added to your casualty loss but may be deducted as miscellaneous expenses if you pass the 2%-of-AGI threshold discussed later in this chapter.

The Role of Insurance

The amount of your casualty or theft loss is reduced, of course, by any reimbursement you receive from insurance. If you have insurance, in fact, you must file a claim or forfeit your right to a tax deduction for the insured part of the loss. Before that rule was written into the law, some taxpayers chose to go for the tax write-off rather than file a claim and risk cancellation of their policy or an increase in premiums.

That's no longer an option.

If you can reasonably expect to be reimbursed for part or all of your loss—through insurance or a damage suit—you must trim your deduction by the amount you expect to get, even if you won't get it until a future year. If you wind up getting less than you expect, the difference is considered a casualty loss in the year of the final settlement. At that time, the amount would again be subject to both the $100 and 10%-of-AGI rules. Since that could easily wipe out any tax benefit, be particularly careful when estimating future reimbursements.

Reimbursement of living expenses

When insurance pays for your living expenses after you lose the use of your home, the payments are not counted as reimbursement for your loss and therefore do not reduce your deduction. In some cases, however, the IRS views such payments as *taxable income* if the money covers normal living expenses rather than extra expenses resulting from the casualty.

Say, for example, that the apartment you rent for $700 a month is damaged by fire and you are forced to live in a motel for two months while your place is repaired. The motel bill is $900 a month, of which your insurance policy pays $850. Because $200 a month pays the extra expense, that part of the insurance payment is tax-free. The other $650 is considered payment of normal expenses and should be reported as income. In a similar situation, a homeowner who had to continue mortgage payments on the damaged house while living in the motel would not report any of the insurance reimbursement as income because the entire motel bill is an added expense.

Used Clothing

● ●

Q: *How do I figure the size of the deduction I should claim for the used clothing I gave to a local welfare organization last year?*

A: Valuing such noncash charitable contributions isn't easy. Your deduction is limited to the fair market value of the clothes at the time of the gift. But as an IRS agent has pointed out, "There's no book value on a used Oxford-cloth shirt." You may want to check used clothing stores in your area to get an idea of the value of various items. It's up to you to come up with a reasonable estimate.

Gaining from Losses

Regardless of how much you suffer from a casualty or theft, the tax law may view you as a winner and demand that you report insurance reimbursement as taxable income. This seemingly hardhearted result occurs when the reimbursement is more than your adjusted basis in the lost or damaged property.

Say, for example, that an item of antique furniture is stolen from your home. Assume you paid $800 for the antique but it was worth much more when it was stolen. Thanks to a rider on your insurance policy, you are reimbursed $3,000. As far as the IRS is concerned, the $2,200 difference between your $800 basis and the $3,000 is taxable income.

Or assume that you have a replacement-value clause in your household insurance policy. After a fire, you determine that your basis in destroyed furniture and appliances is $10,000, but the replacement value paid by your insurance company is $15,000. Taxable gain: $5,000.

There is an important exception to this rule. If you use all the insurance proceeds to buy replacement property—that is, items similar to or having a related use as the lost or damaged property—you don't have to report any of the money as income. To dodge the tax bill on what the IRS sees as excess reimbursement, the replacement property must be purchased within two years of the end of the year in which you are reimbursed.

The basis of the replacement property is its cost minus the amount of "gain" from the insurance. This rule doesn't matter much when you're dealing with things like furniture or appliances, but it's vitally important when your house is involved.

Assume that your home is destroyed by fire and your basis in the house is $50,000. Because it's worth far more at the time of the fire, you receive a $150,000 insurance settlement on the house itself. That's a $100,000 gain—just as if you had sold the house for $150,000. You avoid the tax bill, however, by spending $200,000 on a new home within the two-year replacement period. What's the basis of the new place? It's $100,000: the $200,000 cost minus the $100,000 gain from the casualty. Another way to look at it is that you carry over your original $50,000 basis and add to it the extra $50,000 you put into the new place—over and above the "excess" insurance settlement.

Disaster Areas

There are special rules if you suffer a loss as a result of an event that prompts the President to declare your area a federal disaster area—which often happens in connection with floods, fires, hurricanes, tornadoes and earthquakes.

First, insurance proceeds received for "unscheduled" personal property can't be considered taxable income even if you don't use the money to replace the property. Most of the contents of your home are probably "unscheduled." The exception would be things that are itemized in your insurance policy, such as jewelry or furs for which you have purchased a specific rider.

Second, when it comes to repairing or replacing the home itself, the replacement period is four years, rather than two.

Generally, you deduct a casualty loss on the return for the year the damage occurs. However, when the loss is in a

Tax-Deductible "Vacation"

● ●

Q: *What's the story on these so-called tax deductible vacations that let people deduct the cost of exotic travel? I'd like to get in on such a deal.*

A: You're probably referring to research expeditions sponsored by groups such as Earthwatch and the University of California's Research Expedition Program. They need volunteers to help with projects around the world, most of which focus on animal behavior, anthropology, archaeology and the environment. Participants pay to take part—usually between $600 and $2,500 for ten-day to three-week expeditions. The money supports the research and covers room and board. Participants also have to pay to get to and from the research cite. And, yes, the full cost can qualify as a charitable contribution.

As you may suspect, the IRS isn't keen on subsidizing fun and games, which is why expedition sponsors recoil when their projects are called tax-deductible vacations. While there is no question that the part of the fee paid to support the research is deductible, travel and room and board expenses can be written off only if there's "no significant element" of personal pleasure or vacation involved in the trip. The IRS doesn't say what constitutes "significant" pleasure, but concedes that you don't lose the tax break if you happen to enjoy the expedition.

presidentially declared disaster area,you can write off your loss on the return for the *previous* year. This unusual option is designed to put a tax refund in your hands to help pay for the damage. You can use this provision even if you've already filed your return for the preceding year. You can order your tax-refund check via an amended return (see Chapter 2).

Assume, for example, that a tornado rips through your town in May 1996, causing $20,000 of uninsured damage to your home. Usually, you would wait until you file your 1996 return in the spring of 1997 to claim a casualty loss. But if the President declares your town a disaster area, you could claim the loss by amending your 1995 return. If your 1995 adjusted gross income was $40,000, the casualty-loss deduction for the $20,000 loss would be $15,900—$20,000 minus $100 minus $4,000 (10% of AGI). If you were in the 28% bracket, the amended return would bring a refund of $4,452. An important consideration in deciding which year to claim the write-off is how your adjusted gross income will compare. Because of the 10% rule, your tax savings will be greater in the year your AGI is smaller, unless you're in a lower tax bracket.

Business Property

The $100 and 10% restrictions on casualty and theft losses apply only to personal-use property, such as your own home, car or personal possessions. If you suffer a loss to business property, such as a business auto or a rental house, you can deduct the full loss.

Miscellaneous Deductions

This is the flea market of the tax code, but don't let the all-encompassing sound of this category raise your hopes too high. Although the range of acceptable expenses is broad, it's tough to cash in. Most miscellaneous expenses are now deductible only to the extent their combined cost exceeds 2% of your adjusted gross income.

Although that's not as high as the thresholds for medical and casualty-loss deductions, the 2% test will block enough write-offs that Congress expects it to cost taxpayers about $5 billion a year.

Note, however, that although medical and casualty loss write-offs are exempted from the squeeze on itemized deductions discussed at the beginning of this chapter, miscellaneous expenses aren't so lucky. For high-income taxpayers, the new pinch applies as well as the 2% threshold. Of course, that's all the more reason to tote up all qualifying expenses. They fall in three basic categories:

Bad Debt

Q: *I paid a $2,000 deposit to a builder who went bankrupt before even beginning work on our new house. I've been unable to recover any of the money and have been told I might be able to mitigate my loss by claiming a tax deduction. Is that possible?*

A: If you can show that you tried to recover the money and that there is no chance of doing so, the $2,000 could qualify as a non-business bad debt. If so, it's deductible as a capital loss on Schedule D.

Employee Business Expenses

These are the costs you incur in connection with your job, including the following:

- Automobile expenses

- Home-office expenses

- Job-hunting expenses

- Travel, entertainment and gift expenses

- Educational expenses

- The cost of special work clothes

- The cost of small tools used in your work

- The cost of a physical examination required by your employer

- Dues to professional societies

- Union dues

- The cost of subscriptions to professional journals and trade publications

- Job-security insurance

- Hobby expenses to the extent of your hobby income

    These expenses are discussed in Chapter 13.

Investment-Related Expenses

Money you spend in the pursuit of taxable investment income qualifies as a deductible miscellaneous expense, including the following costs:

- Custodial fees for your individual retirement account

- Safe-deposit-box rental

- Investment management fees

- The cost of subscriptions to investment-advisory newsletters

- The cost of books and magazines you buy for investment advice

- The cost of computer software or on-line services to track your investments

- The cost of travel to see your broker to check on your portfolio or to buy or sell investments

    These expenses are discussed in Chapter 10.

Tax-Related Expenses

Although more and more taxpayers seem to need help coping with the ever-changing tax law, Congress has made it difficult to deduct the cost of help. While what you pay for tax advice and return preparation is still deductible, the cost is a miscellaneous expense subject to the 2% rule. (If you have your own business or a rental activity, what you pay for tax help for those activities is fully deductible on your Schedule C or Schedule E, respectively.)

Make sure you count every dime you can:

- If you hire someone to prepare your return, include the cost.

- If you consult with an accountant about the tax consequences of investments, include the fee.

- If you wind up in court fighting the IRS over a tax bill, include what you pay your lawyer, as well as all filing fees.

- Count any miscellaneous tax-preparation expenses, including what you pay for a return-preparation manual or other tax-planning books (including Cut Your Taxes), the cost of tax-preparation computer software, the cost of long-distance calls to the IRS to answer your tax questions and even the cost of postage to mail in your return.

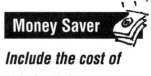

Money Saver

Include the cost of this book in your miscellaneous deductible expenses.

Write-Offs Not Subject to the 2% Rule

Schedule A, the form on which you list itemized deductions, includes a section for miscellaneous expenses not subject to the 2% threshold. You can be certain that qualifying expenses are few and far between. These two are most likely to be of any benefit:

- Amortizable bond premium. The premium is the amount over face value that you pay for certain bonds. This issue is discussed in Chapter 10.

- Gambling losses. This write-off comes with its own restriction. You can't deduct more than the amount of gambling winnings you report as taxable income.

Tax Credits

If itemized deductions are the cake, tax credits are the frosting. How sweet it is! Rather than reduce the amount of income on which you have to pay tax, a credit reduces your tax bill straight away. In the 28% tax bracket, every dollar of deductible expenses saves 28 cents. Regardless of your tax bracket, every tax-credit dollar trims the bill by 100 cents.

There aren't as many credits as there once were. The investment tax credit is gone and, despite a lot of talk, efforts to revive it have floundered. Gone, too, is the credit that refunded part of your contributions to the folks who make the tax law: politicians. So is the credit designed to encourage homeowners to save energy. Still, the law includes several credits that can save you money. Here's the rundown on those most likely to have a place on your tax return.

Child- and Dependent-Care Credit

With the growth of single-parent and two-earner households, Congress created this credit to help cover the cost of child-care you have to pay so you can hold down a paying job…and earn income for the IRS to tax. The credit is based on what you pay for the care of qualifying individuals—including dependent children under age 13 or disabled dependents or a disabled spouse of any age— to enable you to work. The basic rules are the same whether care is provided for children or disabled dependents or spouses, but this discussion will focus on child care because it is the most common.

The size of your credit depends on two things: how

much you pay for care and your adjusted gross income.

The government doesn't really care how much you spend, but there is a limit on how much can qualify for the credit. If you're paying for the care of one child under age 13, the first $2,400 you pay during the year qualifies. If you're paying for the care of two or more children under age 13, the amount doubles to $4,800.

If your AGI is under $10,000, your credit is 30% of your expenses, up to the $2,400 or $4,800 cap. Taxpayers with AGI of more than $28,000 get a 20% credit. Those whose incomes fall in between figure their credit based on the following sliding scale:

Money Saver

Do you invest in international or global mutual funds? Check to see if you deserve a foreign tax credit.

		Top Credit	
		One	Two
AGI	*Credit Percent*	*Individual*	*Or More*
Under $10,000	30%	$720	$1,440
$10,001 to $12,000	29	696	1,392
12,001 to 14,000	28	672	1,344
14,001 to 16,000	27	648	1,296
16,001 to 18,000	26	624	1,248
18,001 to 20,000	25	600	1,200
20,001 to 22,000	24	576	1,152
22,001 to 24,000	23	552	1,104
24,001 to 26,000	22	528	1,056
26,001 to 28,000	21	504	1,008
Over $28,000	20	480	960

In addition to the $2,400/$4,800 caps on qualifying costs, the credit is limited by the amount of earned income you make during the year. (Earned income is basically income from a job or self-employment rather than from investments.) If you earn just $2,000 during the year, for example, that's the highest amount of child-care expenses you can count toward the credit. The IRS doesn't want to be subsidizing your getaway from the kids if you're not earning taxable income.

If you're married, you and your spouse must both work to qualify for the credit, and the earned income limit is the salary of whoever earns less.

Money Saver

Include the cost of kindergarten when figuring your child-care credit. From first grade on, though, the cost of education doesn't count.

If your spouse is in school or disabled

There's a special rule if your husband or wife is a full-time student or disabled. He or she is assumed to have earned income of $200 a month if you're paying for the care of one individual, $400 if you're paying for care for two or more. If your husband is a full-time student all year, for example, his fictitious income for purposes of this test would be either $2,400 or $4,800—the same levels as the regular caps on qualifying costs. If he or she was a student only nine months of the year, though, the assumed amounts drop to either $1,800 or $3,600. Any earnings during the months your spouse is not in school can be included when figuring your credit.

Qualifying Payments

You have almost unlimited latitude in choosing the type of care provided for your children. Until 1988, in fact, you could even count the cost of summer sleep-away camp when figuring the credit. Congress put an end to that, but you still have lots of leeway…including the cost of day camp.

In fact, a recent court case suggests that working parents might be able to count the cost of sending their children to visit grandparents. The case involved a divorced mom who sent her son and daughter to spend school holidays with their grandparents. She included airfare with other child-care expenses when figuring the credit. After all, flying the kids to Grandma's cost less than she would have had to pay for all-day care if the children stayed home. The IRS refused to go along and the matter wound up in court. The judges sided with the IRS, but their reasoning may open the door for other taxpayers. The cost of getting to the grandparents' home didn't count because the care of the children didn't begin until after they arrived. Apparently, if a grandparent had flown with the children, the tax credit would have covered the kids' airfare.

Nursery schools and day-care centers

When you send a child to a nursery school or a day-care center while you work, you can include the entire amount paid when figuring your credit—including the cost of meals provided as part of the care. The cost of attending kindergarten can count, too, but when your child-care choice includes school for first grade on up, the part of the cost allocated to education is not a qualifying expense. If you pay for before- or after-school care, though, that cost can be included when computing your credit. Be sure to get an itemized bill.

In-home care

What you pay for in-home child care counts, too. Even if your care-provider spends a good deal of his or her time on housekeeping chores and cooking, the entire salary is considered to be a qualifying cost as long as those services benefit the child being cared for so that you can work. The IRS draws the line at gardeners and chauffeurs, though. Also not counted toward the credit are amounts you pay to your child under age 19 or any dependent (see Chapter 8 for who qualifies as a dependent).

Remember social security

When you hire someone to come into your home to provide care, you'll become an employer in the eyes of the tax law. That means you'll probably have to pay the employer's share of the social security tax—which is 7.65% of wages paid—and possibly the federal unemployment tax as well (see Chapter 8 for the details). The tax you pay can be included in the amount on which you base your credit.

In response to IRS concerns that many parents were paying caregivers in cash and skipping the social security tax payments, Congress ordered that taxpayers who claim this credit must report the name, address and social secu-

More than Child Care •

Q: *The lady who takes care of our kids also cleans and cooks dinner for our family. Can we include her full salary when figuring the child-care credit, or do we need to break it down between child care and other services?*

A: Assuming that providing care for the children while you work is one of the reasons you hire the caregiver and that the other services performed benefit the children, you can include the full salary.

rity number of the care provider. That will make it easy for the IRS to check whether social security taxes were paid and whether the care provider reports and pays tax on the income.

Dependency requirements

Remember that the person for whom care is provided must be your dependent. Thus, if your disabled father lives with you and you hire someone to care for him while you work, the cost would qualify only if he is your dependent. When your child is involved, he or she must be under age 13. If the child reaches that age during the year, only amounts spent on care before the birthday count. In such a case, though, the full $2,400 or $4,800 expense cap applies.

There is an exception to the rule that you must be able to claim the child as a dependent on your return in order to qualify for the credit. This doesn't apply if you are divorced and have custody of the child but the noncustodial parent gets to claim the dependency exemptions. Also, if you are married, you must file a joint return to claim the credit, unless you otherwise qualify and your spouse did not live with you during the last six months of the year.

You claim the child-care credit on Form 2441, and because it is a credit rather than a deduction, you can get the tax benefit whether or not you itemize.

No Double Dipping

If your employer offers a child-care reimbursement plan, note that the law forbids "double dipping" by taking advantage of that plan and claiming the child-care credit. As discussed in Chapter 6, the law permits employees to funnel as much as $5,000 through set-aside plans to pay for child care, a move that makes that part of their salary tax-free. Before 1989, if additional amounts were paid for child care, those costs qualified for the child-care credit. Now, funds that go through a reimbursement plan reduce the maximum amount allowed for the credit—$2,400 if you're paying for the care of one child, $4,800 for two or more. Exceed those limits in a set-aside plan and your right to the credit disappears, even if you pay much more for child care.

If you have the choice between the credit and a reimbursement plan, the reimbursement plan is probably a better deal. For lower-income workers, however, it's possible that the credit will offer more tax savings. Take the time to weigh which is better for you.

Credit for Overpaying Social Security Tax

This credit is for well-paid individuals who have more than one job or who change jobs during the year. It's designed to protect you from paying too much social security tax.

First of all, you don't have to worry about this issue at all if you have only one job for the entire year *or* if your total wages for the year are less than the amount to which the full social security FICA tax applies: $62,700 in 1996 ($61,200 in 1995).

But if you earned more than that *and* had more than one job, you overpaid the tax and deserve the credit. Here's how it works:

Say you switched jobs in mid-1995 and earned $40,000 at each job. Each employer withheld 7.65% of the full $40,000—$3,060. That means you paid a total of $6,120 in social security tax on your $80,000 of earnings. And, that's too much.

For 1995, the full 7.65% rate hit only the first $61,200 of income. After that, only the 1.45% medicare portion of the tax applied. So, the maximum tax on $80,000 was $4,954.40. That's $4,681.80 (7.65% of $61,200) plus $272.60 (1.45% of the remaining $18,800).

In this example, you deserve a credit of $1,165.60 to refund the excess tax withheld from your paychecks.

You get a credit for that amount when you file your 1995 return. You don't even have to file a special form. Just claim the credit in the section of the Form 1040 for payments. The IRS instructions that come with the tax forms include a worksheet for figuring this credit.

Money Saver

If you have a choice between a child-care credit and a child-care reimbursement account at work, the reimbursement account is likely to be the better deal.

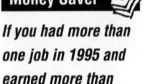

If a single employer goofs and withholds more than the maximum amount of social security from your pay, you can't recoup the difference with this credit. Instead, you'll have to get your employer to refund the overpayment to you.

Credit for Tax Paid by a Mutual Fund

On rare occasions, mutual funds declare capital gains but retain the profits and pay tax on them rather than distributing the gains to shareholders, as discussed in Chapter 10. If this happens, you have to report and pay tax on the income you didn't get. To even the score, you get to claim a tax credit for the amount of tax paid by the fund on your portion of the undistributed profits.

The fund will tell you how much tax was paid on Form 2439, *Notice to Shareholder of Undistributed Long-Term Capital Gains.* You claim the credit on Form 1040 and attach a copy of the Form 2439 to your return.

Foreign Tax Credit

If you paid foreign income taxes—on earnings from overseas employment, for example, or on investments in foreign securities—you may be in line for this credit. It's designed to prevent you from paying tax twice on the same income.

You actually have a choice of either claiming foreign taxes paid as a credit that will reduce your federal tax bill dollar for dollar or including the amount with the state and local taxes you write off as itemized deductions. Although the credit will almost always produce the bigger savings, restrictions on the credit can sometimes make the deduction the better deal. This is most likely to occur only if the foreign tax rate is higher than your U.S. tax bracket and the ratio of foreign income to U.S. income is low.

A certain advantage of taking the deduction route is that you get to avoid the two-page morass of the Form

1116, which is necessary if you claim the foreign tax credit. If you own shares in a mutual fund with substantial foreign holdings, you may be due a credit or deduction for foreign taxes paid by the fund on your behalf (see Chapter 10).

Credit for the Elderly or Disabled

Despite the sound of it, this credit doesn't suddenly become available when you turn 65. It's available only to low-income taxpayers. You must be at least 65 or, if younger, you must be retired on total and permanent disability and have received taxable disability benefits during the year. If you pass either test, your income comes into play. Before you get your hopes up, consider who *can't* claim this credit.

You don't qualify if you are single, a head of household or a qualifying widow or widower with adjusted gross income (AGI) of $17,500 or more, *or* if you receive nontaxable social security or other nontaxable pension or disability benefits of $5,000 or more. (For an idea of how stingy the $5,000 limit is, it limits your nontaxable benefits to just $417 a month.)

If you file a joint return, the rules differ depending on whether one spouse or both meet the age or disability requirements. If only one qualifies, the credit is out of reach if your AGI is $20,000 or more *or* if your nontaxable benefits total $5,000 or more. If both spouses qualify, you can't take the credit if your AGI is $25,000 or more *or* your nontaxable benefits are $7,500 or more.

If you are married filing separately (which is permissible for this credit only

Child's 13th Birthday

Q: *My daughter's 13th birthday was April 8, and I see the rules on the child-care credit say that you can only count expenses for the care of children under 13. Does that mean I lose the child-care credit?*

A: You can still claim the credit, based on the amount you paid for her care during the part of the year before her birthday. Despite the fact that your child qualified for only part of the year, you may base the credit on up to $2,400 of qualifying costs—the same limit that applies to expenses paid for a single child for the entire year.

Time Saver

If you expect to be eligible for the earned-income credit, have your employer include a portion regularly in your paychecks.

if you and your spouse did not live together during the year), you can't qualify if your AGI is $12,500 or more *or* your nontaxable benefits are $3,750 or more.

If you're still in the game after all those restrictions, your credit can be as high as $1,125 on a joint return or up to $750 on a single return. There are other restrictions that can crimp or eliminate the credit, though. You need Schedule R to pinpoint how much, if any, credit you can claim. On the bright side, if you qualify for this credit, the IRS will figure the amount for you. The instructions for Schedule R explain how to request that the agency do the number crunching.

Earned Income Credit

This credit is designed for low-income taxpayers and can actually serve as a *negative* income tax: If the credit is more than your income tax liability for the year, the IRS will send *you* a check.

After being expanded in 1994—including being made available for the first time to taxpayers without children—the earned income credit was the subject of heated debate at our deadline. It appeared likely that Congress would restrict the credit and perhaps once again limit it to taxpayers with children. The description here is based on how things worked for 1995. If Congress changes the rules, the changes will be discussed in the free update you can get by writing the author at the address in the front of this book.

For 1995, the income limits for eligibility and maximum credit size depend on the number of children you have living with you.

If you have no children, the maximum credit is $314, and your right to any credit disappears when 1995 earned income (basically that's income from a job or self-employment) or adjusted gross income (AGI, which can include investment earnings) exceeds $9,230. (This credit is *not* for students with summer jobs that pay less than that amount; you can't claim this credit if you can be claimed as a dependent on someone else's return.)

If you have one child living with you, the maximum possible credit is just over $2,000, and your right to it is completely phased out if your earned income or AGI exceeds about $24,400.

If you have two or more children, the top 1995 credit is $3,100 and your right to it disappears when income passes about $26,700.

As noted earlier, unlike most credits, which can't reduce your tax bill below $0, if an earned income credit exceeds the amount you owe, the excess will be refunded to you. Also, you don't have to wait until you file your return to take advantage of this credit. If you are eligible, you can get your employer to include a portion regularly in your paychecks. To get advance payment of the credit, ask your employer for a copy of Form W-5, *Earned Income Credit Advance Payment Certificate.* That form is filed with your employer, not the IRS.

There is a complicated formula for figuring the earned income credit, but fortunately you don't have to do it yourself. The IRS provides tables showing the size of the credit you should claim based on your earned income or AGI. There's no special form to fill out to claim the earned income credit, but the tax instructions include a worksheet for determining your eligibility.

"I'm ready for the audit any time you are."

Joseph Farris, Cartoonists & Writers Syndicate

Diesel Car Credit

This is one of the least-known tax credits and probably the one of use to the fewest taxpayers. Still, if you qualify, it will knock $102 or $198 off your tax bill.

The credit is designed to compensate buyers of new diesel-powered cars and light trucks for an increase in the diesel fuel tax that went into effect in 1984. Since the tax hike was aimed at commercial users, Congress devised this credit to compensate others for the higher tax. Rather than exempt them from paying the tax in the first place, Congress created the credit, which basically amounts to a one-time payment designed to cover what the extra tax will cost, tankful after tankful.

To qualify for the credit, you have to be the original purchaser of a diesel-powered car, truck or van that weighs less than 10,000 pounds. The credit for cars is $102. For trucks and vans it's $198. You need to fill out Form 4136 to claim the credit.

Year-End
Tax Tips

What part of the year, more than any other, is tax time? If April 15 leaps to mind, you flunk this test, and the consequences can be painful. Mistaking the return-filing deadline for tax time probably means you're paying more income tax than you have to—year after year. The lifetime cost can be enormous.

Taxes are a year-round sport. The borrowing, spending and investment decisions you make from January 1 through December 31 shape the tax bill that's due April 15. Still, one part of the year is especially important: the days between Halloween and New Year's Eve. Think of the final weeks of the year as a cornucopia overflowing with opportunities to trim your tax bill. To cash in, you must invest some time, an ingredient often in short supply around the year-end holidays. But as you draw up your to-do list for this busy time, keep in mind that you can be richly rewarded for carving out time to plan and implement tax strategies. Don't wait until after Christmas to begin. By that time, the doors to many money-saving moves will be closed.

The harvest of savings begins with a survey of where you stand in early November:

• **Tote up your earnings for the year-to-date** from salary, interest, dividends, investment profits, self-employment, rental income and any other sources. Estimate how much more income you expect in each category before the old year gives way to the new.

• **Now figure how much you can shrink that income before the IRS gets a crack at it.** Draw up a list of your *adjustments to income:* write-offs for such expenditures as alimony and IRA contributions that reduce taxable income whether or not you itemize deductions. Next, *estimate your itemized deductions*. The numbers don't have to be precise. Guesses based on your previous year's return and any significant differences you already know about are okay.

- **With a fix on your taxable income, check the tax rates that apply** (see page 65 for 1996 rates; rates for 1995 are in the appendix). That tells you exactly how well you'll be paid for maneuvers that reduce taxable income.

If you are in the 28% bracket, for example, every $1,000 you shave off that income figure cuts your tax bill by $280. In the 36% bracket, your efforts are more valuable, saving $360. This is true even if your adjusted gross income is over $117,950 in 1996 ($114,700 in 1995) and you are hit by the squeeze on itemized deductions. As explained in Chapter 15, the law now takes away a set dollar amount of your deductions based on your income. Since what you lose is set by your income, each additional dollar of deductions can still have full tax-saving power.

Although it's usually best to do what you can to push income down and deductions up, in some circumstances that's a prescription for disaster. If you are likely to be subject to the alternative minimum tax (AMT), which is discussed in Chapter 4, it may pay to accelerate the receipt of taxable income and delay paying deductible expenses. The same goes if you will be in a higher tax bracket the following year.

Savvy year-end tax planning involves looking to the year ahead as well as the one that's winding down. If spending an extra dollar on taxes this year will save you two dollars next year, for example, the standard recommendations stand on their head.

With that caveat in mind, consider these strategies.

Defer Income

The theory here is simple: Income you don't receive until after midnight on New Year's Eve isn't taxed until the following year. Even if you'll be in the same tax bracket, you win by putting off the tax bill.

It's tough for employees to postpone wage and salary income. You can't ask your employer to hang on to your December paycheck until January; nor do you push income into the next year by not cashing your check until then. Income is taxable in the year it is "constructively received." Basically, that means the year you could have had the money if you wanted it. Assume, for example, that in December your boss offers you a choice of receiving a Christmas bonus in December or the following January. Regardless of which you choose, the IRS will expect you to report and pay tax on the income with your return for the year the offer was made. If standard practice in your company is to pay year-end bonuses the following year, however, the income would be taxed in the year you get the check.

If you are self-employed or do free-lance or consulting work in addition to a job, you have more leeway, assuming you use the cash basis of accounting. Delaying billings until late December, for example, can assure you that you won't receive payment until the next year. If you are pressing for payment on an overdue account, it might make sense to give your tardy client a breather. If you own rental property, you may want to be a generous landlord and suggest to your tenants that you wouldn't mind if the December rent check didn't arrive until January. Business considerations certainly come first. But if it's unlikely you have anything to lose by holding off on collections, doing so can push some taxable income into the following year.

Accelerate Deductions

This is the other side of the defer-income coin. It can be just as effective in trimming taxable income—and your tax bill—for the current year.

Medical Expenses

Since medical bills are deductible only to the extent that they total more than 7.5% of your adjusted gross income, timing your payments may be the only way to garner a tax benefit from these costs. Chapter 15 spells out

"The taxpayer—that's someone who works for the federal government but doesn't have to take a civil service examination."

—RONALD REAGAN

Money Saver

If you're close to the 7.5% medical-expense threshold, consider having eye and dental exams and elective work done before December.

which expenses are deductible. By early December, you should have a good idea whether you'll pass the 7.5% test. If it's doubtful, try to hold off paying any medical bills until the following year, when they might have some tax-saving power. On the other hand, if you are close to or already over the threshold, see what you can do to pump up the deduction.

One sure way, of course, is to pay any outstanding medical bills—including health insurance premiums—by December 31. If you charge expenses to a bank credit card or borrow money to pay the bills, you get the deduction for the current year when you pay the bill, regardless of when you repay the debt.

Taxpayers who know they'll get to deduct medical expenses should also consider scheduling, being billed for and paying for elective medical and dental work before the end of the year. That locks in Uncle Sam's subsidy. The same goes if you need new glasses, contact lenses, dentures, a hearing aid, or modifications to a car to enable a handicapped person to drive.

State and Local Taxes

If you make estimated state income-tax payments, mailing the fourth-quarter installment by December 31 earns you the deduction in the current year—even if part of the payment is returned to you via a state tax refund the following spring. As discussed in Chapter 15, the payment has to be based on a reasonable estimate of your actual state-tax bill. You can't inflate your fourth-quarter payment just to hike the write-off on your federal return.

You may have similar flexibility with state and local property-tax bills. In some areas of the country, these bills are mailed out in the fall, for example, but they don't have to be paid until January of the following year. Beating the deadline by paying before year-end lets you claim the tax savings a year earlier.

Interest

Be sure you're up-to-date with your payments on mortgage and home-equity loans that carry deductible interest. You may be able to beef up your home-mortgage deduction by making your December payment before year-end, even if it's not due until the following January. If you make a payment on your mortgage or home-equity loan late in the year, the interest portion might not be included on the Form 1098 that your lender sends you and the IRS to show how much interest was paid during the year. Watch this point carefully. If you mail the check by December 31, you get the deduction in the current year even if the lender doesn't register the payment until the following year. But you'll need to attach a note to your tax return explaining the discrepancy between the Form 1098 and the amount you're deducting.

> # When to Deduct
> •
>
> **Q:** *I gave a check to my church at Christmas, but it wasn't cashed until the following year. Can I deduct the amount for the year I gave the check, or do I have to wait?*
>
> **A:** You can claim the deduction on the return for the year you gave the check.

Points paid on a mortgage to buy your principal residence remain fully deductible in the year paid, assuming the points amount to prepaid interest, as discussed in Chapter 9. If you plan to settle on a home around the end of the year, closing the deal and paying the points by New Year's Eve can give you a big deduction on the tax return you file the following spring.

Charitable Contributions

You have great flexibility in timing your deductible gifts to charities. If you're thinking of making a substantial gift to your alma mater, for example, doing so before the end of the year locks in the deduction for the current year. If you normally give $100 a month to your church, making the January contribution by December 31 boosts your write-off by that amount. If you make a pledge to make future contributions, however, you don't get the deduction until you actually make the gifts.

As discussed in Chapter 15, there's a special advantage to giving away appreciated property—such as stock or mutual fund shares—rather than cash. You can earn a write-off for the current value of the stock and you avoid having to pay tax on the profit that built up while you owned it.

If you routinely go through closets for used clothing to give away, find time for a year-end sweep. Making the donation by New Year's Eve earns you a deduction for the current year.

Miscellaneous Expenses

As with medical costs, you get a deduction in this catchall category only if your expenses exceed a threshold: 2% of your adjusted gross income in this case. The list of qualifying expenses is long—see Chapter 15—but you get no tax savings unless you pass the 2% test. As you get your bearings in November, see how close you are to the threshold. If you're certain to fall short, you should hold off paying qualifying expenses, such as professional dues and the cost of subscriptions to tax or investment publications, or postpone buying small tools for use in your job. If it's likely your expenses will pass 2% of AGI, speed up such spending to exploit the tax subsidy.

Bunching

Before going on a spending spree to hike your deductible expenses, be absolutely certain that you'll be itemizing. Thanks to higher standard deductions—$4,000 for singles and $6,700 for joint returns in 1996—fewer taxpayers than in the past get any benefit from itemizing. (The standard deductions are even higher for taxpayers age 65 and older and those who are legally blind. That point and the standard deduction amounts for other filing statuses are discussed in Chapter 15.) Itemizing pays off only if your qualifying expenses total more than the standard deduction for your filing status.

If you are on the itemize-or-not borderline, your year-end strategy should focus on bunching. This is the practice of timing expenses to produce *lean* and *fat* years. In one year, you cram in as many deductible expenses as possible, using the tactics outlined above. The goal is to surpass the standard-deduction amount and claim a larger write-off. In alternating years, you skimp on deductible expenses to hold them below the standard deduction amount—because you get credit for the full standard deduction regardless of how much you actually spend. In the *lean* years, year-end plans stress pushing as many deductible expenses as possible into the following *fat* year when they'll have some value.

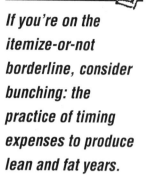

Money Saver

If you're on the itemize-or-not borderline, consider bunching: the practice of timing expenses to produce lean and fat years.

Investments

Your portfolio cries out for special attention as the year draws to an end. Since it's up to you when to sell securities—and convert paper gains and losses to real ones—you can mix and match your trades to deliver the tax outcome you desire.

Begin with an outline of exactly where you stand. Draw up a list of your trades so far during the year and the gains or losses on each. Make another list showing your current holdings and the paper gain or loss to date. In other words, if you sold the securities today, what would your profit or loss be? If you have purchased shares of the same stock mutual fund at different times, track the holding period and paper gain and loss on each block of shares. As discussed in Chapter 10, by selecting which shares to sell you can affect the taxable gain or loss.

Because of the spread between the top tax rate on long-term gains and other kinds of income, you need to distinguish between long- and short-term transactions. Property you own more than a year before selling it produces a long-term gain or loss. Property owned one year or less generates short-term results. (The top rate on short-term gains is 39.6%; the maximum rate on long-term gains is 28%. At our deadline, Congress was consid-

Money Saver

It's up to you when to sell securities—and convert paper gains and losses to real ones. Mix and match trades to deliver the tax outcome you desire.

ering changes that could significantly reduce tax rates on long-term gains. If the law is changed, we'll explain the details in the free update you can get by writing the author at the address on page i.)

Long- and short-term results are shown separately on Schedule D, where you report capital gains and losses. If you wind up with a net long-term gain and a net short-term loss, or vice versa, one offsets the other dollar for dollar before the result is carried over to your Form 1040.

Once you have a clear picture of where you stand as the year winds down, see what you can do to make it brighter.

A strategy for net gain

If your trades to date have resulted in a net gain, take a hard look at the securities in your portfolio that show paper losses. Maybe now is the time to unload some of those stocks, using the loss to offset the gain on other deals and pull down your tax bill. It's not a cockamamy idea to realize losses to save on taxes. After all, you suffered the loss when the securities fell in value. Selling just makes it official and makes the IRS pick up part of the loss.

A strategy for net loss

On the other hand, if your sales so far this year have produced a net loss, perhaps you should go in for some year-end profit-taking. Remember that only $3,000 of net losses a year can be used to offset income other than capital gains, with the tax value of extra capital losses postponed to future years. However, you can benefit from such losses this year by taking gains for the losses to absorb. That lets you take profits, up to the amount of your losses, without increasing your tax bill.

Reconciling Tax and Investment Strategy

Don't let the search for tax savings lead you into bad investment decisions. Your investment goals must be your primary concern. But if a particular investment is on the sell-or-hold borderline, perhaps the tax consequences can be decisive.

What if your tax sense collides with your investment sense? Say you want to sell a stock, but the tax angles make doing so before year-end a costly mistake. Never fear. There are ways to lock in your gain without having to pay tax with your current year's return.

Selling short against the box

This is a classic year-end technique designed to defer recognizing a taxable gain until the following year without having to worry that by January a falling stock price could make the issue moot.

It works this way: You borrow from your broker stock identical to that which you already own, and then sell the borrowed stock at today's price. That locks in your gain, but as far as the IRS is concerned the deal isn't closed for tax purposes until you deliver your shares to the broker to repay the loan. If that's after December 31, you push the taxable gain into the following year. Your holding period basically ends on the date of the short sale, though. Say that in December you sell short against the box some stock that you have owned for 11 months. If you close the short sale the following February that's the year for which you report your gain. But it will be a short-term, not a long-term gain.

Put options

Buying a put—an option giving you the right to sell stock at a set price until a certain date—can also defer recognition of gain while insuring against market loss. A put has a potential advantage over a short sale, too. Rather than lock in today's price, using a put protects you on the downside but lets you claim future appreciation. If the stock price falls, you can exercise the put and sell the stock at the set price. If the price rises, you let the put expire and

Money Saver

If your trades to date have resulted in a net gain, take a hard look at the securities in your portfolio that show paper losses. Maybe now is the time to unload some of them.

sell the shares on the open market for the bigger gain. In either case, the profit is not recognized until you sell. As with a short sale against the box, a put can't be used to convert a short-term gain to a tax-favored long-term gain.

If you exercise the option, the cost of the put is subtracted from your taxable gain; if you let it expire, the cost is considered a capital loss.

Last-minute sales

Since it takes several days to settle a securities trade—between the time you order the sale to the time you get your money—sales during the last few days of the year often straddle year-end. As far as the IRS is concerned, a gain or loss should be reported on the return for the year the trade occurs, regardless of when settlement takes place. That means profits and losses taken as late as the closing bell on New Year's Eve go on the current year's return.

Installment sales

This method lets you hold off reporting taxable income from a sale until you receive the proceeds. Although it can't be used to defer recognition of income from the sale of publicly traded stocks and bonds, the installment method can pay off for individuals who sell a vacation home, for example, or rental property. If the buyer will pay you over a number of years, you can report the income as you get it rather than all at once in the year of the sale. See Chapter 10 for details.

Bond swaps

This is another classic year-end maneuver. The point of the swap is to lock in a tax loss by selling bonds that have fallen in value and reinvesting the proceeds in other bonds. Done right, you can maintain the income stream from your bonds. Consider this example:

Assume you own $100,000 worth of AA-rated bonds with a 7% coupon and a maturity date in 2016. In November, as you begin your year-end planning, the market price of your bonds has slipped to $84,750. If you sell at that price, you'll have a $15,250 loss. At the same time, assume you can buy $100,000 face value of AAA-rated bonds, with a 7% coupon and a 2015 maturity, for $83,612.

If you sell one set of bonds and buy the other, look what happens: Since they have the same par value and coupon rate, your annual income remains the same: $7,000. Your bond rating increases from AA to AAA. You pull $1,138 out of the investment—the difference between what you got for the old bonds and what you paid for the new ones. And you can claim a $15,250 tax loss. If it offsets gains that otherwise would have been taxed at 28%, you save $4,270.

As with much year-end tax planning, the earlier you begin scouting for promising candidates for swapping, the better. The supply dwindles and competition from other investors heats up as the year draws to an end.

Beware the wash-sale rule

What if you'd like to lock in a loss for tax purposes but really want to hold on to the securities you own? Why not just sell to transform the paper loss to a real one and then buy back the same stock or bonds? The wash-sale rule, that's why. A tax loss is disallowed if within 30 days before or after the sale you buy the same or substantially identical securities. Despite all the similarities in the bonds used in the bond-swapping example above, the wash-sale rule does not come into play because different issuers were involved. If you buy bonds of the same issuer, the replacement bonds must have different maturities and coupon rates.

You may be able to accomplish your goal of claiming a loss while maintaining your market position without running afoul of the wash-sale rule. Perhaps, for example, you could trade your stock for that of another company in the same industry that's likely to perform similarly. Your broker may be able to offer recommendations. Or, you could sell shares in one mutual fund for a loss and reinvest the proceeds in another fund that has similar objectives and performance history. If you invest in no-load funds, this method avoids the transaction costs that can offset some of the savings when dealing with individual stocks and bonds.

Money Saver

If you're self-employed and your sales so far this year have produced a net loss, consider going in for some year-end profit-taking.

Interest Income

You have a bit of leeway on when you report interest income, but to capitalize you need to begin long before year-end. Interest earned on a savings account or money-market fund is taxable in the year it is made available to you, regardless of whether you withdraw the cash.

But if you buy a Treasury bill—with a maturity of three, six or 12 months—interest earned isn't taxed until the bill matures. Buy a new six-month bill on July 1 or later, for example, and you put off the tax bill on the interest earned until the following year when the bill matures. The same goes for bank certificates of deposit with a maturity of a year or less. If the interest isn't available to you without penalty until the end of the term, you don't report or pay tax on the interest until the CD matures.

Don't buy a mutual fund tax bill

Mutual funds often pay out most or all of their capital gains and dividends in December. But don't think you're getting a bargain if you buy just before the payout. In fact, that's a tax mistake.

When profits are paid out, share values fall accordingly. But since the payout is taxable, you're better off buying after the year-end distribution—you get your shares at the lower price and you avoid the tax bill on what is essentially a return of part of your purchase price. Before you invest, call the fund to ask for the *ex-dividend* date—and buy after that day.

Business Moves

If you have your own business, whether full- or part-time, you have significant control over the timing of deductible expenses. Bills for qualifying expenses you pay before year-end are deductible on the current year's return; those you hold off until the new year are deductible the following year.

Buying business property at year-end can prove either an advantage or disadvantage.

First, the plus side. The law generally allows you to claim six months' worth of the depreciation in the year you put the property into service, regardless of how late in the year you make the purchase. Even if you buy on the last day of the year, you can earn a substantial depreciation write-off. This *midyear* convention works against you, of course, if you buy your business property early in the year. Even if you buy in January, for example, you still get only half a year's worth of depreciation for the first year of ownership.

Now, the potential problem. You can trip yourself up if you buy too much business property at year-end. If the cost of assets put into service during the final three months of the year exceeds 40% of the total cost of business property put into service during the year, the half-year convention is replaced by a *midquarter* convention. That means depreciation is calculated as though each asset was put into service in the middle of the calendar quarter during which it was first used.

A year-end purchase would earn just six weeks' worth of depreciation, then, instead of six months. However, triggering the midquarter convention rule would also boost write-offs for property put in service early in the year: Assets placed in service during the first quarter would earn 10½ months' worth of depreciation rather than six months' worth. (For more on depreciation of business property, see Chapter 13.)

Expensing

This is the provision of the tax law that lets you immediately write off up to $17,500 of otherwise depreciable property. If you choose expensing, you don't have to bother with the midyear or the midquarter convention. Regardless of how late in the year you put the property into service, you can deduct the full cost of up to $17,500 worth of qualifying items.

Consider how that can boost your deduction. Say you buy $10,000 of business property with a five-year tax life. Under the midyear convention, your first-year depreciation deduction would be a healthy $2,000. Choose expensing,

Money Saver

Mail your fourth-quarter estimated state income-tax payment by December 31, and you earn the deduction in the current year.

though, and you can write off the entire purchase price on the current year's return. Expensing won't let you deduct $17,500 of the business cost of a car all at once, however, regardless of how much the car costs. Under the luxury-car rules, in 1995 the biggest first-year auto write-off was $3,060. The limit for cars purchased in 1996 had not been announced at our deadline. (See Chapter 13 for more on the luxury-car rule.)

Social Security Taxes

Successful efforts to trim your taxable business income can produce double savings. In addition to cutting your income tax bill for the year, you may also save on social security taxes. As discussed in Chapter 3, self-employment income is subject to a 15.3% social security tax. The full tax applies to the first $62,700 of earnings from salary, wages and net self-employment income in 1996. (The limit was $61,200 in 1995). If your self-employment income is subject to this levy, every $1,000 of extra business deductions would save $153 in social security taxes.

Hobby Expenses

If you have to worry about the hobby-loss rules, your strategy may be the opposite of that outlined above. As discussed in Chapter 13, your business write-offs may be limited unless you can show you're in business for profit. The IRS doesn't want to subsidize your hobby. If your endeavor shows a profit in at least three years out of every five, the law assumes you're trying to make money. Fail the three-of-five-year test, however, and it is assumed the activity is a hobby. Unless you can prove otherwise, your deductions are limited to the amount of income you report. You can't claim a loss.

Your year-end planning needs to consider both where you stand on the profit-or-loss front and how you're doing on the three-out-of-five-year test. If you need to show a profit this year to avoid having your activity branded a hobby, you may want to press for collection of any income you're due and put off paying expenses or buying new equipment until the new year.

Rental Property

Owners of rental property can pull down their taxable income by scheduling and paying for repairs on their units before year-end. Be sure, too, that you're up-to-date on paying other deductible expenses, such as property taxes, mortgage interest and insurance premiums. These costs will trim taxable rental income or increase your loss.

As long as you actively manage the property and your adjusted gross income is under $100,000, you can deduct up to $25,000 of rental losses against other income. That $25,000 allowance is phased out as AGI moves between $100,000 and $150,000. Any excess losses generally fall in the category of "passive losses," which can't be deducted unless you have passive income to offset (see Chapter 10).

If your rental losses can't be written off because of the passive-loss rules, forget about speeding up rental expenses. The extra loss will have no current tax benefit.

Passive Investments

As year-end draws near, the pain of the passive-loss rules becomes acute. These are losses from rental activities (except for the $25,000 allowance mentioned above and those incurred by real estate professionals), limited partnerships and any business in which you do *not* materially participate. Such losses cannot be used to shelter other income. Losses generated by passive activities can be used only to offset income produced by passive activities. Any excess loss is suspended for use in future years when you have passive income. (It's possible they'll be worth more to you than they would be currently—if tax rates head back up, for example.)

Year-end planning demands that you focus on losses you can't use. Promoters may try to interest you in a PIG—passive-income generator. These are investments, some are limited partnerships, designed to produce passive income

Money Saver

If you need to show a profit this year to avoid having your activity branded a hobby, press for collection of any income you're due and put off expenses until the new year.

Money Saver

Consider dumping an activity that's producing passive losses. Losses from this—and any losses suspended from previous years—are free to be deducted against other kinds of income.

to soak up passive losses. Be careful not to let your pursuit of tax savings lead you into a bad investment. Any investment touted as "tax-favored" around year-end—when many taxpayers are desperate for tax savings—begs for especially careful scrutiny.

A potential year-end tax-saver would be to unload the activity that's producing the passive losses. When you sell a passive investment, any losses produced during the year—and any losses suspended from previous years—are free to be deducted against other kinds of income.

Christmas at the beach?

Owners of vacation property may have an extra incentive to use their getaways around year-end. If you own property that you rent out part-time, you probably are well-versed in the vacation-home rules: Use the place for more than 14 days or 10% of the number of days it is rented and the house is considered a personal residence. That limits your rental-expense deductions to the amount of rental income. In other words: no tax loss to shelter other income. Limit personal use to pass the 14-day test, though, and the house is considered a rental property. Qualifying it as such lets you deduct losses under the $25,000 rule (*if* you actively manage the place and your AGI is below $150,000 so you're not tripped up by the passive-loss rules).

In the past, the tax subsidy from writing off losses was a key part of financing many vacation homes, so owners were careful not to let personal use tip the scales against them. Now, however, passing the rental-property test can cost you mortgage-interest deductions. The law permits you to deduct all mortgage interest on your principal residence and a second home. If you keep your personal use of the vacation place under 15 days, however, it doesn't qualify as a second home. That means mortgage interest attributed to your use of the house is *nondeductible* personal interest.

If your rental losses are threatened by the passive-loss rules, you may find it advantageous to squeeze in enough extra days of personal use at year-end to qualify the vacation house as a second home. At least that would preserve your mortgage-interest write-off (see Chapter 9).

Retirement Plans

Taxpayers who are considering opening a Keogh retirement plan have to decide by New Year's Eve. If you want to write off a contribution to a Keogh on this year's return, the plan must be established by December 31, although contributions can be made anytime up to the due date of your return (see Chapter 11).

There's no year-end pressure if you're thinking about an individual retirement account. Contributions to accounts opened anytime up to April 15 can be deducted on the previous year's return.

When you take money out of an IRA, much—if not all—of it is taxable. As you consider a withdrawal around year-end, weigh the potential advantage of holding off until the new year arrives. If you can wait to put your hands on the money, you can make Uncle Sam wait an extra year before he gets his share. But if you'll find yourself in a higher tax bracket in the future—due to higher income or increases in the tax rates—you may want to speed up IRA withdrawals to avoid the stiffer tax bite.

Timing of IRA withdrawals might also protect some of your social security benefits from taxation. As discussed in Chapter 12, a portion of your benefits is taxed if income exceeds a certain threshold based on your filing status. For this purpose, *income* includes money you pull out of an IRA. If you're in the range where more income means more benefits are taxed, consider whether it makes sense to increase your IRA withdrawals one year (when the maximum of your social security benefits will be taxed anyway) and hold them down in the next (when doing so might protect the tax-free status of your benefits).

In the year you reach age 70½, the law demands that you begin withdrawals from your IRA, as discussed in Chapter 11. But the first mandatory distribution—the one for the year you turn 70½ can be put off until as late as the following April 1. Holding off trims your taxable income and your tax bill in the current year. But you must double up in the second year. In addition to the withdrawal made by April 1, another has to be made by December 31. If the

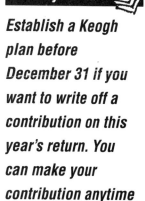

Money Saver

Establish a Keogh plan before December 31 if you want to write off a contribution on this year's return. You can make your contribution anytime up to the due date of your return.

resulting boost in taxable income shoves you into a higher tax bracket, your income-deferral strategy could backfire.

Protect Your Exemptions

With the growing value of exemptions, it's more important than ever to protect your right to claim exemptions for your dependents. In 1996, exemptions are worth $2,550 each, meaning each one knocks $714 off the tax bill of someone in the 28% bracket. (Exemptions were worth $2,500 in 1995.)

Chapter 8 outlines the various tests you must pass to claim someone as your dependent. The two most likely to trip you up—that you can do anything about at year-end—are the *support test* and the *gross-income test*.

The support test demands that you provide more than half of a person's support in order to claim him or her as your dependent. That's usually no problem when your children are involved, but it can be dicey if you are supporting an elderly parent. By November at the latest, you should get a fix on what percentage of your parent's support you've supplied during the year. If it appears that things are going to be close, you may want to beef up your support and have your parent cut back a bit on spending his or her own money.

Money a dependent puts into savings doesn't count as support, but cash that's pulled out and spent on support does. Say, for example, that your father—who you intend to claim as a dependent—wants to tap his savings account to buy a new car. If what he takes out for the car pushes his own contribution to his support over the 50% mark, you lose the tax-saving exemption. Suggesting that your father delay the car purchase until the new year could preserve your right to the exemption.

The gross-income test blocks you from claiming as your dependent someone with gross income that exceeds the exemption amount ($2,550 in 1996). This test does not apply, however, to your children who are either under age 19, or those under age 24 who were full-time students for at least five months during the year.

The exception for children means that here, too, the most likely threat is to dependency exemptions for the taxpayer's parents. But note this: nontaxable social security benefits or other tax-exempt income don't count for purposes of the gross-income test.

You need to keep an eye on the earnings of potential dependents from savings, investments or jobs. It may pay off to recommend that a dependent parent move money out of a taxable savings account and into a tax-free money-market mutual fund, for example, if doing so would preserve the dependency exemption. Your tax savings might outweigh the slightly lower yield your parent would earn in the tax-free investment.

As with all year-end investment decisions, factors other than taxes come into play here. You have to weigh the potential tax savings against other considerations. And remember this: If you can arrange things so that you claim someone as a dependent, that person may not claim a personal exemption on his or her own tax return.

Give Money Away

As discussed in Chapter 18, you can give away as much as $10,000 a year to any number of people without triggering the federal gift tax. The tax-free amount doubles to $20,000 if your spouse joins you in making the gift. You don't get a tax deduction for such gifts unless the object of your generosity is a qualified charitable organization. But there's an important advantage: Assets given away during your life—and any future appreciation—won't be in your estate to be taxed after you die. And income generated by the gift is taxed to the new owner, not to you. (If you give assets to your own children, however, the income can be taxed in your tax bracket until the children reach age 14. That's explained in Chapter 8.)

This issue is raised here, among possible year-end maneuvers, because if you're planning to make substantial gifts, you face a December 31 deadline. If you don't use your $10,000 annual exclusion by that date, you lose it. Each new year presents you with a new exclusion, but

Money Saver

If you mail your mortgage payment check for January by December 31, you get the deduction in the current year even if the lender doesn't register the payment until the following year.

you can't reach back to benefit from a previous year's unused allowance.

Assume, for example, that a couple plans to give $40,000 to their son. If they give it all during one year, $20,000 of the gift would be sheltered from the gift tax, the other $20,000 subject to it. However, if half the gift was given in December and the other half in January, the full $40,000 would be protected.

If you make the gift by check, be sure the recipient cashes the December check before the end of the year. Unlike the rules for itemized deductions—which allow a deduction for the year you give the check regardless of when it is cashed—when a gift is involved, it is considered given in the year the check is cashed.

Give Money to Your Grandchildren?

Q: *I plan to make cash gifts to my grandchildren at Christmas time. Is it true I can deduct up to $10,000 for gifts to each child?*

A: Afraid not, although there is something called the $10,000 annual gift tax exclusion. It has nothing to do with the income tax, though. As discussed in Chapter 18, the gift tax exclusion allows you to give up to $10,000 each year to any number of individuals without having to worry about the federal gift tax. Gifts you make to your grandchildren are not deductible by you on your income tax return.

Get Married, or Not

If you're planning to tie the knot around the end of the year, you may want to check with Uncle Sam before setting the date. Whether you marry in December or January could have a major impact on your tax bill. No, it's not romantic. But playing the tax angle could save enough to pay for a nice honeymoon.

Whether you and your intended are better off married or single at year-end depends mostly on how your incomes compare. See Chapter 8.

If you think weighing the tax consequences of the wedding date is somewhat less than sentimental, how about the folks who consider a year-end divorce as a tax strategy? As far as the IRS is concerned, your marital status on the last day of the year generally determines your filing status. With that in mind, some "shrewd" taxpayers thought they had discovered a way around the marriage tax penalty: Divorce in December and remarry in January. If the tax savings financed a trip to the Caribbean for the quickie divorce, all the better. Alas, it doesn't work. Such a divorce is considered a sham and ignored for tax purposes.

Watch Your Withholding

The federal income tax is on a pay-as-you-go basis. Although the final accounting isn't due until April 15 of the following year, the tax is supposed to be paid as you earn the money. That's why employers withhold tax from your paychecks and why you're expected to make estimated tax payments on self-employment or investment income. If you don't pay enough as you go along, you can be hit by a penalty.

As part of your year-end planning, compare your tax payments so far with what you expect to owe. If your payments will be at least as much as the tax you owed for the previous year or at least 90% of what you'll owe this year, you're probably safe from the penalty. If you will fall short, however, some year-end maneuvering can save you some money.

Estimated tax payments are considered made when you send the money to the IRS, which means you can't make up for an underpayment early in the year by beefing up your final estimated payment, which is due the following January 15. Withholding, however, is treated as though it is paid evenly over the year, even if a big chunk is taken out of your paycheck late in December. That means over-withholding in November and December can make up for earlier underpayments.

If you have a job, then, you have a last-minute opportunity to dodge, or at least mitigate, an underpayment penalty: Arrange with your employer to withhold extra amounts from the final paychecks of the year (see Chapter 7). And, remember in January to have withholding readjusted downward.

Money Saver

Accelerate year-end giving to your church, alma mater, or a charity of choice. That gives you the tax benefit sooner rather than later.

Estate & Gift Taxes

Which came first, the chicken or the egg? That question has confounded generations. Here's an easier one: Which comes last, death or taxes?

You guessed it. Taxes.

After you die, Uncle Sam gets one last crack at the assets you've accumulated during your life. And what a crack it is. The top *official* tax rate is 55%, but it really climbs as high as 60% for some estates. And, as discussed later, a special estate tax can claim even more if you die with large amounts in your retirement accounts. Clearly, the U.S. Treasury can become the primary beneficiary of your legacy.

Fortunately, relatively few estates have to pay this tax. In 1993, just over 60,000 estate tax returns were filed and, all told, those estates paid just over $10.3 billion in tax—for an average tax bill of about $170,000.

The tax kicks in only when the taxable estate exceeds $600,000. Ironically, you'd probably like to have enough to leave to your heirs that you have to worry about this tax. If you do, strategies abound for limiting or eliminating the tax on estates well above the $600,000 level. (Note this: At our deadline, Congress was considering changes in the law that would gradually raise the tax-free level to $750,000 and create new breaks for family-owned farms and businesses. If such changes are made, they will be covered in the free update you can get by writing the author at the address on page i.)

The Basics

First things first. The estate tax applies to the transfer of property at death. The tax is paid by the estate, not by the person who inherits the property.

To avoid a loophole that would let people dodge the estate tax by giving away their property before death, there is a unified system for taxing gifts you make during your lifetime and assets you leave in your estate. The same tax rates apply, and almost everyone gets a credit that permits the tax-free transfer of up to $600,000 worth of assets through gifts made during your lifetime, through your estate after death or by a combination of the two. (However, as explained later in this chapter, you can make gifts of up to $10,000 a year each to any number of recipients without using up any of the credit.)

Don't Underestimate Your Estate

Don't let the $600,000 amount lull you into thinking you'll never have to worry about the estate tax. One of the greatest threats is to underestimate the size of your estate and blissfully ignore planning opportunities.

The fact is, your estate—as the law defines it for tax purposes—may already be much larger than you imagine. It includes the value of your home and other real estate holdings, of course, as well as your savings and the value of your investments, cars, boats, jewelry and other personal property. Also included are benefits from retirement plans, whether an IRA, Keogh or company plan. Another asset that can go into your taxable estate, but which you might not think about because it doesn't exist until after your death, is life insurance. If you own the policy—which you do if you can change the beneficiary or borrow against cash value—its proceeds are considered part of your estate.

Use the worksheet on pages 448 and 449 to get a snapshot of the current net worth, then take a stab at how much it will grow as you grow older.

Money Saver

Nearly everyone gets a $192,800 estate- and gift-tax credit— enough to offset the tax bill on a $600,000 taxable estate.

(continued on page 450)

Adding Up Your Estate

Use this worksheet to size up your estate to see whether your legacy is likely to be threatened by the federal estate tax. *How you own property*—say, solely or jointly—is pivotal to how much of its value will be included in your estate at the time of your death.

In the value column, list the following:

- **The full value of property of which you are the sole owner.**

- **One-half of the value of property that you own jointly with your spouse with right of survivorship.**

- **Your proportionate share of property owned in conjunction with others.** If you and two brothers are equal co-owners of a piece of property, for example, you would include one-third of the value.

- **One-half of the value of community property,** which basically includes assets acquired during marriage in one of the community-property states: Arizona, California, Idaho, Louisiana, Nevada, New Mexico, Texas, Washington and Wisconsin. Gifts or inheritances received during marriage are not considered community property, however, so their full value is included in your estate.

Also include the full value of the proceeds of an insurance policy on your life if you retain "incidents of ownership" in the policy, such as the right to change the beneficiary or borrow against the policy; your interest in pension and profit-sharing plans; and the value of property you have placed in a revocable trust.

Once you know the approximate size of your net estate use the worksheet on page 456 to see how it would be affected by the federal estate tax.

	Value
Assets	
Cash in checking, savings, money-market accounts	$ _____
Stocks	_____
Bonds	_____
Mutual funds	_____
Other investments	_____
Home	_____
Other real estate	_____
Personal property including furniture, cars, clothing, and so on	_____
Art, antiques, collectibles	_____
Proceeds of life insurance policies you own on your life	_____
Pension and profit-sharing benefits, IRAs, Keogh plans, and so on	_____
Business interests (sole proprietorships, partnerships, closely held corporations)	_____
Money owed to you, such as mortgages, rents, professional fees	_____
Other assets	_____
Total Assets	$ _____
Liabilities	
Mortgages	_____
Loans and notes	_____
Taxes	_____
Consumer debt	_____
Other liabilities	_____
Total Liabilities	$ _____
Net Estate *(assets minus liabilities)*	$ _____

Marital Deduction

On the other hand, your taxable estate can be much less than your net worth. If you are married, in fact, you can avoid the estate tax altogether—regardless of how much you're worth. Every dime you leave your spouse is excluded from your taxable estate (assuming he or she is a citizen). This unlimited marital deduction covers bequests made in your will and assets that aren't controlled by it, such as life insurance or retirement benefits of which your spouse is the beneficiary.

The unlimited marital deduction is evidence of the government's patience as much as its generosity. Although the deduction can shield estates of any size from the tax when the first spouse dies, the IRS will be waiting when the survivor dies—unless he or she has remarried. Although leaving everything to your spouse may at first appear to solve your estate-planning worries, that can be a costly mistake, as discussed later.

The Unified Credit

Whether or not you can take advantage of the marital deduction, nearly everyone gets a $192,800 estate- and gift-tax credit—enough to offset the tax bill on a $600,000 taxable estate. We say the credit is available to *nearly* everyone because the benefit of the credit is phased out for estates that exceed $10 million.

When a taxable estate exceeds the $600,000 level, the tax bill mounts quickly, as shown in this table:

Taxable Estate	Tax After Credit
Up to $ 600,000	$ 0
700,000	37,000
800,000	75,000
900,000	114,000
1,000,000	153,000
1,500,000	363,000
2,000,000	588,000
5,000,000	2,198,000

Those staggering sums leave no question about the importance of tax planning as your net worth moves into the vulnerable range. Use the worksheet on page 456 to estimate the tax due on your estate.

Giving It Away and the Gift Tax

Before looking at other basic estate-tax planning strategies, consider the role of gifts and the workings of the gift side of the estate and gift tax.

The gift tax is perhaps the most misunderstood of all taxes. When it comes into play, this tax is owed by the *giver* of the gift, not the recipient. You probably have never paid it and probably will never have to.

The law completely ignores gifts of up to $10,000 each year that you give to any number of individuals. (You and your spouse together can give up to $20,000 a year.) If you have 1,000 friends on whom you wish to bestow $10,000 each, you can give away $10 million a year without even having to fill out a federal gift-tax form. That $10 million would be out of your estate for good. But if you made the $10 million in bequests via your will, the money would be part of your taxable estate and would trigger an enormous tax bill.

Consider a more practical example: Assume that the worksheet on the pages 448 and 449 shows a net estate far above the $600,000 taxable level. To hold down the ultimate estate-tax bill, you initiate a series of annual gifts to your three married children. If both you and your spouse give the full $10,000 to the three children and their spouses, you can distribute $120,000 ($20,000 to each of the three children and three in-laws) *each year* tax-free. Imagine how your tax-free gift total could grow if you also included grandchildren in your beneficence. In addition to removing the gift property itself from your taxable estate, any future appreciation is also spared from any tax in your estate.

How it works when you incur the tax

The rules get complicated if your generosity passes

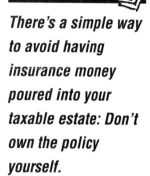

Money Saver

There's a simple way to avoid having insurance money poured into your taxable estate: Don't own the policy yourself.

the $10,000 threshold. For one thing, larger gifts require you to file a gift-tax return. If the gift falls in the $10,000 to $20,000 range and is not taxable because you and your spouse join in making it, you can use the short gift-tax form, Form 709A. If it's not such a gift, however, you must use Form 709, *United States Gift Tax Return,* and figure the tax due on the amount over $10,000.

And to calculate the tax, you must take into account all taxable gifts made in previous years. Here's an example of how it works:

You decide to give your son $50,000 each year for three consecutive years. (For simplicity's sake, assume your spouse does not join you in the gift.) The first

Gift and Estate-Tax Rate Schedule

Taxable Amount		Tentative Tax			
Up to $ 10,000			18%		
$ 10,001 to 20,000		$ 1,800	plus 20%	of amount over	$ 10,000
20,001 to 40,000		3,800	plus 22%	of amount over	20,000
40,001 to 60,000		8,200	plus 24%	of amount over	40,000
60,001 to 80,000		13,000	plus 26%	of amount over	60,000
80,001 to 100,000		18,200	plus 28%	of amount over	80,000
100,001 to 150,000		23,800	plus 30%	of amount over	100,000
150,001 to 250,000		38,800	plus 32%	of amount over	150,000
250,001 to 500,000		70,800	plus 34%	of amount over	250,000
500,001 to 750,000		155,800	plus 37%	of amount over	500,000
750,001 to 1,000,000		248,300	plus 39%	of amount over	750,000
1,000,001 to 1,250,000		345,800	plus 41%	of amount over	1,000,000
1,250,001 to 1,500,000		448,300	plus 43%	of amount over	1,250,000
1,500,001 to 2,000,000		555,800	plus 45%	of amount over	1,500,000
2,000,001 to 2,500,000		780,800	plus 49%	of amount over	2,000,000
2,500,001 to 3,000,000		1,025,800	plus 53%	of amount over	2,500,000
Over 3,000,000		1,290,800	plus 55%*	of amount over	3,000,000

A 5% surcharge applies to taxable estates between $10 million and $21,040,000, making the effective rate 60%. The surcharge is Congress's way of taking back the $192,800 credit that protects the first $600,000 of an estate from taxation. When the estate passes the $10 million mark, Congress figures your heirs don't need that break.

$10,000 gift each year is protected by the annual exclusion. You would report the $40,000 taxable portions and figure the tax as follows:

- **In the first year,** using the rate schedule below, the tax on the first $40,000 gift is $8,200.

- **In the second year,** you add the new $40,000 taxable gift to the previous year's $40,000 and find the tax on $80,000. That's $18,200. From that amount you subtract the $8,200 due on the first gift. That makes the tax on the second gift $10,000.

- **In the third year,** you again add the new $40,000 to the $80,000 of taxable gifts given in previous years. Find the tax on $120,000, which is $29,800, and subtract the combined $18,200 tax on the previous gifts. The tax on your third gift is $11,600.

The point of adding in the previous gifts is to force you to march steadily up the graduated rate schedule. Note that although the same size gift was given in each of the three years in the example, the gift tax rose from $8,200 on the first gift to $10,000 on the second and $11,600 on the third.

Our example assumes that these gifts are the only ones made by you so far, so no tax would actually have to be paid. Rather, your $192,800 unified estate-and-gift-tax credit would be reduced by $29,800 (the bill on the $120,000 of taxable gifts). The remaining $163,000 of the credit would be enough to shelter another $480,000 of taxable transfers, either as gifts made during your lifetime or through your estate.

How gifts affect your estate tax, too

Taxable gifts made during your life also come into play when figuring the tax due on your estate. As you see on the worksheet on page 456, the taxable portion of gifts made after 1976 is included in the amount on which the estate tax is based. That may seem like double taxation, but it's not that sinister. Instead, as with the requirement that previous gifts be taken into account when calculating the gift tax, the point is to prevent you from using the lower estate-tax brackets more than once. Although you have to bring gifts back into the estate, you also get to use the full credit to offset the estate-tax bill—even though part of it was used during your life to shield you from the gift tax.

Assume that during your life you made $600,000 of taxable gifts, using up your entire credit. When you die, your taxable estate is also $600,000. Without the requirement to "gross up" the estate for taxable gifts, the tax on $600,000 would be $192,800. To prevent you from using the 18% through 34% brackets a second time, the law requires you to find the tax on $1.2 million (the total of the taxable gifts plus the taxable estate). Stacked on top of the gifts, the estate is taxed in the 37% through 41% brackets. The bill on $1.2 million is $427,800. Subtracting the $192,800 credit amount leaves your estate with a $235,000 liability.

Although pulling taxable gifts back into the estate may seem to defeat the tax-saving aim, it does not. The assets are counted in your estate at their value at the time of the gift. Any appreciation between that time and your death avoids being taxed in your estate. That can be extremely important, particularly when rapidly appreciating assets are involved.

There may also be income tax advantages to making gifts, as discussed in Chapter 8. But you should be aware of a potential income tax drawback, too. The IRS forgives the tax on any profit that has built up on assets that you own at the time of your death. (This is sometimes called the *Angel of Death* tax break.) Assume that stock you bought for $50,000 is worth $100,000 when you die. That $50,000

Savings-Bond Interest

● ●

Q: *When my father died last year, he owned several thousand dollars' worth of Series E and EE savings bonds that named me as his beneficiary. Do I have to pay tax on the interest that built up on the bonds while he was alive?*

A: Any interest that wasn't reported by your father must be reported as income by you when you cash the bonds. However, interest that had accrued up to the day of your father's death may be reported on his final income tax return. Depending on your father's other income for the year, doing so could significantly reduce the tax due.

profit escapes the income tax. If you were to give away the stock before death, however, the recipient would be responsible for the income tax on the appreciation that accrued while you owned the stock.

Mixing the Marriage Deduction and the Unified Credit

As mentioned earlier, if you are married you can leave everything you own to your spouse free of estate tax. Relying too much on the marital deduction to protect the estate of the first spouse to die, however, could set up the survivor for unnecessary taxes.

To illustrate the potential problem, and a solution for it, consider an example: Assume you have a taxable estate of $1 million and your spouse owns property worth $200,000. If you leave everything outright to your spouse, the unlimited marital deduction will permit it to pass tax-free.

But if the $1 million plus the $200,000 remains intact, when your spouse dies the taxable estate will be $1.2 million. The unified credit will protect just half that amount, letting the IRS claim $235,000 in tax on the extra $600,000. That's money that, with a little planning, could have been passed on to the next generation.

One of the most common estate plans for a couple with more than $600,000 in assets is to make sure the first spouse to die takes advantage of the unified credit as well as the marital deduction. Note that in our example, by relying fully on the marital deduction, the first spouse effectively threw away the $192,800 credit.

To avoid forfeiting that tax break, you can use what's variously known as a *bypass* or *exemption-equivalent* trust. Basically, in our example you would split your estate, putting $600,000 in a trust and leaving the other $400,000 outright to your surviving spouse. (You can split your estate however you choose, of course, but the goal is often to make maximum use of the unified credit.)

Although the money put in this type of trust would

(continued on page 457)

Money Saver

Couples: Protect more of your estate by making use of both the marital deduction and the unified credit.

Federal Estate-Tax Worksheet

Depending on how much you leave behind, Uncle Sam might squeeze into line as an unintended beneficiary. With the worksheet on page 449 you can estimate the projected size of your estate. The worksheet below and the tax rates provided on page 452 can give you a snapshot of the potential estate tax.

Begin with the estimated size of your net estate and subtract the value of all property left to your spouse and sheltered from tax by the unlimited marital deduction.

Next, subtract the value of assets bequeathed to charity.

Then add the value of gifts made after 1976 that exceeded the $10,000 annual exclusion ($20,000 if your spouse joined in the gift).

The total is your estate-tax computation base. Find the tentative tax on that amount using the rates in the table on page 452.

From that amount, subtract any gift tax you actually paid during your life—that is, any gift tax beyond that covered by the $192,800 unified credit.

The result is the tax on your estate.

Before you write a check to the IRS, though, you get to subtract your unified credit and perhaps other credits, such as those for death taxes paid to a state.

(States differ in the way they tax estates. A few impose an estate tax similar to the federal levy. Others impose an inheritance tax directly on those who inherit property, with the lowest rates and highest exemptions often reserved for your spouse and children. More than half the states levy a "pickup" tax, which applies only to estates with a federal tax liability. This tax doesn't really increase the total amount of tax due on your estate because it equals the amount of the credit you're allowed on the federal estate tax return for death taxes paid to a state.)

	Sample Estate		Your Estate
Net Estate	$ 1,070,000	$	_____
Less marital deduction	300,000	-	_____
Less charitable bequests	20,000	-	_____
Plus taxable gifts made after 1976	12,000	+	_____
Estate-Tax Computation Base	$ 762,000	$	_____
Tentative tax from table on page 452	252,980		_____
Less gift tax paid after 1976	0	-	_____
Tax On Taxable Estate	$ 252,900	$	_____
Less unified credit*	192,800	$	192,800
Estate Tax Due	$ 60,180	$	_____

Other credits may be available to reduce the tax, such as the credit for death taxes paid to a state.

not qualify for the marital deduction, it would be protected from tax by the credit. The $400,000 left outright to your spouse would be shielded from tax by the marital deduction. As in the first example, then, no tax is due on the death of the first spouse.

A key feature of the bypass trust is that income from the trust can go to your survivor—just as if he or she inherited the assets outright—but at his or her death the principal would be distributed to other heirs, such as your children, without being included in your spouse's estate.

In our example, that estate would include the $400,000 left under the marital deduction plus the $200,000 of personal assets. The unified credit would shelter the full amount from the estate tax. Bottom line: the family comes out $235,000 ahead.

QTIP Trusts

Until recently, to qualify for the estate-tax marital deduction, assets had to be left to the survivor in a way that permitted him or her to control their ultimate distribution. In other words, if you left $1 million to your wife, she'd get to decide who would inherit what remained at her death.

Now, however, you can use a qualified terminable interest property (QTIP) trust that qualifies for the marital deduction without giving away ultimate control of the property. A QTIP trust gives your surviving spouse income for life and possibly some principal, but after his or her death the distribution of the assets is controlled by your wishes in the trust document rather than by your spouse's will.

Although the QTIP trust is similar to the bypass trust in that the survivor receives income for life and assets are then passed on according to the trust, there are two key differences. One is that the QTIP protects property from the estate tax with the marital deduction rather than the unified credit used by the bypass trust (and, therefore, the transfer of other property can be protected by the credit). And, unlike a bypass trust, assets in a QTIP trust are included in your survivor's taxable estate.

QTIP trusts may be especially appropriate for those who have children from a former marriage. A husband, for example, can use such a trust to provide for his second wife while ensuring that when she dies, the assets will pass on to the children from his first marriage. Childless couples can also use QTIP trusts so that either spouse can be sure that, after providing for the survivor, his or her blood relatives will ultimately inherit specified assets.

Joint Ownership of Property

Married couples often own a significant part of their estate together, either by joint tenancy with the right of survivorship or tenancy by the entirety. The key is that when one owner dies, the other automatically becomes sole owner of the property. That promise and the concept of owning things together rather than individually is appealing to married couples. Beyond the harmony and peace of mind such economic unity can promote, property owned jointly bypasses probate when the first spouse dies, saving time, hassle, publicity and expenses.

Many people also think that because jointly owned property dodges probate, its value also escapes the estate tax. That's only half right. When the first spouse dies, half the value of jointly owned property is included in his or her estate. The unlimited marital deduction will protect that amount from the estate tax. So, what's the problem?

Owning too much property jointly can foul up planning efforts to hold down the tax on the estate of the second spouse. Only property you own individually can go into a bypass trust; jointly owned assets go automatically to the survivor. Estate planners generally like to see at least enough separately owned property to take full advantage of the unified credit. If joint ownership makes that impossible, you are considered to be turning down part of Uncle Sam's $192,800 generosity.

If your projections of future net worth suggest that you may benefit from a bypass trust, pay particular attention to how you take title to property. As with all estate planning, you are almost certain to need professional advice to ensure that your efforts produce the outcome you desire. Seek the help of an experienced professional, such as an attorney or certified public accountant, who specializes in this area.

Life Insurance

Proceeds of a policy on your life could be the asset that pushes your estate into the taxable range. It doesn't matter who the beneficiary of the policy is, if you own the policy when you die, the money is considered part of your taxable estate. However, if your spouse is the beneficiary, the proceeds would be shielded from the estate tax by the marital deduction.

But there's a simple way to avoid having the money poured into your estate at all: Don't own the policy yourself. If you give the policy to your spouse or adult children, for example, the proceeds bypass your estate.

Don't overlook the cost of this move though: Giving up ownership means giving up control of the policy. If you retain any *incidents of ownership* of the policy, the proceeds go into your taxable estate. To avoid that, you have to give up the right to change the beneficiary and forsake your right to borrow against the policy. If the arrangement permits you to change your mind and regain control of the policy, you are not considered to have ever given up ownership.

Giving the policy away doesn't always work, either. If you die within three years of the gift, the proceeds of the policy are brought back into the taxable estate.

Rather than give a life insurance policy to an individual, another option is to put the policy into an irrevocable life insurance trust. Again, that would mean giving up control of the policy. Proceeds of the policy would go into the trust and be controlled by its provisions. Income could go to your surviving spouse, for example, with the principal

> ## *Life Insurance Payments*
> •
>
> **Q:** *After my elderly aunt died, I learned she had named me beneficiary of a $25,000 life insurance policy. Is that money taxed, and if so, where do I report it on my return?*
>
> **A:** The proceeds of the policy are free of income tax.

going to your children after the survivor's death. This arrangement would prevent the proceeds from being taxed in the estate of either spouse.

If You Own a Business

The best-laid plans for passing a business from one generation to the next can collapse if you fail to consider the demands of your invisible partner: Uncle Sam. The value of your business could be the bulk of your estate. If you fail to plan for the potential estate-tax liability, your family could be forced to give up control. Even if your heirs planned to sell out, they could be forced to accept a fire-sale price in the scramble to pay the tax.

The first step in preserving options for the next generation is to have a realistic estimate of the value of the business and the potential estate-tax bill. The IRS has stunned some families with a tax bill based on a value far higher than they dreamed the business was worth. Once you have a handle on what your business is worth, you have a basis for estate planning.

One option is to buy enough life insurance to cover the potential estate-tax bill. Another is to leave the business to your spouse to take advantage of the marital deduction. Keep in mind, though, that there will be no similar protection when it comes time to pass the business on to the next generation.

You could also begin giving away interest in the business, taking advantage of the annual $10,000 gift-tax exclusion for each recipient and preventing future appreciation from winding up in your taxable estate.

Another alternative is to build a buy/sell agreement into your estate plan. That would obligate someone, perhaps your partners or key employees, to buy your share of the business and obligate your estate to sell it at a price set under methods spelled out in the agreement. To make certain the survivor has the funds to cover the price, parties to the agreement often buy insurance policies on each other's lives.

There is also a special estate-tax break for the part of your interest you leave to an employee stock-ownership plan (ESOP). Also, you may be able to take advantage of rules designed to prevent families from being forced to sell closely held businesses in order to satisfy the estate-tax law.

If you qualify and your interest in the business represents 35% or more of your taxable estate, the tax bill can be paid over 14 years, with only interest due during the first four years. And the estate gets a break on the interest charged on the postponed tax bill— it's just 4% of the tax due on the first $1 million of the taxable estate attributable to the business. (As noted at the beginning of this chapter, at our deadline, Congress was considering creating special estate tax breaks for family-owned businesses and farms.)

"Have a seat. Taxes is in with him now."

An Extra Hit on Retirement-Plan Assets

As discussed in Chapter 12, if there's "too much" in your retirement plans when you die, your estate can be hit with a surtax equal to 15% of the excess amount. How much is *too much* depends on your age when you die. Basically, you find how much it would cost someone at your age to buy an annuity that would pay $155,000 for the rest of his or her life expectancy. For someone age 65, that's about $1 million. So, if you die at age 65 with more than that amount in retirement plans—including company pension and profit-sharing plans, Keogh plans and IRAs—the excess would be hit by the extra 15% tax. The trigger point drops as you get older. For someone age 75, for example, it's about $850,000. (That $155,000 annual amount is supposed to rise in the future to keep up with inflation.)

You can't use part of the unified credit to offset this surtax, but if your surviving spouse is the beneficiary of your plans, this tax can be delayed until he or she dies. By that time, the surtax might be or eliminated if the amount in the accounts has been drawn down.

This abbreviated discussion of the estate-tax rules is designed to alert you to the options that may be available for limiting your estate-tax liability. Deciding which strategy will work best for you demands expert professional help. The earlier you begin planning, the more choices you have.

Inherited Stock

Q: *I inherited some stock last year and sold it for several thousand dollars. Do I have to pay any tax on the amount I received from the sale?*

A: Perhaps, but the sale might actually result in cutting your tax bill. Your basis in the stock—that is, the amount from which you figure your gain or loss—is probably its value on the date the previous owner died. On rare occasions an alternative valuation date is used. In either case, the executor of the estate should be able to pinpoint the value. If you sold the stock for more than that amount, you must pay tax on the difference. If you sold for less, you have a deductible capital loss.

Surviving a
Tax Audit

The odds are reassuring. Of more than 113 million individual tax returns filed each year, the IRS audits just over 1% of them. That means there's only about a one-in-one-hundred chance that the IRS will demand that you back up what you put down on your forms. The odds are even slimmer that you'll go eyeball-to-eyeball with an auditor because the IRS handles more than one-third of the audits by mail. Still, each year more than 1 million of your fellow citizens win (or should we say lose) the audit lottery. To them, the IRS says: **Prove it!**

The IRS doesn't randomly choose returns, of course, and the odds of being audited vary with the type of return you file and the amount of income you report. As the following table shows, the odds increase dramatically if you have a business and file a Schedule C with your return or use a Schedule F to report farm income and expenses. Here are the latest numbers from the IRS:

Type of Return	Amount of Income	Odds of Audit
1040A	Under $25,000	1 in 96
1040	Under $25,000	1 in 114
	$25,000 to $50,000	1 in 189
	$50,000 to $100,000	1 in 139
	More than $100,000	1 in 34
with Schedule C	Under $25,000	1 in 23
	$25,000 to $100,000	1 in 33
	More than $100,000	1 in 28
with Schedule F	Under $100,000	1 in 86
	More than $100,000	1 in 57

If your return is one of those selected, why were you singled out and what's in store?

Computer analysis selects most of the returns chosen for audit. The IRS plugs the data from your return into a computer that scrutinizes the numbers every which way and ponders how the picture you paint of your financial life jibes with what it knows about other taxpayers. The computer tries to spot the returns that are most likely to produce extra tax if put through the audit wringer. The computer's choices are reviewed by a human being who can overrule them if, for example, an attachment to your return satisfactorily explains the entry that set the computer all atwitter. Short of such a veto, your name will go on the list.

No Protection in Filing Late

Q: *I've been told that one way to reduce the chances of an audit is to file right at the deadline. The theory is that because of the last-minute rush, the IRS has less time to scrutinize the return. Any truth that that?*

A: No. Returns are chosen for audit by a computer months after the April 15 deadline. Whether you file in February or in August, the numbers on your return will have to run the computer gauntlet.

Even if your return survives the computer's scrutiny, you're not necessarily safe. You may have listed an investment in a tax shelter the IRS is particularly interested in, for example, or the agency might decide to take a closer look at your return because it's auditing the forms sent in by a business associate.

And there's always the chance that someone has fingered you as a tax cheat. The IRS encourages such tips and even pays a bounty on those that pay off in extra tax.

Or you could be the unfortunate prey of a random audit. That's how the IRS collects data that serve as the computer's frame of reference for selecting returns that seem to be the juiciest audit targets. These *Taxpayer Compliance Measurement Program* (TCMP) superaudits are exhaustive, with agents zealously verifying every bit of information on the return—even if it means eyeballing a marriage certificate to see whether a taxpayer deserves to file a joint return, or asking for birth certificates to prove the existence of the children claimed as dependents.

In the Fall of 1995, about 150,000 taxpayers got a stay of execution when the IRS—under pressure from Congress—decided not to launch a planned TCMP attack on 1994 returns. At our deadline, it was not clear when, or even whether, the "audits from hell" would be revived. It's possible that the IRS will have to come up with another way to get the information it needs to program its computers.

Don't Panic

Whatever the reason you're chosen for an audit, it's chilling to get the word that the IRS wants to examine your return. After all, everyone knows that the IRS was able to do what J. Edgar Hoover and all the G-men of the FBI couldn't do: put Al Capone behind bars. Even if you have no reason to think you did anything wrong, you can't escape the anxiety that accompanies an audit notice. For one thing, the return being audited is likely to be the one you filed at least six months and probably 18 months earlier. Where are the records?

Still, it's important not to panic. Steel yourself with the knowledge that the odds of getting through the audit without owing extra tax are far better than the odds of your being picked for the audit in the first place. Nearly 25% of correspondence audits—in which you're asked to mail the IRS proof of entries on your return—result in no change in the taxpayer's bill. And, about one-in-ten face-to-face examinations wind up with the IRS accepting the original return as accurate. You might even hit the jackpot and win a refund. The latest figures show that in 1994, about 90,000 taxpayers walked out of audits with a total of almost $450 *million* in refunds.

But, face it, most folks called in for an audit come out the poorer. The latest IRS statistics show that the average office audit results in the payment of just over $3,000 in extra tax and penalties. And, even if you escape without owing an extra dime in tax, the time, hassle and stress involved are indisputably costly.

Time Saver

At the last minute, the IRS called off the "audits from hell" it had planned for 150,000 taxpayers.

How It All Begins

You'll get a letter announcing your fate. The simplest audit—a correspondence audit—requires only that you mail in the records needed to verify a specified claim on your return. In a field audit, an IRS agent comes to your home or place of business to go over your records. Most common, though, are office audits, which involve getting yourself to a local IRS office. You'll probably have at least a couple of weeks to prepare. If the appointment is set for an inconvenient time or you find that you'll need extra time to get your records together, call the IRS promptly to request that the audit be rescheduled.

The written notice will identify the items on your return that are being questioned—usually such broad categories as employee business expenses or casualty losses—and outline the types of records you'll need to clear up the matter. Office audits are usually limited to two or three issues, so you won't be expected to haul in all your records. What kind of evidence do you need? The answer to that question was put succinctly by a retired IRS official with thirty year's experience putting tax returns through the wringer: "I expect to see the records you used when you prepared the tax return. You must have had some. Otherwise, how did you know you gave $5,000 to charity?"

Also, beware that auditors are sometimes looking for more than proof of what's on your return. They're also interested in whether income that should have been reported was left off. That could mean a review of your bank records, for instance, in search of deposits that might represent unreported income.

First, Audit Yourself

The best way to begin preparing for your meeting is to pull out your copy of the return being audited. Before the IRS puts your forms to the test, do the job yourself. Pore over the items being questioned and pull together the documents that support your entries.

Of course there will be gaps, but don't automatically concede defeat. Try to reconstruct missing records.

- If, as luck would have it, you can't find the return, call the IRS office that contacted you and ask for details on how to get a copy.

- Get copies of canceled checks from the bank or duplicates of receipts or written statements from individuals who can back up your claims.

- Where you can't come up with written evidence, prepare your oral explanation.

Your records don't have to be perfect. If you have a reasonable explanation for how you came up with a figure that's not fully corroborated by the evidence, the IRS may well accept it. The IRS likes to stress how *reasonable* audit personnel are. The agency's official manual for auditors notes, for example, that on some issues oral statements may be acceptable. "Adequate evidence," the manual says, "does not require complete documentation." However, when you're pulling together your records, remember this: The more thorough your documentation is in general, the more likely an auditor will cut you some slack on an occasional point.

Do You Need Help?

You don't have to go to the audit at all. You can avoid it by hiring someone to go in your place. Such a representative must have written authorization to act for you, and the IRS provides a power-of-attorney form—Form 2848—for this purpose. Whether you go alone or hire a representative to go with you or in your place depends primarily on the issues involved. If they're relatively simple, cut-and-dried matters, you may be able to settle things without help. When matters are more technical or require interpretation of the law, however, it's more likely you'll need assistance. You have to make this judgment, and it will turn in part on how you feel about going head to head with the IRS. If you're scared, by all means get someone to go with you or in your place.

Time Saver

You don't have to go to the audit yourself; you can send someone in your place.

If someone else prepared your return, let him or her know about the audit and ask for tips on how to get ready for it. Whether or not you want this person to go along may depend on how much it will cost you. Although the IRS prefers to wrap up cases with a single meeting, if you don't agree with the auditor's conclusions or need time to round up extra evidence, you can schedule a follow-up meeting. Unless you fear you might capitulate if you go to the audit alone, you may want to try to settle as many issues as you can by yourself.

If disagreements remain and the amount of money at stake justifies the expense, you can take an adviser along to the next session. That way you'll have help when you really need it but won't have to pay for hand-holding while you clear up routine matters.

And note this, the Taxpayer Bill of Rights gives you the right to stop an audit in its tracks if you decide you want representation. If the audit begins to veer from the topics you are prepared to discuss, for example, you can call a halt to the proceedings and seek help if you need it.

The Big Day

The key to success is being well-prepared. Forget the old slapstick routine of dumping a box of canceled checks and ratty receipts on the auditor's desk. That suggests your records are sloppy, and that's the last impression you want to give. Remember it's up to you to back up the information on your return.

Establish credibility.

The better organized your records, the more smoothly things will go. Try to develop credibility right from the start. Say, for example, that the audit notice announces that your interest deductions, charitable contributions and travel and entertainment write-offs will be reviewed. If you're solid on interest and contributions but a little shaky on T&E, try to steer the audit to your strongest suits first. If you establish credibility early on, there's a better chance a gap later may be overlooked.

Don't go into the session looking for a fight, but don't equate being cooperative with giving in whenever the auditor raises an eyebrow, either. If the agent tells you your records don't substantiate a deduction, for example, ask what might suffice. Perhaps you can mail it in later.

Don't get chatty.

Be on your guard against chatting your way into a problem. Keep in mind that the agent is trained to zero in on tax issues. A comment you consider totally unrelated to your return might lead you into a thicket. Defending a deduction by saying you've taken it in the past, for example, could prompt a review of previously filed returns; discussing the family's cross-country driving vacation might lead the agent to recalculate the business/personal ratio of your car's use; or bemoaning the problems that led a child to drop out of college could cost you a dependency exception. Fear that taxpayers will talk themselves into trouble is the key reason many advisors recommend that taxpayers send a representative rather than showing up at the audit in person.

If you do go, above all, keep your wits about you. Don't be pressured into settling an issue just to bring the audit to an end. The IRS argues strenuously that it doesn't judge its agents on how much extra money their audits produce. Even so, the fact is that one of the best guides to an agent's efficiency is the amount of additional tax he or she generates without going through all the formal assessment procedures or litigation.

There may be room for compromise on the issue at hand. It may save time and money all around to agree on some in-between point or even for one side to give up on one disputed item in order to win on another.

Most office audits take from two to four hours. You'll spend a lot of that time watching the agent crunch numbers. When it's over, you'll get the auditor's decision—which in most cases is that you owe more tax. He or she should explain each proposed change to your return and the reason for it.

If you agree, that's fine. But remember that the audi-

Money Saver

Try to steer the audit to your strongest suits; you'll establish credibility for when you get to a shaky area.

tor doesn't have the final say. Often, in fact, auditors make mistakes that cost taxpayers money. If you disagree with a finding, tell the auditor so and restate your position. He or she may be willing to compromise to close the case promptly.

Battling the IRS

If you and the auditor come to an agreement, you'll be asked to sign a form saying so. Within a few weeks you'll get a bill for the extra tax, plus interest and any penalty. Most audits end this way.

If you can't come to a meeting of the minds, tell the agent so and go home. You'll receive a report explaining the proposed adjustments to your return. At this point, in the less-heated environment of your own home, you might decide it's not worth the time or trouble to carry on your dispute. If so, you can simply agree to pay the bill.

Appeals

You have several options if you decide to fight on, and at this point you may want to seek professional help. You can ask for another meeting with the auditor to present additional evidence, for example, or you can make an informal appeal to the auditor's boss. If you're still unhappy, you can go to the IRS regional appeal level. At any point, you can take your case to court.

If you want to appeal within the IRS, you have 30 days after you receive the audit report to request a conference. After that, you'll probably have at least a couple of months to prepare. The IRS handles regional appeals informally, and its statistics indicate that taxpayers who appeal do very well. Don't assume that means an appeal guarantees a better deal. One important factor behind the favorable statistics is that generally only taxpayers with strong cases take their cases to this level.

Tax Court

If you're still dissatisfied after an appeal, your only choice is to go to court. Most tax disputes are settled in the U.S. Tax Court, although you can also take your case to the U.S. District Court for your area or the U.S. Claims Court in Washington, D.C. One important difference is that you can go to the Tax Court before paying the disputed amount of tax; otherwise you must pay the tax and go to court for a refund of what you think you were overcharged.

The Tax Court, which hears cases at sites around the country, has a special procedure for cases in which the disputed amount is $10,000 or less. With relatively informal procedures, you can represent yourself in a small tax case. However, unlike regular Tax Court cases and those heard by other courts, decisions by the small-claims division can't be appealed.

If you wind up going to court and winning, there's a chance that the government will pay your legal fees. To be reimbursed for your costs, you must "substantially prevail" in court and be able to show that the rejected IRS position was unreasonable. You must also have tried to settle the matter within the IRS before resorting to court.

With the Taxpayer's Bill of Rights, Congress gave taxpayers a number of safeguards. First of all, if you arrange for a representative to go to the audit for you, the IRS can't demand that you appear, too. In addition, if you go to the audit, you can make a tape recording of the proceedings, as long as you advise the IRS ahead of time. Also, if you can show that an error on your return resulted from your having followed written advice from the IRS—a response to a specific request—it can't penalize you for the mistake. (You'll still have to pay any extra tax, though.)

The Bill of Rights also puts additional restraints on the IRS when it comes to seizing a taxpayer's property to satisfy a tax bill. If you receive notice of an IRS levy, promptly seek legal advice to protect your rights. Taxpayers also now can sue the IRS for damages if an IRS employee "recklessly or intentionally" disregards the law in collecting a tax liability.

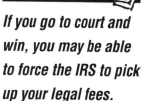

Money Saver

If you go to court and win, you may be able to force the IRS to pick up your legal fees.

Repetitive Audits

What if the IRS computer decides that you should be audited year after year for the same item? Believe it or not, there's a procedure to short-circuit repetitive audits on the same issues. If you receive an audit notice that targets the same items that were examined in either of the two previous years—and that audit resulted in little or no change in your tax liability—call the IRS office that sent you the notice. There's no guarantee that you'll escape the new audit. But it will be suspended while the IRS considers whether there's any reason to believe the audit results are likely to be different this time around. If not, you may be spared.

How to Say No to the IRS

An audit is not the only way the IRS tries to get more money out of taxpayers. Far more common, in fact, are the millions of penalty notices spewed out by the agency's computers. In any year, there's about a one-in-five chance that such a dispatch will land in your mailbox. If it does, don't even open the letter until you remind yourself of three things *not* to do:

- **Don't automatically send off a check.** View any demand for extra tax or penalties with skepticism. The IRS makes lots of mistakes.

- **Don't ignore the letter.** The IRS knows where you live, where you work, where you bank. It will not go away.

- **Don't go ballistic.** It does no good, for your health or your case, to dash off a nasty letter or make an angry phone call.

In a recent year, the IRS sent out over 6 million CP-2000 notices, calling on taxpayers to pay almost $5 billion in extra taxes and penalties. These notices announce that the IRS has discovered a discrepancy between what you reported on your return and what other sources, such as your employer or banks and mutual funds, reported about your income.

Nobody knows how many of those notices are wrong, but even the IRS admits there are plenty of opportunities for error: You might have reported the "missing" income on the wrong line; a mutual fund might have reported as your income dividends that really belong to (and were reported by) a parent with whom you have a joint account; a company you've never heard of might have accidentally used your social security number when reporting someone else's income; or a clerk might have hit the wrong key when typing your numbers into the IRS computer.

If you get a CP-2000 notice, check your records. If you find that you failed to report some income, the notice will show how much the government figures you owe in tax, interest and penalties. If you agree, sign the form and send it back with your check.

The notice also makes it easy to disagree. If you reported the income in question—or if it wasn't yours to report—the form has a space to indicate that the IRS is off base. Return it along with a written explanation. One study found that about 20% of the taxpayers who challenged CP-2000 notices were right.

Deflecting Penalties

More threatening than a CP-2000 is a notice slapping you with a penalty for some transgression. And the IRS has a full arsenal of penalties to keep taxpayers in line. There are fines for filing late, for paying too little or too late, for being negligent, for sending in a rubber check, and on and on. In a recent year, the agency sent out over 20 million notices demanding over $4 billion in penalties. But a lot of those penalties were never paid...nor should they have been.

In that year the agency *abated* (IRS speak for forgave or removed) 1.2 million penalties worth more than $560 million. A lot of those penalties shouldn't have been assessed in the first place. As for the rest, taxpayers were spared because they had good excuses.

A valid excuse is one that shows there was a reasonable cause for the problem. If you file late, for example, you can get the penalty abated if you show the return was

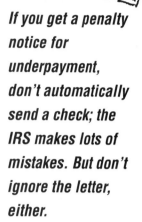

Money Saver

If you get a penalty notice for underpayment, don't automatically send a check; the IRS makes lots of mistakes. But don't ignore the letter, either.

lost in the mail, you sent it to the wrong service center, a fire destroyed your records, or a death or serious illness in the family prevented you from filing on time.

If you think you have a viable excuse, don't pay the penalty. Instead, write the IRS a brief letter explaining the situation and asking that the penalty be abated. If you're turned down, the IRS rejection letter will explain how you can appeal that decision.

Getting Satisfaction

What if your efforts bring frustration rather than resolution? Some cases *do* drag on interminably. In fact, the IRS has a special system just for handling cases that fall through the cracks. It's the *Problem Resolution Program* (PRP), and it's designed to come to the rescue of taxpayers who are getting the runaround. Problem resolution officers around the country can reach down into the bureaucracy, wrest a case from an intransigent computer and give it a quick, objective review. At least that's the idea.

You're supposed to try, and fail, with the regular procedures before trying the PRP. If your initial contact with the IRS is unsatisfying, turn to the PRP. It handles nearly 400,000 cases a year. For the phone number of the nearest PRP office, call 800–829–1040. If you don't get satisfaction, take your complaint to the head of the program: The taxpayer ombudsman. As this book went to press, that job is held by Lee Monks. You can write him at Room 3003, Internal Revenue Service, 1111 Constitution Ave. N.W., Washington, D.C. 20224. His direct phone number is 202–622–6100.

A last resort is to contact your congressional representatives. Your senators and representative won't change the tax law for you, but they'll probably add their voices to yours to get the PRP's attention. Contact a local congressional office or call the Capitol switchboard at 202–224–3121.

NORMAN WILSON
1908 – 1976
NEVER AUDITED

Stuart Leeds

Drawing by Stuart Leeds;
© 1984 The New Yorker Magazine

1995 Tax Rates

Taxable Income	Tax
Single	
Up to $23,350	15% of every dollar
$23,351 to $56,550	$3,502.50 plus 28% of amount over $23,350
$56,551 to $117,950	$12,798.50 plus 31% of amount over $56,550
$117,951 to $256,500	$31,832.50 plus 36% of amount over $117,950
Over $256,500	$81,710.50 plus 39.6% of amount over $256,500
Married Filing Jointly and Surviving Spouses	
Up to $39,000	15% of every dollar
$39,001 to $94,250	$5,850 plus 28% of amount over $39,000
$94,251 to $143,600	$21,320 plus 31% of amount over $94,250
$143,601 to $256,500	$36,618.50 plus 36% of amount over $143,600
Over $256,500	$77,262.50 plus 39.6% of amount over $256,500
Heads of Household	
Up to $31,250	15% of every dollar
$31,251 to $80,750	$4,687.50 plus 28% of amount over $31,250
$80,751 to $130,800	$18,457.50 plus 31% of amount over $80,750
$130,801 to $256,500	$34,063 plus 36% of amount over $130,800
Over $256,500	$79,315 plus 39.6% of amount over $256,500
Married Filing Separately	
Up to $19,500	15% of every dollar
$19,501 to $47,125	$2,925 plus 28% of amount over $19,500
$47,126 to $71,800	$10,660 plus 31% of amount over $47,125
$71,801 to $128,250	$18,309.25 plus 36% of amount over $71,800
Over $128,250	$38,631.25 plus 39.6% of amount over $128,250

Tax Forms & IRS Publications

Here's a list of the tax forms you're most likely to need to settle with Uncle Sam. Don't be intimidated. Millions of taxpayers get by with a single form; most of the rest need just a few. Following the list of forms is an inventory of IRS publications that address various tax issues. These booklets often include several hypothetical examples that can be particularly helpful to understanding the issue at hand.

Each year, you should receive from the IRS a package including the basic forms and instructions for filling them out. There's a good chance, however, that you'll need additional forms. You can get any of those listed here, as well as any of the informational publications, free.

To order, call the IRS toll-free at 800–TAX–FORM or write the forms distribution center for your area at the address listed below. You should get the forms in the mail within two weeks. If you need them sooner, contact your local IRS office (it's listed in the "U.S. Government" listings in your telephone book) or check with a bank or local library. Libraries often have copies of Package X, the multivolume collection of IRS forms, and you can photocopy the forms you need. Or, if you have a computer and modem, you can download the forms from the IRS site on FedWorld (703–321–8020) or on the World Wide Web at *http://www.ustrea.gov.*

If You Live in	Order from IRS Forms Distribution Center
Alaska, Arizona, California, Colorado, Hawaii, Idaho, Kansas, Montana, Nevada, New Mexico, Oklahoma, Oregon, Utah, Washington, Wyoming, Guam, Northern Marianas, American Samoa	Rancho Cordova, CA 95734-0001
Alabama, Arkansas, Illinois, Indiana, Iowa, Kentucky, Louisiana, Michigan, Minnesota, Mississippi, Missouri, Nebraska, North Dakota, Ohio, South Dakota, Tennessee, Texas, Wisconsin	PO Box 8903 Bloomington, IL 61702-8903
Connecticut, Delaware, District of Columbia, Florida, Georgia, Maine, Maryland, Massachusetts, New Hampshire, New Jersey, New York, North Carolina, Pennsylvania, Rhode Island, South Carolina, Vermont, Virginia, West Virginia	PO Box 85074 Richmond, VA 23261-5074
Puerto Rico	PO Box 25866 Richmond, Va 23286-8107

IRS Forms

IRS Form	Use
Form W–2	Form on which your employer reports income to you, and you report income you paid household employees
Form W–4	Controls amount employer withholds from your pay
Form W–4P	Controls amount withheld from pension or annuity payments
Form W–5	Requests advance payment of earned-income credit
Form 1040	Basic tax return
Form 1040A	Simplified version of basic return
Form 1040EZ	Simplest version of basic return
Form 1040 TEL	For taxpayers who file over the phone
Form 1040X	Amends previously filed return
Form 1040–ES	Make estimated tax payments
Schedule A	Claim itemized deductions
Schedule B	Report interest and dividend income
Schedule C	Report income, expenses, and profit or loss from a sole-proprietorship business or profession
Schedule C-EZ	Simplified business return
Schedule D	Report capital gains and losses from sale of securities or other assets
Schedule E	Report "supplemental" income, including rents, royalties and income or loss from partnerships, S corporations, estates and trusts for real estate mortgage investment conduits (REMICs)
Schedule F	Report farm income and expenses
Schedule H	Report household employment taxes
Schedule K–1	(Form 1065) Shows partners' share of income, credits and deductions from partnership interest
Schedule R	Claim the credit for the elderly or permanently and totally disabled
Schedule SE	Compute the social-security tax on self-employment income
Form 1116	Claim foreign tax credit
Form 2106	Report deductible employee business expenses
Form 2119	Report the sale or exchange of a principal residence
Form 2120	Claim a dependent under a multiple-support agreement
Form 2210	Figure penalty (or exemption from penalty) for underpayment of estimated tax
Form 2441	Claim the credit for child- and dependent-care expenses
Form 2688	Application for additional extension of time to file
Form 2848	Power of attorney for your representative at IRS audit
Form 3903	Claim moving expense deductions
Form 4136	Claim the credit for the purchase of a diesel-powered car or light truck
Form 4506	Request copies of previously filed returns

IRS Forms (cont'd)

IRS Form	Use
Form 4562	Figure depreciation and amortization deductions; figure expensing deduction
Form 4684	Claim casualty- and theft-loss deductions
Form 4868	Automatic four-month extension of filing deadline
Form 4952	Claim investment interest expense
Form 4972	Figure tax on lump-sum distribution from retirement plan
Form 5329	Figure penalty for early withdrawal from or excess contribution to an IRA or other retirement plan
Form 5500	Annual report for Keogh plan
Form 5500EZ	Report on Keogh plan covering only the self-employed individual who set up the plan
Form 6251	Compute the alternative minimum tax for individuals
Form 6252	Report installment sale of property
Form 8283	Report noncash charitable contributions exceeding $500
Form 8332	Permit noncustodial parent to claim child as dependent
Form 8453	Declaration that electronic return is accurate
Form 8582	Compute limits on passive-loss deductions
Form 8598	Compute limit on mortgage-interest deduction
Form 8606	Report nondeductible IRA contribution
Form 8615	Compute "kiddie tax" on unearned income of children under age 4
Form 8801	Claim credit for alternative minimum tax paid in prior year
Form 8814	Elect to report interest and dividends earned by child on parent's return
Form 8815	Report tax-free savings bond interest
Form 8822	Report change of address
Form 8824	Report like-kind exchange
Form 8829	Claim home office deductions
Form 9282	Voucher to accompany payment of tax if return filed electronically
Form 9465	Request to pay tax in installments
Form 706	Estate-tax return
Form 709	Gift-tax return
Form 709–A	Gift-tax return for couples to report nontaxable gifts of more than $10,000 but less than $20,000

IRS Publications

Number	Title
2	ABCs of Income Tax
538	Accounting Periods and Methods
909	Alternative Minimum Tax for Individuals
917	Automobile, Business Use of
548	Bad Debts, Deduction for
908	Bankruptcy
551	Basis of Assets
535	Business Expenses
587	Business Use of Your Home
547	Casualties, Nonbusiness Disasters and Thefts
584	Casualty Loss Workbook
526	Charitable Contributions
503	Child and Dependent Care Credit
929	Children and Dependents
721	Civil Service Retirement Benefits
555	Community Property
530	Condominiums, Cooperative Apartments and Owners of Homes, Tax Information for
542	Corporations
524	Credit for the Elderly or the Permanently and Totally Disabled
534	Depreciation
911	Direct Sellers
504	Divorced and Separated Individuals
561	Donated Property, Determining the Value of
596	Earned Income Credit
508	Educational Expenses
15	Employers Tax Guide (Circular E)
539	Employment Taxes
463	Entertainment, Travel and Gift Expenses
448	Estate and Gift Taxes
505	Estimated Tax
556	Examination of Returns, Appeal Rights, and Claims for Refund
559	Executors, Survivors and Administrators
557	Exempt Status for Your Organization
501	Exemptions and Standard Deduction
225	Farmer's Tax Guide
514	Foreign Tax Credit
907	Handicapped and Disabled Individuals
936	Home Mortgage Interest Deduction

IRS Publications (cont'd)

Number	Title
926	Household Employer's Tax Guide
523	Home, Tax Information on Selling Your
590	Individual Retirement Accounts
537	Installment Sales
545	Interest Expense
550	Investment Income and Expenses
502	Medical and Dental Expenses
3	Military Personnel
529	Miscellaneous Deductions
521	Moving Expenses
564	Mutual Fund Distributions
536	Net Operating Losses
554	Older Americans, Tax Information for
1212	Original Issue Discount Instruments
541	Partnerships
925	Passive Activity and At-Risk Rules
575	Pension and Annuity Income
583	Recordkeeping, Information for Business Taxpayers
527	Rental Property
589	S Corporations
544	Sales and Other Distributions of Assets
520	Scholarships and Fellowships
560	Self-Employed Retirement Plans
533	Self-Employment Tax
523	Selling Your Home
504	Separated Individuals
334	Small Business (General Guide)
915	Social Security Benefits and Equivalent Railroad Retirement Benefits
4	Students Guide to Federal Income Tax
910	Tax Services, Guide to Free
571	Tax-Sheltered Annuity Programs for Employees of Public Schools and Certain Tax-Exempt Organizations
525	Taxable and Nontaxable Income
531	Tips
463	Travel, Entertainment and Gift Expenses
505	Withholding
919	Is My Withholding Correct?
17	Your Federal Income Tax (General Guide)
1	Your Rights as a Taxpayer

Glossary

The lexicon of the federal income tax can often seem like a foreign language. Here are translations of some of the key terms you'll encounter. For additional information on any subject, see the index for references to other parts of the book

- **Accelerated depreciation.** For most business property, except real estate, the law allows you to depreciate the cost at a rate faster than would be allowed under straight-line depreciation. For example, automobiles and computers are assumed to have a five-year life for tax purposes. With straight-line depreciation you would be permitted to write off 20% of the cost each year; the accelerated method generally lets you deduct 20% of the business cost the first year, 32% the second, 19.2% the third, 11.52% in years four and five, and the remaining 5.8% in the sixth year. It takes six years to fully depreciate the property, thanks to the "midyear convention."

- **Acquisition indebtedness.** Mortgage debt on which the interest is deductible. To qualify, the debt must be used to buy, build or substantially improve your principal residence or a second home and must be secured by the property. There is a $1 million limit on deductible acquisition indebtedness.

- **Active participation.** The level of involvement that real estate owners must meet to qualify to deduct up to $25,000 of losses from rental real estate. Failure to pass this test could make such losses nondeductible under passive-loss rules.

- **Adjusted basis.** Your basis in property is the stepping-off point for determining taxable gain or loss when you sell it. The basis generally starts out as what you pay for the property, although special rules apply to assets you inherit or receive as a gift. Your basis can be adjusted while you own property. When you

buy a home, for example, the basis begins at what you pay for the place. It's adjusted upward to take certain buying expenses into account and is raised further by the cost of any permanent improvements. Basis is reduced by any casualty losses you claim while you own the house and also by the profit from any previous home you roll over into the new place. When rental property is involved, you reduce your basis by the amount of any depreciation you deduct while you own the property. You use your adjusted basis to figure the gain or loss on the sale. When stock or mutual fund shares are involved, your adjusted basis is the cost of the shares plus any brokerage commissions or load fees and minus any return of capital payouts.

- **Adjusted gross income (AGI).** This is your income from all taxable sources minus certain adjustments. The adjustments—sometimes called above-the-line deductions because you can claim them whether or not you itemize deductions—include deductible contributions to individual retirement accounts and Keogh plans, any penalty paid on early withdrawal of savings, the deduction for 50% of the self-employment tax paid by self-employed taxpayers, alimony payments and job-related moving expenses.

- **Alimony.** Qualifying payments to an ex-spouse that can be deducted as adjustments to income whether or not you itemize. The recipient must include the payments in his or her taxable income.

- **Alternative minimum tax (AMT).** A special tax designed primarily to prevent the wealthy from using so many tax breaks that their regular tax bill is reduced to little or nothing. The AMT ignores certain tax benefits allowed by the regular rules and applies special tax rates to more income than is hit by the regular tax.

Glossary (cont'd)

- **Amended return.** A revised tax return, filed on Form 1040X, to correct an error on a return filed during the previous three years. An amended return can result in added tax being due or in a refund, depending on the mistake you are correcting.

- **Audit.** As if you didn't know, this is a review of your tax return by the IRS, during which you are asked to prove that you have correctly reported your income and deductions.

- **Bargain sale to charity.** Selling property to a charity for less than the property's actually worth. Depending on the circumstances, this could result in a tax deduction or extra taxable income.

- **Basis.** See Adjusted basis.

- **Below-market-rate loans.** If you make an interest-free or bargain-rate loan to a friend or relative, you may be required to include in your taxable income some of the interest the IRS figures you should have charged.

- **Bond premium.** The amount over face value that you pay to buy a bond paying higher than current market rates. With taxable bonds, a portion of the premium can be deducted each year that you own the securities.

- **Capital expenditure.** The cost of a permanent improvement to property. Such expenses increase the property's adjusted basis.

- **Capital gain or loss.** The profit or loss from the sale of such property as stocks, mutual-fund shares, real estate and collectibles. If you owned the property for more than one year before selling, the profit or loss is considered long-term. A short-term gain or loss results if you sell property owned one year or less. While short-term gains are taxed in your top tax bracket, the law sets 28% as the maximum tax rate on long-term gains, a provision that benefits taxpayers in the 31%, 36% or 39.6%

bracket. At our deadline, Congress was considering changes that would significantly change the taxation of long-term gains. If a change is made, it will be covered in the free update you can get by writing the author at the address on page i.

- **Capital-loss carryover.** Capital losses can be used to offset capital gains, and up to $3,000 of any excess loss can be deducted against other income, such as your salary. Losses not currently deductible because of the $3,000 limit can be carried over to future years.

- **Casualty loss.** Damage that results from a sudden or unusual event. Such losses are deductible to the extent that they exceed 10% of your adjusted gross income.

- **Charitable contribution.** A gift of cash or property to a qualified charity for which a tax deduction is allowed.

- **Child- and dependent-care credit.** A tax credit available to offset part of the cost of providing care for a child or disabled dependent while you work. The credit can shave as much as $720 off your tax bill if you pay for the care of one individual or as much as $1,440 if you pay for the care of two or more.

- **Child support.** Payments made under a divorce or separation agreement for the support of a child. The payments are neither deductible by the person who pays them nor taxable income to the person who receives the money.

- **Constructive receipt.** A concept of tax law that taxes income at the time you could have received it, even if you don't actually have it. A paycheck you could pick up in December is considered constructively received and taxed in that year, even if don't get and cash the check until the following January. Also, interest paid on a savings account is considered constructively received and taxable in the year it is credited to your account, whether or not you withdraw the money.

- **Consumer interest.** See Personal interest.

- **Deductions.** Expenses you are permitted to subtract from your taxable income. All tax-payers may claim a standard-deduction amount—$6,550 for 1995 and $6,700 for 1996 joint returns, for example. If your qualifying expenses exceed your standard deduction, you may claim the higher amount by itemizing your deductions. Although no records are needed to back up your right to the standard deduction, you must maintain records of qualifying expenditures if you itemize.

- **Dependent.** Someone you support and for whom you can claim a dependency exemption on your tax return. For each dependent you claim, the exemption knocked $2,500 off your taxable income in 1995. The value increases each year with inflation and is $2,550 in 1996.

- **Depreciation.** A deduction to reflect the gradual loss of value of business property as it wears out. The law assigns a tax life to various types of property, and your basis in such property is deducted over that period of time.

- **Direct transfer.** A method to move funds from one IRA or Keogh plan to another. You can also use this method to move money from a company retirement plan to an IRA. With a direct transfer, you order one sponsor to transfer the money directly to your new IRA; you do not take possession of the funds. There is no limit on the number of times you can move your money via direct transfer. However, if you take possession of the funds and personally deposit them in the new IRA, the switch is considered a rollover. You can use the rollover method only once each year for each IRA account you own. The direct transfer method must be used to move funds from a company retirement plan to an IRA or else 20% of the money withdrawn from the company plan will be withheld for the IRS.

- **Earned income.** Compensation, such as salary, commissions and tips, you receive for your personal services. This is distinguished from unearned or investment income, such as interest, dividends and capital gains.

- **Enrolled agent.** A tax preparer who, by virtue of passing a tough IRS test or experience as an IRS employee, can represent clients at IRS audits and appeals.

- **Estate tax.** The federal tax that applies—beginning at a 37% rate—when a decedent's taxable estate exceeds $600,000.

- **Estimated tax.** If you have income not subject to withholding, such as investment or self-employment income, you may have to make quarterly payments of the estimated amount needed to cover your expected tax liability for the year. You can be penalized if estimated payments, combined with withholding from wages, don't come within $500 of 90% of the tax owed.

- **Exemptions.** You can claim a personal exemption for yourself. On joint returns a personal exemption is claimed for each spouse. You also get an exemption for each dependent you are eligible to claim on your return. (See Dependent.) Each exemption reduced taxable income by $2,500 in 1995; that amount rises to $2,550 in 1996.

- **Expensing.** Also known as the Section 179 deduction, expensing lets you treat up to $17,500 of expenditures that normally would be depreciated over a number of years as current business expenses to be deducted immediately.

- **Filing status.** Your status determines the size

Glossary (cont'd)

of your standard deduction and the tax rates that apply to your income: single, married filing jointly, married filing separately, head of household, or qualifying widow or widower.

- **Five-year averaging.** A special tax-computation method for lump-sum distributions from company retirement plans. It is available only to taxpayers age 59 ½ or those born before 1936. If you qualify, part of the distribution may be completely tax-free. At our deadline, Congress was considering abolishing five-year averaging. If it does, the change will be covered in the free update you can get by writing the author at the address in the front of this book.

- **Fixing-up expenses**. Costs incurred to spruce up your home prior to its sale. If certain requirements are met and you replace the home with a house that costs less than the one sold, fixing-up expenses can reduce the tax due on the sale. The costs have no impact if you buy a replacement home that costs more than the one you sold.

- **Flexible spending account.** See Reimbursement account.

- **401(k) plan.** An employee retirement savings plan through which employees divert part of their pay to a tax-deferred investment account. Salary put in the plan is not taxed until it is later withdrawn, presumably in retirement. Employers usually match part or all of the employees deposits.

- **Gift tax.** To prevent people from avoiding the estate tax by giving their property away, the law includes a gift tax, too. You may give up to $10,000 yearly to as many people as you want without worrying about this tax. Larger gifts are taxable, but a tax credit offsets the tax on the first $600,000 of taxable gifts. When the gift tax is owed, it is owed by the giver, not the recipient.

- **Gross income.** All of your income from taxable sources, before subtracting any adjustments, deductions or exemptions.

- **Head of household.** A filing status with lower tax rates than apply to single individuals, available to unmarried taxpayers who pay more than half the cost of maintaining a home for a dependent relative or unmarried child. Generally, the taxpayer and dependent must live in the same home.

- **Hobby-loss rule.** One requirement for deducting business losses is that you show you are trying to make a profit. The law presumes you're in business for profit if you report a taxable profit for three years out of any five-year period. Otherwise, your activity is assumed to be a hobby, unless you can prove otherwise. The distinction is important because if the expenses of a hobby exceed the income, the difference is considered a personal expense, not a tax-deductible loss.

- **Holding period.** The time that determines whether profit or loss when you sell an asset is a long- or short-term gain or loss. The holding period that distinguishes long- and short-term results is one year. (See Capital gain or loss.)

- **Home-equity loans.** Debt secured by your principal residence or second home—such as a second mortgage or home-equity line of credit—that are not used to buy, build or substantially improve the property. Although interest on most loans is no longer deductible (see Personal interest), interest on up to $100,000 of home-equity debt remains deductible.

- **Household employee.** Someone who works in your home—providing child care, perhaps, or domestic services—who is considered your employee rather than a self-employed worker or the employee of a service. Generally, if you pay a household employee $1,000 or more during the year, you are responsible for paying social security and medicare taxes for him or her. You may also be required to pay unemployment taxes.

- **Imputed interest.** Interest you are considered to have earned—and therefore owe tax on—if you make a below-market-rate loan. The term is also used to refer to the interest income you must report on taxable zero-coupon bonds. Although the bonds pay no interest until maturity, you must report the interest as it accrues.

- **Indexing.** To prevent inflation from eroding certain tax benefits—including standard deductions and exemption amounts and the beginning and end of each tax bracket—they are automatically adjusted for increases in the consumer price index.

- **Individual retirement account (IRA).** A tax-favored account designed to encourage saving for retirement. If your income is below a certain level or you are not covered by a retirement plan at work, deposits into an IRA can be deducted. The maximum annual contribution—deductible or not—is $2,000 or 100% of the compensation you earned during the year, whichever is less. The tax on all earnings inside the IRA is postponed until you withdraw the funds. In most cases there is a penalty for withdrawing funds before you reach age 59 ½. At our deadline, Congress was considering changes that would enhance the tax benefits of IRAs. If the changes are made, they will be covered in the free update you can get by writing the author at the address on page i.

- **Installment sale.** With an installment sale you agree to have the purchaser pay you over a number of years, and you report the profit on the sale as you receive the money

instead of all at once in the year of the sale.

- **Investment interest.** Interest paid on loans used for investment purposes, such as to buy stock on margin. You can deduct this interest up to the amount of investment income you report.

- **Itemized deductions.** See Deductions.

- **Keogh plan.** Also known as an H.R. 10 plan, this is a tax-favored retirement plan for the self-employed. As much as 20% of self-employment income can be deposited in a Keogh, and contributions can be deducted. There is no tax on the earnings until the money is withdrawn, and there are restrictions on tapping the account before age 59 ½.

- **Kiddie cards.** A reference to the social security cards needed by any child you want to claim as a dependent on your return. For 1995 returns, you must report the social security number for any dependent two-months old or older at the end of the year. For 1996 and future years, you need the number for any child at least one-month old.

- **Kiddie tax.** The tax—at the parents' tax rate—imposed on unearned income of children who are under age 14 at the end of the year. The kiddie tax applies to the child's unearned income in excess of $1,300 in both 1995 and 1996.

- **Like-kind exchange.** The tax-free exchange of similar assets, such as real estate for real estate.

- **Limited partnerships.** Investments—in real estate and oil and gas, for example—that pass both profits and losses on to investors. By definition, limited partnerships are passive investments, subject to the passive-loss rules.

- **Listed property.** Certain kinds of depreciable property—including automobiles, cellular telephones, cameras and computers—that come under special restrictions if they

Glossary (cont'd)

are not used more than half the time in business.

- **Long-term gain or loss.** See Capital gain or loss.

- **Lump-sum distribution.** The payment within one year of the full amount of your interest in a pension or profit-sharing plan. To qualify as a lump-sum distribution—and for favorable five- or ten-year averaging—other requirements must be met.

- **Luxury-car rules.** The restriction that limits annual depreciation deductions for business automobiles that cost more than $15,300 in 1995.

- **Luxury tax.** A 10% tax on the amount by which a car's price exceeds $34,000 in 1996. The trigger point was $32,000 in 1995. This tax is collected by the car dealer; it doesn't show up on your tax return.

- **Marginal tax rate.** The share of the highest dollar of your income that will go to the IRS. It's not necessarily the same as the rate in your top tax bracket, as explained in Chapter 5. Knowing your marginal rate tells you how much of each additional dollar you make will go to the IRS and how much you'll save for every dollar of deductions you claim.

- **Marital deduction.** The deduction that allows any amount of property to go from one spouse to the other—via lifetime gifts or bequests—free of federal gift or estate taxes.

- **Market discount.** The difference between what you pay for a bond and its higher face value. The tax treatment varies depending on whether the bond is taxable or tax-free and whether you redeem it at maturity or sell it before that time.

- **Master limited partnerships.** Similar to regular limited partnerships, but MLPs shares are traded on the major exchanges, making for a much more liquid investment. Although limited-partnership losses are con-

sidered passive, income from an MLP is considered investment income rather than passive income. That means passive losses can't be used to shelter MLP income.

- **Material participation.** The test used to determine whether you are involved enough in a business to avoid the passive-loss rules. To be considered a material participant, you must be involved on a "regular, continuous and substantial basis." One way to pass the test is to participate in the business for more than 500 hours during the year.

- **Medicare tax.** The portion of the social security tax—1.45% for employees and 2.9% for self-employed taxpayers—that pays for Medicare. While the retirement portion of the tax stops when wage or self-employment income exceeds $62,700 in 1996, there's no limit on the medicare tax.

- **Midmonth convention.** The rule that treats certain kinds of depreciable property, including real estate, as though it were placed in service in the middle of the month it was first used.

- **Midquarter convention.** In general, business property is depreciated under a midyear rule that allows half a year's depreciation for the first year, whether you buy property in January or December. However, if you buy more than 40% of the business property you put into service for the year during the fourth quarter, the midquarter convention takes over. With it, you depreciate each piece of property as though it were placed into service in the middle of the calendar quarter in which it was purchased. You claim just six weeks' worth of depreciation for property put in service during the final quarter, for example.

- **Midyear convention.** See Midquarter convention.

- **Millionaires' surtax.** The provision that creates the 39.6% bracket on taxable income exceeding $263,750 in 1996 (no one said you had to know math to be in Congress).

- **Mortgage interest.** A term used to refer to deductible interest paid on debt that qualifies as acquisition indebtedness or home-equity debt.

- **Multiple-support agreement.** An agreement under which two or more taxpayers who together provide more than half the support for someone else agree that one will claim that person as a dependent and the others will not.

- **Original issue discount (OID).** The amount by which the face value of a bond exceeds its issue price. Part of the discount on taxable bonds must be reported as taxable interest income each year that you own the securities.

- **Passive-loss rules.** Passive activities are investments in which you do not materially participate. Losses from such investments can be used only to offset income from similarly passive investments. Passive losses generally can't be deducted against other kinds of income, such as salary or income from interest, dividends or capital gains. Generally, all real estate and limited-partnership investments are considered passive activities, but there is a limited exception for rental real estate in which you actively participate, and another exception for real estate professionals. Losses you can't use because you have no passive income to offset can be carried over to future years.

- **Personal exemption.** See Exemption.

- **Personal interest.** Basically, this is interest that doesn't qualify as mortgage, business or investment interest. Included is interest you pay on credit cards, car loans, student loans, life insurance loans and any other personal borrowing not secured by your home. Personal interest cannot be deducted.

- **Points.** Charges connected with getting a mortgage. Each point is equal to 1% of the mortgage amount. Points paid on a mortgage to buy or improve your principal residence are generally fully deductible in the year you pay them. Points paid to refinance a principal home or to buy any other property must be deducted over the life of the loan.

- **Preference items.** Tax breaks allowed under the regular income tax but not under the alternative minimum tax.

- **Premature distributions.** Withdrawals from company retirement plans subject to a 10% penalty if you're under age 55 (if you've left the job) or under age 59½ (if you're still employed). The same penalty applies if you withdraw funds from an IRA before age 59½.

- **Qualified plan.** An employee benefit plan—such as a pension or profit-sharing plan—that meets requirements designed to protect employees' interests.

- **Reimbursement account.** A fringe benefit, sometimes called a flexible spending account or salary reduction plan, that allows an employee to divert part of his or her salary to a special account that is used to reimburse the employee for medical or child-care expenses. Funds channeled through the account escape federal income and social security taxes and, in almost all states, state income taxes as well.

- **Rollover.** The tax-free transfer of funds from one individual retirement account to another. If you take possession of the funds, the money must be deposited in the new IRA within 60 days. You can also use a rollover to transfer funds from a company plan—when you receive a lump-sum distribution at retirement, for example—to an IRA. The tax bill

Glossary (cont'd)

is delayed until you withdraw funds from the IRA. (See also, Direct transfer.)

- **S corporation.** A corporation that generally pays no tax because profits and losses are passed on and taxed to the shareholders.

- **Salary reduction plan.** See Reimbursement account.

- **Section 179 deduction.** See Expensing.

- **Self-employment tax.** The tax due on self-employment income to pay for social security retirement and medicare benefits. For 1995, the rate was 15.3% on the first $61,200 of earnings and 2.9% on the amounts above that level. For 1996, the full 15.3% rate applies to the first $62,700 and income above that level is hit by the 2.9% medicare tax.

- **Short-term gains and losses.** See Capital gain or loss.

- **Standard deduction.** See Deductions.

- **Standard mileage rate.** The deductible amount you can claim for each mile you use your car for business, charitable or medical purposes without having to keep track of the actual cost. The rates are announced by the IRS early each year.

- **Stepped-up basis.** The basis of inherited property is stepped-up to its value on the date of death of the owner. In other words, tax on any appreciation during his or her lifetime is forgiven. The heir uses the higher basis to figure his or her gain when the property is ultimately sold.

- **Taxable income.** Income that is taxable (such as wages, interest and dividends) rather than tax-exempt (such as the interest on municipal bonds). On tax returns, it is your income after subtracting all adjustments, deductions and exemptions—that is, the amount on which your tax bill is computed.

- **Tax bracket.** Each tax bracket encompasses a certain amount of income to be taxed at a set rate: 15%, 28%, 31%, 36% or 39.6%. You are said to be in the 28% bracket if your highest dollar of income falls in that bracket. Even if you're in the 39.6% bracket, part of your income is taxed at the 15% rate.

- **Tax-exempt interest.** Interest paid on bonds issued by states or municipalities that is exempt from the federal income tax.

- **Ten-year averaging.** A special tax-computation method for lump-sum distributions from pension and profit-sharing plans, available only to taxpayers born before January 1, 1936.

- **Unearned income.** Income from investments, such as interest, dividends and capital gains. See Earned income.

- **Wage base.** The level of earnings to which the full social security tax applies. For 1995, the full 15.3% tax applies to the first $61,200 and the 2.9% medicare portion applies to additional income. For 1996, the 15.3% rate hits the first $62,700 of wages and all income above that level is hit by the 2.9% tax. (Employers and employees each pay 50% of this tax; self-employed taxpayers have to pay the full amount themselves.)

- **Wash sale.** The sale of stocks, bonds or mutual fund shares for a loss when, within 30 days before or after that sale, you buy the same or substantially identical securities. The law forbids the deduction of the loss.

- **Withholding.** The amount held back from your wages each payday to pay your income and social security taxes for the year. The amount withheld is based on the size of your salary and the Form W-4 you file with your employer.

A

Above the line deductions. *See* Adjustments to income
Accelerated Cost Recovery System, 233
Accelerated deductions
 charitable contributions, 429–430
 interest, 429
 local taxes, 428
 medical expenses, 427–428
 miscellaneous expenses, 430
 state taxes, 428
 year-end tax planning, 427–430
Accident insurance. *See* Health and accident insurance
ACRS. *See* Accelerated Cost Recovery System
Adjustable rate mortgage, 176
Adjusted gross income
 adjustments to income and, 356
 allowable IRA deduction and, 262–263
 bubble brackets and, 67
 itemizing deductions and, 363–364
Adjustments to income, 356–362, 425–426
AFR. *See* Applicable federal rate
Aggregation, 266–267
AGI. *See* Adjusted gross income
Alimony, 72, 133–135, 361
Alternative minimum tax, 35, 51–57, 221–223
Amended returns, 43–46
 audit risk, 46

for casualty loss in disaster area, 410
caused by government error, 45–46
preparation instructions, 44–45
stepped-up basis, 194
Amortizing bond premiums, 215–217
AMT. *See* Alternative minimum tax
Annuities, 248–250
 commercial annuities, 304
 death of owner, 301–302
 early withdrawal penalty, 249
 joint-and-survivor, 301–302
 life expectancy table, 302
 optional method, 302–303
 taxation of, 301–304
Appeal of audit, 470
Applicable federal rate, 245
Appraisals for charitable contributions, 399–400
Audits, 463–474
 amended returns and, 46
 appeals, 470
 establishing credibility, 468–469
 filing late, 464
 odds of, 463
 penalties abated by IRS, 473–474
 power-of-attorney form, 467
 preparing for, 466–467
 random audits, 464–465
 refunds from, 465
 repetitive audits, 472
 representation, 467–468
 table, 463
 tape recording, 471

tax court, 471
Taxpayer Bill of Rights, 468, 471
Taxpayer Compliance Measurement Program, 464
Automatic exemptions to filing taxes on time, 26–27
Automobile expenses, 316–325
 actual-cost method, 317–318
 basis of, 318
 business trips, 336
 claiming deductions, 325
 depreciation, 318–320
 first-year write-off reducer, 319–320
 leasing a business car, 322–324
 license tags, 383
 luxury-car rule, 320–322
 personal vehicle used for business, 320
 record keeping, 324–325
 sampling method, 325
 standard-mileage rate, 316–317
 table, 320
Automobile rebates, 75
Average basis, 202
Averaging. *See* Five- and ten-year averaging
Awards, 72

B

Backup withholding on interest or dividend payments, 99
Bad debts, 129–130
Bargain sales, 398–399
Barter income, 73

Basis of property
  average basis for mutual
    fund, 202
  business automobile, 318
  community property, 193
  convertible bonds, 217
  definition, 191
  discount bonds, 212
  dividend reinvestment
    plan, 210–211
  divorce, 194
  first in/first out method, 202
  gifts, 191–192
  home converted to rental
    property, 240
  inheritance, 192–194
  IRA accounts, 265–266
  municipal bonds, 223–224
  mutual funds, 199–203
  premium bonds, 212
  purchases, 191
  return of capital
    distributions, 200
  shifting basis, 194–195
  specific identification
    method, 201–202
  stepped up basis, 193–194
  stocks, 207–208
  tax-free exchange of real
    estate, 242–243
  tax planning, 195–196
Beneficiaries
  age of, 275, 302
  of IRAs, 281
  life insurance, 459
Blind taxpayer standard
    deduction, 366–367
Blood donations, 393
Bonds, 211–230
  bond swaps, 224–225
  convertible, 217
  corporate bonds, 212–217
  discount bonds, 212
  Ginnie Maes, 218–219
  inherited bonds, 230

market-discount bonds,
    213–214
municipal bonds, 78,
    219–224
mutual funds, 225
original-issue discount
    bonds, 213–214
par bonds, 212
premium bonds, 212
premiums, 215–217
purchased at discount,
    213–214
sold between interest dates,
    212–213
tax-saving tips, 39
Treasury notes and bonds,
    218
U.S. government
    obligations, 217–219
year-end tax planning,
    431–435
zero-coupon bonds, 214–215
  See also U.S. savings
    bonds
Brokerage statements, 29
Bubble brackets, 67–70
Bunching deductions,
    367–368, 430–431
Business expenses
  automobile expenses,
    316–325
  business trips, 336
  casualty or theft loss, 410
  cellular phones, 328–330
  child-care credit, 414–419
  computers and software,
    326–328
  conventions, 343–344
  deducting interest, 384
  educational expenses,
    347–350
  estate taxes, 460–461
  expensing, 328–329,
    437–438
  gifts, 355

health insurance for the
    self-employed, 353
hobby-loss rules, 350–353,
    438–439
home-office expenses,
    330–338
job-security insurance, 355
loss of business property,
    410
miscellaneous, 354–355
office equipment, 328–330
passive investments,
    439–440
physical exams, 355
professional expenses, 355
rental property, 439
small tools, 355
social security taxes, 438
travel and entertainment,
    338–346
work clothes, 354
year-end tax planning,
    436–440
Bypass trust, 455, 457

C

Cafeteria plans for fringe
    benefits, 80–81
Capital-gain property,
    396–398
Capital gains and losses
  bubble bracket, 70
  carrying over losses to
    future years, 190
  distribution of, 186
  50% exclusion for small
    company stock, 189–190
  holding period, 188
  long-term gains, 187–189
  mutual funds, 206
  new legislation, 187
  rollover to SSBIC stock, 190
  short-term gains, 187–189
  tax-saving tips, 32–33, 40
  28% tax rate cap, 188–189

undistributed, 199–201
  See also Basis of property
Car-pool receipts, 75
Carryover loss, 190
Cash or deferred arrang-
    ments. *See* 401(k) plans
Casualty and theft losses,
    402–410
  business property, 410
  determining loss, 405–406
  disaster areas, 409–410
  gaining from losses, 408–409
  insurance, 406–407
  nonbusiness bad debt, 404
  proving losses, 406
  qualifying losses, 403–405
  reimbursement of living
    expenses, 407
  10% threshold, 402
Casualty insurance proceeds, 75
CDs. *See* Certificates of deposit
Cellular phones, 328–330
Certificates of deposit,
    250–252, 361
Charitable contributions,
    388–402
  accelerated deductions,
    429–430
  alternative minimum tax
    and, 55
  appraisals, 399–400
  appreciated property,
    396–398
  bargain sales, 398–399
  canceled checks as proof
    of, 401–402
  deducting expenses, 383
  donating property,
    394–398, 400–401
  donating services, 392, 397
  fair market value of
    property, 395
  foster care, 393
  getting a benefit in return,
    391

life insurance, 400
limit on deductions, 389–390
lottery tickets, 391
nondeductible donations,
    389, 392–393, 394
over $500 value, 396
qualified organizations, 389
raffles, 391
receipt requirements,
    401–402
record keeping, 390–391
scoutmaster's uniforms, 384
tax-deductible vacations,
    409
tax-saving tips, 38–39
travel expenses, 393–394
used clothing, 407
visiting students, 393
volunteer work, 392
Child-care credit, 41, 353,
    414–419
  after age thirteen, 421
  day-care centers, 416–417
  employer-provided
    reimbursement plan,
    418–419
  in-home care, 417
  nursery schools, 416–417
  qualifying payments,
    416–418
  social security tax, 417–418
  table, 415
Child support, 75, 133–135
Children
  equity sharing, 183–185
  exemptions for after
    divorce, 136
  gifts of assets to, 124–125
  hiring the family, 125–127
  income splitting, 123–127
  interest and dividend
    income, 41
  interest on savings bonds,
    226–228
  IRAs, 262

kiddie tax, 119–122
renting home to, 127
savings accounts, 251
social security numbers for,
    117
special filing rules, 3, 4
taxability of child-care costs,
    81
using savings bonds for
    college tuition, 228–229
  See also Child-care credit;
    Child support;
    Dependents
Cliff vesting, 297
Closing costs, 151–155
Cohan rule, 324
College tuition, 228–229
Combat pay, 76
Commercial annuities, 304
Commercial tax preparers,
    16–21
CPAs, 18, 20–21
  enrolled agents, 18, 19–20,
    21
  fees, 19
  national firms, 16–17
  selecting, 20–21
Community property, 193,
    448
Company matched
    contributions, 292–293
Company-provided car, 81–82
Computers
  business expenses, 326–328
  depreciation table, 326
  expensing, 328–329
  on-line forms, 8
  software for tax prepara
    tion, 8
Constructive receipt, 427
Consulting work, 281–289
Contributions. *See* Charitable
    contributions
Conventions, 343–344
Convertible bonds, 217

Corporate bonds, 212–217
Correspondence audits, 466
Credits. *See* Tax credits

D

Damages won in lawsuits, 73, 76
Day-care facilities, 333, 416–417
De minimus fringes, 82
Deadline for filing returns,
    23, 24
Death
  of annuity owner, 301–302
  basis of assets, 192–194
  of business owner, 460–461
  of dependent, 117
  of family member, 137–141
  of IRA owner, 280–281
  of Keogh plan owner, 288
  of retirement plan holder,
    313–314
  of savings bond owner, 454
Deferring income, 426–427
Dependents
  death of, 117
  dependency requirements,
    418
  dependent-care credit,
    414–419
  exemptions for, 112–117
  if spouse is in school or
    disabled, 416
  standard deductions, 367
  unrelated persons, 112
  See also Children; Elderly
    persons
Depreciation
  Accelerated Cost Recovery
    System, 233
  alternative minimum tax
    and, 53–54
  business automobile,
    318–320
  computers, 326–327
  midmonth convention,
    234–236

office equipment, 328–330
  recapturing, 244–245
  rental property, 232–236
  software, 327–328
Diesel car tax credit, 423–424
Direct transfer, 272
Disability
  tax credits, 421–422
  taxability of payments, 76
Disability insurance, 381
Disaster areas, 409–410
Discount bonds, 212
Dividends
  ex-dividend date, 205–206
  mutual funds, 199, 205–206
  ordinary dividends, 210–211
  reinvestment plan, 210–211
  return of capital
    distributions, 211
  stocks, 210–211
  tax-saving tips, 39
Divorce, 132–137
  alimony/child support,
    133–135
  basis of property, 194
  exemptions for children, 136
  IRAs and, 269
  legal fees, 136–137
  property settlements, 135
  selling a home and, 167
Double-category method,
  202–203
Dues, 339, 355

E

Earned income credit, 422–423
Education expenses, 347–350
Educational assistance
  programs, 82
  See also Scholarships;
  Students
Elderly persons
  special filing rules, 3–4
  standard deduction for, 366
  tax credits, 421–422

Electronic filing, 13–14,
  21–23, 25
  See also Telephone filing of
    1040EZ form
Employee benefits. *See* Fringe
  benefits
Employee death benefits, 76
Employee discounts, 82
Employee expenses
  automobile expenses,
    316–325
  child-care credit, 353
  deducting, 411–412
  education expenses, 347–350
  job-hunting expenses,
    346–347
  2% rule, 315
Employee stock-ownership
  plan, 461
Employee stock purchase
  plans, 82–83
Employer-provided travel, 83
Entertainment expenses. *See*
  Travel and entertainment
Equity sharing, 183–185
ESOP. *See* Employee stock-
  ownership plan
Estate taxes, 446–462
  effect of gifts, 453–455
  employee stock-ownership
    plan, 461
  estimating estate, 447–449
  inherited stock, 462
  joint ownership of property,
    458–459
  life insurance, 459–460
  marital deduction, 450,
    455, 457
  owning a business, 460–461
  QTIP trusts, 457–458
  retirement plan assets,
    461–462
  tax rate schedule, 452
  unified credit, 450–451,
    455, 457

worksheet, 448–449, 456
Estimated tax payments, 36,
    100–105
    calculating, 101
    deadlines for, 103–104
    exceptions, 101–103
    farmers and fishermen, 103
    forms for, 100, 104
    penalties, 101, 103, 104–105
    underpayment penalty,
        101, 103
Ex-dividend date, 205–206,
    436
Exemption-equivalent trust,
    455, 457
Exemptions, 31–32, 111–119
    dependent tests, 112–117
    gross-income test, 442
    support test, 442
    table, 118
    year-end tax planning,
        442–443
Expensing
    business expenses,
        437–438
    luxury-car rules, 438
    office equipment, 328–329
Extension for filing, 24

F

Failure to file, 24–25
Fair market value of charitable
    contributions, 395
Family loans, 128–130, 181
Federal Insurance Contribution
    Act tax. See FICA tax
Fellowships, 78, 127
FICA tax, 47
Field audits, 466
FIFO method. See First in/first
    out method
Filing returns by mail, 42
    See also Electronic filing;
        Late filing; Tax
        return preparation

Filing status, 31, 106–110
    standard deductions, 366
    table, 106
First in/first out method, 202
First-out rule, 386
Five- and ten-year averaging
    Keogh plans, 287–288
    lump-sum distributions,
        306–309
    tax rates table, 307
Fix-up expenses before selling
    a home, 167–168
Fixed annuities, 248
Flexible-spending accounts, 81
Foreign tax credits, 35, 420–421
    alternative minimum tax
        and, 56
    mutual funds, 206–207
Forms. See Tax forms
Foster care, 393
401(k) plans, 291–295
    company-matched
        contributions, 292–293
    early withdrawal penalty,
        294
    hardship withdrawals,
        293–294
    loans from, 294
    taxation of benefits, 295
403(b) plans, 295–296
Free-lance work, 281–289
Fringe benefits, 79–87
    See also specific benefits
Fuel-tax credits, 36

G

Gambling winnings
    taxability of, 73–74
    withholding and, 98–99
Garage sale income, 76
Gift tax
    exclusion, 443–444
    gift-tax return, 452–453
    $10,000 annual exclusion,
        451

unified credit, 450–451
Gifts, 77, 125
    basis of, 191–192
    deducting as business
        expenses, 355
    depreciating, 348
    effect on estate taxes, 453–455
    tax rate schedule, 452
    year-end tax planning,
        443–444
    See also Charitable
        contributions
Ginnie Maes, 218–219
Glossary, 481–488
GNMA. See Ginnie Maes
Government National
    Mortgage Association.
    See Ginnie Maes
Group term life insurance,
    83–84

H

Hardship withdrawals, 293–294
Head of household status,
    108–109
    standard deductions, 366
    tax rate table for 1995, 475
Health and accident insurance
    employer-paid, 85
    self-employment deduction,
        359–360
    taxability of benefits, 77
    See also Life insurance;
        Medical and dental
        expenses
Hobby-loss rules, 350–353
    three-of-five year profit test,
        350–351
    transforming hobby into a
        business, 352
    vacation homes, 182
    year-end tax planning,
        438–439
Home equity loans, 158–161,
    388

Home-office expenses,
330–338
business percentage of
house, 333–334
day-care facilities, 333
deducting rent, 335–336
depreciating a gift, 348
direct expenses, 334
exclusive use test, 331
indirect expenses, 334
interest, 334–335
limit on deductions,
336–337
principal place of business
test, 331–333
property taxes, 334–335
record keeping, 337–338
rollover of gain and, 337
saving records from, 30
Homeownership
closing costs, 151–155
converting home to rental
property, 239–241
equity sharing, 183–185
fix-up expenses, 167–168
home buyer's subsidy,
148–151
home equity loans, 158–161
home-office expenses,
330–338
improvements and repairs,
156–158, 164–165
moving expenses, 185
$125,000 exclusion, 171–173
owner financing, 173–174
permanent rental, 175–176
points, 151–152, 162
prepaid interest and
property taxes, 153–154
real estate agent's
commission, 154
record keeping, 151–156
refinancing, 161–164
renting to your children,
127

reporting home sales,
170–171
rollover of gain, 165–167
seller-paid points, 152–153
selling for a loss, 177
selling your home, 164–177
tax basis, 151
tax deduction when buying
or selling, 382–383
taxability of profits from
sale of home, 78
temporary rental, 174–175
withholding and, 100
See also Mortgages; Real
estate; Vacation homes
Household help, 141–147
earned income credit, 145
employee and independent
contractor distinction,
142–143
social security for, 144
state taxes, 147
tax-saving tips, 36
unemployment tax, 145–146
withholding for, 144–145
H&R Block, 16, 22, 91

I

In-home care for children,
417
Inability to pay taxes owed,
25–26
Incentive stock options,
54–55, 84
Incidents of ownership, 459
Income splitting, 119, 123–127
Indexing capital gains, 187
Individual retirement
accounts, 256–281
adjusted gross income and
allowable deduction,
262–263
aggregation rule, 266–267
annual yield of, 268
basics of, 257–258

contribution deadline, 260
custodial fee, 259
deadlines, 277–278
death of owner, 280–281
deductions for, 34, 357
direct transfer, 272
divorce and, 269
early withdrawal, 278–280
early withdrawal penalty,
267, 268–270
exception to 10% penalty
for early withdrawal,
278–280
excess contributions,
259–260
income test for write-offs,
262–264
investment options,
270–272
Keogh plans and, 285–286
life expectancy table, 275,
280
mandatory withdrawals,
277–278
minimum withdrawal
schedule, 274–277
non-deductible
contributions, 264–266
payouts, 33
penalties, 277–278
pension plan rollovers,
297–300
restricted write offs, 261–267
rollover method, 272–274,
305–306
saving statements from, 30
spousal account, 259
table, 258, 275
tax incentives, 267–268
taxability of withdrawals
from, 74
temporary loans, 273
timing contributions, 260
trustees, 271–272
withdrawals, 273–280

withholding and, 97–98
Inheritances
  basis of, 192–194
  retirement benefits,
    313–314
  stock, 462
  tax-saving tips, 40
  taxability of, 77, 141
  U.S. savings bonds, 454
Installment sales, 243–246
Insurance
  buying replacement
    property, 408–409
  casualty and theft losses,
    406–407
  deducting premiums,
    369–370
  unscheduled personal
    property, 409
Interest
  accelerated deductions, 429
  applicable federal rate, 245
  basic rules for deductibility,
    386–387
  commingling funds, 386
  deducting, 383–388
  first-out rule, 386
  home-equity loans, 388
  minimum charged on
    installment sale, 245–246
  nondeductible, 387–388
  tax-exempt, 55
  tax-saving tips, 32, 38
  tracing rules for deductibility,
    385
  year-end tax planning, 436
  See also Mortgages
Interest-free or bargain-rate
  loans, 84
Internal Revenue Service
  abated penalties, 473–474
  early withdrawal penalty for
    IRAs, 267, 268–270
  forms and publications,
    476–480

interest on refunds not
    paid to taxpayer by
    June 1, 27–28
  life expectancy table, 302
  overpaying taxes and, 9
  penalty notices, 472–473
  Problem Resolutions
    Program, 79, 474
  refund errors made by, 13
  tax preparation help,
    10–11, 15–16
Internet, tax forms, 8
Investment expenses,
    254–255, 412
  deducting interest on
    borrowed money, 384
Investment income
  bond swaps, 434–435
  bonds, 211–230
  capital gains, 187–190
  certificates of deposit, 250–252
  deferring, 123
  distribution of capital gains,
    186
  installment sales, 243–246,
    434
  interest, 252–254
  last minute sales, 434
  life insurance, 246–250
  mutual funds, 196–207
  passive-loss rules, 230–232
  put options, 433–434
  rental property, 232–243
  savings accounts, 250–252
  selling short against the
    box, 433
  stocks, 207–211
  tax-saving tips, 38
  wash-sale rule, 435
  year-end tax planning,
    431–435
  See also Basis of property;
    specific types of investment
IRAs. *See* Individual
    retirement accounts

IRS. *See* Internal Revenue
    Service
ISOs. *See* Incentive stock
    options
Itemized deductions, 363–412
  1040 form and, 7
  AGI threshold, 363–364
  alternative minimum tax
    and, 53
  auto license tags, 383
  average deductions in each
    income group, 364
  bad debt, 411
  bunching deductions,
    430–431
  buying a home and, 148–149
  casualty and theft losses,
    402–410
  charitable contributions,
    388–402
  commingling funds, 386
  deductible taxes, 378–383
  interest, 383–388
  medical and dental
    expenses, 368–378
  miscellaneous deductions,
    410–412
  nondeductible taxes, 378
  personal property taxes, 383
  real estate taxes, 381–383
  restrictions, 363–365
  Schedule A tax-saving tips,
    37–39
  setting up files for, 28–29
  standard deductions,
    365–368
  state and local taxes, 379
  table, 364
  value of labor, 403

J

Job-hunting expenses, 346–347
Job-security insurance, 355
Joint ownership of property,
    192–193, 458–459

Joint returns, 31, 107, 113, 146
Jury fees, 16
   deductions for, 35, 362
   taxability of, 74

K

Keogh plans, 281–289
   death of owner, 288
   deductions for, 34–35, 361
   defined benefit plans,
     284–285
   early-withdrawal penalty,
     286–287
   IRAs and, 285–286
   kinds of, 282–285
   lump-sum distribution,
     287–288
   money-purchase defined-
     contribution, 284
   profit-sharing defined-
     contribution, 283–284
   reporting requirements,
     288–289
   required withdrawals, 287
Kiddie tax, 119–122, 226–227

L

Late filing, 15, 23–27
Leasing a business car,
   322–324
Life expectancy, 275,
   278–280, 302
Life insurance, 246–250
   annuities, 248–250
   charitable contributions of,
     400
   estate taxes, 459–460
   group term, 83–84
   single-premium policies,
     246–248, 388
   taxability of, 76, 77
   taxable income table, 84
   See also Health and accident
     insurance
Limited partnerships, 231

Local taxes. *See* State and local
   taxes
Losses. *See* Casualty and theft
   losses
Lottery tickets, 391
Lump-sum distribution
   direct rollover, 305
   five- or ten-year averaging,
     306–309
   Keogh plans, 287–288
   minimum-distribution
     allowance table, 307
   rollover to IRA fund, 305–306
   tax-saving tips, 41
   taxation of, 304–309
   withholding and, 97–98
Luxury-car rules, 320–322, 438

M

Marginal tax rates, 64–66
Market-discount bonds,
   213–214
Married couples
   estate taxes deduction, 450
   filing separately, 109–110
   standard deductions, 366
   surviving spouse, 107–108
   tax penalty for, 130–132
   tax rate table for 1995, 475
   unified credit and marital
     deduction, 455, 457
   year-end tax planning,
     444–445
   See also Divorce; Joint
     returns; Working
     couples
Material-participation test,
   231–232
Meals and lodging expenses
   standard allowance, 345–346
   taxability of employer-
     provided, 85
Medical and dental expenses
   accelerated deductions,
     427–428

basic definition of medical
   care, 368–369
damages, 378
hair transplant, 367
health insurance for self-
   employed, 353, 370
home improvements as,
   370–372
insurance premiums,
   369–370
itemizing deductions,
   368–378
miscellaneous deductions,
   376–377
nursing homes, 373–375
reimbursement, 368, 375,
   378
7.5% threshold, 368
special schools, 373–375
swimming pools as,
   370–372
tax-saving tips, 37
timing deductions, 375
travel expenses, 372–373
See also Health and accident
   insurance
Medicare, 48, 49
Midmonth convention,
   234–236
Midyear convention, 326
Miscellaneous expenses
   accelerated deductions, 430
   business expenses, 354–355
   itemizing, 410–412
Money-market funds, 204
Mortgages
   acquisition debt, 158–159
   ARM adjustment refund,
     176
   closing costs, 151–155
   deductibility, 149–150, 384
   flat tax and, 168
   home-office deduction,
     334–335
   payment table, 149

points, 151–152, 162
prepayment, 163–164
refinancing, 161–164
second mortgage, 155
seller-paid points on home
    mortgages, 45–46
tax-saving tips, 37–38
withholding adjustment,
    150–151
year-end tax planning, 429
zero-interest loans, 155–156
See also Homeownership
Moving expenses, 34, 185,
    357–359, 362
Municipal assessments, 382
Municipal bonds
    alternative minimum tax,
        221–223
    gains and losses, 223–224
    mutual funds, 204–205
    social security benefits and,
        223
    tax-free interest and, 223
    tax-free status, 220–221, 222
    taxability of, 78
    taxable-equivalent yield,
        219–220
Mutual funds, 196–207
    annual fund income, 204–207
    basis, 196, 198–199
    bonds, 225
    buying after ex-dividend
        date, 436
    capital gains distribution,
        206
    choosing shares to sell,
        201–203
    dividends, 205–206
    foreign tax, 206–207
    money-market funds, 204
    municipal bonds funds,
        204–205
    reinvesting dividends, 199
    return of capital
        distributions, 200

shifting basis, 199–201
switching, 203–204
tax credits, 420
tax-saving tips, 40
taxable bond funds, 204
undistributed capital gains,
    199–201
wash sales, 203–204
worksheet, 197

N

Nannies. *See* Household help
No-additional-cost services, 86
Nonbusiness bad debts, 404,
    411
Nontaxable distributions, 200
Nursery schools, 416–417
Nursing home care
    deductibility, 373–375

O

Office audits, 466
Office equipment, 328–329,
    330
OID bonds. *See* Original-issue
    discount bonds
Ordinary dividends, 210–211
Ordinary-income property,
    396–398
Original-issue discount bonds,
    213–214
Outplacement services, 86

P

Par bonds, 212
Parking, 83
Passive-loss rules, 230–232
    deducting expenses,
        384–385
    material-participation test,
        231–232
    rental property, 237–239
    saving records and, 30
    table, 238
    tax-saving tips, 33

vacation homes, 180
year-end tax planning,
    439–440
Penalties
    abated by IRS, 473–474
    challenging the IRS,
        472–473
    early withdrawal
        of annuity, 249
        of 401(k) funds, 294
        of IRAs, 267, 268–270
        from Keogh plans, 286–287
        from pension plans,
            297–298
        from profit-sharing plans,
            297–298
        of savings, 361
    estimated taxes, 101, 103,
        104–105
    failure to meet mandatory
        IRA withdrawals,
        277–278
    late filing, 24, 27
Pension plans, 296–300
    early distribution penalties,
        297–298
    IRA rollover, 298–300
    loans, 300
    taxability of, 74
    vesting, 296–297
    See also Retirement plans
Personal interest, 384
Personal property taxes,
    334–335
    deducting, 383
    tax-saving tips, 37
Physical exams, 355
Points, 151–152, 162
Power-of-attorney form, 467
Premium bonds, 212
Premiums for corporate
    bonds, 215–217
Private activity bonds, 54, 55
Prizes, 74, 391
    See also Gambling winnings

Problem Resolutions Program, 79, 474
Professional tax preparation
  commercial preparers, 16–21
  IRS advice, 10–11, 15–16
Profit-sharing plans, 296–300
  early distribution penalties, 297–298
  Keogh plans, 283–284
  loans, 300
  vesting, 296–297
Property settlements, 135
Provisional income, 311
PRP. *See* Problem Resolutions Program
Publications list, 476, 479–480
Put options, 433–434

Q

QTIP trusts, 457–458
Qualified terminable interest property. *See* QTIP trusts

R

Raffles, 391
Rapid-refund loans, 23
Real estate
  deducting taxes, 381–383
  installment sales, 243–244
  municipal assessments, 382
  saving files from home sales, 29–30
  tax deduction when buying or selling, 382–383
  tax-free exchanges, 241–243
  tax-saving tips, 37
  See also Homeownership
Receipts for charitable contributions, 401–402
Record keeping
  automobile expenses, 324–325

buying a home, 151–156
charitable contributions, 390–391
Cohan rule, 324
home-office expenses, 337–338
itemized deductions files, 28–30
office equipment expenses, 330
sampling method, 325
travel and entertainment, 344–345
Refinancing of mortgage, 161–164
Refunds
  amended returns and, 44
  checking status of, 18
  early filing and, 4–5, 9, 27–28
  errors by the IRS, 13
  late filing and, 27
  state taxes, 32, 74, 78, 380–381
Reimbursement accounts, 81
Reimbursement for child-care, 418–419
Rental property, 232–243
  depreciation, 232–236
  home converted to, 174–176, 239–241
  installment sales, 243–246
  other expenses, 236–237
  passive-loss rules, 232–233, 237–239
  points on, 153
  tax-free exchanges, 241–243
  taxability of income from, 72
  temporary rental, 235
  year-end tax planning, 438–439
Replacement property, 408–409
Retirement plans

annuities, 301–304
benefit cap, 309–310
death of plan-holder, 313–314
estate taxes and, 461–462
401(k) plans, 291–295
403(b) plans, 295–296
inherited assets, 313–314
IRAs, 256–281
Keogh plans, 281–289
lump-sum distributions, 304–309
pension plans, 296–300
profit-sharing plans, 296–300
qualified plans, 296
Simplified Employee Pensions, 289–290
social security benefits, 310–313
tax-saving tips, 35–36, 41
taxation of benefits, 86, 301–309
using 1040A short form, 293
year-end tax planning, 441–442
See also specific plans by name
Return. *See* Tax return preparation
Return of capital distributions, 200
Rollover
  direct rollover, 305
  IRA funds, 272–273, 274
  of lump-sum distributions, 305–306
  pension plan to IRA, 297–300

S

Salaries, 71–72
Salary deferral, 295–296
Salary reduction plans. *See* 401(k) plans

Savings accounts, 250–252
Savings bonds. *See* U.S. savings bonds
Scholarships, 78, 127
SECA tax. *See* Self-employment tax
Self-employment
    automobile expense deductions, 325
    deductions, 34, 35
    deferring income, 427
    education expenses, 350
    health insurance deduction, 45, 353, 359–360, 370
    Keogh retirement plans, 281–289, 361
    persons who must file, 4
    saving records from, 30
    tax preparation software programs and, 12
    taxability of income, 72
Self-employment tax, 47–50
    computing, 49–50
    deducting, 359, 378–379
    income cap, 48–49
    income tax deduction, 50
Selling short against the box, 209, 433
Senior citizens. *See* Elderly persons
SEPs. *See* Simplified Employee Pensions
Series EE bonds. *See* U.S. savings bonds
Severance pay, 74
Short sale of stock, 208–209
Simplified Employee Pensions, 289–290
    deductions for, 34–35, 361
Single-category method, 202–203
Single-premium insurance policies, 246–248, 388
Singles status, 475

Small company stock, 189–190
Social security benefits
    bubble brackets and, 69
    categories of, 311
    85% rule, 312
    employer identification number, 143–144
    for household help, 143, 144
    numbers for dependents, 116–117
    provisional income and, 311
    self-employment tax and, 48, 49
    tax planning, 33, 36, 312–313
    taxation of, 78, 310–313
Social security tax
    for child-care provider, 144, 417–418
    tax credits for overpaying, 419–420
    year-end tax planning, 438
Software
    business expenses, 326–328
    depreciating, 327–328
    for tax preparation, 8, 11–12, 13–14
Specialized small business investment company. *See* SSBIC stock
Specific identification method, 201–202
Spousal IRA account, 259
SSBIC stock, 190
Standard deductions, 365–368
Standard-mileage rate
    business use, 316–317
    charitable contributions, 392
    educational expenses, 349
    medical expenses, 372
State and local taxes, 32, 74, 78, 147
    accelerated deductions, 428

    deducting, 379
    disability insurance, 381
    refunds, 380–381
    tax-free status of municipal bonds, 222
    timing fourth-quarter estimated payment, 379–380
Stepped up basis, 193–194
Stocks, 207–211
    from bankrupt company, 230
    basis of, 191–196, 207–208
    bonuses and bargain purchases, 86–87
    dividends, 210–211
    estate taxes and inherited stock, 462
    kiddie tax and, 123
    short sales, 208–209
    stock splits, 208
    wash sales, 209–210
Students
    charitable deduction for visiting students, 393
    exemption from withholding, 95–96
Subscriptions, 355
Super IRAs. *See* Simplified Employee Pensions
Superaudits, 464
Surviving spouse
    as IRA beneficiary, 281
    standard deductions, 366
    tax rate table for 1995, 475

T

Tax advisers. *See* Commercial tax preparers; Internal Revenue Service
Tax audit. *See* Audits
Tax basis. *See* Basis of property
Tax cheaters, 63, 68
Tax court, 471

Tax credits
  child-care credit, 414–419
  dependent-care credit,
    414–419
  diesel cars, 423–424
  disabled, 421–422
  earned income credit,
    422–423
  elderly, 421–422
  foreign income taxes,
    420–421
  overpaying social security
    tax, 419–420
  tax paid by a mutual fund,
    420
Tax-deductible vacations, 409
Tax-deferred annuities. *See*
  403(b) plans
Tax forms
  forms that come in the
    mail, 4
  getting extra forms, 8
  list of, 476–478
  reviewing last year's return, 5
  selecting the right form, 5–8
  See also specific form by name
Tax Foundation, 60–61
Tax-free dividends, 200
Tax-free exchanges, 241–243
Tax-free income, 75–79,
    204–205
Tax Freedom Day, 60–61
Tax gap, 63
Tax planning, 60–70
  basis of property, 195–196
  bubble brackets, 67–70
  inflation adjustments, 66
  marginal tax rates, 64–66
  overpaying taxes because of
    errors, 60
  social security benefits,
    312–313
  tax rate table, 65
  See also Year-end tax
    planning

Tax rates
  gift and estate tax table, 452
  table for 1995, 475
  ten-year averaging table, 307
Tax-related expenses, 412
Tax return preparation, 2–30
  commercial tax preparers,
    16–21
  electronic filing, 21–23
  fear of the IRS and, 8–9
  IRS help with, 15–16
  late filing, 23–27
  persons who must file, 3–4
  record keeping and, 28–30
  refunds, 27–28
  software for, 11–14
  table, 3
  tax forms, 4–8
  written help with, 10–11
  See also Filing returns by
    mail
Tax-saving tips, 31–42
Tax-sheltered annuities. *See*
  403(b) plans
Taxable bond funds, 204
Taxable-equivalent yields,
    219–221
Taxable income, 71–75, 475
Taxpayer Bill of Rights, 468,
    471
Taxpayer Compliance
  Measurement Program,
    464
TCMP. *See* Taxpayer
  Compliance
  Measurement Program
Telephone filing of 1040EZ
  form, 6–7
Ten-year averaging. *See* Five-
  and ten-year averaging
Theft losses. *See* Casualty and
  theft losses
Tips, 75, 96
Tools, 355
Transit passes, 87

Travel and entertainment
  expenses, 338–346
  changes in allowable
    deductions, 338–340
  charitable services
    expenses, 393–394
  club dues, 339
  conventions, 343–344
  cruise ships, 344
  foreign travel, 342–344
  investment seminars, 344
  meals and lodging, 85,
    345–346
  medical expenses
    deduction, 372–373
  mixing personal vacation
    with business trip,
    341–342
  ordinary and necessary
    expenses, 340
  record keeping, 344–345
  travel as education, 349
  travel away from home,
    340–341
  when joined by spouse,
    341–342
Treasury notes and bonds,
    218
Treasury securities, 205
Trustees, 271–272

U

Underpayment penalties, 36,
    101, 103
Undistributed capital gains,
    199–201
Unemployment
  compensation, 75
Unemployment taxes,
    145–146
Unified credit
  for gift and estate taxes,
    450–451
  marital deduction and, 455,
    457

Unmarried partners, 193
Unreimbursed expenses, 383
Unscheduled personal
     property, 409
U.S. savings bonds, 225–229
  income qualifier, 229
  inherited bonds, 230, 454
  kiddie tax and, 123, 226–227
  tax advantages, 225–226
  tax-free college tuition,
     228–229

V

Vacation homes, 177–183
  allocating expenses, 182–183
  14-day/10% rule, 179–180,
     181
  hobby-loss rules, 182
  passive losses, 180
  points on, 153
  year-end tax planning, 440
Variable annuities, 248
Vesting
  cliff vesting, 297
  company-matched 401(k)
     contributions, 293
  company pension plans,
     296–297
  profit-sharing plans, 296–297
  table, 297
Veterans' benefits, 78
Volunteer work, 392

W

W-2 form, 4, 85
W-4 form, 90–94
Wages and salaries, 71–72
Wash sales, 203–204, 209–210,
     434–435
Withholding, 89–105
  adjusting for mortgage,
     100, 150–151
  allowance table, 91
  backup, 99
  bonuses, 99

changing, 92–95
  exemption from, 95–96
  Form W-4, 90–95
  for household help,
     144–145
  itemized deductions and,
     93–94
  mid-year adjustment, 100
  part-year method, 95
  pension payouts and, 97–98
  pension plans, 298–300
  on retirement income, 97
  on tips, 96
  winnings and, 98–99
  year-end tax planning, 445
Work clothes, 354
Workers' compensation, 79
Working-condition fringe
     benefits, 87
Working couples
  special tax credit for,
     131–132
  withholding, 88–89
  See also Married couples

Y

Year-end tax planning,
     425–445
  accelerated deductions,
     427–430
  adjustments to income,
     425–426
  alternative minimum tax
     and, 52
  bond swaps, 434–435
  bunching deductions,
     430–431
  business expenses, 436–440
  deferring income, 426–427
  exemptions, 442–443
  expensing, 437–438
  gifts, 443–444
  hobby-loss rules, 438–439
  installment sales, 434
  interest income, 436

investments, 431–435
  last-minute sales, 434
  local taxes, 428
  marriage, 444–445
  medical expenses, 427–428
  for net gain or loss, 432
  passive investments, 439–440
  put options, 433
  rental property, 438–439
  retirement plans, 441–442
  selling short against the
     box, 433
  social security taxes, 438
  state taxes, 428
  vacation home, 440
  wash-sale rule, 434–435
  withholding, 445
  See also Tax planning

Z

Zero-coupon bonds, 214–215

KIPLINGER BOOKS

To order any Kiplinger product, call toll free, 1–800–727–7015 between 9:00 A.M. and 9:00 P.M. Eastern Time, or send your check to: Kiplinger Books and Tapes, P.O. Box 85193, Richmond, VA 23285–5193.

For information on bulk rates or to order in bulk, call Dianne Olsufka at 202–887–6431.

Please send me:

Books	Price		Quantity	Total
Taming the Office Tiger (paper)	$13.00	B		
Retire & Thrive (paper)	$15.00	C		
Money-Smart Kids (paper)	$12.95	K		
Buying and Selling a Home (paper)	$13.95	T		
Invest Your Way to Wealth (hardcover)	$23.95	G		
Make Your Money Grow (paper)	$14.95	S		
Taming the Paper Tiger (paper)	$11.95	M		
12 Steps to a Worry-Free Retirement (paper)	$14.95	U		
Career Starter (paper)	$10.95	V		
Working for Yourself (paper)	$14.95	N		
Survive & Profit From A Mid-Career Change (paper)	$12.95	D		
Facing 40 (hardcover)	$19.95	R		
Handbook of Personal Law (paper)	$14.95	A		
Cut Your Taxes (paper)	$15.00	E		
Video Guides				
Money-Smart Women	$29.95	W		
Retirement Security	$29.95	I		
Estate Planning	$29.95	Z		
Family Finances	$29.95	J		
Small Business Growth	$29.95	P		
Guide to Mutual Funds	$29.95	Q		
Audios				
Make Your Money Grow (abridged)	$13.00	1		
Invest Your Way to Wealth (abridged)	$15.00	2		
Taming the Paper Tiger (abridged)	$10.00	3		
Money-Smart Kids (abridged)	$13.00	4		
			Subtotal	
			*Sales Tax	
			**Shipping	
			Total	

* **Sales Tax:** DC 5.75%; FL 6%; MD 5%; VA 4.5%

** **Shipping:** $3.50 for the first item; 75¢ for each additional item. For Federal Express delivery within 5 business days: $5.00 for the first item; 50¢ for each additional item.

❑ My check payable to Kiplinger Books is enclosed for $_____.

❑ Charge my: ❑ VISA ❑ MasterCard ❑ American Express ❑ Discover

Card No. ☐☐☐☐☐☐☐☐☐☐☐☐☐☐☐☐

Signature _____

Exp. Date _____ Daytime Phone (_____)

Name _____

Company _____

Address _____ Apt. No. _____

City _____ State _____ Zip _____